CONTENTS

ANGLO-AMERICA AND ITS DISCONTENTS

nmonly referred to as the
m of multiple traditions
ind a few outposts in the

by the United States since
been at the very center of
West, Anglo–America is
st with each other and
tion containing multiple
ica is marked by multiple
notions and practices of
egemony or multilateral-
At its core Anglo-America
is fluid, not fixed.

The analytical perspectives of this book are laid out in Katzenstein's opening and concluding chapters. They are explored in seven outstanding case studies, written by widely known authors, which combine historical and contemporary perspectives.

Featuring an exceptional line-up and representing a diversity of theoretical views within one integrative perspective, this work will be of interest to all scholars and students of American and European affairs, international relations, sociology, and political science.

Peter J. Katzenstein is the Walter S. Carpenter, Jr. Professor of International Studies at Cornell University, USA. His work addresses issues of political economy, security, and culture in world politics.

ANGLO-AMERICA AND ITS DISCONTENTS

Civilizational identities beyond West and East

Edited by
Peter J. Katzenstein

Routledge
Taylor & Francis Group

LONDON AND NEW YORK

First published 2012
by Routledge
2 Park Square, Milton Park, Abingdon, Oxon OX14 4RN

Simultaneously published in the USA and Canada
by Routledge
711 Third Avenue, New York, NY 10017

Routledge is an imprint of the Taylor & Francis Group, an informa business

British Library Cataloguing in Publication Data
A catalogue record for this book is available from the British Library

Library of Congress Cataloging-in-Publication Data
Anglo-America and its discontents : civilizational identities beyond West and
East / edited by Peter J. Katzenstein.
      p. cm.
   Includes bibliographical references and index.
   ISBN 978-0-415-80954-2 — ISBN 978-0-415-80955-9 —
ISBN 978-0-203-12691-2   1. International relations and culture.
2. Civilization, Western–21st century. 3. English-speaking
countries–Civilization. 4. World politics–21st century. 5. East and
West. I. Katzenstein, Peter J.
   JZ1251.A54 2012
   306.2–dc23   2011034973

ISBN: 978-0-415-80954-2 (hbk)
ISBN: 978-0-415-80955-9 (pbk)
ISBN: 978-0-203-12691-2 (ebk)

Typeset in Bembo
by Cenveo Publisher Services

MIX
Paper from
responsible sources
FSC® C004839
www.fsc.org

Printed and bound in Great Britain by
CPI Antony Rowe, Chippenham, Wiltshire

for Anika

FIGURES AND TABLES

Figures

Tables

CONTRIBUTORS

Duncan Bell is Senior Lecturer in the Department of Politics and International Studies, University of Cambridge, and a Fellow of Christ's College. His publications include *The Idea of Greater Britain: Empire and the Future of World Order, 1860–1900* (2007).

Brian Bow is Associate Professor of Political Science at Dalhousie University. He is the author of several books and articles on Canada–US relations, including *The Politics of Linkage*, winner of the 2009 Donner Prize. He is currently working on regional politics and security cooperation in North America.

Peter J. Katzenstein is the Walter S. Carpenter, Jr. Professor of International Studies at Cornell University. His work addresses issues of political economy, security, and culture in world politics.

Audie Klotz is Associate Professor at Syracuse University, where she teaches theories of international relations, qualitative methods, and global migration, with a regional specialization in Southern Africa. Her current research compares Australian, Canadian, and South African responses to migration. She is also co-editor of the book series Palgrave Studies in International Relations.

David MacDonald is Associate Professor of Political Science at the University of Guelph, Ontario. He has written three books and co-edited two with themes centered on international relations, indigenous politics, human rights, and comparative foreign policy. He is currently completing a co-authored political science textbook.

Brendon O'Connor is Associate Professor of American Politics in the US Studies Centre at the University of Sydney. He has published articles and books on anti-Americanism, American welfare policy, presidential politics, American foreign policy, and Australian–American relations.

Louis W. Pauly is Professor of Political Science at the University of Toronto, where he also holds the Canada Research Chair in Globalization and Governance and serves as Director of Research Programs in the Munk School of Global Affairs. His principal research interests lie at the intersection of international and comparative political economy.

Christian Reus-Smit holds the Chair in International Relations at the European University Institute in Florence. He has published widely on international institutions, legitimacy and world politics, the nature and limits of American power, the politics of human rights, and the relation between empirical and normative theory.

Arturo Santa-Cruz is Associate Professor and Director of the Center for North American Studies at the University of Guadalajara. His most recent publication is *Mexico in North America: The Semantics of Sovereignty* (2011).

Herman Schwartz is Professor in the Politics Department at the University of Virginia, and author of *Subprime Nation: American Power, Global Capital and the Housing Bubble*. Earlier publications include *In the Dominions of Debt*, *States versus Markets*, and three co-edited books.

Srdjan Vucetic is Assistant Professor in the Graduate School of Public and International Affairs at the University of Ottawa. His latest publication is *The Anglosphere: A Genealogy of a Racialized Identity in International Relations* (2011).

PREFACE

This book is part of a trilogy exploring civilizations in world politics. The first volume, *Civilizations in World Politics: plural and pluralist perspectives* (2010), developed a particular conceptual approach stressing the plurality and pluralism of civilizations and applied it to six major civilizations. Two follow-on volumes explore civilizational processes and identities in greater detail. Situated in a broader comparative perspective, *Sinicization and the Rise of China: civilizational processes beyond East and West* (2012) inquires into Sinicization during the era of China's peaceful rise. With particular attention to the problematic relationship between liberalism and race, *Anglo-America and Its Discontents: civilizational identities beyond West and East* (2012) analyzes the evolution of civilizational identities of Anglo-America. Drawing on *Civilizations in World Politics*, the conceptual foundation of the trilogy is restated in the largely identical first section of the concluding chapters of volumes 2 and 3. The two subtitles of these volumes convey the central message of both books: we need to move beyond sharp distinctions between East and West.

The intellectual origins of this project lie in the twists and turns of my research and teaching during the last two decades. In the 1990s I tried to understand better the importance of norms and identities in world politics. Addressing general theories of international relations in one book, I applied the approach to Japanese security in another. In the last decade I have also thought some about regionalism and regionalization in world politics. I have remained unsatisfied with how I posed and sought to address the issue of regional identities in East Asia and Western Europe. The history of maps offers vivid illustrations of how regional identities evolve and how the world is being reimagined. Regional borders and meanings remain forever open to political debate and conflict. In both ways, regions resemble civilizations. The language of civilizational politics, I hope, offers a compelling way of capturing that kind of politics.

Indeed, the civilizational level of analysis could be added easily to conventional theories of international relations. This trilogy seeks to better specify the cultural context of world politics, focusing on Sinicization and Anglo-America as examples of complex processes and contested identities normally subsumed under the rubrics of globalization and internationalization. Even though they refer to different objects, for the most part these two concepts are used interchangeably. Globalization describes processes that transcend time and compress space, with novel and trans-formative effects for world politics. Internationalization refers to processes of territorially based exchanges across national borders, reflecting basic continuities in the evolution of the international state system. Globalization favors convergence around common standards as well as a variety of local adaptations to global change. Internationalization permits continued national differences in national practices. In this view, contemporary world politics is marked by a mixture of transformative global and incremental international effects that shape and reshape the international system.

A focus on civilizational processes and identities invites us to move from a generic to a more specific characterization of global and international contexts that illuminates the distinctive characteristics of intercivilizational engagements and encounters, as well as occasional civilizational clashes. Contextual specificity is a complement to rather than a substitute for international relations theory. Our theories tell us a number of things at a level of generality that is unhelpful for understanding or engaging the world. This trilogy does not seek to develop precise implications of the civilizational turn for the theoretical debate in international relations. It is an exercise in pattern recognition rather than in the specification of particular puzzles and scope conditions, or the articulation of alternative explana-tions and indicators helpful for quantitative analysis. My hope is to illuminate the broad contours of world politics and thus to create novel perspectives that invite more probing and precise inquiries by others.

Ever since the publication of Samuel Huntington's famous 1993 article in *Foreign Affairs*, his clash of civilization thesis has been required reading in the large introduction to International Relations that I regularly teach at Cornell. That article has remained a perennial student favorite and is typically included among the top three of the close to 50 readings that I assign. A decade ago when the impact of religion on world politics became one of my research interests, I encoun-tered Shmuel Eisenstadt's concept of multiple modernities, in some ways an antidote and in other ways a complement to Huntington's analysis. Finally, a few years ago I developed a new course on American foreign policy. In preparing a new set of lectures I became reacquainted with the broad corpus of Huntington's writings on America and recognized both its affinity to Louis Hartz's views and its consistency with Huntington's civilizational writing. I also learned that Eisenstadt's concept of multiple modernities had a close cousin in Rogers Smith's powerful, multiple-tradition critique of Hartz's (and Huntington's) view of America's liberal tradition. America, and some of its kin countries, I concluded, could be viewed quite profitably through lenses that differed from those deployed by my realist and liberal friends and colleagues. America is not only the most powerful state in the international system and the leading capitalist democracy in global markets; it is also a civilization in its own right.

What is true of any book is also true of this trilogy – it remains unfinished. If the initial spur for this project was Huntington's cultural realism, at the end the limits of liberal internationalism became my central concern. Like cultural realists, liberals continue to adhere to by now outdated aspects of a nineteenth-century Eurocentric model of world politics. Then as now, the civilized or advanced countries set the standards for the uncivilized or developing ones. My engagement with liberal theory and practice forced me to think specifically about the racial dimension of world politics. Born at the end of World War II in Nazi Germany and liberated by U.S. soldiers, many of whom had sacrificed their lives so that I could live freely, this was a topic fraught with intimations of the Holocaust from which I had shied away for a long time. Furthermore, my deep admiration of and attraction to the United States had made me gloss over the problematic and ungainly aspects of a country that had adopted me with so much generosity and that I had come to embrace so fully.

Even though their politeness made them downplay the fact in the presence of an American-German *gaijin*, over many years I learned from my colleagues in East Asia that they considered race to be a salient factor for any serious analysis of world politics. I realized early on that my American colleagues who studied international relations were either uninterested in or openly hostile to inquiries into the relation between liberalism and race. Arguably they live in a society that continues to bear the very visible and ugly scars of a never forgotten racism; but for the most part they regard this to be a non-issue in the era of multiculturalism and human rights. Liberal theorists reformulate Wilsonianism to make this basic policy approach relevant to our times. Alternatively, realist critics of Woodrow Wilson seek to diminish his far-reaching impact on world politics by characterizing him as an unrealistic idealist. Neither spends even a passing moment to reflect on the significance that as a man of the South, Wilson the liberal was also a racist. I thus conclude the trilogy by reflecting on the similarities and differences between the global reach of Anglo-America and Islam; inquiring into the limits of international liberalism; and searching for historical analogies that can help us grasp more fully the movement to what I call "polymorphic globalism." Although that globalism contains within it close links to liberalism, it goes further to deal with a humanity larger and more diverse than that of the West or Anglo-America.

I eventually found my interest in civilizational analysis being met with more than a healthy dose of skepticism by various audiences. Those interested in the cultural terrain of the modern world in particular showed a visceral aversion to the concept of civilization, overladen for that audience by the connotations of Eurocentric racism. While they were often sympathetic to the main parts of my argument, their most persistent question was, "why bother with this concept?" Would it not be better to rely on a different and less contaminated conceptual language? Eventually I prepared two answers to that question. First, I would offer my critics a wager. They should do a content analysis of a reasonable sample of the front page of any number of newspapers, count the times their personal or favorite research project was mentioned, and compare that symbol count to the invocation of the concepts of "East" and "West." To date nobody has taken me up on my offer. I remain confident that common language use shows these civilizational concepts to be ubiquitous. Second, I would mention the reading preferences of Cornell undergraduates referred to above. On both scores I think it is important for scholars to engage public discourse on its own terms rather than to hide behind neologisms or disregard the opinions of their students.

I got a different reaction from scholars of international relations. Realists would simply shrug their shoulders. Typically uninterested in the cultural aspects of world politics, they are convinced that Huntington has been proven wrong decisively. Clashes occur for the most part within rather than between civilizations. That reaction overlooks Huntington's most enduring contribution – to alert us to the fact that, with the end of the Cold War, the cultural context of international relations had undergone a fundamental change. Liberals had a very hard time accepting that the insistence on universal standards of good governance rooted in liberal principles had a deep and troubling affinity with nineteenth-century civilizational analysis, as I argue, and that international liberalism is not sufficiently capacious to encompass the full normative reach of the emerging world order.

My ideas for *Anglo-America and Its Discontents* jelled after many years at the dinner table as I listened to and learned from Mary, my life's love and partner, about her work on American politics. Eventually, in a speech I prepared for the 2008 annual meeting of the American Political Science Association, I tried to articulate a position that encompassed both the domestic and international opportunities and the challenges of liberal thought and practice. For this project I convened two authors' workshops in conjunction with the 2010 annual meetings of the International Studies and the American Political Science Association, where authors and I presented analytical outlines and first drafts of papers. In May 2011, the Munk Center at the University of Toronto hosted a major conference with substantial financial support. I would like to thank Center Director Louis W. Pauly in particular for his generous and unflinching support on top of all his many other obligations, and the Center's staff for its efficient help in all matters large and small. The costs for the first two meetings and the balance for the conference expenses were covered by Cornell's Walter S. Carpenter, Jr. Professorship.

I would like to acknowledge with enormous gratitude the generous financial support that I received in 2009–10 from the Louise and John Steffens Founders' Circle Membership at the Institute of Advanced Studies in Princeton. The year was crucial for giving me the quiet and uninterrupted time to refine the arguments I advance in the trilogy and to do a large amount of reading in literatures that led me in many different directions, with unexpected findings along the way.

Finally, I would like to thank my co-authors, who were already or have now become close companions and friends. I have learned much more from them than

I can convey either here or in the acknowledgments to my chapters. Their many ideas and suggestions, their comments on my paper drafts, and their own papers all deepened and sharpened enormously my understanding of the subjects discussed in these two books and, more generally, many aspects of world politics that I had not understood well or thought about at all. The pleasure of working together was deep and intense, and I shall miss our conversations as we, Melville's wandering seafarer Ishmael, set our sails once again, on the lookout for new cargos and new companions. Both books reminded me once again that the process of creating new knowledge is deliciously social *and* solitary.

I dedicate this book to Anika, whose lusty crying in the last stages of revising this manuscript conveyed an unmistakable message: "my way – not the highway." I hope it will be so when she grows up.

Peter J. Katzenstein
Ithaca, N.Y.
July 2011

1

THE WEST AS ANGLO-AMERICA[1]

Peter J. Katzenstein

Anglo-America is a clearly identifiable part of what is commonly referred to as the West. The West exists, this book argues, in the form of multiple traditions that have currency in America, Europe, the Americas, and a few outposts in the Southern hemisphere.[2] Led by the British Empire until the beginning and by the United States since the middle of the twentieth century, Anglo-America has been at the very center of world politics. Bridging the European and the American West, Anglo-America is distinctive, not unique. These multiple Wests coexist with each other and with other civilizations, as parts of one global civilization containing multiple modernities. And like all other civilizations, Anglo-America is marked by multiple traditions and internal pluralism. Once deeply held notions and practices of imperial rule and racial hierarchy now take the form of hegemony or multilateralism and politically contested versions of multiculturalism. At its core Anglo-America is fluid, not fixed.

Anglo-America is, in the lexicon of contemporary conservative political supporters in the major English-speaking countries, called the Anglosphere. In the tradition of Winston Churchill it enjoys today support among conservatives as a community of states that is united by traits such as liberal values, Protestantism, individualism, an achievement culture, a life of private grace testified to by worldly success, the use of the English language, common law, Parliamentary rules, and other ancient British traditions. Supporters of this conservative project oppose other forms of the West, such as the European Union.[3] Left-wing critics see in the Anglosphere instead a neoliberal, imperialist, and at times furtively racist project. These critics can point to George Orwell's nightmarish novel *1984*, which detailed the tyrannical rule inside Oceania, conceived of as a political amalgam of Britain, the United States, Latin America, and Africa.[4] The political Left has therefore put its energy behind the support of the United Nations and some of the new transnational governance institutions. All political disagreements aside, the historical record shows that Anglo-America has won all major wars since the late seventeenth century. In the twentieth century, in hot and cold global wars, Anglo-America defeated challenges from both the Fascist Right and the Communist Left. Despite local and temporary setbacks, Anglo-America has been a central axis around which international politics has revolved for more than three centuries.

The West is frequently invoked in public discourse as the most encompassing source of collective identity that tells us who we are, where we came from, and where we should be going. Yet Sigmund Freud argued in his essay *Civilization and Its Discontents* that the individual Self is not unitary but continues inward without any sharp delineations.[5] And so it is for civilizations. As political constructions, civilizational complexes have a direct bearing on core concepts of international relations such as empire, race, sovereignty, and interdependence, as well as on political practices such as diplomacy and alliance formations. This is not to argue that Western civilization in its different manifestations is the only source of collective identity. Nations and their various regions or localities, as well as group, family, and individual identities, are also significant in situationally specific ways. Incessantly invoked, the "West" remains, however, the most general social category that provides elites rather than mass publics with a sense of direction as they seek to understand what they believe in and what governments, groups, and individuals should do. As a modern equivalent to the now outdated concept of "Latin Christendom," invoking the "West" can serve different political purposes, such as highlighting its distinctive contributions to or detractions from humanity, or extolling some of its values as inherently superior or inferior to others.[6]

After briefly discussing the existence of many Wests, I develop two arguments in this chapter. First, with specific reference to Louis Hartz's and Samuel Huntington's insistence on the unity and singularity of America and Western civilization, I argue for the pervasiveness of multiple traditions. Referencing the chapters in this book, I then sketch Anglo-America's gradual evolution away from race and empire, analyzing varieties of international communities and three different patterns of internal multiculturalism typifying contemporary Anglo-America. I end with a brief conclusion.

Many Wests

Winston Churchill is proof of the West's internal tensions and contradictions. When, as a lieutenant, he stepped in front of a ballroom crowd in the Waldorf Astoria eager to hear about the Boer war, he was introduced by Mark Twain, no friend of Britain's imperialist exploits in Africa or America's against Spain: "We have always been kin: kin in blood, kin in religion, kin in representative government, kin in ideals, kin in just and lofty purposes; and now we are kin in sin, the harmony is complete, the blend is perfect, like Mr. Churchill himself."[7] It was Churchill the racist who supported and participated in campaigns of ethnic cleansing and the establishment of detention camps in British colonies. And it was Churchill who hated Gandhi and Hitler equally, a fact that may help explain his callousness during the great 1943 famine in Bengal – which was caused largely by Britain's mismanagement, then under Churchill's leadership.[8]

This was Churchill's first face. His second was the fearless and eloquent leader of Britain and the West, the man who helped greatly in defeating Hitler and the Nazis. At the dawn of the Cold War, Churchill argued in his Fulton, Missouri, speech:

> Americans and British must never cease to proclaim in fearless tones the great principles of freedom and the rights of man which are the joint inheritance of the English-speaking world and which through Magna Carta, the Bill of Rights, *habeas corpus*, trials by jury and the English common law find their most famous expression in the American Declaration of Independence.[9]

For Churchill and his intellectual followers, the English-speaking peoples are the specific manifestations of Anglo-America and the loftiest representation of the West – as discussed by Duncan Bell in Chapter 2.[10]

Drawing on the second of Churchill's faces, a unitary conception of the West still enjoys wide currency today, especially in conservative quarters. The "special partnership" between Britain and the United States, for example, was very much in evidence in the first decade of the twenty-first century. During the run-up to the attack on Iraq, Prime Minister Blair was the USA's most important comrade-in-arms, ready to pay the "blood price."[11] In 2007, President Bush called the ties between the United States and Britain the "most important bilateral relationship … primarily because we think the same, we believe in freedom and justice as fundamentals of life."[12] Blair reminded Bush of Churchill: "I heard of Winston Churchill in my friend's voice."[13] And Gordon Brown's visit to the United States in March 2009 was explicitly designed to revitalize the special relationship tarnished by an unpopular war and American high-handedness.

Yet the White House this time around invoked a "special partnership" rather than a "special relationship," which raised eyebrows in London.[14] President Obama had written at length about his grandfather's accounts of having been tortured by British soldiers in Kenya; and he had the bust of Winston Churchill removed from the Oval Office and returned to Britain. Prime Minister David Cameron acknowledged new political conditions during his first visit to Washington after becoming prime minister in 2010. Undermining the notion of Britain as America's Trojan poodle, Cameron sought to replace misty-eyed emotion with hard-nosed national interest in a "partnership of choice" as the foundation of Britain's special relations with the United States.[15]

"The West" is often referred to in the singular as a civilizational complex that differs from "the East." This is implausible. After all is said and done, it is not clear why 1,700 miles and three flight hours to the west of Athens, Rabat is part of the Orient. Conceived as unities, East and West are inaccurate labels that offer a profoundly misleading view of the world. Although they invite questions about demarcations that can undermine their persuasiveness, more specific regional designations such as "Europe" or "Asia" encounter similar problems. Europeans find themselves in fundamental disagreement over whether Russia and Turkey are parts of Europe. And the concept of Asia, in the singular, makes no sense in trying to impose a unity on South, Southeast, and East Asia that simply does not exist for the peoples living in these disparate parts of the world – except in the powerful imaginations of popular pundits and pan-Asian political theorists. The story is no different when we talk about the West. In the singular, it does not exist and needs to be replaced by the idea of many Wests that, often in tension, coexist with one another.

Maps representing civilizations in single colors suggest a social homogeneity that is misleading compared to more complex visual representations.[16] Focusing specifically on the writings of Louis Hartz and Samuel Huntington, I argue here for pluralist notions of Anglo-America. The substantive chapters in this book illustrate great variations in what we mean by Anglo-America and what the politics of Anglo-America look like in practice. In the nineteenth century it was widely believed that there existed only one Anglo-American standard of civilization.[17] Furthermore, Anglo-America served the purpose of a liberalism suffused by racist and imperialist ideas. Those ideas have lost much of their credibility in a multi-civilizational world in which complex sovereignty, diplomatic cultures, and special relations mark the international relations of Anglo-America. In recent decades, across the various parts of Anglo-America, we are witnessing the democratic politics of multi-racialism, embryonic triculturalism, and contested multiculturalism.

Besides Anglo-America, there exists a second conception of the West, as in the New World of the Americas. Building on the work of Arthur P. Whitaker, Arturo Santa-Cruz delineates the Western Hemispheric Idea as a distinct sphere of communication, interaction, and interest that constitutes what is considered legitimate in politics.[18] Ever since Jefferson, the idea of a not necessarily peaceful pattern of interaction has grown up around the notion that the New World is different from the Old. Over time, the internal division of the Western Hemisphere has diminished, as illustrated by the pan-American movement. Starting with the Washington Conference of 1889, the modern inter-American system dates back to the very moment at which US interventions in Central America and the rise of anti-Yankee feelings were on the upswing. Tensions and disagreements about the normative order of the American version of the West did not abate until President Roosevelt initiated the "Good Neighbor Policy" in 1936, with the USA accepting unconditionally the principle of non-intervention. At that time, the USA affirmed with all its partners in the Americas the commitment to democracy, peace, and justice. The self-proclaimed distinctiveness from Europe thus had given way to an expression of shared solidarity based on the principles of representative democracy, expressed subsequently in the Bogotá Charter as the founding document of the Organization of American States in 1948. The Western Hemispheric Idea as a distinct version of the West thus is based on the principle of rights-based representative government (supported most forcefully by the USA) and non-intervention (supported by the states of Latin and Central America fearing the USA), with both principles informing but not determining political practices – which have often deviated from these lofty ideals.

Shmuel Eisenstadt, Edmundo O'Gorman, and Jeremy Smith have offered complementary arguments of the Americas that reconfirm and illuminate the idea of many Wests from a more explicitly civilizational perspective. As the point of departure, they reject out of hand Louis Hartz's Eurocentric theory of the Americas as "frozen fragments" of Europe.[19] European patterns were instead radically transformed in the process of transplantation from the Old World to the New. Like that of Santa-Cruz, Eisenstadt's comparative analysis stresses both commonalities and differences of American civilization.[20] He points to the relative weakness of primordial criteria such as language and territory. Instead, new collective identities emerged among the settlers, imbued by a universalist ethos in the United States and a formal hierarchical one in Latin America. The principles of social order offered mirror images of each other. Equality, achievement, and transient, reformist protest orientations prevailed in the British North; clientelism, ascriptive social status, and cyclical, radical protest in the Hispanic South. In their relationship with the old European world, the two American variants were not clashing as much as they were undergoing divergent processes of self-differentiation from kindred European societies. Transplanted to the Americas, the impulses of the Reformation and Counter-reformation were affected deeply by what British and Hispanic settlers shared: the experience of European colonialism and the confrontation with indigenous populations. O'Gorman adds that the originality of the American political project rather than the colonial imitation of the mother countries' political institutions and practices in Latin America led to the identification of the USA with all of America and made US citizens Americans par excellence.[21] Smith, finally, disaggregates American civilization further by analyzing distinctive Canadian and Caribbean variants that Eisenstadt bypasses, and by adding America's indige-nous civilizations and perhaps the American South as further variants to illustrate the existence of many Wests.[22]

Finally, there exists the enduring debate about the relations between Europe and America. Even in moments of externally induced crisis and in times of change, the two are viewed as distinct though deeply related. For example, President Kennedy's speech, delivered in Philadelphia on July 4, 1962, invoked a transatlan-tic partnership founded on a new declaration of interdependence between the United States and Europe. Competing American and French universalisms also illustrate the existence of a plural and pluralist West. The core values motivating the French revolution – *liberté, egalité, fraternité* – remain of utmost importance to France's sense of self and the projection of that self, through language and institu-tions, in the world, particularly in Africa.[23] Republican values, French officials hoped, would secure French influence in its "special relation" with Africa even after decolonization. Lacking the resources necessary for pursuing its self-proclaimed universalist *mission civilisatrice*, during the Cold War Sub-Saharan Africa in particular acquired great civilizational significance for France. Always the political realist, De Gaulle cut the political links to North Africa early in the

Fifth Republic. But he saw France's *grandeur* as deeply enmeshed with Black Africa. Africa was thus an essential partner in the universalist Western values embodied in the French revolution.[24] For decades, French officials feared increasing American (and Soviet) involvement in what they regarded as an exclusively French African sphere of influence. This was one of the many deep-seated sources of French anti-Americanisms.[25] It finds its American analogue in the periodic outbursts of anti-French sentiment, as in the renaming of French fries into freedom fries on the US Congress' cafeteria menu at the height of the 2003 crisis over the American invasion of Iraq. In light of historical facts pointing to the existence of many Wests and multiple Americas, singular and unified theories of America and the West deserve close scrutiny.

America and the West: not unified, not singular

During the last half-century, various analysts have written as if America and the West were unified and singular. Louis Hartz and Samuel Huntington are two scholars in particular who have shaped profoundly our thinking of the category of "America" and "the West." Hartz, the political theorist, first articulated a compelling argument about the omnipotence of America's unitary liberal tradition, before putting what might have appeared to his readers as an exceptionalist argument in a broader, Eurocentric context. The liberal offshoot that implanted itself on the American soil, Hartz argues, was comparable to other fragments of Europe's political ideologies that took root in other parts of the West constituting Anglo-America. What all of these fragments shared was the experience of having remained frozen, lacking the vitality of an intellectual dialectic that might have propelled them forward. As a new and more global world strips away the protection from these Anglo cocoons, that vitality is now being imported from other civilizations, themselves offshoots of the intellectual vitality of European theories and ideologies. Huntington, the social scientist, advanced an argument about a civilizational clash between "the West" and "the rest" that prompted his critics to ask *Who are We?* (the title of his last book).[26] As he moved from a general civilizational argument to a more specific American one, Huntington continued to take a unitary view of both civilizations and American culture. In both of his books, and in contrast to Hartz, Huntington's objective was explicitly political and prescriptive as he sought to advance a conservative view on questions of identity. Despite the richness of their insights and the argumentative power of their writings, I argue here that both Hartz and Huntington fall prey to the fallacy of thinking in unitary and singular categories.

Hartz[27]

More than half a century ago, Louis Hartz developed an argument that has remained foundational for how we understand America today.[28] Hartz proposed a consensus view of American culture and identity. Without a reactionary, feudal past, America lacks a revolutionary socialist future. Lockean liberalism has snuffed out all alternative political traditions and imaginations. And American liberalism is a frozen fragment of bourgeois liberalism, transplanted from the Old World to the New. The American South, to be sure, resembled Europe in several ways. But after the Civil War it was relegated to a position of political marginality. America thus remained in the iron grip of a tyrannical liberal tradition.

Hartz's insistence on the dominance of a single tradition in the United States is flawed. Rogers Smith has reworked an older scholarly perspective on dueling traditions, such as Jeffersonianism and Madisonianism, that preceded Hartz's book. In so doing he has developed the multiple-traditions perspective now closely associated with his name.[29] Addressing, among others, both Hartz's and Huntington's single tradition theories, Smith observes in his analysis that American political development was marked not only by egalitarian values of liberal democracy but also by inegalitarian and illiberal ideas that yielded substantial and serious clashes over America's reigning ideas and practices. "At its heart," he argues, "the multiple-traditions thesis holds" that not any one tradition but a "more complex pattern of apparently inconsistent combinations of the traditions" has shaped American history.[30]

Specifically, Hartz's argument overlooks America's republican and racial traditions. For Hartz, conflict in America occurs within the liberal tradition – between majority rule and minority rights, and between democratic and property rights. He thus discounts America's strong republican tradition. The rejection of monarchism led to the support of popular republicanism informed by Rome and by ideals of civic virtue.[31] This republican tradition had strong effects on Jeffersonian and Jacksonian conceptions of politics and a distinctive form of American communitarianism. Furthermore, Hartz's liberal tradition argument has very little to say about the issue of race. In semi-feudal Latin America, slaves were placed at the very bottom of the social hierarchy, but they were not robbed of their humanity. In America's non-feudal culture, slaves were denied their humanity and made pieces of property. Liberal slavery was thus more vicious than feudal slavery. But Hartz went on to argue that once humanity was granted, liberalism was more generous, since it did not have within its own intellectual tradition arguments that could stop the demand for equality. The elimination of slavery was necessary to establish the hegemony of liberalism in Hartz's argument; yet Hartz slighted the importance of race in American politics, a fact he reportedly regretted subsequently.[32]

Hartz's second major book internationalizes and puts into comparative perspective his analysis of American liberalism.[33] This is a daring book of comparative intellectual history, grounded in the core assumption that as in the United States, the political imagination and traditions of the West in Latin America, South Africa, Canada, and Australia are also all fragments of European culture and ideology. In Hartz's treatment the West, America, and Europe are indelibly fused into one unitary European core. Taking with them various seeds of theory and ideology, European emigrants implanted them in foreign soil and then watched them mature into a peculiar intellectual immobility that escaped altogether the European contagion of intellectual self-renewal. This affected in equal measure, Hartz argues, Europe's feudal fragments in Latin America and French Canada; its bourgeois ones in the United States, Dutch South Africa, and English Canada; and its radical ones in Australia and British South Africa.[34] Spread across the full arc of Europe's intellectual revolution, these seven fragments evince "the immobilities of fragmentation."[35] The escape from the European past was also an escape from the future enemies of Europe. Only now, after two centuries of stasis, has the decolonization movement hurled back at these fragments the "very Western revolution they originally fled ... these societies in the midst of the variations they contain, are governed by the ultimate experience of the American liberal traditions."[36] Whether feudal, liberal, or radical, all fragments are conservative. Challenged by global intellectual developments since the middle of the twentieth century, they are all forced to transcend their conservatism. To be sure, the fragments have at times tried to recoil into isolationism, exploit their nationalism, or erupt into hysteria. But in the end, such reactionary responses did yield to being reconnected with the European intellectual imagination now playing itself out on a global scale.[37]

European ideology thus refurbished was extended to its African and Indian relationships to instill a series of racial formulations altogether outside of the original European ethic.[38] Transplanted fragments of European ideology thereby became moral absolutes, national essences, and different ways of experiencing racial lives. Extricating themselves from the intellectual battles and sources of renewal in Europe permitted the conservative fragments to unfold their own potentialities beyond the theoretical imagination of the Old World. Pruning the fragments' intellectual possibilities did not stop new grafts from taking hold. Admittedly, since European ideologies were ignorant of first-hand experience with racial issues, the fragments experienced political battles over how to apply their different ideologies to questions of race. In feudal fragments, debates about the incorporation of racially different groups of people focused on how to absorb them in a hierarchical society. In liberal and radical fragments, the practice of racial rule was harsher in practice than in feudal fragments; under slavery the focus was on total exclusion and the denial of the slave's basic humanity. The racial question was thus swept into the traditionalism of each fragment's politics, challenged by non-Western ideas and practices. And thus the indigenous evolving ethic of each fragment became the "exclusive defender of the Western faith ... with only one imaginable way of dealing with the man outside the West."[39] The stasis of these fragments, the lack of challenges they faced, and their unmistakable European descent in an intellectually Eurocentric world all speak to Hartz's eloquent restatement of his basic single-tradition theory on a grander scale.[40]

Huntington[41]

With the end of the Cold War, Samuel Huntington saw a new cultural context in which states would henceforth act.[42] The old ideological confrontation between capitalist democracy and communist totalitarianism, he argued, was replaced by a new kind of clash between the "West" and the "Rest." With the end of the Cold War, civilizations were destined to become the most salient cultural context for international relations. Ascriptive traits now define the identity of individuals and states and thus help shape their interests. Compared to ethnic groups, nations, or language communities, civilizations operate at a higher level of inclusiveness. Since their building blocks are variable constellations of religion, culture, language, values, traditions, and memories, Huntington concedes that civilizations cannot be defined easily and with any degree of precision. Like Doctor Dolittle's pushme-pullyou, Huntington's argument appears to have two heads and thus can take on all comers. Under the wide umbrella of civilization, identities are contested and can be reconstructed through a politics that is forever in flux. Kemalist reformism thus can be explained within the context of Islam, as can significant reform efforts in Mexico, Australia, or Russia.[43] Yet this is not the central thrust of Huntington's argument, which stresses instead that the basic factors defining civilizations are objective and unchanging. Underneath civilizational multiplicity Huntington discovers, instead, a profound civilizational division. Civilizations are culturally unified contexts that are increasingly tending toward clash.

Huntington often writes as if civilizations themselves were actors which, just like culturally coherent nation states, balance and bandwagon. In this formulation, civilizations appear to be coherent and compact. They operate as both the deepest of all cultural structures, most resistant to penetration from the outside, and the broadest of all cultural contexts. Viewing civilizations as billiard balls, Huntington insists that contacts between civilizations have been intermittent at best and normally non-existing. In Huntington's conceptualization, core states are carriers of particular civilizations; other states line up behind such core states and support them for reasons of civilizational identity. This is Huntington's argument about the United States as the leader of Western civilization. After the Cold War, conflicts within civilizations will decrease, conflicts between civilizations will increase, and the most violent conflicts will occur along the fault lines separating civilizations. Furthermore, Huntington predicts a decline of the West and of American power. The superficial tokens of America's power, for example in the domain of popular culture, activate in other civilizations a backlash that is stronger and politically more consequential than the thin veneer of the globalized culture that America is producing. As non-Western routes to modernity become better traveled, America and the West will be engaged in civilizational struggles with other civilizations.

Many scholars and practitioners have disagreed, both with Huntington's specific assignments of different parts of the world to different civilizations and with his overall argument. A number of statistical and qualitative studies refute his predictions that intercivilizational clashes and wars are more significant than intracivilizational ones.[44] Other critics have countered him by emphasizing other factors in world politics.[45] But the most telling criticism of Huntington's conceptualization has been directed against his view of civilizations as unitary cultural complexes that act and clash. Historically, for example, the relationship between Islam and the West has encompassed many peaceful and enriching exchanges that simply cannot be covered by the concept of "clash."[46] Even today, Islamic jihadist movements are only a tiny part of a world civilization of enormous variety.

Recognition of the plurality that inheres in all civilizations is an indispensable first step if we want to avoid the mistake of assigning to all non-Western civilizations a compact "otherness" that relegates them to the status of being inescapably different from the West. Civilizations are most similar in the differences they contain. The precise normative content of the West illustrates the point. The list of traits that Huntington enumerates – the legacy of Greece and Rome, bicephalic religious communities, multiple languages, separation of Church and state, rule of law, social pluralism, representative bodies, and a tradition of individualism – is highly selective. It extols the tradition of Western Enlightenment rather than the legacy of racial supremacy and genocidal warfare.

A final criticism focuses on Huntington's highlighting of clash over all other forms of encounters or engagements. Donald Puchala offers a more nuanced set of categories encompassing multiple kinds of encounters between fully developed civilizations, fully and partly developed civilizations, and civilizations and other political communities.[47] This more fine-grained conceptualization allows Puchala to offer a comparative analysis that covers many significant encounters during the last two thousand years. Based on his survey of seven different cases, Puchala concludes that: civilizations do not often clash, although mature civilizations sometimes do; cultural borrowing is often uni-directional; advanced civilizations tend to be culturally resilient; and empires associated with civilizations tend to engage in different kinds of intercivilizational relations.

In defense against his many critics, Huntington asserts boldly that his is not a perfect theory but one that is better than any of its alternatives. The binary distinction that informed Cold War theorizing (East–West and North–South) no longer works. Thinking of the world as divided into a handful of civilizations is the right level of abstraction to capture a more complicated and nuanced reality. Huntington offers illustrative evidence in support of his argument and, for the most part, sidesteps or ignores most of the quantitative and qualitative empirical tests that tend to undercut his main claims. He insists, however, that whatever its conceptual shortcomings and empirical weaknesses, his paradigm beats all rivals and thus cannot simply be dismissed.

At the center of the disagreement between Huntington and his critics lies the issue of cultural cohesion. Clifford Geertz writes that

> cultural systems must have a minimal degree of coherence, else we would not call them systems; and by observation, they normally have a great deal more. But there is nothing as coherent as a paranoid's delusion or a swindler's story. The force of our interpretations cannot rest, as they are now so often made to do, on the tightness with which they hold together, or the assurance with which they are argued.[48]

And so it is with civilizations as loosely coupled, internally differentiated systems of social meaning. They provide important multiple contexts for world politics, as Huntington correctly establishes. But they lack the cultural coherence with which his cultural realism seeks to imbue them.

That coherence view is central to Huntington's view of America.[49] While his perspective has shifted over time, Huntington has consistently advanced different versions of a single tradition theory.[50] Initially he defined the American Creed first and foremost in terms of political ideals of rights, democracy, and the rule of law. In this view, the American Constitution is the main source of liberal political ideals and a secular, constitutional patriotism. Twenty-five years later, in his last book *Who Are We?*, Huntington rejects this view as insufficient, as the Constitution simply lacks sufficient Creedal power.[51] The glue that holds America together is not the Constitution but a culture of seventeenth- and eighteenth-century dissenting Anglo-Protestant sects expressing Christian religious commitments, adherence to a common language, and English concepts of the rule of law, the responsibility of rulers, and the rights of individuals. That culture empowers individualism, supports a strong work ethic, and creates a duty for individuals to create heaven on earth.[52] This more recent view of the American Creed is broader in the sense of incorporating both cultural and political components, and narrower in the sense of including fewer types of people. Huntington now argues that his original conception, inspired by Hartz, is inadequate for building or rebuilding America's walls. The thrust of his civilizational argument is division and clash; the focus of his Creedal argument is assimilation and exclusion.

Conclusion

Unitary and singular accounts stress the crystallization of a broad consensus around core values and uncontested identities. This is the view of Hartz and Huntington discussed above. And many have followed their lead. Robert Kagan's analysis of a deeply fractured West, for example, is based on a unitary view of the United States.[53] The United States is a dangerous nation marked by mild family quarrels between liberals and conservatives who are equally ignorant of and dangerous for the world. In this liberal reading of the domestic sources of American foreign policy, conspicuously absent is "race," with the book's index lacking even a single entry. Although for Kagan the West is deeply divided, America is fundamentally united. Similarly, Stephen Krasner has built a powerful explanation of US foreign policy based on the Hartzian consensus theory of liberal America.[54] And Walter Russell Mead argues that the United States as the center of Anglo-America is marked by selective racial–religious controversies that have maintained and animated its WASPish core. In this formulation, only Jews have succeeded in joining the white, Protestant ruling elite.[55] Neglecting white race theory, Mead titles one of his chapters "how they hate us" and writes at length about the world of the "Waspophobe." He assumes, erroneously, that "them and us" are defined by unambiguous and unchanging boundaries.[56] This argument is empirically inaccurate in the specific case of Anglo-America and analytically flawed when applied to civilizations in general; varieties of anti-Americanisms, for example, include liberal versions.[57] America and the West thus illustrate a general truth: civilizational world politics is inescapably plural and pluralist.

Anglo-America's slow exit from supremacy and imperial rule

Neither the West nor Anglo-America is immutable. To prove this point it might be instructive to analyze renegade or marginal parts of the West – Germany in the first half of the twentieth century and Russia at the beginning of the twenty-first. Alternatively, one could analyze the West from one of its self-proclaimed alternative centers or extended peripheries – France and Latin America. Such inquiries would likely lead to conclusions similar to those reached in this book. Anglo-America incorporates competing and changing conceptions of identity, and multiple and evolving discourses, practices, and policies. I anticipate below this book's central arguments.

Race and empire

In the late nineteenth century, theories of white racial supremacy were part and parcel of widely held theories of imperialism and Anglo-Saxon supremacy. The long history of the political construction of the white race was grounded in the institution of slavery, including white slavery first practiced on a large scale by Vikings and Italian city-states. Later, Britain took a leading position among Europe's imperial powers in selling its own peoples into bondage in faraway lands – convicts and children prominently among them. Before the eighteenth-century boom in the African slave trade, 300,000–400,000 people, more than half of the British immigrants to the Western Hemisphere, came as unfree laborers.[58]

Despite this long history of what amounted to white slavery, in the late eighteenth century the doctrine of the supremacy of the Anglo-Saxon race was widespread. Anglo-Saxonism had a long political history reflected in English literature, law, and religion.[59] In the nineteenth and early twentieth centuries, these constructs of the Anglo-Saxon past merged with a scientific racism that placed Anglo-Saxons at the apex of the white races, ahead of all others. As the embodiment of the nineteenth-century American renaissance, Ralph Waldo Emerson's formidable intellect and prodigious literary output made him the "philosopher king of American white race theory," as Nell Painter argues in her deeply researched and carefully argued book.[60]

The binary distinction between white and non-white replaced the recognition of a multiplicity of races, religions, and nations – such as Caucasian, Aryan, Chinese, Hindu, Malay, Black, Muslim, Japanese.[61] Transnational in inspiration and identification, the political project of whiteness was nationalist in methods and goals. White settlers claimed their racial superiority as grounds for Aboriginal dispossession and genocide first and racist immigration controls later. With 50 million

Chinese and the same number of Europeans, as well as 30 million Indians migrating to new homes around the world in the nineteenth century, "whites only" became a widespread global color line. Education and literacy tests first used in Mississippi in 1890 to disenfranchise black voters were promulgated by self-styled Anglo-Saxonists like Henry Cabot Lodge and served as models for federal immigration restrictions in the United States, Natal and other British Dominions, as well as Nazi Germany. In the United States, the social fact of racial inequality was pervasive well into the twentieth century, illustrated by the re-enslavement of large numbers of black Americans between the Civil War and World War II, and legally sanctioned racial segregation well into the 1960s.[62]

Laws and policies based on mono-racial categories were undermined by a complex set of factors and series of events, including universalistic liberal principles that promised equality and growing numbers of racially mixed peoples.[63] Cast for the most part in biological terms in the nineteenth century, racist theories were reformulated in sociocultural terms in the twentieth. It is a much debated question whether this shift from biology to culture has ended racism or shifted it to new terrains.[64] In practice, the difference between what is biologically innate and what is culturally deeply ingrained is by no means clear. Although the language in which race is discussed publicly has changed greatly, there exists considerable continuity in political discourses, use of stereotypes, and targeted groups. Many conservatives argue that the causes of inequality between the races and differential rates of social mobility are due to the deficiencies of disadvantaged groups or developing societies. For them, the causal efficacy of historical inequities rooted in slavery, racism, and imperialism have lost their force in global markets and under conditions of equal opportunity. The sources of individual and societal failures are to be found in values and habits. Biologically equal, individuals and groups array themselves hierarchically in terms of culture. What needs to change is not the system in which individuals and groups operate, but the help they mobilize for themselves. Progressives insist that while traditional racist hierarchies have been dismantled, their delayed impact on the social conditions of individuals and groups has not. This historical legacy requires constant reform and action. Economic, political, structural, and institutional causes recreate persistent inequalities along racial, class, and other lines; this legacy needs to be addressed through incessant political reform or radical transformation. It is pointless to adjudicate this deep-seated disagreement in the abstract. What matters to me is its persistence. Publicly sanctioned racism is a thing of the past. But deep internal divides over questions of race persist, and they are a powerful force for a pluralist politics.

Around the turn of the twentieth century, theories of empire and racial conceptions of Anglo-America illustrated sharp racial and ethnic boundaries coexisting with the blurred lines of an imperial politics organized around various kinds of colonies, and subsequently, Dominions and the Commonwealth. Nineteenth-century British imperialism occurred in close interaction with evolving visions of Anglo-America. The idea of an encompassing Anglo-American political association incited the imagination of a growing number of British and

American commentators.[65] Some form of a Greater Britain would be desirable to help Britain extend its dominant position well into the twentieth century. The animating source of British discussions was unease and anxiety about the rapid changes transforming technology, economy, society, and Britain's place in the modern world. America was the object of both admiration and scorn. The question of the future of Britain and its empire, a possible union of all English-speaking peoples, and the prospect of the Anglo-Saxon race were all deeply intermingled. "A range of arguments pointed to Anglo-America as a unified racial–political order: a singularity."[66]

To date, historians disagree on the character of that vision. Some see it as an extension of Anglo-America's Lockean logic. Others view this as the period in which a rapacious liberalism conquered the world by whatever means necessary. But for most of the nineteenth century, reality was probably more complicated. The British Empire, Bernard Porter argues, was globe-spanning. But the motives leading to its acquisition were mixed; its spirit was ambivalent; and its impact on the world was uneven, more so than either its supporters or its critics have been willing to acknowledge.[67] One reason was the very different types of colonies Britain controlled: India, the British West Indies, trading posts, naval stations, and settlement colonies. Another reason was the fact that the acquisition and rule of many of the colonies was relatively easy and did not require an inordinate straining of either British resources or will. Toward the end of the nineteenth century, however, Britain's policy and public sentiment turned more explicitly and enthusiastically toward clearly imperialist ventures, embracing the idea of Anglo-America.

In Chapter 2, Duncan Bell tracks the intellectual contours of the political–racial thought that accompanied and spurred on Anglo-America and British imperialism during the Victorian era. Theories of civilization and empire illustrate conceptions that had a powerful hold on political imaginations. Many voices advocated the creation of a Greater Britain that would encompass Anglo-America, either in one union of all settler colonies under British leadership or, more radically, in the unification of the American with the British empires. These theories were fully racialized and envisioned preferred political orders dominated by Anglo-America. Although some observers emphasized connections with the settler colonies, others focused on America. Unity, especially racial unity, was widely considered important and desirable. And the Anglo-American world was widely believed to extend Britain's imperial rule under the guise of an all-embracing global polity. The Anglo-American idea was more than an instrumental construct. Bell argues that as political discourse, this world order argument can be interpreted as a utopian space made possible by technological innovation. A racial–political order dominated by Anglo-Saxons and Anglo-America held the promise of bringing justice and peace to a world convulsed by modernity and violence. Shorn of its explicit racial content, Bell argues, this vision has continued to find a strong echo in the twentieth century: in American Cold War discourses of world federalism, in Cold War Atlanticism, and in a global "Concert of Democracies" to institutionalize the democratic peace.[68]

Herman Schwartz provides in Chapter 3 a materialist argument that complements Bell's analysis. Metaphorically speaking, Anglo-America has played the role of suburban sprawl to Europe's core city and Asia's working-class slums. Owners of undeveloped land create capital using debt such as mortgages; interest on capital is paid by streams of future income derived from future land cultivation; and land and debt draw in large pools of labor. The availability of vast tracts of land, the labor that this land attracted, and the capital that it generated all prevented a sharp demarcation of domestic from international affairs as the dynamic relations between the imperial center and settler societies evolved, first in a series of boom-and-bust cycles and later in relations marked by other powerful transnational factors. Economic growth thus creates the racial, cultural, and ethnic identity politics so characteristic of Anglo-America. With Britain as a partial exception in terms of the sources of immigration, Schwartz traces three institutional forms that characterize Anglo-America as it transforms land into capital and draws in labor: the classic, absolutist sovereign state that controls overseas plantation economies and relies on coerced labor, exemplified first by Britain in Ireland; the decentralized and locally controlled state attracting immigration eventually from all quarters of the world, first showcased in the northern states of the USA; and the partially autonomous Dominion states populated for a long time largely by immigrants from Great Britain.

Schwartz's analysis resonates with James Belich's bold and brilliant book on settler societies. Helped by rapid technological advances in communications and transportation, the size of Anglo-America exploded in the nineteenth century.[69] Without belittling other revolutions, the importance of institutions, or the role of imperial networks, Belich focuses our attention on the settler revolution. The very term "settler" misleads us into thinking "stability." Our stereotypes of "nomadic" hunters and "settled" farmers, however, have it the wrong way around. "It is agricultural societies that tend to be on the move," Hugh Brody points out; "hunting peoples are far more firmly settled."[70] European empires, writes Belich, dominated one and a half continents; European settlements ended up dominating three and a third continents, including Siberia. Settlement, not empire, powered Europe's expansion. And nowhere more than in Anglo-America.[71] Cultural hybridity that draws from and generates multiple traditions is the shared characteristic of all successful settler societies.[72]

In various "Wests" across various continents, the settler revolution followed its own rhythm, varying between the compression of time that accompanied "explosive colonization" and the compression of space that came with "re-colonization." Explosive colonization was spurred by mass transfers of settlers, funds, goods, and ideas, creating a boom mentality. After the inevitable bust, the reintegration of settler colony and metropolis converted settler communities into long-range staples exporters, virtual hinterlands of the two megacities of Anglo-America – London and New York. As migrants and money flowed easily across existing political boundaries, agricultural exports from the Great Plains fed both of those cities; London eventually listed more American stocks than did New York. Social ties grew, as the elite marriage market brought women from New England to Great Britain. The zenith of Britain's empire coincided with the Boer War (1899–1902) as a potent symbol of its unmistakable vulnerability. Too weak to intervene militarily on the European continent, Britain's empire had difficulty holding on to its extra-European colonies. The question is not why that empire declined and eventually fell apart, but why it lasted as long as it did. Belich's answer holds that explosive colonization and stabilizing recolonization made the United States into a superpower and extended Britain's status as a superpower by half a century.[73]

In Chapter 4, Audie Klotz shifts our perspective on Anglo-America. Her central argument is based on an inversion of the conventional Self–Other distinction in contemporary analyses of international relations, as reflected in contemporary theorizing about international security communities. Conventional thinking holds that common interests, over time, generate the collective identities that make war unthinkable as a means for resolving political disputes. In this view, a united national community eventually is able to bridge the traditional divides that inhere in international politics. Building on the work of Karl Deutsch, Bruce Russett has made the case specifically for Britain and the United States, while Emanuel Adler and Michael Barnett have developed the general argument.[74] Klotz argues the inverse case, paying particular attention to the positions of South Africa, India, and Ireland in the British Empire. In the first half of the twentieth century one distinctive aspect of the Anglo community was the tension between a racially white "external Self" and a racially non-white "internal Other." Identity threats that emerged from encountering indigenous populations that immigrants experienced as foreign and threatening were thus countered by a transnational community based on racial identification. Klotz charts two subsequent stages in the evolution of that transnational community: the search for a contained political autonomy by the Dominions first; and the emergence of a genuine multi-racial Commonwealth later. Klotz's chapter examines three periods: growing demands for political autonomy in the British Empire, subsequent demands for autonomy or independence by members of the League of Nations during the interwar period, and political bargaining in the United Nations and the Commonwealth after 1945. The community between motherland and colony was at first deeply felt. But kinship eventually gave way to a sense of strategic partnership between Dominion nationalism and British imperialism – with two notable exceptions, the Boers and parts of Francophone Canada. Britain and the Dominions pursued foreign policies reflecting a security community based on political choice rather than imperial loyalty. And during the twentieth century, South Africa moved from being a contested part of the imperial Self (during the Boer War) to an external Self (during the decades of Dominion and Commonwealth politics) and an external Other (during its pariah period between 1961 and 1994); Ireland and India also traversed deeply contested terrain over the boundaries between internal and external Self and Other, with outcomes that differed from those in South Africa.

Srdjan Vucetic argues in Chapter 5 that Anglo-America is a vital bequest of the British Empire. The gradual loosening of Britain's imperial bonds and the empire's eventual disappearance left in its wake a number of peoples and states committed to liberal democracy, capitalism, common law, and the English language. Despite the lack of formal bonds, or perhaps because of it, Anglo-America continues to punch above its weight in an international order once dominated by London and, for the time being, by Washington and New York. Vucetic shows how the meaning of Anglo-Saxon identity has changed over time. He examines two historical moments: the late nineteenth century as revealed in the political discourses of Anglo-Saxon liberals, and a century later in the 1980s during the patriation of the Canadian constitution of 1982 and the Australian bicentenary of 1988. In the late nineteenth century, he argues, racial politics was brutally direct in creating political hierarchies that were exclusionary. Today, multicultural politics struggles with opaque borders of inclusion and exclusion.

The conceptual world that informed Anglo-America has changed dramatically over time. In the late nineteenth century most students of international relations believed that Americans of British descent were innately superior to all other races. They thought of Anglo-America as predestined to bring good government, economic prosperity, and Christian religion to all of the other, inferior and less fortunate peoples of the world. Racial theories were the foundation of international analysis in the academy in Australia and the United States.[75] In America, the nascent discipline of "imperial relations" was informed by the biological rather than the territorial division of the world. The justification for racial hierarchy and exclusionary policies was widely believed to rest on evolutionary theory rather than imperialist history. The predecessor of the journal *Foreign Affairs*, founded in New York in the 1920s, was the *Journal of Race Development*.[76] In short, race was very much present at the creation of Anglo-America and of the Anglo-American discipline of international relations. Not so today, when it cannot be found even at the margins of the rationalist categories that inform liberalism and realism.

Anglo-American varieties of international communities and domestic multiculturalisms

World War II, the Holocaust, the break-up of the British Empire, and the decline of the Commonwealth altered beyond recognition imperial and race-based notions of the Anglo-American West. Transnational opposition movements helped bring about change as they worked for the principle of racial equality and human rights and organized pan-African and pan-Asian movements. In 1919, the British Empire and the United States defeated the Japanese bid to have a racial equality clause included in the Versailles treaty. After 1945, however, the tide turned decisively. The adoption of the Universal Declaration of Human Rights in 1948 and the decolonization movement of the 1950s and 1960s provided a very different political context for civilizational politics on a global scale.[77] With a few exceptions, justifications for empire have played a much smaller role than advocacy of hegemony and multilateralism. Furthermore, explicit invocation of race has all but disappeared from public speech even though the language of modernization and economic development has provided political space for the articulation of views with a lineage to older race-based arguments.[78]

Anglo-American communities: complex sovereignties, shared diplomatic cultures, and special relations

These historical developments have permitted Anglo-American relations to become the exemplar for conditions of complex interdependence and transnational relations, which arguably typify international relations in the age of globalization. This, at least, was the core claim of Robert Keohane and Joseph Nye's foundational book first published in 1977.[79] Keohane and Nye identified complex interdependence as a novel condition in world politics. The source of interdependence among actors could be military, as conventionally understood. But it could also refer to the vulnerability or sensitivity in non-military issues, measured by the costs of pursuing alternative policies or change under existing policies. Complexity refers to the existence of multiple channels, the absence of hierarchy among issues, and the relative insignificance of military force. Finally, complex interdependence generates distinctive political processes in world politics. Conceived as two ideal types, complex interdependence contrasts sharply with realism. Neither type is readily identified in world politics. The main explanatory claim of Keohane and Nye holds that as the character of world politics is shifting from the "high politics" of security to the "low politics" of prosperity, traditional realist theories of world politics fail to explain observable changes in international regimes. With their empirical focus on US–Canadian and US–Australian relations, this logic helps us understand the politics within Anglo-America, which approximates complex interdependence more than conventional power politics.

Louis W. Pauly and Chris Reus-Smit argue in Chapter 6 that, like other conceptual tools of international relations – hegemony, power, and autonomy among them – the concepts of complex interdependence and transnationalism do not capture adequately the changing nature and tensions that mark relationships within Anglo-America. The reason is simple: They elide and overlook issues of collective identity and political legitimacy that have been central to how Canada and Australia have constructed and reconstructed themselves, both in the light of history and often in explicit or implicit dialogue with the United States. Pluralist practices, bequeathed in substantial part by their shared Anglo heritage, manage unfinished internal conflicts, attempt to recast collective identities, and effectively reshape bilateral relations with the United States and other states. In the Canadian case, the changing character and meaning of a shared border reflects a continuous and increasingly complicated negotiation. For Australia, the practices associated with the contemporary outreach to Asia provide insight into what has been a continuous and subtle process of social and political reconstitution. Convergence and divergence with norms promoted by the United States suggest in both cases that complex interdependence no longer captures the essential political and cultural drivers of bilateral relations.

If they were writing *Power and Interdependence* today, Keohane and Nye would probably agree with such an assessment. In a critical self-review of their own book, they acknowledged the importance of domestic factors, the lack of which, they write, "weakened the prospects for a deeper analysis of complex interdependence" and left the concept "hanging."[80] Returning to that very challenge, the analysis of Pauly and Reus-Smit bolsters the argument that internal and external practices are both at work in the reconstruction of identity, autonomy, and legitimacy. They characterize the transnational relationships within Anglo-America in terms of leadership, followership, and shared purposes. Complex sovereignties are negotiated in the context of networks, as Canada and Australia manage their identities and autonomy.[81] Flexible border controls permit letting in what is considered desirable and keeping out what is considered undesirable, especially for the case of the United States and Canada. Maximum feasible autonomy, not strict independence, is the policy maxim. If there is convergence, it is around the acceptance of political practices that create workable governing arrangements while at the same time making it possible to accept enduring diversity. The politics of complex sovereignty, they argue, remains as open-ended as the boundaries around a manifold West.

Relations inside Anglo-America belong to the category of "warm" peace, part of a broad range of peaceful relations that also encompass "normal" and "cold" peace.[82] It was not always so. The model for all others, the special relations between the USA and the UK, for example, dates back only to the peaceful resolution of the diplomatic conflict over Venezuela in the 1890s.[83] Since then, however, Anglo-America has evolved the distinctive diplomatic cultures and special relations analyzed in Chapters 7 and 8.[84] Brian Bow and Arturo Santa-Cruz trace in Chapter 7 the variable social content or relative "thickness" of specific diplomatic cultures. They map this variation through the United States' emplacement within two different versions of the West, transatlantic and Western Hemispheric. Canada ties Anglo-America to the old European West, Mexico to the new American one.[85] Within each of these spheres, they argue, Americans' ideas about sociocultural affinity support distinctly different bargaining norms and practices, as revealed within the US–Canada and US–Mexico bilateral relationships. The ideas of American elites about how the USA relates to either country shape neighborly relations and conceptions of identity and purpose. Based on different senses of compatibility, trust, and obligation, distinctive diplomatic cultures have evolved over time. In North America, sociocultural affinity or distance trumps geography. Both Canada and Mexico try to secure US self-restraint, and both have succeeded to a very large degree, if on different terms. More extensive and reflexive than with Mexico, US restraint with Canada is predicated on mutual identification and a sense of obligation. With Mexico, there exists no such affinity. Instead, the USA exerts a self-restraint that is calculated and thus more circumscribed. To be sure, the robustness of a well-understood quid pro quo sets its relations with Mexico apart from those with other Latin American countries. However, these relations lack the foundation for building the more intimate cooperation that exists between the USA and Canada. Diplomatic practices are thus constantly challenged by both the underlying cultural and ideological diversity within each society, and by the practical demands of bilateral diplomacy.

David MacDonald and Brendon O'Connor amplify the same point in Chapter 8, with specific reference to the "special relations" between the United States, Australia, and New Zealand, with Britain fading into the background in the American century. Strong bonds of common historical experience, shared interests and purposes have had demonstrable and durable effects on a strategic culture that supports the notion of special relationship, first with Britain and later with the United States. Special relations reflect conceptions of interest. But the strategic culture typifying them creates also a political language of sentimentality that at times can counter interests when they point away rather than toward Anglo-America. The notion of specialness is important because political constructions of cultural similarity, a strong sense of shared history, and emotional identification are important for legitimation − which the utilitarian calculus of *Realpolitik*, pragmatism, and the personal chemistry between individual leaders often fail to provide. For American foreign policy, religious imagery and the imagination of modernity offer master narratives of American politics and culture that help define the special relevance or irrelevance of particular relationships. The story of the two antipodean allies of the United States, Australia and New Zealand, illustrates this central point.

Anglo-America: three patterns of internal division and pluralism

Despite its remarkable openness and internal pluralism, a unified conception of the West with Anglo-America at its center has been a favorite theme of a number of mostly conservative writers.[86] The view of an unbroken lineage, however, is problematic. Much of the historical evidence points toward different genealogies and multiple understandings of the West. Focusing on the political, violent, and unplanned synthesis of classical, Christian, and Germanic influences between the fifth and the eighth centuries CE, for example, David Gress has traced a ruptured evolution of Western values, identities, practices, and institutions that stretches "from Plato to NATO."[87] For Samuel Huntington, the unity of the West is instead a very recent product. Since its beginning, America was the New World, which defined itself in opposition to the corrupt and evil ways of the Old. Freedom, equality, opportunity, and the future reigned on one side of the Atlantic; repression, class conflict, hierarchy, and backwardness ruled on the other.[88] More recently, students of political economy have identified clear differences between Anglo-America's liberal market economies and the coordinated market economies on the European continent. And Robert Kagan's analysis of the West is built around a profound split between the Kantian European world of legalistic norms and the Hobbesian American world of power politics.[89] Unified conceptions of the West thus encounter inconsistencies when looking at its history, and contradictions when analyzing the concrete case of contemporary Anglo-American international relations. As is true of unified conceptions of Islam and Huntington's argument about clashing civilizations, they are the result of explicitly political projects that reify political categories and attribute to them essential characteristics that crystallize around core values.

Distinctive of Anglo-America are three different multicultural patterns. First is the deep racial divide that characterized all of Anglo-America at the beginning of the twentieth century and that, in attenuated and different forms, has continued to shape internal politics in the United States, South Africa, and Mexico. Second is New Zealand's current transformation from its traditional White–Māori biculturalism into a new triculturalism that blends characteristics of the indigenous population with those of old British settlers and new Asian immigrants. Third is the contested multicultural politics of Australia and Canada, which centers around longstanding, principled conflicts and ever-changing political practices yielding pragmatic accommodation.

The United States, South Africa, and Mexico offer ready examples for the first pattern of multiculturalism. Half a century after *Brown vs. Board of Education*, in an era of sharp political polarization and mobilization, Barack Obama's presidency illustrates that America's race problem has not been solved as much as it has been reconfigured in important ways.[90] What was once unimaginable – the election of an African-American as President – has come to pass, opening up new political possibilities and activating ancient prejudices and hatreds. For better and for worse, that single event has effected a seismic change in America's collective imagination. The election of a Catholic John F. Kennedy in 1960 was important, and so are the prejudices that Mitt Romney, a Mormon, encountered in 2008 when running for the Republican nomination for the Presidency. But these religious milestones and millstones are dwarfed by the significance of Obama's election as an indelible marker in American history.

Similarly, South Africa's history of race relations in the twentieth century was marked by the 1948 decision of the Afrikaner National Party to institutionalize a regime of *apartheid* in the very year that the Universal Declaration of Human Rights was adopted. About forty years later, Mandela's South Africa emerged from stigmatized, pariah statehood. When the African National Congress won the first free elections in 1994, it initiated a new set of political choices, based on existing traditions and newly emerging ones, that made it possible to conceive of South Africa as a multi-racial democracy. Mexico, finally, like South Africa, is living at the periphery of Anglo-America, not in its midst. Like all of the Americas, Mexico with its Hispanic legacy has an indigenous population that makes race a relevant political category, as illustrated during the last two decades by the Chiapas rebellion. Yet, historically, Mexico has tried to elide its race question and bury it altogether during the revolution by embracing the notion of Mexico as a *mestizo* or mixed race society. As a member of an alternate West, Mexico thus fits the general pattern of contested identity politics and multiple traditions that also characterizes Anglo-America.

New Zealand illustrates a second, very different pattern of Anglo-America's multiculturalism, which David MacDonald and Brendon O'Connor discuss in Chapter 8. New Zealand bridges the differences among its Māori, Pacific Islander or Polynesian, European, and Asian populations. Non-European groups are now growing so fast that by 2025, almost half of the country's population will be non-European. Open to external influences and living in a benign international setting, New Zealand has been relatively open to a large influx of immigrants from Asia and the Pacific Islands. China's rise is likely to reinforce rather than wall off that openness. Although it maintained restrictive quotas for Asian immigrants into the 1950s, in contrast to Australia New Zealand never adopted a "whites only" immigration policy. Before 1908, Chinese were considered "friendly aliens" who could be naturalized as British subjects. Between 1908 and the 1950s, Chinese and Asian immigration almost stopped, but it has since increased greatly so that Asians are now as numerous as Māoris. The indigenous population was marked by a strong culture, a unified language, and a fairly unified political movement on the North Island. The 1840 Treaty of Waitangi is the founding document of the enduring myth of racial equality between Māori and white New Zealanders. The promises of sovereignty over Māori land, access to resources, and legal protection were often broken. Compared, however, to other indigenous groups in Anglo-America, Māoris fared better. They had a large numerical preponderance throughout the country, a strong military tradition, internal cohesion, and discipline. It was their power, not the generosity of white settlers, that made their lives under white rule comparatively comfortable. This is not to argue that the Māori population is economically and socially as well off as whites. And it does not enjoy institutional parity in contemporary politics. But Māoris have their own political parties, enjoy considerable political influence, own a national television station, have national funding to support Māori culture, and have succeeded in making theirs one of New Zealand's two official languages. Race relations are far from ideal in New Zealand, but they compare favorably with those in other parts of Anglo-America.

With rising Asian immigration, the growing economic pull of China cannot help but be of great significance in shifting the country's underlying identity politics. New Zealand recognized the People's Republic of China (PRC) early in December 1972. It was the first to sign a bilateral trade agreement after Hong Kong's return to China in August 1997, to recognize China as a market economy in April 2004, and to sign a free trade agreement with China in April 2008. Asia is no longer viewed as an undifferentiated Other, as was true as late as the 1950s. Instead, New Zealand has for economic reasons become "Asia-literate." With economic ties, tourism, and student exchanges all growing, and with the number of immigrants from Asia rising fast, China is now funding language and culture programs in 26 Auckland schools. These educational efforts enjoy the full support of the New Zealand government, which sees Kiwi ignorance as the greatest impediment to securing the country's position at the edge of high-growth Asia. What is likely to evolve is not a third Asia-in-New Zealand identity, but a New Zealand–Asian hybrid identity that would be bolstered by the varieties of immigrants from different parts of China and Asia. New Zealand's traditional White–Māori biculturalism thus could evolve into a grudge (for the skeptics) or genuine (for the optimists) triculturalism, or a pluri-culturalism characterized by the spread of hybrid identities overlaying distinct cultural poles.

A third multiculturalism typifies Canada and Australia. As Louis W. Pauly and Chris Reus-Smit argue in Chapter 6, in both countries the conflict between the descendants of English-speaking settlers, indigenous populations, and, in the case of Canada, French Canadians leaves unresolved the tension between the communal identities invoked by eighteenth-century nationalism and the individualism of nineteenth-century liberalism. Canada has managed to live with both, as Quebec has carved out a lasting opposition, based on communal terms, to the multiculturalism that is Canada's official policy. Australia meanwhile is trying to hitch indigenous memories and Asian realities to Anglo-American sensibilities that retain a perceptible skepticism about the multiculturalism the country has come to espouse.

In recent decades, Canada's internal pluralism has revolved around traditional ethno-nationalist and linguistic lines. After the end of the first global war in the eighteenth century, the descendants of French explorers and settlers found themselves part of a British colony that gradually moved toward political autonomy and in 1982 severed its last legal bonds with the British Parliament. In sharp contrast to the English-speaking majority, French-speaking Quebec insists, like ethnic minorities in other Western societies, that its distinct ethno-nationalist identity should not be submerged in an all-embracing post-national Canadian multiculturalism. Prime Minster Trudeau's bold move to redefine Canadian identity along multicultural lines in the 1970s had to accommodate a murky compromise with the ethno-nationalist realities of a Quebec that insisted on the legitimacy of its territorial and group cohesion and refused to be dissolved into an atomized post-national society. On the question of Quebec, Canada has thus evolved a contested multiculturalism that both celebrates enjoyment in diversity and experiences sullen indifference.[91] Quebec's and Canada's future is far from clear. Separation within Canada, secession from Canada, or submersion in North America all seem possible, as does a continuation of the status quo. Stuck between a rhetorical multiculturalism and a de facto biculturalism, Canada's internal pluralism is beyond question.

Australia's self-understanding and institutionalized practices underwent a momentous shift in the 1970s. What had been a white, culturally defensive Anglo society that denied its indigenous people full rights and citizenship experienced nothing short of a revolution in social policy with the extension of full citizenship to the Australian Aborigines, an activist policy of multiculturalism, and a change in immigration policy. Yet, the vast majority of the Australian population has virtually no contact with the Aborigines, who account for less than 3 percent of the population, live in larger concentrations only in the outback of three states and a few urban ghettos, and have had relatively small direct impact on Australian identity. This is in contrast to their large indirect effect through the shaping of Australian self-understanding. Few politicians challenge multiculturalism openly, and debate focuses on its meaning rather than its merits. As it espoused a more assimilationist version of multiculturalism than had the Labor Party it replaced, some culture and history wars erupted under the conservative Howard Government starting in 1996. Conservatives are skeptical about grand identity debates and have an inclination to just get on with things unquestionably Australian. They favor a relaxed and comfortable manner that does not have to confront constantly thorny issues such as offering an apology to atone for past violence or discrimination, or debating the representation of Australia's past in a new National Museum. Since many multicultural practices such as land rights and affirmative action have become fully institutionalized, this can create an uncomfortable tension between institutions and still current attitudes. The internal pluralism of Australia, however, is by now beyond question. In short, these internal issues, rather than the relations with their Anglo-American partners, have posed the most serious political challenges for both countries. Viewed through Australian and Canadian looking-glasses, complex sovereignty is a constitutive element of the Anglo-American West. Unresolved differences over individual autonomy and group legitimacy, and the conflicts and accommodations they engender, thus blur the boundary between Anglo-America and a larger global civilization that witnesses similar struggles.

Internal divisions and international engagements

Internal divisions yield different kinds of international engagement. Depending on their audience, Canadian government officials will play up commonalities when talking to US officials, or differences when addressing domestic audiences. During the last century Canadian foreign policy has come to emphasize a community of fate of white Anglos less, and shared Western values more. At times, Canada's internal divisions lead the country's foreign policy establishment to adopt high-minded rhetoric and broadly liberal poses, while critics on the right routinely call for a closer "special relationship" with the United States and critics on the left insist on tangible commitments to multilateralism and anti-militarism. Australia's international engagement has also changed with the country's domestic transformation. The sense of a white settler society stuck at the edge of Asia had instilled a sense of insularity mitigated by traditional security alliances. Economic globalization and radical transformation of Australia's national identity have led to a vigorous integration with Asia that has not been halted by domestic contestations over Australian identity. Internal transformation has been accompanied by liberal internationalism. A new openness marks both the domestic and the foreign policies of the new Australia. In contrast, Mexico's internal divisions have been much less important in shaping its international engagements. Still, Mexican elites play on the theme of similarities with the USA by stressing differences with Europe, a republican form of government, and the optimistic and future-oriented outlook of the Americas.

There has been less of a need to stress differences with the USA that are in plain sight for all to see; for instrumental political reasons, however, anti–Americanism is often manipulated by elites who invoke US hyper-imperialism and capitalism. In the case of America and Mexico, distance is predicated on perceived sociocultural differences. These ideas have been challenged, both by demographic flows across state boundaries and by diversity and ideological divides within them. Canada has tried to accommodate differences through multiculturalism. It continues to struggle with the issue of unity – due to ongoing political challenges from its assertive Francophone minority and its profoundly marginalized native communities. Mexico has long denied its own diversity through the *mestizaje* myth, which since 1994 has been unsettled by the eruption of an indigenous insurrection in the south. And the influx of Mexican migrants to the USA highlights America's pluralist character. These domestic political tensions, and their anchoring within multiple Wests, thus have profound consequences for the international relations and diplomatic cultures of Anglo-America. Finally, New Zealand's tricultural turn in domestic and foreign affairs has led to a partial distancing from the USA, a strong embrace of Pacific Island states, an incomplete turn toward Asia, and continued sibling rivalry with Australia.

In sum, in three different patterns, Anglo-America exhibits a diversity which yields identity politics and international engagements that are both complicated and vibrant. Taken together, they point to Anglo-America's relative openness as a distinctive quality – openness to transnational influences and domestic political arrangements. Different patterns of internal multiculturalism have produced different terms of international engagement. Always attuned to the requirements of reaffirming the legitimacy of their evolving and contested multiculturalism, Anglo-American states have sought to maximize their political autonomy while at the same time furthering deeper global integration. In doing so they offer vivid illustrations of a pluralism that characterizes both Anglo-America and a global civilization of multiple modernities that pose vexing questions for both.

This predicament is illustrated most clearly in the inner core of Anglo-America. Internal divisions in the USA also affect its terms of international engagement. Since the late 1970s there have existed two competing policy alliances, organized around contrasting color-blind and race-conscious principles, each of which claims to be the true heir of the civil rights movement.[92] A near universal repudiation of white supremacist attitudes has given way to a polarized, partisan politics. Political divisions run very deep and cover a remarkably broad spectrum of policy issues. President Obama searches for a pragmatic middle ground that embraces diversity and finds ways of uniting around the pursuit of common endeavors. Yet it remains unclear whether Obama will be able to give specific content to the unifying social purpose and to the collective national experience that has brought Americans to this point in their history. "The need for some forms of unity is real," write Rogers Smith, Desmond King, and Philip Klinker; but the source of that unity is far from clear.[93] This daunting multicultural challenge at home, they argue, is matched by an analogous cosmopolitan challenge abroad. Obama's international charisma is rooted in a mixture of races, religions, and regions in world politics. At the same time he also stands for dominant though contested forms of American identity: Christianity over Islam or secularity, American patriotism over foreign allegiances, and racial unity over racial separatism. Is there a pragmatic middle way that combines the celebration of national greatness in an era of declining American primacy with the embracing of multilateralism and internationalism in an era of fragmentary globalization? The necessity for conversation and compromise must be reconciled with the existence of competing and irreconcilable absolute truth claims.[94] For that task the continuous reinvention of America as a shining city on the hill and the celebration of Americans as the new Adam (and Eve) of Western culture can open up unexpected eddies and channels; but they can also create dangerous rapids and dams. To navigate that narrow passage from liberal America as a New World to a New World Order that will contain and go beyond liberal America will require more than the pragmatic politics of American ingenuity and imagination.[95] If it can be navigated at all, it will be by a politics that, though closely linked to America's national affairs, will have to transcend it.

Conclusion

Sustained by a domestic liberalism steeped deeply in racism, over the last century Anglo-America has shifted from the pursuit of racial supremacy and empire abroad to an interdependent community of states marked by complex sovereignties, shared diplomatic cultures, and special relations, grounded domestically in distinctive forms of democratic capitalism and multicultural politics. Then as now, the substance and form of international engagements have been closely tied to domestic politics.

Illustrating this important fact, contemporary analyses of international politics are enriched by acknowledging both the historical evolution of liberal internationalism and the contested nature of its core concepts. In the 1950s, for example, Karl Deutsch and his colleagues developed the concept of "security community."[96] Extending Deutsch's path-breaking work on nationalism to the international realm and grounded in a series of historical case studies of national integration, the main empirical and normative finding supported the notion of "pluralistic" security communities. Roughly conterminous with the North Atlantic Treaty Organization (NATO) as the center of the West, a North Atlantic security community was developing in which war among Western states was becoming increasingly unthinkable. With the end of the Cold War and the disintegration of the Soviet Union, this concept experienced a renaissance in the 1990s as scholars sought to better understand a new world politics that combined global and international elements.[97] As they did, political concerns shifted away from the exclusive preoccupation with national or state security to encompass broader notions of human security. A large body of research established a robust, though not uniformly accepted, empirical finding that was consonant with Deutsch's substantive work. Democracies rarely have fought each other.[98] In this view it was not the Cold War but the dynamics of democratic politics that secured the democratic peace. This was the ground on which neoconservative politicians and scholars of liberal internationalist persuasions proposed the creation of a "league" or "concert" of democracies, thus moving some distance toward the amalgamation of security communities that Deutsch had warned against.[99]

Is the century-long evolution of the Anglo-American West from racialized empire to multicultural community a matter of plain empirics, historical narration, or a combination of both? And if it is both, what is the balance between the two? There exists no quick and easy answer to that question. Furthermore, it also remains an open question whether liberal multiculturalism has eliminated traditional race-based hierarchies (by emphasizing the idea and practice of cultural diversity in the era of human rights); whether it merely conceals the racial–liberal symbiosis in a new kind of politics (which appears to accommodate diversity at the surface only to resist ever more strongly a more far-reaching transformation of its traditional core);[100] or whether it accommodates itself to various sources of opposition through a series of pragmatic compromises. These are difficult questions and our answers are, at best, tentative speculations. It seems safe to venture here only one guess. In its protean politics the West appears always at risk of sliding back into deplorable, old practices of exclusion and unjust rule; and it always holds forth the promise of evolving admirable, new practices that search out emerging commonalities in evolving diversities.

Notes

1 Earlier drafts of this chapter were presented at the 2010 annual meetings of the International Studies Association and the American Political Science Association, and a May 2011 conference hosted by the Munk Center at the University of Toronto. I would like to thank the discussants at these meetings: Duncan Bell and Andrew Gamble at the ISA meeting; Robert Keohane, Ron Krebs, Jennifer Mitzen, and Herman Schwartz at the APSA meeting; and a large number of colleagues who participated in the Toronto conference. I thank Martin Bernal for his detailed criticisms and suggestions. And most importantly I thank the contributors to this book, from whom I have learned enormously and who have been generous to a fault with their comments, suggestions, and friendly criticisms. For their excellent research assistance I am indebted to Emma Clarke, Elisa Charbonnel, and Jill Lyon. Sarah Tarrow has, as always, helped smooth my prose. Finally, I would like to acknowledge with enormous gratitude the generous financial support that I received in 2009–10 from the Louise and John Steffens Founders' Circle Membership at the Institute of Advanced Studies in Princeton.
2 Katzenstein 2010a; Browning and Lehti 2010b.
3 Churchill 1956–58; Roberts 2007; Bennett 2007a.
4 Vucetic 2010b, 1.
5 Freud 1961, 13.
6 Melleuish 2009, 239.
7 *The Economist* 2008a, 71.
8 Toye 2010, 234–7, 315; Hari 2010.
9 *The Economist* 2004, 39.
10 Churchill 1956–58; Roberts 2007.
11 *The Economist* 2008b, 66.
12 *The Economist* 2008a, 71.

13 Bush 2010, 246.

14 Burns 2009. At the beginning of his speech in Westminster Hall in June 2011, President Obama again referred to the relationship as "special."

15 *The Economist* 2010a.

16 Huntington 1996, 22–7; Abu-Lughod 1989, 34.

17 Gong 1984; Aydin 2007; Bowden 2009.

18 Whitaker 1954; Santa-Cruz 2005, 6–8, 17–18, 34–42. See also Jones 2007.

19 Hartz 1964.

20 Eisenstadt 2002b.

21 O'Gorman 1961.

22 Smith 2010. In addition, he emphasizes that cross-civilizational engagements is a central category for comprehending the dynamism of the multiple Americas. On the American South, see Knöbl 2006, 2007.

23 Stanley 2006; Chipman 1989.

24 Tensions between assimilation and association were a constant in France's relations with Africa. They were mediated by the acceptance of a tiny portion of the African elite into French society. In general, though, the principle of human rights based on racial equality, embedded in the core values France held dear, clashed plainly and painfully with French racist discourses, practices, and policies. See Stovall and van den Abbeele (2003) and Peabody and Stovall (2003). Whatever their other differences, on this point the similarities between French and Anglo-American incarnations of the West are striking.

25 Meunier 2007; Mathy 1993.

26 Huntington 2004.

27 The next paragraphs draw on Katzenstein 2010c.

28 Hartz 1955; Abbott 2005.

29 Smith 1988, 1993, 1997, 1999, 2007. For a review of liberal theory that places Smith in the context of two subsequent interpretations, liberalism as exclusion and liberalism as multiplicity, see Stears 2007.

30 Smith 1993, 558.

31 Pocock 1975.

32 Hartz 1955, 17, 50, 55; Hulliung 2010, 5.

33 Hartz 1964; Braudel 1993, 507–23. David Hackett Fischer (1989, 783–898) develops a related argument to explain the "voluntarism" of American society in terms of the four British folkways, or "freedom ways," associated with four distinct waves of English-speaking immigrants between 1629 and 1775.

34 Hartz does not discuss or reference New Zealand. But, as I do in this book, he would probably have grouped it with Australia.

35 Hartz 1964, 3.

36 Ibid., 3–4.

37 Ibid., 22–3, 44–8, 63–5.

38 Ibid., 6, 9, 17–19, 49–63.

39 Ibid., 19.

40 In an opaque and problematic book manuscript that wrestled with the writing of world history, Hartz (1984, 264–85; see also Barber 1986, Riley 1988, and Roazen 1990) returned briefly to central themes of his first two books, placing them, tragically and unsuccessfully, in a much broader civilizational and global context.

41 This section develops further arguments made in Katzenstein 2010c, 7–10.

42 Huntington 1996, 1993a, 1993b.

43 Huntington 1993b, 24, 42–4, 48.

44 Chiozza 2002; Senghaas 1998, 71–102; Fox 2001; Henderson and Tucker 2001; Russett, Oneal, and Cox 2000; Esposito 1995, 188–253; Fox 2004, 158, 167–8, 175–226; Melleuish 2004, 237; Hobson 2007, 153–4; Ferguson 2007, 192–5; Schimmelfennig 2003, 150; Neumayer and Plümper 2009; Ferguson 2011, 312–14.

45 Fox 2004, 161–5; Jackson 2006, 1–12.
46 Collins 2004; Melleuish 2004, 240–1.
47 Puchala 1997; 2003, 117–42.
48 Geertz 1973, 17–18.
49 The next two paragraphs are adapted from Katzenstein 2010a.
50 Huntington 1981. I would like to thank Rogers Smith for pointing out some changes in Huntington's thinking.
51 Huntington 2004.
52 As Alan Wolfe (2005) argues persuasively, the empirical evidence, both historical and contemporary, puts into question some of Huntington's most important claims.
53 Kagan 2007.
54 Krasner 1978.
55 Mead 2007.
56 Ibid., 54–82.
57 Katzenstein and Keohane 2007.
58 Painter 2010, 40–2.
59 Horsman 1981; Frantzen and Niles 1997.
60 Painter 2010, 151, 151–89.
61 Lake and Reynolds 2008, 4, 5, 9.
62 Blackmon 2008.
63 Basson 2008, 2.
64 McCarthy 2009, 11–13.
65 Bell 2007a.
66 Bell 2011, 2.
67 Porter 2006, 17.
68 Ikenberry and Slaughter 2006.
69 Belich 2009.
70 Brody 2001, 7.
71 Belich 2009, 23.
72 Ibid., 42, 67–70.
73 Ibid., 435, 548–59.
74 Russett 1963; Deutsch et al. 1957; Adler and Barnett 1998c.
75 Cotton 2009, 643–4. In Australia, the pervasiveness of racist thought created tensions with the statist realism and societal liberalism that dominated scholarship at the outset of the twentieth century. The problem persists, as current rationalist theories of international relations and foreign policy often fail to acknowledge the centrality of racial categories when analyzing world politics around the turn of the twentieth century.
76 Vitalis 2005, 2010.
77 Lake and Reynolds 2008, 335–56.
78 McCarthy 2009, 4.
79 Keohane and Nye 2001.
80 Keohane and Nye 1987, 740.
81 Grande and Pauly 2005.
82 Press-Barnathan 2009, 9–13.
83 Kupchan 2010, 73–111; Vucetic 2011, 22–53; Feng 2006. More generally see Krotz 2007, 2010, 2011; Schoenbaum 1998.
84 Dumbrell 2006; Dumbrell and Schäfer 2009b.
85 O'Gorman 1961.
86 Browning and Tonra 2010.
87 Gress 1998.
88 Huntington 1996, 46–7.
89 Kagan 2003.
90 Hochschild and Weaver 2010.

91 With regard to Canada's aboriginal peoples, the outcome is even less hopeful.
92 Smith, King, and Klinker 2011.
93 Ibid., 132.
94 Ibid., 227–8.
95 This formulation is taken from the subtitle of Ghaneabassiri 2010. For a more conventional international liberal argument, see Ikenberry 2011a, 2011b.
96 Deutsch et al. 1957.
97 Adler and Barnett 1998c.
98 Doyle 1986.
99 McCain 2007; Ikenberry and Slaughter 2006.
100 Balibar 1991; Novkov 2007; Short and Kambouri 2010.

PART I

PART I

2

THE PROJECT FOR A NEW ANGLO CENTURY

Race, space, and global order[1]

Duncan Bell

> I believe that the twentieth century is par excellence "The Anglo-Saxon Century," in which the English-speaking peoples may lead and predominate the world.
>
> (Dos Passos 1903, vii)

Prophets have long dreamt of schemes to govern a violent and unpredictable world. This chapter sketches a synoptic intellectual history of a prominent variation on the theme: the attempt to unify the constituent elements of the "Anglo-world" into a single globe-spanning community, and to harness their purported world-historical potential as an agent of order and justice.[2] Since the late nineteenth century numerous commentators have preached the benefits of unity, though they have often disagreed on the institutional form it should assume. These are projects for the creation of a new Anglo century.

The opening two sections of the chapter explore overlapping elements of the *fin de siècle* Anglo-world discourse. The first section focuses on the relationship between Britain and its colonial empire, while the following one turns to intersecting arguments over the future relationship between the empire and the United States. The third section traces the echoes of these debates through the twentieth century, discussing the interlacing articulation of imperial–commonwealth, Anglo-American, democratic unionist, and world federalist projects. Despite important differences between them, most versions of these grand supranational schemes were heirs of the earlier debates. In the final section I discuss contemporary accounts of Anglo-world supremacy. While none of the most radical plans came to fruition, the evolving debate over the nature of the Anglo-world formed a central element in the cultural construction of the "West," and highlights the extravagant hopes that have been invested in the "Anglo-Saxons" over the course of a brutal century.

This constitutes, then, an important strand in the history of modern political thought.

Empire, nation, state: on Greater Britain

To govern, Foucault argues, is "to structure the possible field of action of others."[3] The second half of the nineteenth century saw a radical transformation in both the scale of the field of action and the ways in which it could be structured. It witnessed the emergence of a novel governance *episteme* – an imaginative regime wherein established conventions and presuppositions about political order were overturned.

Daniel Deudney aptly labels this the "global industrial period." The spread of the industrial revolution was a "primal development" for global politics, as new technologies intensified interactions across the planet, reshaping the material and imaginative contexts in which debates over the future took place. "As the scale and tempo of human affairs changed, a major and tumultuous reordering of large-scale political relationships and institutions seemed imminent and inevitable."[4] The thinkers of the time – the "industrial globalists" – proselytized a wide array of schemes for transcending the anarchic international system, including pan-regional imperial structures, European union, the federation of the British empire, and even the future development of a world state. The debates about the Anglo-world were an integral element of this more general discourse.

This period also saw the rearticulation of the global politics of race – a subject to which the field of international relations (IR) remains largely blind. In 1900, at the meeting of the Pan-African Congress in London, W.E.B. DuBois predicted that the "problem of the twentieth century" would be "the problem of the color line."[5] Fears about racial contamination were rife. A civilizational dividing line was constructed between "white" peoples and others, resulting in the initiation of numerous exclusionary practices, including xenophobic immigration controls. This was a paradoxical process: "The imagined community of white men was transnational in its reach, but nationalist in its outcomes, bolstering regimes of border protection and national sovereignty."[6] Those debating the future of the Anglo-world insisted on carving out a space *within* the general identity of whiteness, establishing a stratified geo-racial imaginary. Usage of the term "race" was highly imprecise, but it typically designated a combination of cultural markers – historical mythscapes, habitus, shared language, cultural values, and political ideals – circumscribed by "whiteness." It was simultaneously cultural and biological. The French, the Germans, the Russians, and the Hispanics were all considered inferior to the Anglo-Saxons. They in turn ranked higher on the scale of civilization than other non-white racial constellations populating the world outside the Euro-Atlantic zone and its diasporic outposts. In this conception of world politics, the basic ontological unit was race, and political institutions, including the state, were only of derivative importance.

The sweeping debate over the future of the British colonial empire was conducted under the sign of "imperial federation," while the assemblage of communities under discussion was frequently labeled "Greater Britain."[7] This debate formed a key building block in the ideological construction of the twentieth-century Anglo-world. It was driven by two intersecting imperatives. Fear that British relative power was threatened by the rise of formidable states – notably Germany, Russia, and the United States – led many commentators to argue for the construction of a globe-spanning political association, encompassing Britain and its settler colonies in Australia, Canada, New Zealand, and (more ambivalently) South Africa, either to balance the new threats or to deter them from attempting to compete. These geopolitical concerns were reinforced by anxieties about the onset of democracy, with many imperial observers fearing that an expanding electorate would fail to recognize the importance of the empire, concentrating its energies and ambitions on domestic reform. It was feared – prematurely as it turned out – that a democratic polity would invariably be anti-imperial. Creating a federal Greater Britain, and populating it in part through an accelerated program of "systematic" emigration from the "mother country," was thought to be one way of neutralizing these threats. Yet even some radical and liberal admirers of democracy, including J.A. Hobson, H.M. Hyndman, and Keir Hardie, saw benefits in imperial federation. For them, Greater Britain could simultaneously hasten the peaceful development of the international system and help to democratize Britain itself through the importation of progressive practices from the more egalitarian colonies.[8]

For Hobson, great federal political communities would dominate the future, and it was thus essential to erect a "Pan-Saxon" one. As he proclaimed in *Imperialism*, a text often mistakenly read as anti-imperialist, "Christendom thus laid out in a few great civilizational empires, each with a retinue of uncivilized dependencies, seems to me the most legitimate development of present tendencies and one which would offer the best hope of permanent peace on an assured basis of inter-Imperialism."[9] Hobhouse, meanwhile, argued that imperial federation "is a model, and that on no mean scale, of the International State."[10] These arguments illustrate the two broad temporal logics that underpinned debates over Anglo-union deep into the twentieth century. In one of them, union represented the terminal point of future political development: the polity would take its place among other competing pan-racial or regional units. In the other, Anglo-union was figured as a transitional institutional formation, one that could serve as a template, catalyst, and leader of a future global political association.

Time was of the essence. Haunted by memories of the American revolution, many feared that the rapidly expanding colonies would secede, either establishing independent countries or fusing with another state – most likely the United States – thus further weakening Britain. The imperial advocates were determined to refute Alexis de Tocqueville's prediction, made in the closing lines of *Democracy in America*, that Russia and America would dominate the future.[11] Greater Britain was their answer.

A significant number of British unionists fantasized about the incorporation of the United States within an imperial federation, though most of them recognized that this was unrealistic (at least in the short term). Nevertheless, America played a crucial role in imperial discourse. First, it was regarded as a potential challenger to British supremacy, thus motivating the call for action. This was especially apparent in the wake of the McKinley Tariff of 1890, which incited the demand throughout Britain and its colonies for the creation of a system of imperial preference.[12] Second, the turbulent history of American–British relations, and in particular the War of Independence, preoccupied British imperial unionists, teaching them that the demands of colonial subjects had to be treated seriously. This meant ascribing them greater political autonomy. And finally, the United States demonstrated the power of federalism as a political technology by proving that individual liberty was compatible with vast geographical extent. This was welcome in an age in which it was commonly believed that the future belonged to huge omni-competent political units. The radical politician Charles Dilke, author of the influential *Greater Britain*, cautioned that "[i]t is small powers, not great ones, that have become impossible."[13] Three decades later Joseph Chamberlain, arch-federalist and Secretary of State for the Colonies, concurred: "[t]he days are for great Empires and not for little States."[14] Size mattered.

The debates over Greater Britain generated hundreds of proposals, differing in ambition, detail, and rationale. Three general institutional models were discussed.[15] The least ambitious was "extra-parliamentary" federation, wherein a group of distinguished individuals – organized as an imperial Advisory Council – would offer the British parliament non-binding advice on imperial affairs.[16] A more constitutionally far-reaching model was "parliamentary federalism," in which the colonies were to send elected representatives to sit in Westminster. This had been a common exhortation since the late eighteenth century, though it was much less popular in the closing decades of the Victorian age. Finally, "supra-parliamentary federalism" connoted the formation of a sovereign federal chamber supervening on the individual political assemblies of the empire. This model followed the example, above all, of the United States.[17]

The leading constitutional scholar A.V. Dicey observed that many imperial federalist proposals implied the creation of a "new federated state."[18] According to prevailing conceptions of statehood, all supra-parliamentary schemes – and indeed most parliamentary ones – could be viewed as demanding the creation of a globe-spanning Anglo-state, a polity composed of people belonging to the same nation and/or race, governed by a system of representative institutions subordinate to a supreme federal legislative chamber. The local legislatures would have a high degree of autonomy over specified domains of policy, though supreme authority would reside in either a newly created imperial chamber (sometimes labeled a "senate") or a reconfigured parliament in Westminster. This body would determine questions of war and peace, trade, and any other general issues that concerned the whole polity. The case of the extra-parliamentary advocates is less straightforward, for they were simply trying to reanimate the existing structure and were far less willing to promote significant constitutional engineering. Many of them did, however, predict radical developments in the future.

Yet not all advocates of Greater Britain proposed the creation of a vast federal polity. For many of them the key to the future lay in the shared identity of the British people spread across the world, and they argued that further institutionalization was unnecessary – it either fell outside the scope of "practical politics" or it was counterproductive. Instead, they maintained that it was essential to nourish the existing connections. This was the course that the British government ultimately followed. Dilke and Goldwin Smith, both leading public intellectuals and critics of imperial federal schemes, extolled the superiority of the British "race" and promoted a vision in which the Anglo-Saxons, acting as a collective of independent states, would shape the future. They supported the independence of the British settler colonies, but as a means to the end of Anglo-unity, not its termination. For Dilke, the "strongest of arguments in favour of separation is the somewhat paradoxical one that it would bring us a step nearer to the virtual confederation of the English race."[19] Both of them also included the United States in their vision. The cultural–racial conception of "virtual confederation" proved the most enduring; it remains an important factor in world politics to this day.

Arguments about both Greater Britain and Anglo-American union were premised on a cognitive revolution, a fundamental transformation in the perception of time and space. It was this, above all, that shaped the new governance *episteme*. In his *Considerations on Representative Government*, John Stuart Mill argued, in an idiom common throughout the eighteenth and much of the nineteenth centuries, that physical distance thwarted the union of Britain and its settler colonies. It contradicted the principles of "rational government" and precluded the necessary degree of communal homogeneity.[20] From the 1860s onwards, new communications technologies radically altered the way in which individuals perceived the physical world and the sociopolitical possibilities it contained, spawning fantasies about the elimination of geographical distance that prefigure late twentieth-century narratives of globalization. H.G. Wells declared that "modern mechanism" had created "an absolute release from the fixed conditions about which human affairs circled." For J.R. Seeley, the leading intellectual of the imperial federalist movement, the "unprecedented facility of communication which our age enjoys seems to be creating new types of state."[21] A Greater British state was now realizable. Techno-utopianism underpinned arguments about the existence of a trans-planetary British political community. "When we have accustomed ourselves to contemplate the whole [colonial] Empire together and call it England," Seeley proclaimed, "we shall see that here too is a United States. Here too is a homogeneous people, one in blood, language, religion, and laws, but dispersed over a boundless space."[22] Previously viewed as immutable, nature was now open to manipulation, even transcendence.

All of these projects depended on claims about the common identity of the dispersed Anglo people(s).[23] The argument assumed two main forms. One insisted that the social ontological foundation of the people was *race*. They were, above all,

Anglo-Saxon or members of the "English race." This view was compatible with (but did not entail) an argument that the populations of the individual colonies were coalescing into new nationalities, and that the United States already comprised a distinct nation. The other account accepted the centrality of race, but emphasized the idea of a singular *nationality*: the (relevant) population of Greater Britain was the British (or "English") nation writ global. Both conceptions sanctioned extensive discrimination. The indigenous populations of the settler colonies, and the vast majority of the people that Britain ruled over in the Caribbean, Africa, the Middle East, and Asia – and that the USA came to rule over in Hawaii and the Philippines – fell outside the scope of either account of the singular people.

The "nationality" view prevailed among late Victorian imperial thinkers. Seeley was only the most prominent to claim that "Greater Britain is homogenous in nationality."[24] During the Edwardian years, a multinational commonwealth vision began to eclipse the Seeleyean global nation state. This alternative option was not without precedent, for Lord Rosebery, the future British prime minister, had argued in 1884 that the empire should be regarded as "a commonwealth of nations."[25] This position became increasingly popular over time, not least because it mirrored the views of the political elites in the colonies. Greater Britain morphed into a post-national (or multinational) political association. In 1905 W.F. Monypenny, a leading journalist with *The Times*, conceived of the colonial empire as a "world state" that "transcends nationality" while allowing separate nationalities to flourish within it.[26] The idea of an Anglo-Saxon commonwealth was central to the influential Round Table movement (founded in 1909–10) because, as Lionel Curtis wrote in 1916, the colonies had acquired a "national consciousness of their own."[27] Both the nation-centric and the race-centric accounts, however, centered on an argument about the singularity of "the people."

The imaginative extension of the scope of the people was conjoined with an expansion of the compass of the public – of the set of individuals within the totality of the people regarded as politically significant. Arguments promulgating the unification of the British colonial empire (and also Anglo-America) embodied a claim about the existence or potentiality of an ocean-spanning public. This was a racially delimited precursor to the idea of a global public sphere.[28] Indeed one of the most conceptually innovative features of the discourse, prominent especially in the early twentieth century, was the effort to inaugurate a system of Greater British imperial citizenship.[29] It is possible to view the Anglo-racial imaginary as an example of what Arjun Appadurai terms "translocal" affiliation – of an emergent cartography that escaped the topological imperatives of the modern territorially bounded nation state.[30] As time and space were reordered, so it was increasingly argued that a strong sense of identity and belonging bound Britain and its colonial populations. However, whereas many of the examples explored by Appadurai are "counterhegemonic" – seeking to challenge extant power structures and sources of authority – the attempted reworking of "Anglo-Saxon" racial–national consciousness in the Victorian age was a hegemonic project, an effort to prolong British supremacy through novel articulations of political identity. It involved a double process of deterritorialization and reterritorialization.[31] The British polity was no longer to be conceived of as a small group of islands lying off the north-west coast of continental Europe (deterritorialization). Instead, it was to be seen as encompassing a vast range of territories in North America, the Pacific, and Southern Africa (reterritorialization). A similar geo-racial logic also helped underpin arguments about Anglo-American unity.

The reunion of the race: on Anglo-America

The unity of the Anglo-world was not preordained. For much of the nineteenth century, relations between the British empire and the United States were antagonistic. Resentment about the colonial past, incessant disputes over the Canadian border, the bitter divide over the Civil War and its aftermath, pervasive cultural condescension from the British, and widespread Anglophobia in American public life: all fanned the flames of antipathy. Mutual suspicion was the norm. It was only during the last two decades of the century, and in particular during the late 1890s, that relations thawed. This "rapprochement" – and the subsequent creation of an Anglo-American security community – has long been the subject of intense scrutiny by diplomatic historians and IR specialists. Yet insufficient attention has been paid to the political thought of the episode.

It was during the 1890s that the debate over Anglo-American union moved to the center of political debate. The Venezuelan boundary dispute (1895–96) led to acrimonious exchanges between Washington and London, but it also prompted anguished commentators on both sides of the Atlantic to recoil from the prospect of war. Numerous proposals for Anglo-American union appeared. The clamor for racial unity was in part a result of America's new assertiveness, for although the United States had been engaged in imperial conquest since its founding, the annexation of Hawaii and the Spanish–American War (1898) signaled its first sustained burst of extra-continental imperial activity. This was seen as marking a new phase in American history: either a moment when the country assumed its predestined role as a great power, or when it betrayed the founding principles of the republic. Many observers on both sides of the Atlantic insisted that the British and Americans should be united, not divided, under conditions of global imperial competition. Arguments ranged from a minimalist position that simply encouraged deeper political and economic cooperation between the two "kindred" powers, through intermediate proposals seeking a formal defensive alliance, to maximalist plans for uniting the two countries in a novel transatlantic political community.

Plans for a formal alliance blended "realist" concerns over shared security interests with assertions about underlying cultural affinities. The British imperial commentator Arthur Silva White declared that schemes for a comprehensive political union were "at present impossible," but that there "remains but one expedient – an alliance, or accord, which would pave the way to concerted action in the future."[32] Yet many commentators were skeptical about such an alliance, either because they opposed closer connections in the first place,[33] or because they thought it would instrumentalize (and potentially distort) a more fundamental form of unity. The esteemed American naval strategist Alfred T. Mahan argued that it was vital to "avoid all premature striving for alliance, an artificial and possibly even an irritating method of reaching the desired end." Instead, he continued, "I would dwell continually upon those undeniable points of resemblance in natural characteristics, and in surrounding conditions, which testify to common origin and predict a common destiny."[34] A British military writer concurred, warning against the "artificial and temporary arrangements miscalled 'alliances,' which provide occupation for European chancelleries."[35] The "organic" bonds of "kinship" were sufficient. Fearful that talk about the Anglo-Saxons was dangerously triumphalist, Benjamin Harrison, the former US president, insisted that friendship was quite enough. "Are not the continuous good and close relations of the two great English-speaking nations – for which I pray – rather imperilled than promoted by this foolish talk of gratitude and of an alliance, which is often made to take on the appearance of a threat, or at least a prophecy, of an Anglo-Saxon 'paramountcy'?"[36] This was a prescient warning.

At the core of the Anglo-American vision lay a novel set of arguments that ruptured the isomorphic relation between state, citizen, and political belonging. Advocates of racial unity frequently decoupled the state from both citizenship and patriotism. Citizenship was reimagined as a political institution grounded ultimately in racial identity, not state membership. Dicey offered the most sophisticated elaboration of the idea of common citizenship, arguing in 1897 for "the extension of common civil and political rights throughout the whole of the English-speaking people." Rejecting the idea of a transatlantic (or imperial) federation, he insisted that "reciprocal" citizenship would be enough to secure permanent unity. The idea was, he averred, simply a return to a prior condition, for such a connection had existed before the Anglo-Saxon peoples were ripped apart by the War of Independence.[37] Patriotism, meanwhile, was also reconfigured as a form of allegiance owed, in the first instance, to the race. Arguments about "race patriotism" – a term usually associated with Arthur Balfour, a future prime minister – circulated widely.[38] They implied that people were enmeshed in a concentric circle of belonging and affect, the outer (and most important) ring of which was the race. Alfred Milner, a leading imperial thinker and official, summed it up neatly: "My patriotism knows no geographical, but only racial limits … It is not the soil of England, dear as it is to me, but the speech, the tradition, the spiritual heritage, the principles, the aspirations of the British race."[39] Quoting Balfour, Charles Beresford, a British Tory politician and senior naval officer, observed that

> [I]n addition to our domestic patriotism and our Imperial or American patriotism, we also have an Anglo-Saxon patriotism, which embraces within its ample folds the whole of that great race which has done so much in every branch of human effort, and in that branch of human effort which has produced free institutions and free communities.[40]

Traditional notions of state citizenship and patriotism were thus seen as acceptable only insofar as they were compatible with attachment to the wider racial encompassing group.

Andrew Carnegie, the Scottish-born industrialist, argued repeatedly for racial fusion and the "reunion" of Britain and America. Though usually lauded or reviled as an anti-imperialist, Carnegie, like Hobson, highlights how opposition to certain kinds of imperial activity – in his case, British occupation of India and Africa and the American assault on the Philippines – was consistent with ardent support for projects of racial unity or superiority. Carnegie dismissed the idea of an Anglo-American alliance as failing to grasp the far more important issues at stake. "Alliances of fighting power form and dissolve with the questions which arise from time to time. The patriotism of race lies deeper and is not disturbed by waves upon the surface." "[M]y belief," he declared, is that "the future is certain to see a reunion of the separated parts and once again a common citizenship." This federated "British-American Union" would constitute a "reunited state." Yet this vision was irreconcilable with imperial federation: the British had first to grant independence to their settler colonies, which would then be welcome to join the union as equal members.[41] Although perturbed by the South African War, and by the exuberant imperialism of the American administration, he never lost faith in the transformative potential of the Anglo-Saxon race.

Skeptics were quick to point to the empirical inadequacies of unionist plans. One of their main complaints focused on the pertinence of arguments about racial unity. America, they complained, was simply not an "Anglo-Saxon" lineal descendent of Britain. "There is," one critic observed, "no fundamental reason rooted in human nature by virtue of a community of blood and religion why Americans as a nation should regard England with instinctive sympathy and friendship."[42] Another stressed the multi-ethnic composition of the American population. "What about the descendants of French men, of Germans, of Slavs, and of Scandinavians, who do not admit Anglo Saxon superiority?" And what about the Irish or African-Americans?[43] But such demographic arguments failed to register with the proponents of unity, not least because their conception of race was fluid. As one unionist observed,

> It is quite true that, if the census of descent were taken as the test, the sons or descendants of Englishmen by no means make up the majority of American citizens. But there is descent other than that of birth and a lineage beside that of blood. The unity of language, literature, and law between England and America is a threefold cord that cannot be broken. To have our English Bible, our English Shakespeare, our English Blackstone all absolutely American in reverence and influence outweighs, outvotes and overwhelms all questions of racial compositeness.[44]

In general, then, what identified the United States as an Anglo-Saxon country was its dominant political culture – its White Anglo-Saxon Protestant (WASP) institutions, values, and ideals. Pointing to his own Portuguese origins, Dos Passos celebrated the American polity as a machine for turning (white) immigrants into Americans, and thus into adherents to an Anglo-Saxon creed. The "foreign element," he argued, "disappears, almost like magic, in the bosom of American nationality."[45] Carnegie, meanwhile, suggested that immigration had barely altered the racial composition of America: "in race – and there is a great deal in race – the American remains three-fourths purely British. ... The amount of blood other than Anglo-Saxon or Germanic which has entered into the American is almost too trifling to deserve notice, and has been absorbed without changing him in any fundamental trait."[46] Moreover, skepticism about racial commonality did not preclude support for political union. The eminent Anglo-American archaeologist Charles Waldstein argued that the notion of "Anglo-Saxon" racial identity was both misleading and dangerous: "it opens the door to that most baneful and pernicious of modern national diseases, namely, Ethnological Chauvinism." Yet he was adamant that Britain and the United States shared enough features in common to constitute "one nationality," and he toasted the future creation of "a great English-speaking Brotherhood."[47]

Cecil Rhodes was another formidable proponent of Anglo-American unity. At the heart of his vision lay an account of the fractured nature of history: its progressive course had been diverted by the catastrophic estrangement of the United States and Great Britain. This could only be put right if the two great institutional expressions of the race were reunited permanently. As a self-proclaimed "race patriot," Rhodes was largely agnostic about whether Britain or the United States should lead the Anglo-Saxons in fulfilling their destiny, suggesting that a "federal parliament" could rotate between Washington and London.[48] Rhodes's main practical contribution to the dream of global racial dominance was the establishment of the Rhodes Trust, endowed following his death in 1902 with the intention of strengthening bonds between the elites of the Anglo-world, as well (initially) as Germany, that other Teutonic power. The radical journalist W.T. Stead agreed with his friend Rhodes that the "English-speaking race is one of the chief of God's chosen agents for executing coming improvement in the lot of mankind," and he utilized his position as a prominent author and editor to preach the gospel of Anglo-unity, seeking to "constitute as one vast federated unity the English-speaking United States of the World."[49] Like many of his contemporaries, Stead sensed a gradual intra-racial shift in the balance of power. In *The Americanization of the World*, he argued that the Americans had overtaken the British in most aspects of social and economic life, observed that Britain itself was slowly Americanizing, and determined that those ruling in London now faced a stark choice: ally with the United States in a grand project of earthly redemption, or become increasingly irrelevant as the empire slowly weakened and the settler colonies sought independence and looked to Washington for leadership. This was a cause for celebration: "there is no reason to resent the part the Americans are playing in fashioning the world in their image, which, after all, is substantially the image of ourselves."[50] American success was an expression of British power, institutions, and values. This was a common trope in British accounts of Anglo-America, with Dilke, for example, boasting that "[t]hrough America, England is speaking to the world."[51]

H.G. Wells also dreamt of an Anglo enunciation of modernity. In *Anticipations*, published in 1902, he prophesized the emergence of a world state ruled over by a new techno-managerial class of "efficients" – the "kinetic men" of the future.[52] This was a theme he was to pursue, in one way or another, until his death in 1946. In this early vision, the unification of the "English-speaking" peoples assumed a central role: they were to serve as pioneers of the world-state-to-come. By the year 2000 the English-speaking people would constitute a federal state, united by "practically homogenous citizenship," with its headquarters in the United States. They would govern all the "non-white states of the present British empire, and in addition much of the South and Middle Pacific, the East and West Indies, the rest of America, and the larger part of black Africa."[53] His vision was vanguardist in a double sense. Not only were the English-speaking peoples to lead the way to a further global "synthesis," but this drive was itself led by a select group of individuals, men (*sic*) of energy, determination, and drive, who would help to dissolve – either through social revolution or in the wake of war – the remaining barriers to its realization found in "deliquescing" modern societies. The New Republicans would act as a largely uncoordinated "Secret Society" to help inaugurate a new dawn in human history. This notion of a clerisy acting behind the scenes to secure race unity was echoed by Rhodes and Stead.

Wells was not the only fiction writer to propagate Anglo-unity. Arthur Conan Doyle was another enthusiast, dedicating his historical novel *The White Company* to "the Hope of the Future, the Reunion of the English-Speaking races." He even enlisted Sherlock Holmes, who declaimed that history should not prevent "our children from being someday citizens of the same world-wide country whose flag should be a quartering of the Union Jack with the Stars and Stripes."[54] Henry James, meanwhile, observed that "I can't look at the English-American world, or feel about them, anymore save as a big Anglo-Saxon total, destined to such an amount of melting together that an insistence on their difference becomes more and more idle and pedantic."[55]

While many of the proposals for unity were motivated by pragmatic security concerns, an equally large number made drastic claims about the world-transforming potential of racial unity. We can thus interpret aspects of the pre-1914 Anglo-race discourse as expressions of utopian desire.[56] A political project can be considered utopian, I submit, if and only if it invokes or prescribes the transcendence or elimination of one or more fundamental practices, structures, or ordering principles that shape human individual and collective life. These include poverty, inequality, war, the state, the biochemical composition of the environment, or the ontological constitution of human beings, including death itself. Utopianism is not best employed as a synonym for any ambitious project of political change – as the term is frequently used in IR – or seen as a general feature of the human condition, a universal striving for a better life. Rather, it identifies a particular species of transformative social and political thought.

The utopianism of this racial vision resided in the belief that if the United States and Greater Britain were properly aligned, the "Anglo-Saxon" race would help to bring peace, order, and justice to the earth. Carnegie argued that the "new nation would dominate the world and banish from the earth its greatest stain – the murder of men by men." Lyman Abbott, a prominent American Congregationalist theologian, dreamt of an Anglo century – even millennium. "[T]hese two nations, embodying the energy, the enterprise, and the conscience of the Anglo-Saxon race, would by the mere fact of their co-operation produce a result in human history which would surpass all that present imagination can conceive or present hope anticipate."[57] For Albion Tourgée, American soldier, diplomat, and judge, the Anglo-Saxons were, quite simply, the "peacemakers of the twentieth century." Rhodes once wrote: "What an awful thought it is that if we had not lost America, or even if now we could arrange with the present members of the United States Assembly and our House of Commons, the peace of the world is secured for all eternity!" In 1891, he predicted that union with the United States would mean "universal peace" within one hundred years. Stead agreed, envisaging that "war would by degree die out from the face of the earth."[58] This, then, was the promise of an Anglo-racial utopia.

Afterlives of empire: Anglo-America and global governance

During the twentieth century, proposals for supra-national political unions were divided among (at least) five models. One of them emphasized regional federation, and centered above all on combining the states of continental Europe. It was this vision that ultimately had the most practical effect, though only after the cataclysm of a genocidal war. The other four – which I will label imperial–commonwealth, Anglo-American, democratic unionist, and world federalist – placed the transatlantic British–American connection at the core of global order. All were descended, in part or wholly, from the earlier Anglo-world projects. Some offered only minor modifications to earlier imperial schemes, while others pushed out in new directions. Perhaps most importantly, though, the majority of the interwar and mid-century projects regarded the "Anglo" powers as a nucleus or vanguard. And even those schemes that expanded beyond the institutional limits of the Anglo-world were almost invariably liberal democratic and capitalist in form, and as such they exemplified, even embodied, the values and institutions on which the Anglo-world was based, and over which its advocates claimed paternity.

The imperial–commonwealth model focused on the continuing role of the British empire. During the Edwardian years and beyond, the Round Table and other British imperial advocacy groups continued to campaign on behalf of Greater British unity. The imperial federalist project reached its zenith during the First World War with the creation of an Imperial War Cabinet in 1917, which incorporated the prime ministers of the Dominions. This was the nearest the dream of a politically unified Greater Britain came to fruition. Yet the war also accelerated calls for further independence in the colonies. While the efforts of the imperial federalists did not go completely unheralded in the United States,[59] they found, perhaps ironically, a more receptive audience in continental Europe, with a number of them – notably Philip Kerr (Lord Lothian) – playing an important role in shaping the ideological foundations of European union.[60]

During the 1920s, power continued to shift within the British empire and as the colonies were granted further autonomy, they frequently came into conflict with London.[61] In the interwar period it became increasingly popular to reimagine the empire as the "British Commonwealth" – the two terms were often used interchangeably – and to see it either as a self-contained system capable of balancing other great political orders, or as the embryonic form of a future universal political system. Britain and its settler colonies remained at the center of the model, although India and other elements of the empire were sometimes allotted subordinate roles. In the second half of the twentieth century, following decolonization, the imperial–commonwealth vision morphed into a postcolonial international organization.[62] Today it lingers on, a pale shadow of the hopes and dreams once invested in it.

The Anglo-American model centered on the Anglo-Saxon – or "English-speaking" – peoples, and in particular on a British–American axis. Relations between London and Washington continued to strengthen in the wake of the late Victorian "rapprochement," and the alliance was cemented during the First World War when the United States joined the Franco-British cause in Western Europe. It remained close for the rest of the twentieth century, though not quite as close as many of its cheerleaders, then as now, like to boast. The First World War had a catalytic effect on American foreign policy discourse, spawning the development of a powerful, though often fractious, East Coast policy elite oriented towards greater American involvement in world politics, in cooperation (even alliance) with Britain.[63] During the interwar era a variety of institutions and informal networks were created to foster closer links between America and Greater Britain. They constituted an emergent epistemic community dedicated to emphasizing the importance of Anglo-world global leadership. The Council on Foreign Relations in New York and the International Institute of International Affairs (Chatham House) in London served as institutional hubs of Anglo-world thinking, in both its Anglo-American and British imperial–commonwealth articulations.[64]

While the 1920s saw constructive cooperation between Britain and the United States, relations during the 1930s were strained; it was only with the outbreak of war, and especially between 1940 and 1942, that the two powers were forced into a tight embrace.[65] This peaked with the signing of the Atlantic Charter in August 1941, dedicated to the promotion of "certain common principles in the national policies of their respective countries on which they base their hope for the common world," though tension continued between London and Washington over the future of the British empire. As American power increased, and it became clear that Britain would be a junior partner in any future relationship, so once again the dream of an Anglo-American order faded. Perhaps its last gasp can be found in Churchill's "iron curtain" speech in March 1946, in which he popularized the term "special relationship" and insisted that peace was impossible without "the fraternal association of the English-speaking peoples."[66] Like the contemporary Commonwealth, the "special relationship" in the postwar years was a weak imitation of the ideal that had inspired many British, and even a few American, commentators over the previous decades.

Another model envisioned the creation of a league (or concert) of democracies. Before 1945 this essentially meant a transatlantic union of the United States, Great Britain, and assorted western European countries. As such, it moved beyond the "racial" limits of the Anglo-world. In the 1950s this idea sometimes mutated into an Atlanticist vision centered on the NATO countries. Perhaps the most influential interwar democratic unionist vision was propounded by Clarence Streit, a journalist with the *New York Times*. In *Union Now*, he proposed a federation, on the model of the constitution of 1787, of the 15 democracies of the Atlantic world. The union would serve three main purposes:

> (a) to provide effective common government in our democratic world in those fields where such common government will clearly serve man's freedom better than separate governments, (b) to maintain independent national governments in all other fields where such government will best serve man's freedom, and (c) to create by its constitution a nucleus world government capable of growing into universal world government peacefully and as rapidly as such growth will best serve man's freedom.[67]

He followed this up with *Union Now with Britain*, in which he argued that the creation of an Anglo-American union would guarantee the defeat of the Axis.[68] Streit's later work highlights the way in which the Cold War constrained the imagination of democratic unionists. The West, figured as an "Atlantic community" – a term first used by Walter Lippmann[69] – took center stage. In 1961 Streit published *Freedom's Frontier*, suggesting that the 15 countries of NATO already constituted the nucleus of an immanent Atlantic federal state: "Atlantica."[70] This fed into a popular Atlanticist current of thought. Expressing a common view, Livingston Hartley, a former State Department official, demanded "the political integration of the Atlantic community, the citadel and the powerhouse of freedom."[71] For many, European union and Atlantic union went hand-in-hand, the development of the former helping to strengthen the viability of the latter.[72] For others, though, the creation of a European union threatened the more desirable goal of Atlantic union. For Streit, avatar of Atlanticism, America needed to take the lead in creating a new order, "preferably teamed closely with Canada," while European integration threatened transatlantic division.[73]

The veteran British peace campaigner Norman Angell followed a similar trajectory to Streit. An early advocate of democratic federal union as a precursor to world federation,[74] during the Second World War he too emphasized the vital leadership role of the Anglo-states (and the British empire) in this future global order. Like so many other post-state visionaries, he insisted that a "nucleus of authority" was required to catalyze and then direct the transition to world federation, and that this nucleus "must be the English-speaking world," by which he meant the United States and the "British peoples."[75] Rather than the latest manifestation of Anglo-Saxon imperialism, he was adamant that this Anglo core could act as the embryo of a true universalism. The empire should, then, be transformed into a "nucleus of integration" rather than dissolved into independent sovereign states.[76] By the late 1950s, in Streitian vein, he was arguing that "the West" as a whole should act as the advance guard in any future transformation. "A world government would have to work on the basis of 80 or 100 nationalisms, emphasizing widely differing cultures and ways of life." The common social basis for political unity did not (yet) exist. As such, he concluded, the adoption of the "federal principle" was necessary to unify the West in the face of Soviet totalitarianism, and as a necessary step on the road to a more wide-ranging union.[77] The unionist axis had shifted from the British empire, through Anglo-America, to the West as a whole, but the Anglo-world remained at the heart of the project.

The major difference between "Anglo" and "Democratic unionist" models concerns the identity claim on which they are based. The Anglo model is confined to a finite set of British diasporic communities; its potential spatial extent is bounded by a specific historical trajectory. A league of democracies is in principle more expansive, designating a community that shares a minimal set of political values and institutions, all of them hypothetically exportable. Yet in practice, at the heart of this picture, were (and are) the Anglo-states. Moreover, the values and institutions associated with such a community – the architecture of liberal–democratic capitalism – were either implicitly or explicitly ascribed by contemporaries to the British and American intellectual traditions. Once again, social science offered authoritative epistemic support. The empirical analysis, and the normative affirmation, of the Anglo-world were high on the agenda of early postwar behavioral political science. Perhaps, most notably, the hugely influential idea of a "security community" was forged in the crucible of Atlanticist politics. Pioneering political scientist Karl Deutsch argued, for example, that the North Atlantic security community was anchored in the most highly integrated states, namely the United States, Canada, and the United Kingdom.[78]

The final model was a universal world polity. Ideas about world government have percolated through the history of political thought, ebbing and flowing in popularity.[79] The 1940s witnessed an efflorescence of utopian political thinking, catalyzed by the old Kantian premonition that the route to perpetual peace would most likely wind its way through the valley of death; that a brutal war might, once and for all, force people throughout the world to recognize the necessity of federation. Advocates of a global polity typically conceived of it as a long-term ideal rather than something within immediate grasp.[80] Nevertheless, many of them called for a federal institutional structure with an Anglo nucleus, while numerous advocates of democratic or Anglo-racial union saw their own more limited goals as temporary steps on the road to – and often agents in the creation of – a universal federation.

Perhaps the most famous world federalist was Wells, who proselytized on behalf of a post-sovereign cosmopolitan order in a seemingly endless stream of publications. After the First World War he increasingly turned his attention to the creation of a functionalist world state, suggesting in rather vague terms that a future world polity would result from the coagulation of regional and racial groupings.[81] Like most of his contemporaries, his account of a cosmopolitan world state never escaped the ethnocentric assumptions that had marked his earlier writings. Evolving through various iterations, his vision of a future global order was rooted in the purported superiority of the Western powers, and in particular the Anglo-Americans. He longed for the (re)union of the English-speaking peoples. In 1935, for example, he argued that "the commonsense of the world demands that the English-speaking community should get together upon the issue of World Peace, and that means a common foreign policy." It also meant economic unification, for "the world revival" would not materialize "unless we homologize the financial control and monetary organization of our world-wide group of people."[82] Wells exemplified the technocratic aspect of the world federalist project, even flirting with fascist methods during the 1920s and 1930s in order to help bring about a new global order.

World federalist thinking flourished in Britain and the United States in the 1940s and early 1950s, drawing in a wide array of intellectuals and politicians, from Albert Einstein and Aldous Huxley to Henry L. Stimson and John Foster Dulles.[83] Campaigning organizations – notably the United World Federalists (1947) – were formed, politicians lobbied, newsletters and pamphlets circulated. Wendell Willkie's *One World* sold over two million copies.[84] Henry Usborne, a British Labour MP, created a Parliamentary Group for World Government and signed up over 200 MPs.[85] Under the leadership of its president, Robert M. Hutchins, the University of Chicago created a Committee to Frame a World Constitution.[86] House Concurrent Resolution 64, in 1949, proposed as a "fundamental objective of the foreign policy of the United States to support and strengthen the United Nations and to seek its development into a world federation." It secured 111 votes, including those of John F. Kennedy, Gerald Ford, Mike Mansfield, Henry Cabot Lodge, and Henry Jackson.[87] The movement peaked in early 1950, with 150,000 members worldwide.[88]

In the shadow of the bomb, political realists had their own one world moment. John Herz and Hans Morgenthau, among others, argued that human survival demanded the creation of a world state, though both were skeptical of its plausibility.[89] The world federalist movement was stifled by the onset of the Cold War.[90] The dream of world federation struggled on, finding a variety of intellectual outlets, including the World Orders Model Project most closely associated with Richard Falk.[91] But it was an early victim of bipolar ideological confrontation. Once a topic of mainstream concern for scholars, public intellectuals, journalists, and politicians, Thomas Weiss argues that today ideas about a global federal state are "commonly thought to be the preserve of lunatics."[92] Yet there are signs of a revival of interest in the idea, at least among scholars.[93] In IR, for example,

Alexander Wendt and Daniel Deudney have offered theoretically sophisticated accounts of the plausibility, even inevitability, of a world state.[94]

The proponents of democratic leagues and world federation often drew inspiration from – and shared personnel with – the imperial federal movement. Lionel Curtis is a prominent example. An enthusiastic advocate of imperial and then world federalism over the course of five decades, his political thought was riddled with the tensions between universalism, Atlanticism, and imperialism.[95] Curtis's magnum opus, the sprawling politico-theological treatise *Civitas Dei*, posited that a federated British empire could serve as a kernel and a model for a future universal commonwealth of nations, because of all extant political communities it offered the most appropriate space for human personality to find its fullest expression.[96] The most difficult stage in creating a world federal state was the first one; the "most experienced commonwealths" needed to show leadership. He identified the core of the new global order in the union of Great Britain, New Zealand, and Australia.[97] The Second World War only reinforced his belief in the necessity of political transformation. In the early 1950s Curtis angrily denounced intellectuals for upholding the myth of sovereign statehood; they were, he charged, "responsible for the bloodshed of this century" and "answerable for the suffering, poverty, and death that millions are now facing."[98] Federation, with an Anglo core, was the only way to escape the killing machine. An arch Anglo-supremacist who died in 1956, Curtis was frequently hailed as one of the pioneers of the world federalist movement.[99]

A notable aspect of the debates over global order, in both the nineteenth and the twentieth centuries, was that America often served as a template for the future. Both American political experience and political philosophy were routinely cited as inspirational, even formative. Streit modeled his plan for an Atlantic union of democracies on the US Constitution. Indeed, he went so far as to call for a Federal Convention, similar to its namesake in Philadelphia in 1787, to deliberate over the desirability and potential form of a Transatlantic Union.[100] This proposal gained the support of the Canadian Senate and dozens of US senators.[101] Twentieth-century British imperial federalists, meanwhile, regularly invoked the genius of the American founders, often interpreted through the prism of F.S. Oliver's *Alexander Hamilton*.[102] Curtis, for example, was explicit about his debt to the Federalist papers; they taught him, he recorded, about both the problem of political order and the best (federal) solution to it, fundamentally influencing his views over half a century of federalist agitation.[103] America was both model and motive. Indeed, many world federalist plans can be read as demanding the Americanization of the planet.

Millennial dreams, or, back to the future

While today there are few advocates of a global federal state outside of universities and think tanks, the vision of a "concert" or "league" of democracies has resurfaced in public life. "Democracy" has supplanted "civilization" as the defining feature in discourses of global governance. Democratic unionist arguments have been given a powerful boost by the popularity of theories of the "democratic peace," once again highlighting the complex entanglement of twentieth-century social science with projects for global order. This line of reasoning is directly descended from the mid-twentieth-century discourse. Michael Doyle, for example, identifies Streit as the first modern commentator to point to "the empirical tendency of democracies to maintain peace among themselves."[104] Uniting liberal internationalists with neo-conservatives, the idea of a league of democracies has wide ideological appeal among members of the American political elite, even if it has resonated far less in Europe. Advisors to both Barack Obama and John McCain promoted the idea during the 2008 election campaign, and McCain endorsed it.[105] It has found its most systematic articulation in the Princeton Project on National Security, coordinated by Anne-Marie Slaughter and John Ikenberry, which proposes the creation of a global "Concert of Democracies" to "institutionalize and ratify the 'democratic peace.'"[106]

Recent years have also witnessed a brief flurry of arguments focusing on the Anglo dimension of world politics – the imperial dream that never expires. They are variations on the earlier themes of imperial federation and Anglo-American unity. In addition to the old rubric of the "English-speaking peoples," a new term (coined in a science fiction novel) has entered the lexicon: the "Anglosphere."[107] Advocacy of Anglo superiority has assumed different forms. One popular version, outlined in a bestselling book and a popular television series, is Niall Ferguson's paean to British imperial power, and the necessity of the American empire assuming the responsibility – the old "White Man's burden" – of hegemonic stabilizer and civilizing agent.[108] Other widely discussed proposals have emanated from the American businessman James Bennett and the British historian Andrew Roberts.

Echoing earlier discussions about the world-historical function of the telegraph, Bennett contends that the Internet can serve as a medium through which the geographically scattered but culturally and politically aligned members of the "Anglosphere" can come into closer communion, and act together for the planetary greater good.[109] He sees this as both desirable and necessary, given the likely development of other competing network "spheres" – Sino, Luso, Hispano, and Franco. He concludes that the inherited political and economic traditions of the Anglosphere mean that it is uniquely equipped to thrive in the coming century. Roberts, meanwhile, seeks to pick up where Churchill finished his own bombastic history of the English-speaking peoples.[110] Rather than advocating formal union, he outlines a vision, grounded in a hubristic reading of twentieth-century history, in which the English-speaking peoples are united by "common purposes" and in defeating waves of totalitarianism, today exemplified by Islamic fanaticism. Superior political institutions mean that when they act in unison, the whole world benefits. Roberts's vision of the English-speaking peoples is limited to the United States, the United Kingdom "and her dependencies," New Zealand, Canada, and Australia, as well as the British West Indies and Ireland – though of the latter two, the first is largely ignored while the second is routinely assailed for failing to live up to the standards set by the others. Reproducing earlier arguments about race patriotism, Roberts decenters the state: the ontological foundation of his argument is a singular people, while the political units of this singularity play a secondary function. "Just as we do not today differentiate between the Roman Republic and the imperial period of the Julio-Claudians when we think of the Roman Empire, so in the future no one will bother to make a distinction between the British Empire-led and the American Republic-led periods of English-speaking dominance."[111] The book secured him an invitation to George W. Bush's White House.[112]

None of these authors proposes a formal political union, instead hymning the powers of shared culture, traditions, and interests. But the vision of an institutionalized Anglo-union has not disappeared completely. Robert Conquest, eminent poet and historian, has called for the "English-speaking" countries of the world to join a "flexibly conceived Association," something "weaker than a federation, but stronger than an alliance." A "natural rather than artificial" association, this "Anglo-Oceanic" polity would act as a progressive hyperpower.[113] Like Roberts, Conquest is driven in part by a sense of anger at the duplicity of British politicians signing up to European integration, and thus betraying their true kin in the dominions and across the Atlantic.

There are notable continuities between the contemporary projects for an Anglo century and their predecessors. All have been framed by war or imperial action. While Cuba, the Philippines, and South Africa set the context for the first outburst of writing on Anglo-America, and the rise of Hitler, the Second World War, and then the onset of the Cold War helped initiate the second, today it is Iraq, Afghanistan, and the "War on Terror" that provide the general ideological milieu. All of them depend on a form of "othering," an imaginative geography of fear and loathing. Over time, the Anglo-Saxons have been arrayed against Japan, France, Russia, Germany, the Soviet Union, and now an amorphous "radical Islam." Each phase has also been predicated on hyperbolic claims about the power of new communications technologies to transform the nature and scope of political association. Since the late nineteenth century, radical visions of formal political union have been accompanied by more modest proposals for strengthening existing connections and fostering close cooperation. Yet all of these varied projects, however ambitious, have been based on claims about translocal identity and belonging. They have insisted that the members of the Anglo-world share much in common – a language, a history, a set of values, political and economic institutions, and a destiny.

But there are also some notable differences. The *fin de siècle* and mid-twentieth-century debates about supranational political unions were much wider ranging and more prominent; they drew in many of the leading public intellectuals, journalists, and politicians of the day. While the current debate over the league of democracies has a high profile, the ambitions of its proponents are far more limited than those dreamt of by their mid-twentieth-century precursors. They do not seek to transcend the state system, only to carve out a powerful coalition within it.

The contemporary Anglospheric discourse, meanwhile, is a pale imitation of previous iterations. This is partly because of its ideological coloring. Whereas the older debate crossed political lines, the contemporary discourse is almost exclusively confined to the political right, and in particular to neo-conservatives. Another significant difference is that the utopian dimension of the earlier projects is largely absent. In the reheated version, the Anglosphere is figured as a force for good in the world, securing and helping to spread freedom, democracy, and liberal capitalism – it upholds the new civilizing mission. This is arguably a form of imperial idealism, but it is not equivalent to the earlier claims that the unity of the Anglo-Saxon race would eliminate war, or that it would inaugurate a universal world state. The messianic impulse has ended.

Conclusion

The last one hundred and fifty years have seen the elaboration of numerous projects to unify or coordinate the scattered polities of the Anglo-world. Initially they centered on British imperial federation, before the focus switched to the Anglo-American relationship. Proposals for a league of democracy, Atlantic union, even world federalism were heirs of this Anglo discourse, not discrete and incompatible models of global order. They emerged from the earlier imperial–racial debates, and many of the proposals for transcending the existing system were similar in form and ambition to the projects for Anglo-world imperium. To chart the "growth of nations," Tocqueville once wrote, it is an imperative to remember that they carry with them "some of the marks of their origin."[114] The same is true of projects of global governance. We have yet to escape the will to empire and the seductive call of the civilizing mission.

Notes

1 I would like to thank the following for comments on earlier drafts of this chapter: Peter Katzenstein, Ron Krebs, Jennifer Mitzen, Casper Sylvest, Anthony Lang, and all the other contributors to this book.
2 For the term "Anglo-world," see Belich 2009.
3 Foucault 1983, 221.
4 Deudney 2007, 215, 219.
5 Cf. DuBois 1903.
6 Lake and Reynolds 2008, 4.
7 I expand on the argument in this section in Bell 2007a.
8 Bell 2010a; Claeys 2010. The idea of importing reform from the colonial periphery was prevalent in wider social reform debates: Rodgers 2000.
9 Hobson 1997 [1902], 332.
10 Hobhouse 1994, 116. Note that Hobson later abandoned his support for imperial federation (Bell 2010a; Cain 2002).
11 Tocqueville 1862, 456–7.
12 Palen 2010; Cain and Hopkins 2002, ch. 7.
13 Dilke 1868, I, 274, 48.
14 Chamberlain 1902, 177.

15 This schema is derived from Martin 1973.
16 E.g. Lorne 1885.
17 E.g. Labillière 1894.
18 Dicey 1915, lxxxiv. On Victorian ideas about statehood, see Bell 2007b.
19 Dilke 1868, II, 157.
20 Mill 1861, ch. 18; Bell 2010c.
21 Wells 1999 [1902], 38, 44; Seeley 1883, 62.
22 Seeley 1883, 158–9.
23 For further details, see Bell 2010b.
24 Seeley 1883, 49.
25 Bennett 1962, 283.
26 Monypenny 1905, 23, 27.
27 Curtis 1916, 68; cf. Morefield 2004.
28 I discuss this conception in greater detail in Bell 2010b.
29 Gorman 2006.
30 Appadurai 1996.
31 Ibid., 54.
32 White 1894, 492–3; see also Besant 1896.
33 E.g. Lodge 1895. Indeed Lodge, a Massachusetts senator, regarded the British empire as a dangerous geopolitical competitor.
34 Mahan and Beresford 1894, 554.
35 Clarke 1899, 141.
36 Harrison 1901, 354. On the history of the concept of the "English-speaking peoples," usage of which originated in the 1870s and peaked during the early decades of the twentieth century, see Clarke 2011.
37 Dicey 1897, 458.
38 On Balfour's "race patriotism," see Tomes 1997, chs. 2–4. On Milner, see Thompson 2007.
39 Milner 1925.
40 Beresford 1900, 809.
41 Carnegie 1899, 5–6; Carnegie 1893, 9; Carnegie 1896, 132.
42 Hazeltine 1896, 597.
43 Fleming 1891, 254.
44 Doane 1898, 318.
45 Dos Passos 1903, 101, 104.
46 Carnegie 1893, 9.
47 Waldstein 1898, 225, 230, 238.
48 Rhodes 1902, 73.
49 Stead 1901, 100, 397.
50 Ibid., 2.
51 Dilke 1868, 318.
52 Wells 1999 [1902], ch. 8. On Wells, see also Deudney 2007.
53 Ibid., 146.
54 Doyle 1891, 1892.
55 James, cited in Allen 1954, 19.
56 For more on this argument, see Bell 2012.
57 Carnegie 1893, 12–13; Abbott 1898, 521.
58 Tourgée 1899; Rhodes 1902, 73, 66; Stead 1901, 435.
59 E.g. Smith 1921; Burton-Adams 1919.
60 Kendle 1997, ch. 6; Bosco 1988; Burgess 1995, Pt. III; Turner 1988.
61 MacMillan 2001.
62 Shaw 2008.
63 Roberts 1997.
64 Cull 1996; Roberts 2009; Parmar 2002; Williams 2003.
65 Reynolds 1981, 1986.

66 James 1974, 289. Churchill advocated a common citizenship between Britain and the USA. See Ryan 1987, ch. 3; Toye 2010, 240.
67 Streit 1938, 2.
68 Streit 1941.
69 Lippmann 1943, 83.
70 Streit 1961.
71 Hartley 1965, 92.
72 Strauz-Hupe et al. 1963.
73 Streit 1953, 8. While Streit routinely talked of uniting "all democracies," he also stressed "Atlantic Union," thus leaving unclear the role of the non-Atlantic parts of Greater Britain.
74 Angell 1918.
75 Angell 1942, 10.
76 Angell 1943.
77 Angell 1958.
78 Deutsch et al. 1957; see also Russett 1963.
79 Heater 1996; Bartelson 2009.
80 Pemberton 2001; Wooley 1988.
81 Wells 1925, 708.
82 Wells 1935, 24.
83 Dulles 1939.
84 Willkie 1943.
85 Baratta 2004, 162–4.
86 Hutchins et al. 1948; cf. Borgese 1953.
87 Weiss 2009, 258.
88 Baratta 1999, 342.
89 Craig 2003; Deudney 2007, ch. 8.
90 Baratta 2004. This transition was mirrored in the mutation of an "astrofuturist" discourse that focused on the possibilities of the exploration and conquest of outer space. This discourse emerged in the interwar years in the USA, Germany, Britain, and Russia, and flowered in the second half of the century, chiefly in the USA. It reached its apotheosis with the moon landing in 1969. During the interwar period it had been largely internationalist in orientation – albeit infused with the justificatory strategies of imperialism – whereas its post-1945 fortunes saw it tied increasingly to the priorities of the national security state. Kilgore 2003.
91 Falk 1975. Falk drew on Sohn and Clark 1958.
92 Weiss 2009, 258.
93 Cabrera 2010.
94 Wendt 2003; Deudney 2007.
95 On his life and religious views, see Studdert-Kennedy 1995; Lavin 1995.
96 Curtis 1937.
97 Curtis 1939, 309; cf. Curtis 1937, vol. III. Curtis also expressed admiration for Streit's alternative Atlanticist plan (Curtis 1939, 310; 1951).
98 Curtis 1951, 284.
99 E.g. Streit 1956, 10.
100 Streit 1953.
101 Curtis 1951, 275–76.
102 Oliver 1906.
103 Curtis 1939, 302–7. Daniel Deudney's (2007) fascinating discussion of republican security is also modeled on American experience.
104 Doyle 1986, 1162n2; cf. Ikenberry 2001, 178–9.
105 McCain 2007. See also Daalder and Lindsay 2007; Fukuyama 2006; Huntley 1998.
106 Ikenberry and Slaughter 2006, 7.
107 For an insightful analysis, see Vucetic 2011.
108 Ferguson 2004.

109 Bennett 2007a.
110 Roberts 2007. Cf. Churchill 1956–58. On the term "English-speaking peoples," see Clarke 2011.
111 Ibid., 381.
112 Weisberg 2007.
113 Conquest 2000.
114 Tocqueville 1862, 13.

3

ANGLO-AMERICA AS GLOBAL SUBURBIA

The political economy of land and endogenous multiculturalism[1]

Herman Schwartz

> It would be difficult to describe the avidity with which the American rushes forward to secure this immense booty that fortune offers ... [with] a passion stronger than the love of life. Before him lies a boundless continent, and he urges onward as if time pressed and he was afraid of finding no room for his exertions. ... Fifty years have scarcely elapsed since Ohio was founded; the greater part of its inhabitants were not born within its confines; its capital has been built only thirty years, and its territory is still covered by an immense extent of uncultivated fields; yet already the population of Ohio is proceeding westward, and most of the settlers who descend to the fertile prairies of Illinois are citizens of Ohio. These men left their first country to improve their condition; they quit their second to ameliorate it still more; fortune awaits them everywhere, but not happiness.
>
> (Alexis de Tocqueville, *Democracy in America*)[2]

Anglo-America is the suburban sprawl of the global economy. That is, Anglo-America has a political economy in which land development creates both sides of the balance sheet simultaneously, and out of nothing. Capital emerges from debt on relatively depopulated lands whose streams of income are largely in the future, rather than from current streams of income. In turn, this new capital draws in a corresponding pool of labor to validate itself. In-migration driven by land development thus makes the constant renegotiation of internal racial and cultural boundaries, described in the other chapters, endogenous to economic growth in Anglo-America. Britain constitutes a partial exception. The formative moments for Anglo-American states involve the establishment of a legal and institutional framework for dealing with the transformation of land into capital. These frameworks in turn motivate a search for labor.

This chapter thus addresses the core issues of identity and sovereignty found in the other chapters from a political economy point of view in order to show how

Anglo-America differs from continental European societies on the one hand, and from non-frontier, non-European societies on the other. If Anglo-America is the world's suburban sprawl, continental Europe constitutes its core cities and Asia its working-class slums. Each area thus exhibits a distinct pattern of development that interacts and is interdependent with the other two. At the same time, Anglo-America is not a unified whole, but rather exhibits three distinct sub-patterns of sovereignty and land development. This political economy-based understanding of Anglo-America excludes countries whose legal system or linguistic character qualifies them for membership in James Bennett's "New Anglosphere."[3] Their economic development follows a different dynamic flowing from the prior presence of a settled population.

I make three key points about Anglo-America. First, three different Anglo-Americas exist, with three different kinds of sovereignty and logics of state power. These Anglo-American states exist as hybrids, rather than pure forms. They are institutionally layered, producing the complex sovereignty Pauly and Reus-Smit identify in Chapter 6 and the divergent patterns of US–Canadian and US–Mexican relations Bow and Santa-Cruz depict in Chapter 7. Second, divergent patterns of state power in these three different Anglo-Americas animate and reflect different kinds of politics around land. The analyses by Bell, Klotz, and Vucetic (Chapters 2, 4, 5, respectively) partially reveal these patterns of domestic and external sovereignty. Third, efforts to populate the land in Anglo-America generate(d) the multilayered sets of conflicts between different generations of coerced and free immigrants we see today. This combines with continual pressure to develop new land to produce the pervasive and perpetual liminality Klotz and Vucetic identify. Anglo-America's external and internal borders constantly expand, drawing ever newer and different groups of people into its domains.

New groups mean new conflicts and forms of accommodation. The specifics for these conflicts and accommodations vary from place to place depending on the timing of settlement and expansion, and the kind of state power present. While the political economy of Anglo-America generates multicultural societies, it does not determine the specific form that multicultural policy will take. Yet the connection between growth and labor inflows means that mutual enmities in the Anglo-Americas can be papered over with access to property. Just so, the recurrent eruption of nativist social movements during economic downturns shows how growth lubricates social relations across different groups. Anglo-American multiculturalism is as much about mutual tolerance in the shared pursuit of goods as it is about moving past enmity to some notionally true shared identity.[4]

After a brief overview, the first three sections of the chapter correspond to these three points. The final section ties them together by suggesting that identity politics in Anglo-America is not free-floating but instead has a substantial and common material basis. Nothing surprising there: Alexis de Tocqueville had already identified the strong connections between land, migration, and the state in 1831. This political economy account focuses on the why and not the what of Anglo-American multiculturalism. But it is not intended to be totalizing, that is, to argue that all the ideational factors noted in the other chapters are ineluctably based on some "hard," "real," or economic factor. As John Weaver and James Belich both argue, Anglo-American ideas about the proper acquisition, use, and development of land powerfully shaped the political economies I sketch below.[5]

Three kinds of states in Anglo-America

Anglo-America encompasses three different sorts of states created at different times. These states are sometimes overlaid on one another, as in the United States and Canada, but they are distinct enough to treat as different species. These different states align with different kinds of elites, different yet similar orientations toward land as an asset, and different patterns of immigration. The oldest Anglo-America is the classic absolutist, sovereign state controlling a set of overseas plantation economies using coerced labor. The second emerged from the new England in America that overthrew control by that prior absolutist state, creating a more decentralized, locally controlled state. A wide range of immigrant labor populated this Anglo-America from early on. The youngest Anglo-America is the set of partially sovereign Dominions that Britain deliberately created in response to its failure to control the second Anglo-America. Predominately populated by immigrants from greater Britain, this Anglo-America did not get the much more heterogeneous mixture seen in the United States (or even Canada) until much later. Each of these Anglo-Americas has a different political economy over land, a different relationship to indigenous people, and a different form of multiculturalism emerging from its specific pattern of immigration. Despite these differences, they exhibit the strong commonalities the other chapters stress, as well as having disproportionately high levels of investment in and integration with each other's economy.

These three state forms emerged as part of the expansion of a Britain- and then northwest Europe-centered global economy in the seventeenth through nineteenth centuries. Yet this expansion only meant that individuals, firms, and states would face incentives to acquire land at the frontier.[6] It did not determine the form that expansion might take, or even that expansion was a certainty everywhere. Non-Anglo Europe and China also experienced an internal expansion into lightly or un-settled areas and an intensification of production at this time. What made the Anglo-American expansion different from this more general process? Belich argues that the prevalence of permanent migrants rather than sojourners distinguished British colonial settlement from that of other European societies.[7] This is partially true with respect to Britain's competitors in the Americas, but misleading with respect to internal migration in Europe and China.

China also had British-style expansion of agricultural production through permanent migration of ethnically related peoples into sparsely settled areas. Indeed, the migration of Han people out of the Yangtze River valley into the geographic "China-island" limned by northern and western deserts, western and southern mountains, and the eastern sea defines much of Chinese history. This migration produced *the* classic ancient agrarian empire but not Anglo-America's characteristic multiculturalisms and immigration. Belich carefully limits his discussion to Chinese expansion into Xinjiang, the "far west," which conceals this divergence. Similarly, the European expansion into its own internal hinterlands (including Belich's Siberia) involved filling in pockets of contiguous land with families drawn from identical cultural and linguistic backgrounds.[8] European peasant societies reproduced themselves literally at their margins – moving excess population into neighboring marginal lands. Where they did not – vide the 80 percent of German emigrants who went into eastern Europe rather than to the Americas[9] – they produced the same kinds of multicultural societies and tensions found in Anglo-America, until the two World Wars re-sorted eastern Europe into relatively homogeneous nation states. What made Anglo-American expansion different was the combination of modern, forward-looking forms of capitalism, two novel kinds of state, and diverse *sequential* streams of immigrants.

A classic sovereign state confronts a settled population

The oldest Anglo-America is the original British Crown, understood as encompassing both the monarchy and the commercial landed elite controlling that monarchy through Parliament after the mid-1600s.[10] This state combined classic, absolutist sovereignty with despotic power, in Michael Mann's sense of despotic – a reliance on coercion rather than self-motivation to induce action by subjects.[11] As Cain and Hopkins and also Brenner have argued, this state expanded its domain at the behest of commercial landed elites.[12] It constructed an inner ring of new domains – in the sense of demesnes, land acquired without debt and fully owned by that commercial aristocracy – and an outer ring in the Caribbean.

Ireland was the original field of play for these elites. They sought a stable labor supply out of the existing local population for market-oriented production on their new demesnes. They subjugated the local population, steadily squeezing it out of land ownership. At the same time they kept their large estates intact through entail, rather than having a modern land market. Most attention is usually focused on the plantation system that emerged in the northern Irish counties. There, the British invaders attempted to clear out the local Irish population and replace them with British Protestant settlers, foreshadowing the later displacement and extermination of native populations in the other European settler colonies. But this overstates the degree to which Ulster was the model for the future, and simultaneously obscures why it was the model. The first Virginia Plantation occurred in 1607, essentially the same time as either the formal private (1606) and royal (1609) plantations in Ireland. Ulster was a negative model, highlighting the difficulty the Crown and its associated elites faced in displacing and subjugating a dense, relatively developed native population in the rest of Ireland.

The plantation system was secondary to the larger engrossment of land in Catholic Ireland. Even in the Ulster plantations, settlers initially simply displaced Catholic Irish enough to make them into a useful labor force. Massacre and formal segregation occurred well after the Ulster plantation's initial implantation.

Instead, violent dispossession from land, and resistance to that dispossession, is the one constant in pre-1922 Irish history. The Catholic-owned share of land in Ireland fell from 59 percent in 1641 to 5 percent in 1776.[13] From the Irish point of view, this was undoubtedly far too fast. But in comparison to expansion in north America, it was pitifully slow. There, for example, settlers expelled native Americans and occupied the Ohio and Kentucky territories, an area roughly three times as large as Ireland, in roughly 20 years. The Ulster plantation's ultimate failure in destroying and replacing the local population reveals the contradiction inherent in the simultaneous acquisition of land and labor in a colonial system. Any place where conquest was easy was also a place where labor would be scarce. By contrast, while a large local population with a pre-existing sense of common identity might provide an immediate labor force, it would be an intractable labor force, perhaps more expensive to police than slaves would be.

The difficulty in containing a restive local Irish population locked the British state into an overt and despotic mode of control that parallels that in the slave societies of the Caribbean and southern North America. The British state in Ireland faced continual insurgency and responded with constant violence. Efforts to let Protestant Ireland govern itself under a parliament in Dublin – though one already subordinate to the British Parliament after Poynings Law in 1494 and excluding Catholics through the Penal Laws from 1607 onward – proved increasingly problematic after some Catholics received the franchise and greater security of land tenure from 1771–93. Loosening of the Penal Laws at the end of the century encouraged the first of many Home Rule movements, basically slow-motion rebellions. In the context of the French and American revolutions, Home Rule risked rebellion in Britain's backyard, so even a limited degree of autonomy was intolerable. The British state bribed and bullied Ireland into a union and thus direct rule in 1801.

The expansion of a commercial agriculture controlled by an aristocracy and oriented towards Britain shaped the subsequent evolution of state, economy, and population both in Ireland and, in a different way, in the rest of Anglo-America. The British market strongly shaped Irish land use and thus the degree to which the local population constituted an economic resource or not, and in turn whether that population stayed put or migrated. Growing British demand for foods, and competition from cheaper food sources in Europe and the Americas, meant that Irish agricultural exports shifted from extensive cattle grazing (for salted meat) to wheat and then finally to dairy and fresh meat.[14] Cattle required grazing land, which accounts for the first displacement of Irish peasants (and to a lesser degree Protestant Ulster settlers) onto smaller and smaller plots of land. In the 1600s and even more strongly in the 1700s, "cattle ate men." But from the late 1700s through the mid-1800s, the area tilled for grain increased eight-fold, peaking at 440,000 hectares in 1847, or nearly a fifth of all tilled land. In the 1780s Ireland had been a marginal net exporter of grain; by the 1800s it exported ten times more grain than it imported and provided half of British grain imports. Where low-quality cattle had displaced peasants in the 1700s, grain now displaced both in the early 1800s. Cattle returned after the 1850s, but as dairy animals and for live slaughter in Britain. Two million acres shifted from cultivation back to pasture. In turn, milk and butter accounted for one-fifth of agricultural output and the entire animal sector for 60 percent by 1900.

These shifts had a profound effect on the Irish population via the demand for labor, and thence on Anglo-America via the supply of ready Irish immigrants. Extensive cattle grazing required much land but little labor. This compressed the existing population onto ever smaller plots and helped start the first, heavily Ulster Protestant wave of out-migration to both Britain and the Americas. The shift to wheat exports increased labor requirements, primarily for harvesting, and dampened out-migration. But the final shift back to animal husbandry drastically reduced labor demand and available land, producing a huge wave of out-migration in the 1800s. During the 1800s a net outflow of 7 million people meant that the Irish constituted between 18 and 25 percent of the population of the Americas, Australia, and New Zealand by 1890.[15] A further 2–3 million Irish migrated to Britain, though largely at the end of the century, and with a large seasonal component. Remarkably, Ireland was one of the few western European locations to lose population during the European population explosion of the 1800s, falling from a peak of 8.5 million in the 1830s to roughly 4 million by 1930. In other words, Ireland's 1930 population barely exceeded that already attained in 1790 in the United States (including slaves). By contrast, the Irish-born and descended population of the United States alone probably amounted to 10 percent of the total US population of 123 million in 1930.

In Britain and particularly England, this huge inflow of Irish created a permanent if small underclass. As in the southern USA and other parts of the empire where English came into contact with "natives," "white" Britons constructed classic racial hierarchies excluding the Irish.[16] Though this did not rise to de jure segregation, in the larger industrial towns with a substantial Irish presence (e.g. Liverpool), de facto segregation was the norm.[17] As Klotz points out in Chapter 4, Ireland's constitutional status was always in doubt. While it was theoretically ruled from and represented in Westminster, the fact that the Colonial Office handled day-to-day administration shows that the imperial state could not figure out if Ireland was part of the metropole or the empire in our conventional understanding of those terms.[18]

The export-oriented and exploitative agriculture using a dense local population, racial hierarchy, and overt state coercion pioneered in Ireland forms one package of social relations in Anglo-America. Its details are repeated in Europe everywhere that an ethnically and religiously distinct aristocracy exploited a peasant population in order to construct a classic absolutist, fiscal state possessing a relatively large military and considerable direct state control over the economy. With commercial agriculture and out-migration, these processes occurred everywhere European empires encountered relatively dense populations outside Europe. The British state also replicated this package in its tropical empire, albeit abjuring settlement in favor of rule through local intermediaries, as in India. They also did so in ways that accommodated labor shortage rather than labor surplus in the Caribbean and the US slave states. This extension into north America came into conflict with the different kind of state created by a population fleeing that highly exploitative and coercive empire in what became the northern United States.

"A government out of sight" and immigration in North America

By contrast with the first Anglo-America, Anglo-American north America possessed two novel and related features: first, expansion into non-proximate areas that were essentially devoid of population; second, the construction of a new form of modern state by local elites rejecting the constraints imposed by the oldest, most coercive Anglo state. Both novelties rested on modern markets in land, and equally important, modern capital markets around land. In turn, these novelties drove a massive and unprecedented immigration mirroring the equally large-scale flight from modernizing economies in absolutist Europe. Immigration occurred in sequential waves that generated recurrent conflict between older and newer groups of immigrants. Where British engrossment of Ireland produced a backwash of immigration, terror, and a national liberation movement, immigration into north America produced nativism, hybrid identities, and a jus soli understanding of citizenship.

This second Anglo-America initially grew rapidly on the basis of local population growth.[19] Efforts by the Crown to control expansion and in particular to limit claims on the Crown's military resources – which amounted to the issue of how fast and how thoroughly the extermination of natives should occur – provoked a backlash by an already "multicultural" settler community that had already begun to develop its own distinct identity. This produced fully sovereign secessionist states in a double movement, with 1776 and 1860 as the starting points. The second revolution was an effort to remove the lingering aspects of the first Anglo-America, namely the slave south, which was a hybrid combining the first Anglo-America's coercive economy with the second Anglo-America's orientation towards modern land markets and expansion into thinly settled territory.

Although it took two revolutions cum civil wars – 1776–83 and 1860–65 – to emerge fully, the second type of Anglo-American state departed considerably from the typical contemporaneous European model. Contrary to Alexander Hamilton's desire for a visible and active European-style state, the United States built "a government...out of sight."[20] But out of sight did not mean out of mind. America was no libertarian paradise in which order emerged spontaneously from voluntary market transactions. Rather, conscious of its inability to coerce compliance, this new state created a system of property relations precisely in order to generate voluntary adhesion to itself. This framework favored debt-financed expansion of agricultural production.

Where European states homogenized people, the new US state homogenized space through massive internal improvements, the Public Land Survey System, and a new legal framework for transferring land from the state to individuals. The new state then let individuals operating inside this framework work out the optimal pattern of production. Markets homogenized individuals as producers, and those producers offered up loyalty to the new state. "Homesteaders (and homeowners) into Americans" characterized the United States rather than "*Peasants into Frenchmen*"; survey and regulation preceded settlement and production rather than being imposed on extant and heterogeneous populations.

In the Caribbean and the US south, the original, coercive imperial state constructed a set of economies that were the mirror image of Ireland. Native populations either died off or could not be forced to work, so planters imported various forms of bonded labor, including transported Irish rebels, before settling on slaves from Africa. They reproduced Ireland, but without a population whose prior social ties and identity made them intractable. These areas hybridized some features of the classic sovereign state found in Ireland, including strict racial hierarchies or color bars and an openly coercive state, with a social structure based on free sale of land. Free sale of land and a modern mortgage market made expansion economically possible.

The point of contact fusing the interests of slave and free states in the colonial and post-revolutionary United States was a desire for westward expansion, that is, more land.[21] Britain sought, through the Proclamation of 1763, to contain westward expansion in order to limit expensive conflict with Indian nations to the west of the Appalachian Mountains. Further, the Treaty of Paris terminating the Seven Years War gave Britain sovereignty over the lands from the Appalachians to the Mississippi River. Britain used this power to attach the lands north of the Ohio River to Quebec in the Quebec Act of 1774. Areas south and east of the Ohio and west of the Proclamation line were reserved to the Indians (or contested with Spain). Combined with a prohibition on direct private land purchases from Indians, the Proclamation sharply curtailed the possibility for western expansion and for local self-government.[22]

From the British side, this seemed a prudent limit on the increasingly restive American colonies. Just so, the difficulties involved in domesticating French and Catholic Quebec made the British increasingly reluctant to countenance immigration to the colonies by people from outside the empire. Although Britons (and, of course, Africans) constituted by far the largest ethnic groups, Germans accounted for about 8 percent of the non-African population at the time of the Revolution, and more Germans than English (albeit not Britons) emigrated to the colonies in the 1700s.[23] There were substantial Dutch, Swedish, and Irish populations, and worse, they lived in geographically concentrated settlements conducive to rebellion. The same was true of various non-Anglican religious groups. From the side of expansion-minded American elites, restrictions on westward movement and immigration were intolerable. Expansionists won the Revolution, which in part was a civil war between themselves and those Loyalists who fled to upper Canada.

The new American state had a different attitude towards land, (immigrant) labor, and governance than the old imperial state. Unlike the old imperial state, the new American state had to compete with Britain (via Canada), its own possibly independence-minded westward-bound settlers and, to a lesser extent, France and Spain for settlers' loyalty.[24] Much as in the original Thirteen Colonies, the key issue was access to land. Settlers would align themselves with whoever offered them secure tenure, more land, and self-governance. And as a century of events from Bacon's Rebellion in Virginia (1676) through to the American Revolution (1776) had confirmed, settlers were likely to abandon or destroy elites who tried to stem their westward outflow. Wakefieldism – limiting access to land so as to assure landowning elites a steady supply of cheap labor – worked better in theory than in practice.

The new Anglo-Americas in north America thus bid for settler loyalty with land, rather than coercing loyalty. This competition produced a curious isomorphism, first between Ontario and the United States and then later in the prairies. While the 1862 Homestead Act seems archetypically American, Britain first offered free land to settlers in the Ontario peninsula. Though these were largely loyalist refugees, they also included large numbers of politically indifferent Americans simply seeking free land. Canada's governor (1791–96), John Simcoe, saw land grants as a way to bid away population from the new United States and thus simultaneously weaken it while strengthening British Canada.[25] His land grants tripled Ontario's population from the Revolution to 1800. He also sought to use Ontario's strategic position on the Great Lakes to consolidate control over the Mississippi River watershed, blocking further westward expansion by the new Republic. Meanwhile, aside from military tracts in upstate New York, the new United States was selling land at $2 per acre upset price in the Northwest territories (that is, Ohio, Indiana, and Michigan).

At that time, Simcoe's strategy made sense, as the loyalties of the majority of settlers and traders in the Great Lakes littoral and upper Mississippi were in play.[26] Neither state could project enough pure military force into the region to control it without first securing the loyalty of the existing settler population.[27] As Hatter points out, much of the American militia in Detroit was composed of nominally British citizens.[28] At the same time, the post-revolution, post-Constitution government in the United States saw westward expansion as the relief valve for its current domestic class conflicts.[29] So the new republic had multiple incentives to offer secure property title to potential and actual settlers. Successful imposition of a regulatory structure favoring settlers reversed the population flow into Canada; an estimated fifth of Canada's natural increase and immigrants, amounting to approximately 2 million Canadians, flowed into the United States from 1850–90.[30] Some Americans, and American firms, also flowed north, making Canada less like its other dominion siblings.

The new US state also seemingly inverted the usual European top-down governance structure. States (and in some cases local governments) predated the Constitution and, unlike corporate European towns, were not creatures of the Federal government, except insofar as the Constitution established a procedure for admitting new states. But local independence or self-governance only occurred inside the larger framework established by the Federal government. States and townships were at liberty to find their own economic path so long as they stayed within the parameters set by the Federal government. States and localities were implicitly and explicitly in competition with each other for immigrants and capital. They did not hesitate to use their revenue and regulatory capacity to chase both.

Internal and external security thus rested on the new state's ability to deliver land to migrant and immigrant settlers, and, in the south, to control slaves. As with European states, this required revenues and military force. But the new state had different relative proportions for these. Where European states confronted established land-owning nobilities, the new US Federal state pre-empted ownership of most trans-Allegheny land. Federally owned land in the Northwest Territory amounted to 200 million acres, and the Louisiana Purchase, Texas, and California comprised an additional 1 billion acres.[31] Land sales provided on average 13 percent of Federal revenue from 1806 until 1846. In the 1830s it averaged about 23 percent of Federal revenue, and in 1836 land sale revenue actually exceeded customs revenue.[32] By contrast, customs and excise taxes and state monopolies provided the bulk of European state revenues. The Federal state bought policy compliance and economic integration from the states (provinces) by allocating 5 percent of land revenue to them for road construction, and of course, the famous grant of one township section out of every 36 sections to fund primary education. Federal revenue sharing rose to 14 percent of land revenue by the 1860s,[33] and in 1862 the Federal government granted yet more land to the states to fund agricultural colleges. But a fuller discussion of the relationship between transport infrastructure and immigration comes naturally after a consideration of the dynamics of slavery and the financial infrastructure.

To be sure, the Federal government maintained a military presence at the frontier, tacitly and often overtly aiding the states in the dispossession of Indians. But its army engaged in only one sustained traditional campaign of expansion, against Mexico in 1848. Even that was brought on by the steady in-migration of Anglo and German settlers into Texas and California, which was rather different from, for example, a contest over settled lands along the Rhine or Isonzo. The signature events in US expansion were instead the Louisiana or Alaskan purchases rather than overseas empire or unification of a group of ethnically and linguistically related states through war. Even there, the acquisition of New Orleans was intended as much to secure the loyalty of settlers upstream in the Northwest territories as it was to remove the French and Spanish as strategic threats. As Jefferson himself noted, internal threats like Aaron Burr's conspiracy found little support from settlers already well served by the Federal government.[34]

Why expand? As in Ireland, each successive increase in British import demand affected production in north America. But unlike Ireland, the frontier moved outward with each increase. For example, cotton production rose from 3,000 bales in 1790 to 4.5 million bales in 1860, moving steadily across the southeast from Georgia to Louisiana.[35] Each increase thus brought in train an expansion of extensive production at the frontier, an intensification of production in former frontier zones, and rising labor demand in both. In Ireland, conquest simultaneously obtained land, labor, and output. Investment and expanded production could occur without recourse to capital markets, though at the cost of increased coercion of the Irish. But in the US south, conquest (the expulsion of native Americans) created only the possibility for new production units, and those units lacked labor and any prior improvements. Creating a labor force, buying land from the state, and putting up basic structures required borrowing in advance of production.

The Federal state abetted local (southern) states' efforts to create access to this borrowing by permitting free banking by default.[36] Legislation in New York in 1838 permitted banks to use Federal or state bonds, rather than specie, to back notes. This system spread to the frontier states to accommodate planters' desires to capitalize new production. By 1860, 17 out of 33 states had free banking, and another four a modified form.[37] Booming demand for cotton created new demand for land and slaves. Land sales rose from an average of 359,000 acres per year in 1800–14, to 5.5 million acres in 1819 and eventually 20 million in 1836. But all of this activity was based on expectation rather than established production. It required credit creation, rather than simple credit intermediation. The southern states were able to "bootstrap" development in a kind of Ponzi scheme that funded mortgages on land whose stream of income lay in the future, by using state bonds whose revenues ultimately also relied on that future stream of plantation income.

The contemporaneous Secretary of the Treasury, William Crawford, acknowledged this bootstrapping, saying many banks were incorporated "not because there was capital seeking investment…but because men without active capital wanted the means of obtaining loans, which their standing would not command."[38] Would-be planters, particularly in Louisiana, Mississippi, Arkansas, and Florida, founded banks to extend themselves mortgages. Ultimately, the banks needed specie to fund actual purchases of slaves and other capital goods. These came not from deposits but from a flow of capital organized by their own states. The pre-Civil War southern states gave planters' banks state bonds. The banks sold those bonds in the global capital market, receiving British pounds, which they could then lend to factors, who in turn lent to planters trying to capitalize production. The new southern states thus bootstrapped their economies. Just as individual planters borrowed against the coming year's crop, their states borrowed against the coming year's revenues. These states borrowed $732 million in the 1830s.

Expanding debt on one side of the balance sheet had a corresponding asset in the expanding number of slaves. Slaves in the abstract are a form of capital good. But in their absence there would be no labor force, and owners would not be able to repay loans against their land and slaves. These slaves were purchased from slower growing areas, like Virginia. The roughly 700,000 slaves present in the New United States in 1790 grew to nearly 4 million by 1860. But their numbers grew because slavery in the old, upper South had become a *relatively* benign condition as compared with, say, sugar production in Brazil. Life expectancy for US slaves was about double that for Brazilian ones.[39] This burgeoning slave population created a mobile labor force that could be redistributed as production moved westward towards the Mississippi River. Traders moved roughly 200,000 slaves per decade from the upper South (primarily Virginia) to the cotton South in the 1800s. Thus while Virginia contained 42 percent of the US slave population in 1790, by 1860 both Alabama and Mississippi rivaled it at around 11 percent.[40] Had Virginia maintained its share of the US slave population, it would have contained 1.7 million slaves in 1860 rather than 491,000.

Slaves represented an additional increment to the capital investment needed to start cotton production. In 1805 the estimated value of the US slave population was $300 million. By 1860 it had risen to $3 billion, implying a rising price per head.[41] The combined need to borrow for both land and a labor force disguised as a capital good meant that rapidly growing southern slave states had very high levels of credit creation, as Figure 3.1 shows by comparing bank credit to real income in the Northwest territories, old south, and new south. Both sets of southern states had very high levels of debt the 1840s. By contrast, producers in the old northwestern territories, which did not need to borrow to buy slaves, had very low levels of debt. Figure 3.2, by contrast, shows the prominent place that slaves occupied on the asset side of the South's balance sheet.

Settlement of the non-slave territories in north America gives us a purer form of the second Anglo-America. Here, successive waves of increasing demand pushed the frontier out in discernible increments. Each new increment drew in a new wave of immigrants, with a new predominant ethnic or national group. The same cotton boom that propelled slave agriculture across sub-tropical America also caused the Northwest territories to boom on the basis of secondary demand. Immigrants constituted one-sixth of total white population growth during the 1830s–1940s

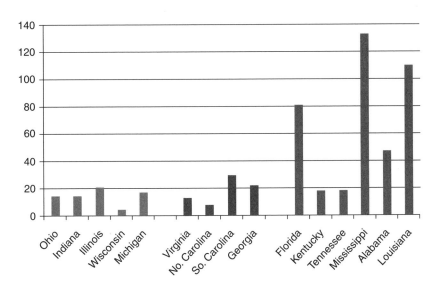

FIGURE 3.1 Ratio of bank credit to real income, 1840
Source: Bodenhorn, 2002, p. 68.

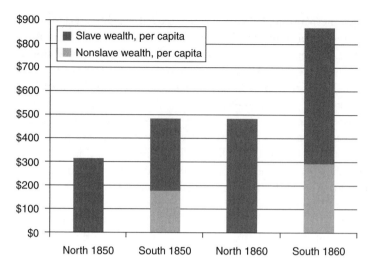

FIGURE 3.2 Proportions of slave and non-slave wealth in per capita wealth, 1850 and 1860
Source: Wright 2006, 60.

boom.[42] But this immigration deepened the existing ethnic heterogeneity of the North, as only 25 percent of immigrants were British. Instead, Germans, mostly from the Rhineland, and Irish provided a third each. Expansion of the wheat production frontier into Illinois, Wisconsin, and Kansas likewise expanded the catchment zone for new immigrants to Francophone Europe and Scandinavia, driving the British share down to 20 percent. By 1860, 22 percent of the northern population was foreign born; in northern Eastern seaboard cities it was as high as 50 percent.[43] Naturally, not all immigrants ventured west. But the inflow made it economically rational for some native born Americans to do so.

These immigrants had the same economic effect as the rising population of slaves. By populating lands emptied of native Americans, they enabled borrowing against that land. That borrowing validated the same kind of bootstrap investment in infrastructure that had occurred in the south. The Federal and "provincial" states provided infrastructure more aggressively than did European states.[44] Not only did the Federal government build infrastructure in advance of production, it also built publicly at a time when Europeans built privately. It then reversed course, promoting private construction at a time when Europeans moved to public construction.[45] In the North, states provided about 40 percent of all railroad capital in the 1830s.[46] Revenue and infrastructure were organically connected, as indicated above. The Federal General Survey Office was housed in the Treasury Department rather than at a ministry of the interior. Land and infrastructure were also organically connected. A Federal land grant funded construction of the Illinois Central Railroad, which was intended to connect the Upper Mississippi at Galena, Illinois, to the

Gulf of Mexico at Mobile, Alabama. This system was generalized in the 1862 Pacific Railway Bill.

The land grant railroad system is the archetypical instance of the new state, and in many ways typical of American industrial policy ever since. The Federal state wanted a railroad network that would tie the entire continent together. Rather than designing it from the top down, the Federal government gave fledgling railroad firms alternating sections of land along their planned routes. This policy put the onus of land development on the railroad company. They could not make money unless the land adjacent to the rail generated sellable commodities to be carried by the system, nor could they raise capital without mortgaging their land grant. So both land and infrastructure were organically connected to immigration, as land was worthless without labor. The Illinois Central Railroad (ICR) received 2.6 million acres of land. But these had to be sold within ten years or forfeited at auction. So the ICR offered seven years' credit to settlers and small down payments to buyers. It did so through its own land development company, which distributed advertisements in Europe and engaged agents to seek emigrants.[47] More generally, private firms like the American Emigrant Company tried to indenture potential immigrants so as to increase their number.[48]

Railroad expansion, production expansion (including industrial products for and from agricultural production), and immigration were thus tightly connected. Each bump out of production brought a wave of new immigrants. These waves were non-random in two ways. First, each new wave of production brought in a different wave of immigrants. Most Europeans migrated in search of substantially higher wages than they could get at home. The flow of migrants inward and the flow of cheap food outward tended to reduce the gap between European and US wages. As migrants streamed out of a given area, they reduced the labor supply there, raising wages. As cheap food streamed in, real wages rose. As in the United States, railroads and steamships mediated this process. They made moving cheaper but also brought in cheaper food. Europe's rail networks built out eastwards in parallel to the westward build out in the United States. Second, chain migration meant that immigrant waves clustered in specific locations. Put simply, immigrants from a given region in Europe tended to migrate to US regions that already had migrants from their family, village, or province. This reduced the transaction costs for migrating.

The combination of the moving frontier and chain migration produced large-scale regional clusters of immigrant communities still visible a century later in the United States: Norwegians in the upper prairies; Swedes in Minnesota; Finns in Washington State and the Michigan Upper Peninsula; Poles in Wisconsin, Michigan, Illinois, and New York; Dutch in New York and Western Michigan; Italians in greater New York City; Hungarians in western Pennsylvania and eastern Ohio; Czechs in Texas and Nebraska; Danes in Nebraska and southern Minnesota; non-Jewish Russians in North Dakota; Chinese and Japanese on the West Coast. Germans of course dominate much of the old northwest, northern prairies, and Texas, but the data are not fine grained enough to identify areas of origin within Germany. Table 3.1 shows some of the heterogeneity in the foreign-born population that still prevailed as late as 1920 in six non-southern states selected for geographical representation and different periods of settlement.

This pattern of immigration had political consequences. As Kevin Phillips noted, regardless of specific issues, political conflicts in most American congressional districts typically revolved around a struggle for power between earlier and later groups of immigrants, as with Catholic Germans and Lutheran Scandinavians in the upper Midwest.[49] But the heterogeneity of the immigrant population in any given area often meant that immigrants from the same regions (and religions) often ended up in different parties at the national level. The political economy of immigration thus makes America's peculiar multiculturalism differ from that in Canada, and even more so Australia or New Zealand. There, as we will see, later migration and greater controls over inflows created less heterogeneous populations until quite recently.

The second Anglo-American state and society thus differs from the first on two important dimensions. In terms of sovereignty, the state's control over society was less coercive and much more indirect (with the important regional exception of the slave states). The state ruled by establishing frameworks in which market contestation would produce the outcome the state desired, rather than through dirigisme or state-owned enterprise. In terms of population, the second Anglo-America was an immigration-receiving country, rather than a primarily sending country. It attracted a huge but sequential variety of immigrants. Those immigrants came in order to validate the exploitation of new lands opened up through land grants. These two distinct features were intertwined, as those land grants were a form of indirect state building or economic planning.

Dominionization and partial sovereignty as the third Anglo-America

British determination to avoid a repetition of what they saw as a geopolitical disaster in north America strongly shaped state structures and immigration in the third

TABLE 3.1 Share of foreign-born population in total foreign-born population, selected states, 1920 (%)

Kansas		Michigan		Ohio		Oklahoma		Pennsylvania		Washington	
Germany	21.1	Canada	20.1	Germany	16.5	Germany	17.6	Italy	16.1	Canada	16.2
Scandinavia	13.2	Poland	14.3	Hungary	10.8	Mexico	16.8	Poland	12.8	Sweden	13.9
Mexico	12.3	Germany	11.8	Poland	10	Russia	12.5	Russia	11.6	Norway	12.1
Russia	10.9	Britain	8.5	Britain	9.3	Britain	10.3	Britain	10	Germany	8.9
Britain	10.5	Scandinavia	8.4	Italy	8.9	Canada	6.2	Austria	8.8	Britain	8.3

Source: United States Bureau of the Census (1921–23).

and final Anglo-America. The 50-year process of dominionization addressed the issues that troubled British relations with the 13 US colonies up to 1776: population, responsible government, control over land (which also meant control over relations with the indigenous and quasi-indigenous populations), and taxation. A settler society was already forming in upper Canada. Could the British empire continue to control this society as well as what became the seven Australian colonies, the Canadian Prairies, and southern Africa? As in the second Anglo-America, settlers in all these societies lusted after land, spilling over the frontier set by the authorities. As in the second Anglo-America, they needed labor to make that land valuable. As in the second Anglo-America, centrally set limits and taxes created some danger of disenchantment.

A British state determined not to have a replay of the US revolution created the dominions by devolving just enough control to local governments to avoid irritation, and abjuring taxation.[50] But Britain retained control over all the important external aspects of sovereignty: foreign affairs, defense, and the law. Thus the dominions emerged from the nineteenth century with semi-sovereign states, capable only of looking inward and not outward. In turn, this affected how in-migration connected to land development.

First, with respect to immigration, the dominions deliberately refused to add new and potentially disloyal streams of immigrants from outside an imaginary Anglo-Aryan and indeed Anglo-Saxon community. This kept the imagined community with Britain stronger than in the rebellious polyglot, polytheist, poly-ethnic American colonies. Indeed, as Belich points out, by the end of the century Anglos in the new dominions considered themselves "better Britons" than those in the metropole.[51] While this started as a government policy, the narrower emigration pipeline into the dominions, and the fierce (and often failing) competition with the United States, meant that the labor force ended up more homogeneous than that in the USA.

In turn, greater solidarity allowed labor to exert more political power in all these societies. Organized labor used this in part to further restrict immigration and thus wage competition from low-wage areas of Europe and especially Asia, as in the unofficial and official versions of White Australia. Asian exclusion thus ran parallel to and reinforced relative homogeneity in the dominions. While large employers were more than happy to bring in Chinese and South Asian labor in large numbers, workers and small firms in European settler communities all around the Pacific Rim correctly saw Asian immigrants as a threat to wage levels and small enterprise.[52] They pressed their governments to restrict Asian immigration by any means. The British empire theoretically assured free movement to all subjects within the empire. But the dominions used dictation tests, bars on direct passage, residency taxes, and other opaque barriers to restrict Asian inflow. The United States also barred large-scale Asian immigration in 1882, following a series of California laws attempting the same thing. Asian exclusion shows the limits to the suction empty land exerted on free bodies in other countries. Like America's postwar segregated suburbs and modern gated communities, nineteenth-century Anglo-America made sure that Asians stayed in the working-class slums.

Multiculturalism thus took on a different valence in the dominions. Instead of the extreme heterogeneity of the United States – still probably the most diverse large country in the world – the dominions were instead more bifurcated societies until after World War II. On the one hand, the new dominions all faced substantial and indigestible communities of others – Māori in New Zealand, Irish in Australia, Africans and Afrikaners in the Cape, and Quebecois in Canada. Africans aside, all these groups had a better status than ex-slaves in the southern United States, which prevented the extreme polarization found there. Unlike the United States, where the indigestible "second society" was a disenfranchised population of ex-slaves, the second societies in the dominions all attained a significant degree of cultural, legal, and political autonomy, including control over large politically defined territories. The defensive cohesion these prior communities exhibited enabled them to avoid becoming just one more item in a list of hyphenated peoples. This permitted those second societies to retain and maintain a distinct identity in a way that, for example, the Irish in America did not. On the other hand, postwar import substitution industrialization in Australia and New Zealand created the diverse European populations America and Canada already enjoyed in the prior century. Continued export of raw materials funded that postwar industrialization, however, creating an echo of the earlier dynamics. What was new was literal suburbanization, with industrialization and a growing population validating land values in new housing tracts.

Second, with respect to land, policy differed in several critical respects from that in the United States, and this in turn allowed immigration to be more selective. Ontario aside, the dominions were at the outer edges of the agricultural production zones supplying Britain and Europe as compared with the United States during the nineteenth century. The dominions thus engaged in more extensive, and thus less labor-intensive, production processes. While Australia and New Zealand were expanding sheep grazing for wool exports in the 1860s–1880s, the old Northwest territories and New York in the United States were shifting to more intensive dairy, meat, and orchard production. So while the dominions needed labor imports to valorize land, they needed proportionately less than the United States did.[53] At the same time, the dominions, except Canada, had to subsidize immigration. New Zealand's subsidies amounted to roughly 45 percent of the annual wage for a family of four.[54] Subsidies allowed the dominions to be more selective than the United States. Tellingly, one of the classic economic histories of New Zealand, by M.F. Lloyd Prichard,[55] has a table of immigrant origins from 1861–76 and lists only two categories: United Kingdom and British possessions; while a second one[56] covering a later period simply lists emigration from Britain.

At the same time, the Dominion governments metered land into the market after the early experiment with free land in Ontario. In New South Wales, Australia, for example, the upset price for land sales in the 1860s was set at £1 per acre.[57] At about $4.85, this is well above the initial $2 per acre sale price for land in the US Northwest territories, about five times the later $1 per acre price, and of course infinitely more expensive than a homestead grant. As in the United States, land sales were expected to help provide part of the cost of building infrastructure. And indeed, in New Zealand for example, land-related revenues, including quitrents, provided roughly one-third of revenue in the 1870s and 1880s.[58] But the critical difference between the United States and the dominions was the use of public debt to build and operate publicly owned railways, or directly subsidized private railroads, as in Canada.

Metering the flow of land into the market in order to strike a balance between local expansionism and indigenous rebellion was only moderately successful, as recurrent conflict with the *Métis* in Canada shows. In Southern Africa, the Boer proved uncontrollable until after the Boer Wars. In Australia, squatters engrossed critical water supplies that gave de facto control over much larger areas (as also happened in South Africa).[59] In New Zealand the great rush of immigrants from 1860 to 1880 sparked the "Land Wars" with the Māori. And in Canada, competition with the United States induced a land grant policy once the US Homestead Act created a magnet for land-hungry settlers. Canada's Dominion Lands Act (1872) is thus the great departure from the dominion pattern of land sales rather than grants.

Even so, its weaknesses relative to the US Homestead Act reveal a different attitude towards settlement. The Lands Act only applied to Canada's prairie provinces, and initially only to land more than 20 miles from a railroad. This reduced the uptake of land, as it made commercial farming unprofitable until the widespread use of motor vehicles.[60] In 1882 this requirement ended, and the next decades saw an explosion of new settlement. This settlement followed the logic already seen in the United States. Land grants and direct subsidies to railroads created an incentive to develop land; development required settlers; railroads thus imported bodies.[61] As in the United States, this meant that Canada imported whatever bodies were available at the moment, rather than the sturdy Britons of yore. Eastern Europeans and particularly Ukrainians settled the prairie grain belt. While immigrant diversity did not reach US levels, the same sort of cohesive "bloc settlements" emerged in specific locations (and survive today, like the Albertan Doukhobor). Thus Saskatchewan and Manitoba had large German, Scandinavian, Dutch, and Ukrainian populations, and Alberta similarly had large Ukrainian and Russian populations. Until recently, all were more religiously diverse than the rest of Canada. Canada thus ended up more like the United States than either Australia or New Zealand, because the political economy around land was more like that in the United States.

New Zealand presents the model dominion case and so merits a few words. Permanent European settlement in New Zealand started as a set of planned "Wakefield" style settlements in which the quantity and quality of immigration would be tightly controlled and linked to land development (see also the discussion of Wakefieldism in Chapter 8 by MacDonald and O'Connor). Edward Wakefield correctly assessed a central problem of social order in both the United Kingdom and the colonial Americas. Britain had too many people without land, who threatened to become an unstable rabble. The colonial Americas had too much land, which made it impossible for aristocratic or large landholders to find adequate – cheap and servile – labor. His solution was to export Britain's surplus bodies to the colonies, but to prevent those bodies from acquiring land once there. The New Zealand Company created six settlements – all still among New Zealand's 15 largest cities today – of groups of English and Scottish settlers replicating the existing British society.

Although Wakefieldism failed – apparently more lower- than upper-class people were willing to migrate to New Zealand and consort with sheep – immigrants helped push the European population to 1 million by 1900. But these migrants remained overwhelmingly non-Irish British, producing an unparalleled cultural homogeneity. As late as 1950, New Zealand had a spirited debate over whether it would be possible to assimilate 5,000 Dutch refugees. The resulting population was thoroughly loyal to the Crown; unlike in Australia, no referendum bill on establishing a republic has ever passed parliament.

New Zealand also remained semi-sovereign much longer than the other dominions, if we look at the core issues of lawyers, guns, and money. The Statute of Westminster was not adopted until 1947. Despite that Act, the British Parliament theoretically could legislate for New Zealand all the way up until the Constitution Act of 1986. That constitution was adopted in consequence of a domestic constitutional crisis rather than any positive effort to cut ties with Britain. Military forces were similarly limited to militias and coastal navies (authorized under the Colonial Navy Defence Act 1865). These coastal navies, and implicitly any future blue-water forces, were subordinated to the Commonwealth Naval Force after 1901. Appeal to the Privy Council was not abolished until 2003. And the Colonial Office encouraged New Zealand to adopt a tariff structure favoring British producers. Relations with the Māori also showcase the constraints on local sovereignty. The Treaty of Waitangi of course created an explicit accommodation with the Māori. But similar treaties in north America did little to contain the westward rush of settlers. The Crown's willingness to supply enough troops to displace the Māori set the real limit on the scale and speed of settler expansion. And the correlation of forces favored the Māori more than the Canadian *Métis*, given the distances involved.

The dominions thus entered the twentieth century with less diversity and less sovereignty than the United States. In effect, Britain had applied to the dominions the policy the United States government applied to its states and their peoples. In each case, subordinate states had autonomy over local issues and could use this autonomy to build out their local economies *in competition with the other localities*. Local autonomy and competition combined to deliver loyalty to and dependence on Britain. British investment in the dominions and the United States comprised 54 percent of all British overseas investment in 1914, split 34 percent and 20 percent.[62] These investments were the counterpart to a vast outflow of railroad equipment and shipping services from Britain to the dominions. The interest payments on those investments were considerable. Net overseas property income rose from 7 to 21 percent of all British property income, 1864 to 1913, paralleling the increased share of foreign assets in total assets from 12 to 33 percent.[63] So a partial economic sovereignty paralleled the partial political sovereignty documented in the other chapters in this volume. And as Hatter and Weaver show, Anglo-American capital was fused right from the start.[64]

Second, the later and more extensive build out of the dominion economies meant that they ended up with a different kind of multiculturalism, a different sort of legal relationship to native societies, and the different language issues present in Canada and South Africa as compared with the United States. (However, the rising and geographically concentrated Spanish-speaking population in the United States may create something akin to South Africa's old Afrikaans/ English divide.) As in the United Kingdom and the United States, the nature and timing of land development baked a different kind of multicultural population into the dominions from the start. The differences in the timing of land development and states' varying ability and desire to control immigration means there cannot be one single Anglo-American pattern of multicultural policy, even though multiculturalism is endogenous to economic development in each society. The sequencing of development creates the pluralism noted in Katzenstein's concluding chapter.

Conclusion

What about suburban Anglo-America in comparison to the world's inner cities and working-class slums? Relatively speaking – and it is always about relativities – the much larger weight of land development in the Anglo-Americas forms a significant part of the specific qualities that mark the differences between Anglo-American liberal market economies (LMEs) and the "European" coordinated market economies (CMEs) so central to the *Varieties of Capitalism* approach. Anglo-American economies are based on deep and liquid capital markets, mobile labor, and financialization of much economic activity. These factors stem from the deep history of the Anglo-Americas as a set of settler capitalisms. As a set of lands without people (mostly), settled by people without land (mostly), the expansion of production into empty lands allowed those who claimed land to create capital out of thin air. Production on top of the land that was otherwise worthless could create capital gains for those holding that land. By shifting or enticing populations to move onto emptied lands, owners could create financial capital out of nothing by mortgaging the land. This made the second and third Anglo-American capitalisms intrinsically about credit, not savings. By contrast, European or CME capitalism was based on savings out of an existing production structure, rather than the use of credit to anticipate new earnings. Savings could be recycled as bank credit to existing enterprises. The Anglo preference for equity finance similarly reflects an orientation towards future earnings and capital gains. The differences between LME Anglo-America and CME Europe, though, should not be read as privileging one over the other. Like modern suburbia and central cities, they are fundamentally dependent on each other. As the 2007–10 global financial crisis showed, CME Europe relied on LME mortgage financed growth to drive its own growth.

Land development and its associated multiculturalism continue to differentiate Anglo-America. While none of the Anglo-Americas has remained a purely agricultural economy, land development remains an important part of their economic growth and of their pension systems. Space prevents a full scale analysis of the relationship between pension plans and home ownership, but put simply, a system of private pensions creates long-term liabilities (or assets, from the pensioner's point of view) whose natural balance sheet counterpart is assets in the form of long-term residential mortgages. And metaphorically speaking, people continue to move out of the denser areas of the global economy into Anglo-American suburbia, guaranteeing continual pressure to develop more housing.

Multicultural populations are thus endogenous to the Anglo-American economies, as each seeks to entice a constant flow of new bodies into their empty lands. The oldest version of the Anglo-Americas did this through slavery and indenture but now is being reshaped by the same kind of backwash of bodies from its formal empire that occurred after the absorption of Ireland. The second one did it through voluntary migration. The youngest version did it through assisted migration and continues to exert a higher degree of selectivity about in-migration. But all three end up having to deal with race and assimilation/multiculturalism in different degrees and mixtures as they match demand for labor to sequential land booms. This also produces the kinds of external renegotiations the other chapters describe. As a truly WASP elite gave way to a more variegated bureaucratic and state elite in each country, real and manufactured warm feelings around Anglo-Saxon cultural norms necessarily gave way to a different form of cooperation in which, for example, the professional norms, practices, and training exercises in the intelligence and military community that Bow and Santa-Cruz describe in Chapter 7 produce a new form of imagined community around organizational routines and shared enemies. Similarly, Anglo-American firms, capital markets, and economies are interconnected in ways that continental Europe is only beginning to approach.

Flows of capital and labor into empty land are one major material basis for the sense of shared identity among the three Anglo-Americas. Negatively, they set the Anglo-Americas off from other civilizations based on longstanding peasant settlement. Positively, they create a set of shared practices around housing, economic development, pensions, and state regulation of the market through frameworks permitting experimentation rather than direct determination of outcomes. Considerable differences also exist among the three Anglo-Americas analyzed here. These can be understood as the consequence of differences in the onset of land development, and they have produced different stews of immigrant populations nd thus different flavors of multiculturalism. All suburbs are not alike, but suburbs are intrinsically different from cities.

Notes

1 Thanks to Brian Balogh, James Bennett, Richard Bensel, Peter Katzenstein, Audie Klotz, Jeffrey Kopstein, Kees van der Pijl, and Srdjan Vucetic for comments and criticism. All errors remain mine.
2 Tocqueville 1904, 316.
3 Bennett 2007a, 1–3.
4 I thank Brian Balogh for this point.
5 Weaver 2003; Belich 2009.
6 Schwartz 2009.
7 Belich 2009, 29–30.
8 Slicher van Bath 1963.
9 Taylor 2001, 318.
10 Lachmann 2002; Brenner 2003.
11 Mann 1986.
12 Cain and Hopkins 2002; Brenner 2003.
13 O'Hearn 2001, 41.
14 Schwartz 2009, 108–10.
15 Belich 2009, 60.
16 Lebow 1976.
17 Pooley 1977.
18 Lustick 1993, 57–70.
19 Belich 2009.
20 Quoted in Balogh 2009, 3.
21 Egnal 1988.
22 Ibid.; Taylor 2010.
23 Taylor 2001, 317–20.
24 Taylor 2010; Hatter 2010.
25 Taylor 2010.
26 Ibid.; Balogh 2009, 66; Hatter 2010.
27 Cf. Emmanuel 1972, more generally on settler societies.
28 Hatter 2010, 109–15.
29 Egnal 1988, 329–31.
30 Jackson 1923.
31 Gates 1960, 52; Balogh 2009, 143.
32 Dewey 1915, 216–17.
33 Gates 1960, 53.
34 Balogh 2009, 191.
35 Schwartz 2009, 128.
36 Hammond 1934, 1936, and 1948; Sylla 1972, 214–15.
37 Bodenhorn 2002, 262.
38 Quoted in Gates 1960, 57–8.
39 Fausto 1999, 20.
40 United States Census Office 1791 and United States Department of the Census 1860.
41 Gunderson 1974, 922.
42 Zolberg 2006, 128–9.
43 Ibid., 129.
44 Balogh 2009, 126–9.
45 Callendar 1902; Dunlavy 1991; Bensel 2000.
46 Dunlavy 1991, 12.
47 Gates 1968; Gates 1960, 89; Zolberg 2006, 131.
48 Zolberg 2006, 172–5.
49 Phillips 1969.
50 Cain and Hopkins 2002, 98–9, 212–13; Taylor 2010.
51 Belich 2009, 466.

52 Zolberg 2006, 175–84.
53 McMichael 1984.
54 Lloyd Prichard 1970, 107.
55 Ibid., 98.
56 Ibid., 143.
57 Wells 1989.
58 Lloyd Prichard 1970, 106, 140.
59 Weaver 2003.
60 Schwartz 2009.
61 Naylor 1975.
62 Schwartz 2009.
63 Edelstein 1982, tables 2.5, 8.3.
64 Hatter 2010; Weaver 2003.

PART II

4

THE IMPERIAL SELF

A perspective on Anglo-America from South Africa, India, and Ireland[1]

Audie Klotz

In the late 1800s, South African leaders were active participants in "an imagined community of white men" that spanned the British Empire and the United States.[2] They and their counterparts in Australia, New Zealand, British Columbia, and California shared the assumption that democracy required the exclusion of non-white people. As part of expanding self-rule, the Dominions gained the right to regulate immigration, an issue viewed as critical for retaining white superiority.[3] The resulting exclusion of Asians, politically and physically, inscribed a racial hierarchy between whites and non-whites. Ironically, a racist Anglo-American collective identity was thus constructed by advocates of "democracy."

Yet where to draw the line between whites and non-whites, and how to regulate those boundaries, was highly contested. Given the widespread use of steep educational and financial requirements for franchise, few Asians would have qualified to vote anyway, but xenophobes were not satisfied. London regularly reminded its colonists that explicit racial discrimination was unacceptable, even as it encouraged other methods of exclusion. Notably, when the adoption of a literacy test was under consideration in 1897, the Colonial Secretary reaffirmed his sympathy with the settlers and their desire to prevent an "influx" of people who were "alien in civilization, alien in religion, alien in customs." Still, Joseph Chamberlain also underscored the need to "bear in mind the traditions of the Empire," which abjured distinctions based on race.[4]

Negotiating within such imperial rules, advocates of whites–only democracy in these emergent national governments shared "best practices" of the time, but their lightly veiled racism hardly satisfied stauncher critics. Most famously, Mohandas Gandhi, at the time a young lawyer in South Africa protesting widespread discrimination against Indians who were British subjects, also pointed to the Proclamation of 1858 by Queen Victoria, which promised equal treatment regardless of race or creed.[5] By 1914, Gandhi had lost his battle for imperial rights but, due to his innovative strategy of passive resistance, won some concessions for Indians within South Africa that also set the stage for his future role as father of Indian nationalism.[6] Similarly, Japan lost the larger goal of a racial equality clause in the League of Nations but, through Gentlemen's Agreements, won some concessions for its immigrants in Australia, Canada, and the United States.[7] As Srdjan Vucetic also argues in Chapter 5, contemporary controversies over multiculturalism are the latest manifestation of these deep tensions between race and liberalism.

To illuminate the fluid nature and shifting scope of this "Anglo" community during the twentieth century, I trace evolving definitions of an Imperial Self, my label for the crucial transnational "we-ness" theorized in the security community literature. Drawing attention to the ambiguity of national borders and the quasi-sovereignty of the Dominions, I concentrate on the liminal positions of South Africa, India, and Ireland within the British Empire.[8] My aim is not to define who counts as the core of an Anglo-world but to use views from its periphery as a vehicle for exploring relationships among its putative components. To grasp these connections, I concentrate on the epicenter of political authority: imperial institutions. What I seek to capture is a set of assumptions that intersect discourse and practice via administrative procedures.[9] In particular, I assess the degree of subjectivity accorded or denied to these liminal actors by examining the extent to which they are included in or excluded from core institutions.

Thinking about the shifting boundaries within and around an Imperial Self leads me to ask how South Africa fluctuated between a terrain of conflict and a core part of the British Empire. Both India and Ireland offer similar examples of contestation over collective identity, though obviously with different specific outcomes. I start with South Africa not simply because I know its history better. Conflicts over it rippled through London's relationships with its other colonies, especially the Dominions but also Ireland and India.[10] Apartheid certainly played a key role in South Africa becoming an outlier by 1960, but its abiding similarities with the other Dominions challenge the naturalized pairing of Australia and Canada that continues into the twenty-first century.

I demarcate three phases. In the crucial decade between the Anglo-Boer War and World War I, Britain discovered the limits of its naval-based defense, and its self-governing colonies started to assert themselves. Then the interwar period witnessed extensive debates over greater Dominion autonomy, both within the nascent Commonwealth and among the members of the newly formed League of Nations. Irish independence, but also India's abiding subordination, defined the edges of an Anglophone community that fused race and liberalism. The boundaries shifted again in the context of the postwar rights revolution, when Britain and the Commonwealth wrestled with new population mobility and the challenges of multiculturalism. The result is a bifurcated former empire: an Anglo-American alliance and a multiracial postcolonial Commonwealth.

Overall, this rereading of imperial history and theories of identity primarily from the perspective of South Africa, India, and Ireland challenges assumptions about sovereignty and power that inform civilizational analysis, as detailed by Peter

Katzenstein and Duncan Bell (Chapters 1 and 9, and 2, respectively, in this volume). The devolution of Dominion autonomy in the British Empire undermines static or unitary views of identity and reverses key causal arrows in the security community literature. In addition, stressing the legacies of racialized democracy rather than any inherent cultural ties among the Anglophone former British colonies sets the stage for rethinking Anglo-America in Part III of this volume.

Empire as security community

After the collapse of the Cold War, International Relations scholars rediscovered the notion of a security community. Emanuel Adler and Michael Barnett largely blame history for the displacing of the idea, promoted by Karl Deutsch in the 1950s, that "actors can share values, norms, and symbols that provide a social identity, and engage in various interactions in myriad spheres that reflect long-term interest, diffuse reciprocity, and trust."[11] By the 1970s, alternative concepts such as regional integration or interdependence, it seemed, better captured relationships across the North Atlantic and Western Europe. The US-centric nature of the International Relations discipline is also a key factor. After World War II, British experiences got sidelined, practically and conceptually. For instance, as historian Mark Mazower has recently rediscovered, British thinking featured significantly in the design of the United Nations in part due to its profound influence on the League of Nations.[12]

Thus the notion of collective security had earlier roots. Indeed, the term "security community" aptly characterizes the relationship between London and the Dominions through much of the twentieth century, which helps to explain why it was actually a South African who initially promoted the League concept and later wrote the Preamble to the UN Charter. The only colonial leader to serve in two War Cabinets, Jan Smuts truly embodied the notion of an Imperial security community in the interwar period. But the Cape-born Afrikaner was hardly a typical colonial. A Cambridge-trained lawyer, he became a close advisor to Paul Kruger, the irascible president of the South African Republic who was a thorn in the side of ardent imperialists. After commanding insurgents during the Anglo-Boer War, Smuts ultimately had an illustrious political career defending the British cause – despite his inability to reconcile the best of his liberal ideals with the unapologetic racism of his policies as a prime minister of South Africa.[13]

Although Canadian and Australian leaders were not as close to the inner circle of decision-making power as Smuts, their troops and material support were indisputably crucial to British victories. In particular, the central role of the Royal Navy in imperial defense manifests the high degree of trust and integrated militaries that distinguish "mature" security communities.[14] By World War I, the idea that Britain or the white settler colonies might go to war against each other was indeed unthinkable. Anti-Asian sentiment in response to burgeoning migration flows also captures the "tightly coupled" perceptions of external and internal threat that Adler and Barnett suggest is crucial to collective identity.[15] Even though the Dominions were no longer automatically obligated to fight on the British side in World War II, most of them readily did. Grumblings in parts of Francophone Canada, Afrikaans-speaking South Africa, and Catholic Ireland are notable primarily for what they tell us about the limits of shared identity and long-term interests.

Since this relationship foreshadows subsequent work on collective identities, it is not surprising that Richard Jebb, a famous British commentator on imperial governance in the early 1900s, outlined a proposal for what is essentially the concept of a security community. In outlining a "position of equality in a council of nations" for the Dominions within the imperial realm, he argued that the growing autonomy in the white settler colonies could be harnessed into a cooperative defense arrangement that retained a sense of community derived from their common British connections.[16] At the core of this "imperial partnership" was the idea that nationalism and imperialism could be mutually compatible rather than mutually exclusive (the view that has prevailed since widespread nationalist-inspired decolonization). Illustrated in Figure 4.1, this system would be based on choice rather than obligation, calculation rather than blind loyalty. The result, Jebb hoped, would be a vibrant and robust security community that strengthened imperial power in the face of new international realities, not least a rising Japan.

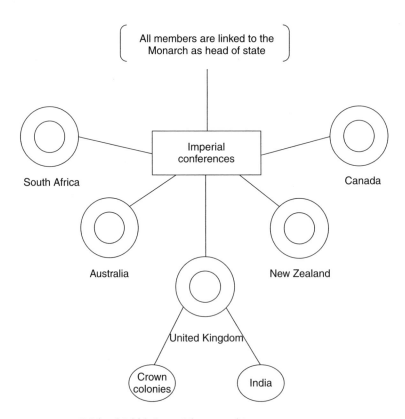

FIGURE 4.1   Richard Jebb's imperial partnership

Jebb's ideas could be lost to future theorists in no small measure because Britain did not adopt his formulation. His failure to persuade politicians despite a prominent pulpit as a journalist illustrates many of the general barriers to creating security communities. Disheartened by a failed campaign for Parliament in 1910, largely due to the unpopularity of his position on tariff reform, Jebb soon withdrew from public life.[17] Britain also did not adopt the proposals of his friendly rivals, avid imperialists who envisioned direct governance of the whole empire.[18] Even Jebb underestimated the strength of the Dominion nationalism that he trumpeted; Canadians and South Africans were as opposed as London to closer commitments, albeit for different reasons. Ironically, in political historian Daniel Gorman's assessment, "imperial citizenship failed because it was expressed, at least by its more progressive proponents, in democratic terms."[19] Yet issues of imperial restructuring continued to dominate British strategic thinking through the interwar period, with strains of Jebb's notion of partnership recurring today.

Although Jebb's vision did not come to pass, at least not in his lifetime or in the particular form that he imagined, history has proven him right: the Dominions did not have to choose between being nationalists and being British. The trajectory of Dominion nationalism over the past century (captured in many other chapters of this volume) demonstrates that the two notions were (and remain) fundamentally intertwined. Thus Jebb's ideas, and the white settler Dominion experiences central to them, fundamentally challenge key assumptions about sequencing in the security community literature. For Adler and Barnett, along with many of their followers, converging national identities and interests provide the basis for building trust, eventually transforming narrower conceptions of the Self into a more diffuse sense of "we-ness." Not for Jebb: British "we-ness," the blind loyalty of kinship, was the starting point for devolving the empire into a security community that would make possible the realization of national identity and the pursuit of national interests. In this alternative formulation, cross-border commonality precedes nationality.

One of the main implications of this reversed sequencing is the need to revisit the role of any essentialized British heritage at the core of an Anglophone community. I start with the Anglo-Boer War (1899–1902) to make my case that the Imperial Self should be considered an example of collective security. After all, a skeptic might argue that the very existence of this conflict contradicts any claim of even a rudimentary "no-war" community within the empire. Keeping in mind that imperialists and Boers alike stressed the cultural and political barriers between their communities, I follow with modified intent Jebb's emphasis on this conflict as "a criterion of progress from colony to nation," contained within the Imperial Self.[20] In his framework, a nationalistic embrace of agency underpinned voluntary solidarity with Britain, in contrast to a sense of obligation that characterized colonialist support of wars based on "the sympathy of kinship."[21]

This imperial history demonstrates twin pillars, race and liberalism, that produce recurring tensions over what it means to be British. These tensions and their legacies are succinctly captured through the intertwined life stories of Smuts, Gandhi, and a third towering figure, Winston Churchill. Half American by birth, Churchill spent a brief stint as a young British officer stationed in India before gallivanting around war zones. As the Parliamentary Under-Secretary for the Colonies, he defended restored autonomy for the former Boer rebels, then as the Secretary of the Colonies negotiated the problematic division of Ireland. Shunned later for opposing the Indian autonomy, Churchill regained stature as prime minister during World War II, coming to symbolize the Anglo-American "special relationship," a term that he coined. Neither Smuts, emblematic of Jebb's ideal nationalist, nor Churchill, the archetypal English imperialist, resolved the ambiguities within British liberalism no matter how often Gandhi brought its racist strains to their attention.

The Imperial Self

Reactions to war in South Africa, more so than the issues driving the conflict itself, reveal the nature and strength of an Anglo-community at the height of imperialism. I stress that the self-governing colonies supplied Britain with troops, albeit based on a mix of motives. It is important to note, however, that few in the imperial public sphere knew or cared much about the South African conflict itself, nor did the press or politicians generally challenge the prevalent portrayal of British liberty and British communities under threat.[22] It is also worth remembering the prediction of a speedy victory, a "one-day event," with no serious thought even to the possibility of a protracted conflict, as actually happened.[23] Thus questions of cost played a relatively small role in Dominion debates. And, as the remainder of this section explains, tensions persisted after the war over the extent of inclusion for Afrikaners, Francophone Canadians, Indians, and Irish. These relationships, evident in the early twentieth-century discourses of race and civilization that permeate the diplomatic archives, are summarized in Figure 4.2.

South Africa

The underlying and proximate causes of any conflict are complex. Some attribute the Anglo-Boer War to the political machinations of the arch-imperialist Cecil Rhodes, twice serving as prime minister of the Cape Colony, rather than to aggression by the Boer-controlled South African Republic. Obviously, the two self-governing British colonies in southern Africa, the Cape and Natal, were on the front lines and contributed in various ways, albeit without allowing non-whites to serve in the military. Some Afrikaners in each colony also sided with the rebels, raising difficulties over whether to punish them for treason. Widespread anti-British reactions to the war in Europe, and especially German support for the South African Republic, is also a reminder of Britain's broad strategic concerns, which helps to explain the significance of southern Africa beyond London's putative mercantilist desire to control supplies of gold.[24]

Ultimately, colonial troops proved to be more proficient than London expected, contributing significantly to victory, in contrast to the ill-prepared and ineffectual

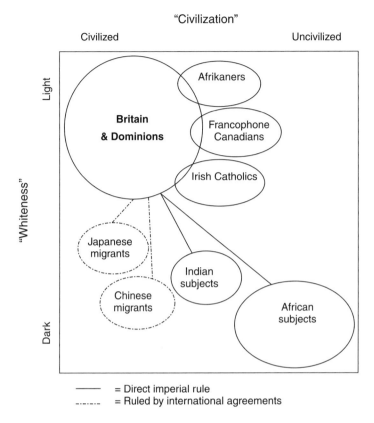

FIGURE 4.2 The Imperial Self

British military that initially came close to losing the war. Even Churchill, traveling in South Africa as a journalist, characterized the British military as initially moving from "blunder to blunder and from one disaster to another," although his early published reports emphasized Boer brutalities instead.[25] In Jebb's scathing assessment, which sought to capture the mood in the Dominions right after the war, the colonial forces were "horsemen, not men on horses," who, "not hampered by aristocratic habits," were "used to thinking for themselves" and "less liable to panic."[26]

Afrikaner defeat secured South Africa's place within the Imperial Self, but in unanticipated ways. By 1907, Smuts persuaded Britain to grant self-government to the Transvaal and Orange River Colony, the former Boer Republics, setting the stage for the unification of South Africa in 1910.[27] Cementing the imperial tie, Smuts and his friend Louis Botha, South Africa's first prime minister, even suppressed pro-German resistance among some of their former commando comrades. Smuts later went to London, where he participated in planning two world wars, commitments that alienated radical Afrikaners.[28] However, the South African nationalism of Smuts and Botha also undermined visions of a stronger imperial federation, because these commitments were made in pursuit of an autochthonous *civic* nationalism that aimed to bridge the extremes of Boer republicanism, based on ethnic nationalism, and imperial jingoism in the style of Rhodes. These policies toward South Africa also simultaneously infuriated and inspired Irish nationalists, who saw a crucial precedent – a reminder of the complex interconnections of collective identity.[29]

Canada and Australasia

According to Jebb, willingness to fund troops or subsidize the Royal Navy marked movement away from the traditional colonialist assumption that London should cover the costs of imperial defense. At the most nationalist end of this spectrum, Canada viewed its contributions of approximately 7,000 troops to fight in South Africa as voluntary, leading both Jebb and subsequent historians to see it as a positive step towards a new mode of imperial cooperation.[30] But a longer historical perspective shows that the controversy over whether to participate in the Anglo-Boer War also sowed the seeds of stronger anti-imperialist nationalism, especially in Quebec, which would temper Canadian enthusiasm for institutionalized cooperation in future decades.

Illustrating the divided sentiments of Francophone Canadians, Prime Minister Wilfrid Laurier supported Britain, but his primary critic, Henri Bourassa, even objected to the compromise (eventually adopted) of voluntary recruits as unacceptable support for imperialism.[31] In Jebb's admiring assessment, "Only the eloquence and known sincerity of a French-Canadian Premier could have kept Quebec in hand."[32] Perhaps, but not for long: Bourassa resigned from Laurier's Liberal Party to galvanize anti-imperial nationalists. Any allegiance to Britain, he argued, should be based not on emotion or pride or duty but on "reason, mixed with a certain amount of esteem and suspicion."[33] In 1909, when Laurier proposed building a navy to protect the coast, Bourassa objected on the grounds of likely entanglements in British wars. In World War I, Canada once again debated whether or under what conditions to contribute troops. Vociferous objections in Quebec led to the controversial adoption of conscription in 1917, a policy that prompted deadly riots and left a long-lasting divide.[34]

Such controversy stands in stark contrast to the debates on the other side of the Pacific Ocean. Despite a much smaller population, the colonies of Australasia contributed over 15,000 troops, primarily based on a mix of colonialist loyalty and growing nationalism. Since the onset of the war preceded Federation in 1901, each of the colonies made separate decisions, partially as the result of competition to outdo each other.[35] Queensland was most enthusiastic and New Zealand most reluctant, although the latter still contributed almost as many troops as all of Canada did. Jebb argued that the war served as a rallying point for those advocating Australian unification, in part because popular sentiment favored nationalist imperialism.[36] In contrast to Canada, it was colonialists who argued against participation, mainly on the basis that the war did not fundamentally threaten core imperial commercial interests or military rivalries. Furthermore, while the Australasian governments contributed to the British response against the Boxer rebellion in China, that conflict garnered little public support even among nationalists, who viewed it as a peripheral concern for the empire.[37]

Overall, then, rising Dominion nationalism supported the British cause in South Africa, with the exception of the Boers themselves and sections of Francophone Canada. Their essential role in imperial defense, with concomitant declining faith in protection by the War Office, produced greater self-confidence. The implications were particularly relevant for redefining the Imperial Self into a security community. Most immediately, victory in the Anglo-Boer War ushered in a new period of intense debate over the constitutional relationship between London and the Dominions, producing greater autonomy for the white democracies.[38] In addition, reflecting their significant role in World War I, most of the Dominions – along with India – attended the peace settlement at Versailles and became founding members of the League of Nations.[39]

India

British regiments stationed in India also played a crucial role in victory over the Boers, both initially and at the end of the conflict. Although few of those units included any Indian soldiers – the conflict was unmistakably viewed in London (and elsewhere) as a white man's war – thousands of Indian non-combatants also served in South Africa.[40] Even Gandhi, a firm believer in British principles of liberty, organized an ambulance corps among pacifist Indians.[41]

Yet we cannot infer much about Indian nationalism from these deployments or Gandhi's views. Unlike the settler colonies, India lacked self-government. The Viceroy, despite the grandeur of his title, was subordinate to the India Office in London, and his advisory council included a mix of elected and appointed representatives, some white, some Indian. Even while extending representation in 1908, the Secretary of State for India affirmed that "if it could be said that this chapter of reforms led directly or indirectly or necessarily up to the establishment of a parliamentary system in India, I, for one, would have nothing to do with it."[42] More like its approach to Africans than to white settlers, trusteeship was the official policy; even Jebb agreed that self-government remained something for the future.[43] Unlike Gandhi, critics of imperialism in the nascent nationalist movement looked to Japan and Ireland for inspiration.[44]

More important than the Anglo-Boer War for fostering Indian nationalism, but garnering only belated attention from Jebb among others, was discrimination against Indians who were imperial subjects.[45] In particular, treatment of Indians in South Africa proved a crucial issue in the early 1900s, with far-reaching implications into the post-World War II era. The roots of the debate over apartheid go back to London's refusal to come to the defense of its darker-skinned subjects, deferring instead to the sensibilities of local white public opinion in the Dominions, especially South Africa.[46] The battles between Gandhi and Smuts have gained almost mythical status, particularly as they were the proving ground for Gandhi's philosophy of passive resistance, *satyagraha*, which he later used to oppose British rule over India.

As for their legacy within South Africa, both the discriminatory policies that Smuts instituted and his suppression of Indian resistance presaged the further development of state capacity that marked apartheid-era authoritarianism. The keystone was London's refusal to protect the imperial rights of its Indian subjects, which made the local rights of Africans even easier to rescind. London's refusal to extend qualified franchise to the Union as a whole, as then practiced in the self-governing Cape Colony, is typically described as whites selling out blacks. While true, this interpretation overlooks the intermediary step of depriving Indians of their imperial rights to franchise and property, which weakened African claims and precluded the availability of stronger non-white allies. Viewed counter-factually, had Gandhi rather than Smuts prevailed prior to Union, Africans would have had a better chance of retaining at least some of their rights.[47]

What the implications of a hypothetical Gandhian victory in South Africa might have been for the future of Indian nationalism is too tenuous to merit speculation, but the controversy in South Africa does offer a window into the status of India within the empire. With the partial exception of George Curzon, rarely did the Viceroy defend the rights of overseas Indians.[48] Typically, the views of the India Office in London prevailed, with some pressure exerted through the growing Indian nationalist movement. Within imperial councils, India shifted only gradually from the status of a colony, excluded from consultation in the 1890s, to occasionally being brought in as an observer at the turn of the century for consultation regarding discrimination against Indians. The 1911 Conference in particular dealt extensively with the issue of discrimination against overseas Indians.[49] Still, Indian nationalists arguably had more representation through two members of the British Parliament who were Indian than through the governing system within India itself.[50]

Ireland

Unlike India, which was of strategic importance but clearly part of the subordinated periphery, Ireland was simultaneously core and periphery, "a bulwark of Empire" and "a significant source of subversion."[51] The territory was administered through a complex system that included the Colonial Office and a Viceroy, indeed setting a precedent for governance of India. Yet Irish representatives had sat in Parliament since 1801, often serving at the highest levels, and sometimes even held the key to coalition government.[52] Therefore, from London's perspective, the prospect of either home rule or an Irish republic threatened the very core of British power.

The Irish Question cut to the heart of how the Imperial Self was defined by intertwined hierarchies of civilization and race. As illustrated by overlapping ovals in Figure 4.2, colonized Europeans, grouped by what we now call ethnicity, were closest to the core at the turn of the century. Although viewed by British imperialists as inferior culturally, French-Canadians and Afrikaners were accepted as part of the white community, ideally to be assimilated into the superior British civilization. In contrast, Indians were clearly outside the core, represented by a line of direct rule in Figure 4.2. Unlike the "uncivilized" Africans, they were of a different "Asiatic" civilization, in the vocabulary of the times.[53] That a few Asian and African elites did adopt British standards actually enabled imperialists to affirm that theirs was a principled position, based on superior ideals of liberty rather than crude prejudice.

Not as clearly inferior as the Indians yet obviously European, the Irish were the ultimate liminal nation. Perhaps they had transitioned economically from being treated as "semi-savages," comparable to "marginalized indigenous peoples," to "semi-settlers" in the macro-historical assessment of James Belich.[54] And they were disproportionately well represented in the British military, including regiments that fought in South Africa.[55] Yet they were typically not as acceptable as even their fellow Catholics, the French-Canadians. Catholics in Canada benefitted from British fears of a potential alliance with the United States. Absent a comparable threat, Britain feared the proximate Irish and viewed them, like the Indians, as unfit for self-government. Therefore, it "failed to address the challenge and opportunity presented by the essentially conservative Irish Catholic elites."[56]

Unassimilated and facing pervasive constraints in a semi-colony, landless peasant-laborers and middle-class Catholics ventured into the wider empire and the United States.[57] Indeed, discrimination fueled emigration from both Ireland and England. Within England, Irish internal migrants were "perceived as an alien invasion," not solely because of their "dangerous" religion; they also organized secret societies in the hopes of mobilizing demands for independence.[58] Although not immune from anti-Catholic prejudices, Irish immigrants were more readily accepted in the Dominions. Many bolstered support for racial exclusions against Asians, but some also supported the nationalist cause back home and would later protest conscription into World War I.[59] In addition, some Irish nationalists in South Africa rallied to Kruger's cause, fueling pro-Boer and separatist sentiments back home.[60] The implications of Irish immigration for the Anglo-American relationship were similarly multifaceted.[61]

Thus the Imperial security community that had emerged on the eve of World War I was not quite along the lines of the voluntary alliance that Jebb envisioned or the cohesive federation that imperialists advocated. "Subordination has melted into partnership," wrote Charles Lucas, former Permanent Under-Secretary for the Colonies, "and the Dominions at the present day are side by side with the mother country as younger partners in a family firm."[62] However, Ireland was not considered a partner in Lucas's imperial family firm, even though it was as invaluable as India in its far-flung construction.[63] And it is these prejudices that fundamentally influenced the increasingly multilateral nature of the international system in the interwar period, another key characteristic of a mature security community, according to Adler and Barnett.[64]

Partnership in practice

Fueled by victory in World War I, debate about Dominion autonomy became even more complicated due to the new League of Nations. Other countries meeting at Versailles objected to their full membership, characterizing the proposal as simply providing Britain with multiple votes. India's comparable status raised the most controversy, as it was the "anomaly of anomalies": not clearly self-governing.[65] Indeed, Woodrow Wilson questioned why the Philippines, then under the quasi-imperial jurisdiction of the United States, should not be a member if India could bolster Britain's position; ironically, Smuts was one of the voices who persuaded him to allow India to join.[66] A second debate over Dominion and Indian eligibility in the Council and the Permanent Court of International Justice also resulted in their inclusion, adding another reason for US opposition to the League.[67] India proved to be a major financial contributor to the organization, certainly less so than Britain (its main underwriter) but more so than even Canada, which was the only Dominion ever to gain a non-permanent seat on the Council.[68]

Despite any inequalities in practice, equal status in principle enabled the Dominions and India to use the League to bolster claims for autonomy, especially in foreign affairs. For example, as part of the postwar process of reallocating German colonies, South Africa gained jurisdiction over South West Africa (Namibia), where it already exercised military control from July 1915.[69] While British hopes of a unified imperial position within the League fueled the concerns of many Europeans, the predominance of Afrikaners among South Africa's representatives dampened that perception somewhat. On balance, then, by providing an alternative venue for the nascent British Commonwealth to pursue a shared worldview, the League appears to have strengthened the Imperial security community based on choice rather than loyalty – Jebb's original vision for nationalism as a positive force within the empire. But again, neither Ireland nor India fits comfortably into the picture.

Ireland

Not unlike reactions in Quebec and amongst radical Afrikaner nationalists in South Africa, World War I contributed to rising discontent in Ireland. Apparent German complicity led to British charges of treason against key republican leaders, and significant funds from sympathizers in the USA created strains with London's new ally. Sinn Fein won widespread electoral support in 1918 but refused to sit in the British Parliament, instead demanding a separate legislature in Dublin. Escalating civil war in 1919 and 1920 prompted a brutal response from Churchill, who was then the Colonial Secretary and a vociferous opponent of republicanism anywhere in the imperial realm. After recognizing the futility of repression, Prime Minister David Lloyd George offered a truce, which Sinn Fein accepted. During this brief calm, the Parliament passed the Government of Ireland Act of 1920, which divided the island into two territories. Much like a Dominion, powers of home rule for the south were strengthened, but defense and foreign affairs remained in London's control.[70]

Yet the republicans, elected again with widespread support in 1921, refused to accept this limited dispensation. Negotiations quickly broke down and fighting resumed. Further negotiations led to an agreement, the Anglo-Irish Treaty of 1921, crafted on the British side by Churchill with Smuts assisting as key advocate for compromise. Essentially, London offered Dominion status: an Irish Free State in the south, with the equivalent of a Governor-General, but no navy and no future neutrality, in light of its territorial proximity and thus strategic location. With minor concessions, the Irish negotiators agreed, knowing it would be controversial back home. In the end, a close majority favored the treaty, the implementation of which dampened but did not eliminate the violence.[71] Ireland thus belatedly joined the League of Nations, which it embraced, like the Dominions and India, as a venue for developing greater independence.[72]

Ireland was not the only part of the empire seeking greater autonomy. Canada in particular had been pushing for the right to negotiate directly with the United States over issues of common concern, rather than relying on British diplomats. London compromised and, once and for all, rejected the idea of an imperial constitution. With the Balfour Declaration of 1926, the Dominions and the Irish Free State, whose status was reaffirmed as comparable to Canada, could sign treaties and establish their own departments of foreign affairs.[73] The Dominions finally resembled sovereign states, as "autonomous" self-governing communities alongside Britain within the empire, "equal in status, in no way subordinate one to another in any aspect of their domestic or external affairs, though united by a common allegiance to the Crown, and freely associated as members of the British Commonwealth of Nations." Henceforth, since London lost the power to disallow Dominion legislation, the Governors-General would be representatives solely of the monarch, not the British Parliament or any department. Britain, in turn, established a new position, that of High Commissioner, so that the government retained direct intergovernmental representation with each of the Dominions.[74]

In deference to Ireland's standing comparable to Dominion status, the 1926 Conference also agreed that the King's title would be modified to delete "United Kingdom" from the phrase "Great Britain and Ireland, and the British Dominions beyond the Seas." Furthermore, by retaining the first "and," the new title left Ireland clustered with Britain rather than with the Dominions. The revised title also underscored that the monarch's role over both Ireland and the Dominions remained distinct from that of the "Emperor of India." Yet "Commonwealth membership resembled the chafing of an ill-fitting shoe," according to historian Deirdre McMahon, because the "waffle" of Dominion status could not compare to the "precision" of a republic.[75] Whereas the former involved an ambiguous quasi-sovereign autonomy, the latter emphatically did not entail any allegiance to the British monarch.

To address the constitutional consequences of the Balfour Declaration, the British Parliament adopted the Statute of Westminster in 1931, with each Dominion free to pass its own enabling legislation. The main exception to formal sovereignty was judicial appeal, the highest level of which remained with the Privy Council in London, since the Dominions retained the monarch as head of state. Little else stood in the way of de facto if not de jure independence. The core of the Imperial security community, white settler democracies, was thus reaffirmed and would carry Britain through World War II. However, questions about its boundaries remained. The Irish Free State was still not satisfied, even after constitutional changes in 1936 further diminished the significance of the monarchy and enabled it to insist on neutrality during the war. Finally, it declared a republic on 18 April 1949 and withdrew from the Commonwealth.[76] Yet even then, Ireland preferred to deal with the Commonwealth Relations Office rather than the Foreign Office, until the two were merged in 1968.[77]

India

Paralleling the League debates, the Balfour Declaration acknowledged the problematic status of India, which had reached the semblance of equality with the Dominions but without self-government. Noting that "in the previous paragraphs we have made no mention of India," it reaffirmed movement towards greater autonomy as set out in the 1919 Government of India Act. It also invoked a 1917 Imperial War Conference resolution that recognized India's importance, accompanied by a generic pledge by the British government to move towards self-government. Important indeed: Indian troops contributed significantly in World War I, and the Indian military remained critical to imperial policy in Asia. With Ireland as a backdrop, London feared that expectations of Dominion status unfulfilled by the 1919 reforms, and unresolved disagreements over the rights of Indians overseas, might even lead to the collapse of the empire.[78] Thus the Balfour Declaration confirmed that issues affecting more than one part of the Commonwealth – an implicit but well-understood reference to disputes over the treatment of Indians in South Africa – should be addressed through intra-imperial consultation.

The administrative structure of the empire also reflected India's abiding liminal status. The India Office existed in parallel to the Dominions Office, which was separated from the Colonial Office in 1925. Through the India Office, London controlled its positions on League policy, including the appointment of its delegation, thus ensuring that neither the issue of discrimination against Indians nor Indian nationalism emerged within the Council or the Permanent Court of International Justice.[79] Even after the India and Dominion Offices were consolidated into the Commonwealth Relations Office – instigated by the wish to eliminate the term Dominion, which implied undue subordination – it remained situated uneasily between the jurisdictions of the Colonial Office and the Foreign Office.[80] Throughout the 1920s, imperial federalists supported upgraded standing for India as a Dominion.[81]

In the face of burgeoning Indian nationalism, London began to shift its perspective by the late 1920s. However, the infamous Simon Commission in 1929 did not include any Indians. In response, credible nationalist leaders boycotted it. Finally, Gandhi and other authentic interlocutors attended a conference in 1930, the first in a series to design Dominion-like status for India, setting off a vociferous debate.[82] The goal for Gandhi was India independent "from the Empire" but "from the British nation not at all," an equal partner along with Britain and the Dominions in the Commonwealth.[83] Churchill, ever the imperialist, led a faction of Conservative Party critics. In response to the Viceroy urging him to reconsider, Churchill declared that "I am quite satisfied with my views on India" – in essence that its diverse population did not comprise a nation and its caste system evinced an unacceptable lack of civilized standards – "and I don't want them disturbed by any bloody Indians."[84]

Gandhi's famous Salt March and his subsequent release from jail escalated Churchill's attacks on the government for its lack of resolve. In his view, Gandhi should be "crushed" because there "is no use trying to satisfy a tiger by feeding him with cat's meat."[85] However, Churchill failed to subvert the negotiations from the opposition benches. Envisioning a federation, the Government of India Act passed in 1935. It too failed due to lack of sufficient support within India. Despite general rejection of Churchill's starkest articulation of it, Indians were still viewed through an imperial gaze: rewards for compliant allies and repression of critics, including more time in jail for Gandhi. And control of foreign policy remained firmly in London: without local consultation, Indian entered World War II by proclamation. Once prime minister, Churchill was well positioned to prevent any further devolution of authority, despite prodding even from his crucial US ally.[86]

In essence, by continuing to subordinate India, Britain and its Dominions reaffirmed the shared identity of a transnational white male governing class.[87] Yet this strong sense of racial community left an unstable military arrangement in which Britain remained heavily dependent upon India, setting the stage for a "disintegration" of the Imperial security community.[88] The strategic implications of the war and its aftermath, including Japan's defeat and US predominance in Asia, are just one explanation for Britain's reassessment of its role in India.

Post-Imperial Selves

All too reminiscent of the bloody Irish partition, Britain finally granted India and a newly established Pakistan self-government in 1947.[89] Three years later, India followed Ireland in declaring a republic. Unlike Ireland, however, India established a new precedent by requesting to remain in the Commonwealth as a republic.[90] This wide array of choices – to retain autonomy short of full sovereignty or to declare republican status, to stay within the Commonwealth or to withdraw – illustrates how many aspects of the Imperial Self had changed. Initially, India played a key role in the divergence of the "New" Commonwealth of former African and Asian colonies from the "Old" Commonwealth of the Dominions.

The "New" Commonwealth

Provoking a new round of intra-community interactions that would soon redefine two distinct Post-Imperial Selves, India succeeded in placing South Africa's discriminatory policies on the United Nations agenda in 1946, after Smuts passed legislation that bolstered segregation (which his successors would take even further as "apartheid"). Intra-Imperial negotiations subsequent to the Balfour Declaration had resulted in agreements that South Africa viewed as confirming its domestic jurisdiction; India challenged this interpretation and, by taking its cause to the General Assembly, turned it into a broader international issue. Britain supported South Africa, and the Dominions also hesitated to criticize since they retained racial restrictions of their own. Into the 1950s, as the full range of South Africa's discriminatory practices came under UN scrutiny, a collective commitment to non-interference in domestic affairs still prevailed over international human rights principles.[91]

By the late 1950s, however, the tide had turned. Due to a confluence of causes, 1960 proved the breaking point. British Prime Minister Harold Macmillan's famous Winds of Change speech, delivered to the South African Parliament in February, relented on domestic jurisdiction. Widespread coverage of the South African government's violent response to protests by blacks, notably the Sharpeville killings in March, transformed the tone of international condemnation. Claims that apartheid was sui generis strengthened, while norms of domestic jurisdiction lost persuasiveness. South Africa made its formal constitutional break with Britain in May 1961, after withdrawing the prior October from a Commonwealth that had become almost uniformly critical of its racist policies.[92] As an Afrikaner-dominated republic, South Africa moved beyond the boundaries of the core Imperial Self.

The apartheid controversy also gave the former British colonies a reason to remain together: to bring about its redemption. In effect, South Africa's withdrawal redefined the Commonwealth as a community based on principles of democracy and non-discrimination. By the mid-1960s its members routinely underscored the group's unique role as a leader in the "application of democratic principles in a manner which will enable the people of each country of different racial and cultural groups to exist and develop as free and equal citizens."[93] Furthermore, the 1971 Declaration of Principles identified "racial prejudice as a dangerous sickness threatening the healthy development of the human race and racial discrimination as an unmitigated evil of society." Amidst an international rights revolution, the Commonwealth affirmed multiculturalism as a foundation for peace and security.

After a democratic South Africa rejoined in 1994, this Post-Imperial Commonwealth confronted something of an identity crisis, with soul-searching about its purpose. Subsequent expulsions and reentries of various members confirm the central place of democracy as the core principle that defines membership and links back to the British parliamentary heritage that justifies its very existence. What to label this quirky collective that follows neither regional nor universal rationales, and even now includes a few non-British former colonies, depends largely on whether "development" counts as "security." Terminology such as "loose" versus "tight" cooperation or "thin" versus "thick" commitments strikes me as incapable of capturing the essence of this New Commonwealth.[94] Perhaps it is more important to acknowledge what the group is not, nor aspires to be: an alliance.

In keeping with theories that stress the multiplicity of identities, it should not surprise us that members of the Commonwealth have frequently pursued their security concerns and economic interests through other avenues. Notably, after South Africa's departure freed the Old Commonwealth to pursue other identities, Britain turned more toward Europe. One consequence was that Australia and Canada lost their special place based on the old imperial racial hierarchy, but a Dominion collectivity was perpetuated under the new guise of Cold War security cooperation. However, that new strategic vision depended as much on the USA as on Britain, leading to the revived and revised notion of a special relationship based on something other than empire (as explored by the chapters in Part III of this volume). At the same time, the New Commonwealth provided Britain and the Dominions with an avenue for affirming their commitments to democracy and non-discrimination. These reconfigurations, with forms of democratic institutions replacing civilizational discourse as a metric of membership, are summarized in Figure 4.3.

The "Old" Commonwealth

The claim that the Old Commonwealth paid only rhetorical attention to liberal principles is a familiar (and sometimes valid) charge against London. For instance, detailed archival evidence shows that, despite trumpeting liberal principles after World War I, both Britain and the United States opposed Japan's efforts to enshrine a racial equality clause in the League of Nations, thus ensuring that immigration was solely an issue of domestic jurisdiction.[95] However, a charge of hypocrisy overlooks the profound role of the strengthened principle of non-discrimination, honed through Commonwealth and UN debates over apartheid, on the shift to multiculturalism as a core feature of the Post-Imperial Self. In the absence of any overarching ethnic solidarity to define their Anglo identity, members of the Old Commonwealth have gradually replaced democracy for white men with multiculturalism as the foundation of civic nationalism.

Canada took the lead in 1960, the first to adopt a Bill of Rights that broke with Westminster tradition and to disavow domestic jurisdiction as a defense for apartheid.[96] However, Canadian multiculturalism policy evolved out of its Anglophone–Francophone biculturalism rather than any aim to overturn its White Canada immigration policies. It was multi-ethnic Saskatchewan that resisted a linguistic dichotomy and insisted on enshrining a bill of rights; and before that, it was protests by Asians in British Columbia that brought civil rights to the national agenda after World War II, including relaxation of some immigration restrictions.[97] Subsequent reforms in the 1960s, notably a skills-based points system and rights-respecting approach to asylum determination, sought to remove any explicit racism.[98]

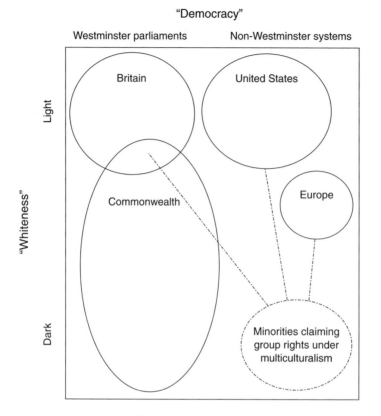

FIGURE 4.3 Post-imperial identities

The Constitution Act of 1982 and the Multiculturalism Act of 1985 further enshrined protections for diversity.[99]

In contrast, Australia adopted multiculturalism and the point system from Canada by the early 1970s as an explicit alternative to the long-acknowledged racism of its White Australia policy. This shift away from an exceptionally homogenous British community, possible only after the arrival of more diverse postwar European immigrants had tamed the worst racist fears, came in response to economic and international pressures. Unintended effects included a significant population of middle-class Asians, starting with a growing number of students arriving in the 1960s, and the path-breaking acceptance of refugees from Southeast Asia in the aftermath of the Vietnam War.[100] As in other liberal democracies, the rise of family unification as a right bolstered immigration from historically underrepresented regions, even in the absence of any formal bill of rights.[101]

Yet, ironically, multiculturalism as a rights-based form of civic nationalism in these settler societies provides the foundation for a reconstructed Anglo-hegemony.[102] Britishness is not simply one ethnicity among many; it is the taken-for-granted majority culture of liberal individualism into which minorities should be integrated. As religion replaces skin color as the acknowledged marker of difference, both Canada and Australia still grapple with the tensions between the racial dimensions of their democratic roots. In Canada, the burgeoning Asian population was an unanticipated consequence that has forced questions about the limits of liberal individualism in disputes over "reasonable accommodation" for ethnic and religious claims, exemplified in the symbolism of a turbaned Sikh Mountie. And in Australia, ambivalence about asylum seekers, especially Muslims despite their minimal numbers, percolates into political pressures to process claims offshore.[103]

Similar debates over group rights have followed a different trajectory at the imperial center. Despite supporting Dominion exclusion of Asians at the turn of the last century, an emigration-oriented Britain itself had minimal restrictions. Even in the 1950s, joining the ranks of European immigrant-receiving countries did not immediately reverse its course. Because Britain lacked a concept of national citizenship that could serve as the foundation for restrictions, imperial subjects, notably from the Caribbean, retained the unfettered right of entry until 1962. As a result, multicultural accommodation has had more to do with non-discrimination in employment and education than with immigration policy.[104] The British Nationality Act of 1981 finally cut the ties of subjecthood in principle albeit not in practice. For instance, in the hopes of forestalling additional immigration from South Asia, Britain refused to enshrine a right of family unification by adopting legislation in 1988 that eliminated any automatic right of entry for spouses.[105]

These variants of multiculturalism demonstrate that the legacies of race and liberalism need not be mutually exclusive or clearly prioritized. As Louis Pauly and Chris Reus-Smit underscore in Chapter 6, Australia and Canada perpetually recalibrate their relationships with Britain and the United States. For instance, multiculturalism was both a prerequisite and a consequence of Australia restructuring its economic ties to Asia. And Britain continually rebalances its Post-Imperial, European, and Anglo-American identities, as evident in 1985 when it subverted an adverse ruling from the European Court of Human Rights into an opportunity to apply further restrictions against immigration.[106] In the days when Gandhi protested South African discrimination, South Asians were ambivalently acknowledged as subjects, whereas the Anglo-American relationship defines them as a fundamental threat. Strands of the Imperial Self remain, but the fabric of a tightly knit Imperial security community has worn thin.

Conclusion

My rereading of imperial history through the lens of liminality places greater emphasis on events such as the Anglo-Boer War and institutions such as the League of Nations that tend to be overlooked in US-dominated theorizing about International Relations. And while I stress the importance of the former Dominions, I also question the centrality of Australia and Canada minus South Africa, which

British-trained scholars tend to accept without much scrutiny. The implications of shifting these standard perspectives are more than empirical: this reinterpretation challenges at least two pieces of conventional wisdom about identity and community in international relations theory.

First, the trajectory of the Imperial Self runs counter to the teleological nature of the security community argument, often associated with liberal theories that imply progressive movement towards a more peaceful world. Implicitly Eurocentric, that literature starts with sovereign states and seeks to explain why alliances sometimes transform into deeper commitments. In contrast, the bifurcation of the former British Empire into "Anglo-America" and the "New" Commonwealth demonstrates an inverse trajectory: the reconfiguration of an intensely connected community. Furthermore, this devolution did not herald a descent into war; it spawned two alternative liberal visions. Both the Anglo-American special relationship and the multiracial Commonwealth, in distinctive ways, have claimed to promote peace.

Second, this bifurcated Post-Imperial Self raises the normative issue of whether security communities are inherently "better" than alliances, as is often implied. For instance, nationalists in South Africa argued that an independent republic was preferable to imperial partnership for many reasons, only one of which was freedom to entrench racial discrimination. Irish and Indian nationalists made similar claims in pursuit of independence, as do contemporary secessionists in Quebec, all of whom are unhindered by the albatross of apartheid that will forever temper any rereading of South African history. These examples of republican skepticism underscore "that democracy itself is value-free, capable of licensing both progressive and exclusionary outcomes."[107] The Imperial Self was not automatically good or necessarily bad, and, without denying the legitimacy of ethical debate, the same can be said of contemporary Anglo-America.

Indeed, in light of the historical taint of racism upon liberalism, the ethical implications of a purportedly progressive, peace-enhancing theory of international relations should be scrutinized more thoroughly. Like multiculturalism at the domestic level, membership in a transnational security community privileges a certain collective identity. As Bell notes in Chapter 2, one dominant iteration is ideas about a "league of democracies" to foster peace, at least among themselves. Clearly, the Old Commonwealth remains within the core of that configuration, as evident in the persistent mistrust guiding US–Mexico relations that Brian Bow and Arturo Santa-Cruz contrast to US–Canada relations in Chapter 7. Yet internal and external identities, even if both are rooted in "democracy," may not always be compatible or synchronized. The result, as David MacDonald and Brendon O'Connor detail in Chapter 8, is inevitable tensions over definitions of the Self among the former Dominions, pulled between Anglo-American special relationships and a rising China.

For better or worse, Jebb made essentially the same point a hundred years ago in his analysis of anti-Asian sentiment as a positive factor reinforcing an imperial partnership among white democracies. Discrimination, he acknowledged, raised questions about the meaning of equality and caused problems with allies. Looking for pragmatic solutions, he admired the lightly veiled racism of a literacy test, because its "elasticity" of application allowed for diplomatic face-saving.[108] Such views are remarkably similar to those surrounding contemporary calls for the use of education tests to assess the suitability of prospective immigrants throughout Anglo-America and Europe in ways that downplay racial difference.[109] Yet the Commonwealth volte-face to multiculturalism confirms that there is no teleology to racism, be it the demise of apartheid or the securitization of Islam. Because the lines between insiders and outsiders remain inherently fluid, "the West" will continue to be contested, domestically and internationally.

Notes

1 I remain indebted to Peter Lyon, who tutored me on the British Commonwealth many years ago. More recently, research assistance by Matthew Smith, Wagaki Mwangi, and Jooyoun Lee helped sort out the institutional complexities of Dominion status. In addition to invaluable feedback from project participants and commentators, I appreciate efforts by Heather Pincock, Paloma Raggo, Herman Schwartz, and Bob Wolfe to improve my understanding of Canada.

2 Lake 2005, 211; also Bryce 1897; Cell 1982; Bell 2007a; Belich 2009; Mar 2010; Vucetic 2011; Bell, Schwartz, and Vucetic, Chapters 2, 3, and 5, respectively, in this volume.

3 Jebb 1908; Huttenback 1976; Brawley 1995.

4 Colonial Conference memorandum, 31 July 1897, reprinted in Ollivier 1954, vol. 1, 138–9; Klotz forthcoming, ch. 2.

5 Bhana and Pachai 1984, 71–2.

6 Bhana 1997.

7 Brawley 1995.

8 The notion of liminality emphasizes the overlay of transnational connections, in contrast to the sharp separation of the internal and external that is embedded in international relations theory and often replicated in studies of national identity (Bhabha 1990; Walker 1992; Neumann 1999; Grovogui 2006; Klotz and Smith 2007).

9 This institutional conception of the relationship between discourse and practice is akin to what Chanock (2001) calls legal culture at the domestic level. Gorman (2006) follows a similar strategy, concentrating on debates over imperial citizenship.

10 Examining additional cases, such as New Zealand, would highlight other aspects, for example indigenous peoples (MacDonald and O'Connor, Chapter 8, in this volume).

11 Adler and Barnett 1998b, 3.

12 Mazower 2009.

13 For example, Smuts 1930.

14 Adler and Barnett 1998a, 37–48.

15 Adler and Barnett 1998a, 55–7. These characteristics are lightly veiled generalizations based on European integration that lack clearly specified theoretical underpinnings. Thus, their subsequently brief discussion of the potential disintegration of security communities (pp. 57–8) offers little analytical guidance on the factors that might weaken the Imperial security community.

16 Jebb 1905, 104; 1911.

17 Gorman 2006, 150–3.

18 Lucas 1915; Headlam 1933; Kendle 1967; Fletcher 2003; Bell 2007a.

19 Gorman 2006, 211.

20 Jebb 1905, 103. I am not blindly following his analysis. For instance, Kendle (1967, 217) claims that Jebb overdraws a dichotomy between the nationalist and colonialist perspectives.

21 Jebb 1905, 105.
22 Ibid., 110–11.
23 Pakenham 1979, 261.
24 Headlam 1933; Pakenham 1979; Hyam and Henshaw 2003, ch. 2; Belich 2009, 380–2.
25 Manchester 1983, 297. Although replete with details of military embarrassments, Pakenham (1979, 571) also notes that all of the imperial forces came under recrimination for brutalities during the guerrilla phase.
26 Jebb 1905, 127.
27 Hyam and Henshaw (2003, ch. 3) challenge as myth this standard interpretation that Smuts actually persuaded the British.
28 Hancock and van der Poel 1966; Belich 2009, 386; Mazower 2009.
29 Fletcher 2003, 251; McMahon 2004, 196, 199–200.
30 Pakenham 1979, 260, 440. To put these numbers in perspective, Britain initially called up 50,000 troops and quickly exhausted its reserves (ibid., 261–2).
31 Jebb 1905, 116–17; Pratte 2011, 99, 136–41. Other critics included Irish nationalists (McMahon 2004, 202–3).
32 Jebb 1905, 123. Pratte (2011, 131–2) portrays Laurier in less-heroic terms, suggesting that he brokered conflicts by seeking to maintain the status quo and by delivering beautiful yet ambiguous speeches.
33 Bourassa in *The Monthly Review*, October 1902, reprinted in Dawson 1937, 137.
34 Pratte 2011, 151–3, 187–93. Laurier, then leader of the Opposition, opposed conscription as a form of coercion that went against liberal principles and as a policy that would destroy national unity. The Liberal Party split, leaving Laurier and Bourassa on the same side of the divide. Other provinces also witnessed opposition to conscription (for example, Mar 2010).
35 Jebb 1905, 125.
36 Ibid., 109–10.
37 Ibid., 125–6.
38 Dawson 1937; Kendle 1967; Belich 2009, 461–5.
39 Dawson 1937; Lloyd 2001, 12; Verma 1968, 6; Belich 2009, 468–9.
40 Pakenham 1979, 94, 525; Metcalf 2007, 85.
41 Fischer [1951] 1982, 74–9; Huttenback 1966, 285–7; Pakenham 1979, 234.
42 Fischer [1951] 1982, 221. In 1929, similar views still prevailed at the highest levels of the India Office (ibid., 316).
43 Gorman 2006, 63–5, 157.
44 Fischer [1951] 1982, 159, 223; Jackson 2004, 142–3; McMahon 2004, 188–9.
45 Jebb 1908; Hancock 1937; Gorman 2006, 167.
46 Fischer [1951] 1982; Huttenback 1966, 1971, 1976; Pachai 1971.
47 Klotz forthcoming.
48 Tinker 1993; Gilmour 2003.
49 Ollivier 1954.
50 Huttenback 1966, 173; Gorman 2006, 22–3.
51 Jackson 2004, 123.
52 Ibid., 124–6, 130–1; McMahon 2004, 183–9; Schwartz, Chapter 3, in this volume.
53 Headlam 1933; Gorman 2006, 62–4.
54 Belich 2009, 446.
55 Jackson 2004, 141–8; McMahon 2004, 192. As a consequence, both militant Irish nationalists and Unionists were well trained for their own deadly battles.
56 Jackson 2004, 151; also Lucas [1912] 1970; McMahon 2004, 187–8.
57 Jackson 2004, 136; McMahon 2004, 184–5; Schwartz, Chapter 3, in this volume.
58 Lucassen 2005, 28–9. I am focusing on the Catholic Irish; the status of Protestant Irish differed, as Lucassen repeatedly underscores.
59 Huttenback 1976; Jupp 2005, 212; Belich 2009, 466–7; McMahon 2004, 195–203; MacDonald and O'Connor, Chapter 8, in this volume.

60 McMahon 2004, 192–8.

61 Ignatiev 1995; McMahon 2004, 197–8; Schwartz, Chapter 3, in this volume.

62 Lucas 1915, 173.

63 Although Lucas did not include Ireland, he certainly recognized parallels between rights granted to French-Catholics in Canada and later debates over Home Rule for Ireland (Lucas [1912] 1970, 318–24).

64 Brawley 1995; Adler and Barnett 1998a, 55.

65 Verma 1968, 21–4.

66 Ibid., 16–17.

67 Ibid., 19, 26–8; Pienaar 1987, 23–30. The League subordinated the autonomous princely states to British India, and the India Office further subordinated all Indians administratively by relying mainly on white male Britons in the Indian civil service (Verma 1968, 240–50).

68 Buell 1929, 715; Verma 1968, 86–8.

69 Later, disputes arose over the interpretation of the League mandate; South Africa expected to incorporate conquered territory, much as a colonial power would (Pienaar 1987, 111–13).

70 Manchester 1983, 714–21; Jackson 2004, 144; McMahon 2004, 205–7.

71 Manchester 1983, 721–8; McMahon 2004, 208–10. Northern Ireland retained many semi-colonial features (Jackson 2004, 151–2).

72 Manchester 1983, 735; Lloyd 2001, 12; McMahon 2004, 211–12.

73 Proceedings of the Inter-Imperial Relations Committee of the 1926 Imperial Conference (E 129/IR 26).

74 Symptomatic of the ambiguity that permeated their subordinate position, the nascent Dominions had dispatched non-diplomatic High Commissioners to London, which only much later evolved into something akin to ambassadors. As Lloyd (2001, 11–12) points out, "it would have been ridiculous for the Queen to give permission for one of her government to be represented in London." In the late 1930s, the Dominions also began to exchange High Commissioners between each other, illustrating a shift to more of a network relationship.

75 McMahon 2004, 211.

76 Ibid., 212–14.

77 Lloyd 2001, 18

78 Fischer [1951] 1982, 222–25, 240–42, 315–16; Millar 1967, 137–38; McMahon 2004, 210; Gorman 2006, 64–65.

79 Verma 1968, 80–2, 96–8, 272–7, 286–92.

80 Kendle 1967; Lloyd 2001, 13–15.

81 Rich 1986, 58–61; Gorman 2006, 62, 157, 207–8.

82 Fischer [1951] 1982, 316–64. Smuts was amongst the many people he met while in Britain (Ibid., 354).

83 Ibid., 357–8.

84 Manchester 1983, 841; McMahon 2004, 213.

85 Manchester 1983, 838–9; Fischer [1951] 1982, 348.

86 Fischer [1951] 1982, 361–4, 373–401, 438–54.

87 Gorman 2006, 8–9.

88 Although giving little attention to the disintegration of security communities, Adler and Barnett (1998a, 53–7) place great emphasis on a core state (or coalition) for stabilizing "ascendant" security communities; Gorman (2006, 147) makes a similar historical claim about a stabilizing equilibrium.

89 "Disastrous" is how Jackson (2004, 143–4) characterizes this explicit application of the Irish model; see also McMahon 2004, 214. British experiences with decolonization would also reflect back onto their approach to Northern Ireland (Jackson 2004, 149).

90 Lloyd 2001, 16. The Indian precedent also fueled periodic discussion of Ireland rejoining (McMahon 2004, 215–19).

91 Wagenberg 1966; Millar 1967, 137–57; Klotz 1995, ch. 3; Bhana 1997, 49–54, 72–88; Hyam and Henshaw 2003, ch. 7. In contrast to the Dominions, Ireland took a tougher stand (McMahon 2004, 216).

92 Millar 1967, 157–64; Klotz 1995, ch. 4; Hyam and Henshaw 2003, ch. 11.

93 Final Communique, Meeting of Commonwealth Prime Ministers, London, 8–15 July 1964. The journal *Round Table* routinely reprinted Commonwealth declarations; recent ones are available on the organization's website: thecommonwealth.org.

94 C.f. Adler and Barnett 1998a, 36; Gorman 2006, 206; Bow and Santa-Cruz, Chapter 7, in this volume.

95 Brawley 1995.

96 "Diefenbaker's Bill of Rights an Act Worth Remembering," *The Star*, 10 August 2010 (thestar.com); Klotz 1995, 59–60.

97 Belich 2009, 410; Mar 2010, 125–30.

98 Kelley and Trebilcock 1998, chs. 9–10.

99 Canadian Department of Justice, laws-lois.justice.gc.ca; Vucetic, Chapter 5, in this volume.

100 Hawkins 1989, 31–4, 93–118; Jupp 2005, 209–16; Pauly and Reus-Smit, and MacDonald and O'Connor, Chapters 6 and 8, respectively, in this volume.

101 Carens (2003) characterizes family unification as a right within liberal democracies, although many others only go so far as to note the political salience of such claims.

102 Mackey 1999; Vucetic, Chapter 5, in this volume.

103 Jupp 2005, 217–23; "It's Just a Jump to the Right," *Mail and Guardian*, 10 Sept. 2010 (www.mg.co.za); "Protection Obligations Determination," Australian Department of Immigration and Citizenship (www.immi.gov.au); Vucetic, Pauly and Reus-Smit, and MacDonald and O'Connor, Chapters 5, 6, and 8, respectively, in this volume.

104 Bevan 1986; Rich 1986; Joppke 1999, ch. 7; Lucassen 2005, ch. 5; Gorman 2006, ch. 1; Hansen 2000, ch. 6; Joppke 2009, ch. 4; Schwartz, Chapter 3, in this volume.

105 Hansen 2000, 242.

106 Ibid., 118–19.

107 Gorman 2006, 211.

108 Jebb 1908, 596.

109 Chebel d'Appolonia and Reich 2008; Joppke 2009.

5

THE SEARCH FOR LIBERAL ANGLO-AMERICA[1]

From racial supremacy to multicultural politics

Srdjan Vucetic

At first centered on the British empire and later on the American imperium, Anglo-America has dominated the world for the past two hundred years, perhaps more.[2] Winston Churchill, the man who in so many ways epitomizes this elastic, loosely bounded, and semi-institutionalized community of societies, states, and nations, preferred the term "English-speaking peoples." What made them so superior in the global society, he argued, was their fierce and unwavering commitment to freedom, democracy, and the rule of law. If we learn anything from Churchill's multi-volume *History of the English-speaking Peoples*, it is that its eponymous protagonists gained power by thinking and acting like good liberals. From their birth on the periphery of Caesar's map to their triumph in the era of empires, the English-speaking peoples worked hard to develop a political system that protected individuals and rewarded cooperation and "conciliation."[3]

This narrative remains influential even today, though in much-refined and expanded forms. Walter Russell Mead begins his *God and Gold* by suggesting that Churchill's book was "too old, too Anglo-centric, and too influenced by the author's political agenda to meet the needs of a twenty-first century public."[4] Churchill was right to stress the centrality of the liberal ideology, but he failed to grasp how liberalism interacted with the Protestant ethic, maritime commercialism, and, above all, capitalism to endow (first) Britain and (then) the USA with the ability to wield the greatest political, economic, military, social, and cultural influence in the global society. In order to better understand the triumph of Anglo-America, Mead suggests, we must in fact stay away from Churchillian reductionisms and teleologies.[5] Kathleen Burk's *Old World, New World* is similarly motivated. In contrast to the "rosy" picture painted by Churchill, Burk describes the Anglo-American relationship as one of "love–hate," but still unique in the presence of "common ideals and common interests."[6]

What is significant for the purposes of this volume is that these newest post-Churchillian histories retain rather Churchillian laudations of liberalism, at least implicitly. In the view of Mead and Burk, what distinguishes Anglo-America is not simply a standardized language that members of the community recognize as common, but also a liberal political culture and/or ideology among its elites. On the one hand, the observation is banal. Basic liberal values saturate laws, public policies, party politics, judicial rulings, and other aspects of Anglo-American political life. And if liberalism is a statement of ends rather than means, then it is easy to appreciate how generations of historians could describe Anglo-America as liberal. On the other hand, the malleability of liberal Anglo-America raises a number of questions. How did its liberal culture and ideology evolve? What were the key contents and contestations? Over time, what means did Anglo-American liberals apply toward freedom and equality as their most desired ends? There are many ways to approach these questions, all of which depend on how one defines liberalism. Any single definition will illuminate some issues but not others.

This chapter focuses on the record of applications and misapplications of liberal equalitarian doctrines. Historically speaking, just who are the English-speaking peoples? On this question, I find that Anglo-American liberalism has long been challenged by exclusionary and hierarchical ideas (and corresponding institutions, practices, and habits). Liberal Anglo-America, I argue, is grounded in racialized meanings at least twice, first in terms of the long shadows of its racist past and then in certain aspects of its multicultural politics.

To make this argument, I examine two historical contexts. First, I consider the world of Anglo-American liberals in the 1880s, focusing on the ideas of those who strove to establish a global order based on the idea of Anglo-Saxon supremacy. Next, I fast-forward a century to a make a comparison between the "patriation" of the Canadian constitution in 1982 and the Australian "bicentennial" in 1988 and show how the debates on citizenship rights in Anglo-America became replete with the politics of cultural and, indeed, racialized recognition.

Before I begin, let me address the main caveats. First, what I examine in this chapter is a small number of historical details in which liberalism appears not as a political and social theory but as a set of evolving ideas regarding human freedom and equality.[7] In defining peoplehood, I follow Rogers Smith to refer to a population that imagines itself to be a political community and so empowers its elites to allocate rights and responsibilities in a legitimate manner.[8] Peoplehood can include anything from the most liberal "myths of civic identity" to the most illiberal myths of race and ethnicity – both serve to order a political community in ways that appear natural, historical, and ethical. The "liberal government of population," to borrow a term from Barry Hindess, emerges in the struggle along the continuum between these two types of myths.[9]

For the purposes of this chapter, race and ethnicity are defined as socially and politically constructed, historically evolving, and cross-culturally variable identities that order human beings on certain ancestral links, whereby race stands out by (more) directly linking ancestry to body morphology. The term racialization, introduced in different contexts by sociologists Michael Banton, Robert Miles, and Michael Omi and Howard Winant, is meant to underscore not only the dynamism, variability, and intersectionality of race-making, but the idea that race is a form of power that operates through distant social relations to establish who is vulnerable/protected and subordinate/privileged in the society.[10] When appropriate, I will return to these and other conceptual issues.

The Anglo-Saxon Atlantic

As a field of study or at least a category of analysis within the discipline of history, Atlantic history focuses on the structures and processes of interaction among the Americas, Europe, and West Africa in the early modern period. Oddly absent from this literature is the subject of Anglo-Saxonism, a collective identity that once rallied all those identified by themselves and others as Anglo-Saxon Protestant males around the flag of racial superiority.[11] This absence may be explained by the subject's bad timing – peaking at the end of the nineteenth century, Anglo-Saxonism fits neither "long Atlantic" nor non-Atlantic perspectives.[12] This is unfortunate because Anglo-Saxonism is one of the most politically consequential ideas to cross oceans in the modern age.

Versions of the racialized Anglo-Saxon identity can be traced back to the early modern period. According to Churchill, the "race had taken shape" in the late fifteenth century.[13] Later, during the English Reformation and the English Civil War, it was Anglo-Saxonism that glued the state and society together: the more England became Protestant and parliamentarian, the more it became Anglo-Saxon. Anglo-Saxonism was similarly helpful in legitimating a rather brittle Britain in the early eighteen century – an isolated English–Scottish union (1707) under a German monarch (1714) thrown among the warring states of Europe. It is also found in the revolutionary American republic. Texts left behind by Thomas Jefferson, John Adams, Benjamin Franklin, and other founding fathers are peppered with claims to America's Anglo-Saxon past, among other pasts. By making these claims, American revolutionaries invariably positioned themselves as "better" and "truer" English than those in England.[14] What all of these stories had in common was an argument that "we Anglo-Saxons" topped all scales of human development and worth. In each case, the intellectual incoherence and inconsistency of the Anglo-Saxon idea melted before the political utility of legitimating state and nation, with class, gender, regional and religious divisions, exclusions, and hierarchies in tow.

In the 1880s, the power of Anglo-Saxonism was on the rise again, but so was its political ambition – "Greater Britain." From the moment Charles Dilke introduced it into the public discourse, the term smacked of a political project: "If two small islands are by courtesy called 'Great,' America, Australia, India must form a Greater Britain."[15] As Duncan Bell has shown in Chapter 2 in this volume and elsewhere,[16] this very idea implied the possibility of an "imperial federation." For some, the federation referred to an Anglo-American political union, while for others it meant the unification of Britain with its settler colonies. The limits of the imagined polity were only moderately elastic, however. Greater Britain sometimes included Ireland and India, as in Dilke's definition, but Irish and Indians did not necessarily constitute the "people." The specificity of the latter was clarified in the first edition of the Canadian magazine *Anglo-Saxon*, in September 1887:

> the nation formed by the union of the Angles, Saxons and other early Teutonic settlers in Britain, from whom the English, the Lowland Scotch, a great proportion of the present inhabitants of Ulster, and the mass of the population in the United States and the various Colonies have sprung.[17]

Though places like India and the rest of Ireland were carefully left out, the word "nation" left much to be desired. *Notes & Queries* (Sixth Series, Vol. 3, 1881), a popular search engine at the time, traced the term Anglo-Saxon from its eighth-century Latin roots (when it served to identify Old English) but never linked it to any form of nationhood. A decade later, *Lloyds Encylopaedic Dictionary* (Vol. 1, 1895) copied the Canadian magazine's definition of Anglo-Saxons almost verbatim, save for an important switch from nation to race. Anglo-Saxons never followed Italians, Germans, and other imagined communities in building a single polity; but much like pre-unification Italy or Germany, Greater Britain was very much a social, cultural, and economic reality. To the extent that the English-speaking "communities," "nations," "peoples," and "race" were interchangeable, we could probably agree with James Belich's observation that in the 1880s, "Greater Britain had made its way into at least middle-class conceptual language."[18]

Bell and Belich have explained how Greater Britain emerged in lockstep with shifts in political participation, transportation, and communication technologies as well as in popular attitudes regarding migration. The intensification of social and economic exchanges across the English-speaking world led to greater imaginations of Anglo-Saxon unity and vice versa. This recursive process owed a great deal – although certainly not everything – to individuals and groups who called themselves "liberals," as in "liberal Anglicans," "liberal Unitarians," "university liberals," "new liberals," "Liberal Unionists," or "liberal Republicans." What they had in common was a belief that American and British citizens had certain rights – especially the right to private property and free enterprise – and that government should work toward securing those rights. The Greater British entity that emerged in the late nineteenth century was predominantly liberal in the sense that its most vocal proponents invoked abstract ideals of the English and Scottish Enlightenments, rather than classical, feudal, or Christian forms of privilege and citizenship.

In this liberalism, real-world political contradictions and inconsistencies existed primarily as abstract philosophical dilemmas. It was widely accepted, for instance, that good liberals must sometimes act illiberally to maintain order; that evolution can modify ethics; or that empire and frontier life should be kept separate from homeland liberty. Dilemmas and distinctions of this sort almost always related to racialized identity. To relate to a theme of Herman Schwartz in Chapter 3, (our) responsible government always corrected (their) irresponsible land use.

Anglo-American liberals argued with their political opponents over the extent to which the success of a polity depended on its commitments to liberal goals and procedures, but the debate was meaningful only in the context of a profoundly racialized worldview. Here, the characteristics of the individual liberal subjects who made up a people were understood as essentially determined by the racial characteristics of that people.

Contemporary science, specifically evolutionary scientism, strongly supported this worldview. In the age of mesmerism, phrenology, telegony, and other pseudoscientific advances, notions of biosocial evolution easily grafted onto the theories of human inequality. All of them underscored race as a permanent or semi-permanent category that determined one's worth and potential. The 1880s saw no consensus on how exactly evolutionism related to race – many argued that it was partly or even fully environmental, not hereditary – but most American and British scientists agreed that Anglo-Saxons stood head and shoulders above everyone else. Francis Galton's essay *Inquiries into Human Faculty and its Development* was representative of a broader trend in which scholars at once furnished explanations of Anglo-Saxon supremacy and offered advice on how this supremacy could be preserved through "viriculture" or "eugenics," a science of "judicious mating."[19] The American state, argued Galton, would do well to turn this science into official policy.

In this intellectual climate, it is not surprising that liberals accepted only a very selective universalism and, in turn, no shortage of human inequality. Immigration and democratization, to name but two examples, were desirable for liberals only on the basis of the prior assumption that certain white men – indeed, gentlemen – had the authority to decide who warranted inclusion instead of exclusion, subordination, or ignorance.[20] Consider the thought of liberal historians, starting with theories about the Anglo-Saxon origins of the state, race, and nation – all three often used interchangeably. In his widely read *History of the Norman Conquest* (1867–69), E.A. Freeman argued that the English race had already developed its winning qualities in Teutonic times. Freeman's Oxford colleagues J.A. Froude, A.V. Dicey, William Stubbs, and J.R. Green advanced roughly the same line focusing on Britain, while James Bryce, Freeman's star student, turned to his native USA. In *The American Commonwealth*, Bryce examined the nature of Greater British political bifurcation and confirmed the "political genius, ripened by long experience, of the Anglo-American race."[21] Bryce was also famous for demonstrating the benefits of denying political subjectivity to the once enslaved American blacks – an argument long embraced by much of the official Anglo-world and beyond.[22]

Cambridge did not lag behind Oxford in the production of Anglo-Saxonism. Henry Maine's *Early Law and Custom* and J.R. Seeley's *Expansion of England*, both published in 1883, each made an instant academic splash; but the latter also went on to become a popular bestseller. Having sold ten printings of his book before the end of the decade, Seeley's logic of blood and belonging clearly resonated with its target audiences: Britain, its self-governing settler colonies, and the USA shared so much in common that they should form a federation.[23] Tellingly, the same logic did not apply to the newly minted German empire. Theories on the Teutonic origins of Anglo-Saxons suggested the existence of significant racial similarities among contemporary Americans, British, and Germans; but Germany rarely, if ever, appeared in the imperial federation schemes.[24]

American Anglo-Saxonism was in some ways autochthonous, partly because it emerged in relation to slavery as well as the Indian and Mexican Wars.[25] As the new transportation and communication technologies compressed the Atlantic, the two Anglo-Saxonisms slowly harmonized with each other, as shown in Freeman's direct influence on Bryce. The supremacist themes discussed above run through the mid-century poetry by Ralph Waldo Emerson and H.W. Longfellow to, in the decade of our focus, texts penned by publicists and novelists Henry James and E.L. Godkin; scientists Nathaniel Shaler and Daniel Garrison Brinton; politicians Henry Cabot Lodge and Nelson Aldrich; and theologians James Freeman Clarke and Josiah Strong. Even those "classical" liberals like Edward Atkinson and William Graham Sumner, who in the subsequent years formed the backbone of America's anti-imperialist movement, defended racial inequality.[26]

Perhaps the most popular writings on the subject in the decade were those by John Fiske, a Harvard philosopher. His Anglo-Saxonist triumphalism was as obsessive as anything produced in Britain's Cambridge: "The day is at hand when four-fifths of the human race will trace its pedigree to English forefathers, as four-fifths of the white people in the United States trace their pedigree to-day."[27] One difference between American and British Anglo-Saxonisms was predictable: for most Americans the USA, not Britain, was the Piedmont of Anglo-Saxon political integration. By the same analogy, if the USA was the Anglo-Saxon Piedmont, then Canada had to be Genoa: at the time, the idea of "Canadian annexation" was broadly related to general calls for political unity among the English-speaking peoples.[28] Had the Anglo unification proceeded, many continental European observers and those elsewhere would have not been terribly surprised. For most late nineteenth-century French liberals, for example, America and the British empire had long looked like a "unified political/cultural bloc."[29] That the French intellectuals regarded the Anglo-Americans as a single people is perhaps ironic. It was France's recognition of the American republic that induced the passage of the Declaratory Act of 1778 by which London relinquished the right to tax settler colonies for revenue. With this act, the motherland in effect seceded from its loyal settler dominions, thus complicating future imperial federation schemas.

Nearly all historical figures mentioned in this section were described by themselves and others as liberals, at least according to the standard sources such as the American National Biography or the Oxford Dictionary of National Biography. But their liberalism rested upon a racist doctrine according to which a people had a fixed membership, in the sense that it corresponded to a racialized community. In this discourse, individual freedoms coexisted with the inequities based on a rather absolute racial hierarchy. The only acceptable qualifier in evaluating the Self versus the Other was to identify an extinct people, like Galton did with Pericles'

Athenians, and argue that Anglo-Saxons were the second most superior race in history. Christopher Parker once described this thinking as "liberal racialism."[30] More recently, Carol Horton and Peter Mandler called it "Darwinian liberalism" and "ethnocentric liberalism," respectively.[31] All of these are useful terms in historicizing liberal Anglo-America. Rather than being made in the image of a progressive Lockean utopia, the Anglo-Saxon Atlantic in the 1880s was more decisively shaped by illiberal ideas, specifically by racism. This world left no place for any liberalism of rights that would divorce America, Britain or, indeed, Greater Britain from its racialized Anglo-Saxon core.

The productive power of late nineteenth-century Anglo-Saxonism was massive.[32] Churchill's *History of the English-speaking Peoples*, recall, was basically a story of how an "island race" overcame various challenges, including regional tensions and civil wars, to achieve trans-oceanic "reconciliation." The trajectory was not simply a triumph of the "liberal peace." By declaring themselves the origin and evolutionary engine of civilizational progress, those at the helm of the American and British empires justified all sorts of racial hierarchies at home and abroad, while simultaneously defusing intramural political clashes.[33] Though tensions, confusions, contradictions, and non sequiturs always abounded in the idea that the English are biologically and/or spiritually continuous with the Saxon immigrants from the fifth and sixth centuries, the notion of the "Anglo-Saxon race" withered and died rather slowly. Whites-only, European stock-preferred immigration laws and policies introduced in the 1880s were duly enacted until the mid-1960s. Differences in implementation and formulation notwithstanding, the anti-racist policy shift first occurred in Canada (arguably, 1962) and the USA (1965), then in Australia (1972). In South Africa, as Audie Klotz explains in the previous chapter, racial supremacy in fact solidified, surviving until 1994.

In a backward reading of history, we can see how liberalism survived its nineteenth-century dalliance with Anglo-Saxon supremacism. As Mandler puts it, "while the universalist creed came under stress, was inflected, even bent, it did not break."[34] The ebbs and flows of this particular history fall outside the scope of this chapter, but it is important at least to point out the plurality of liberal knowledge-claims at the time. For one, circulating in parallel to Anglo-Saxonism were more universalist historical discourses penned in the spirit of the Enlightenment by scholars like Hume, J.S. Mill, Tocqueville, Gibbon, and Macaulay. These thinkers rejected ideas of inherent superiority – humans rise, but empires fall – and pointed to the record of racial mixings. Here, the British peoples were at the very least part Britons, part Saxons, part Danes, and part Normans, while Americans were all that plus much more. For example, David Hume's *On National Characters* (1754) and *History of England* (1754–61) famously denied the idea of fixed races, as did the hyphenated term Anglo-Saxon itself.[35] Good Enlightenment skepticism also applied to the non-hereditary claims of continuity, such as those concerning the links between constitutional liberties, the House of Commons, and the rule of common law on the one side and the Witan – that mythical assembly of self-ruling male patriarchs in the mythical Saxony – on the other. In short, the main conclusion reached by the skeptics was that nations ought to be differentiated by their constitutions and other institutions, not by their biological and spiritual lineages.

It was the same spirit of the Enlightenment that compelled liberals to accept that a commitment to liberalism was a commitment to equality and inclusion of all people, not just certain white propertied men. The so-called mid-twentieth-century human rights revolution – a product of the war against Nazism, decolonization, civil rights movements, second wave feminism, and many other forces – overturned the ideas of racial purity and natural inequality on a global scale. As I show next, by the 1980s, cultural differences that were once unacceptable to state authorities began to gain constitutional recognition and make a major impact on the political life of Anglo-America.

The rise of multicultural politics

If racism defined liberal Anglo-America in the late nineteenth century, then multiculturalism might describe it in the late twentieth. For theorists of "diversity liberalism," multiculturalism relates to the idea that the cultural contexts in which individuals operate shape individual capacity to act autonomously – hence the need for "differentiated citizenship."[36] The first state to declare itself multicultural was Canada. On 8 October 1971, Prime Minister Pierre Trudeau argued before the House of Commons thus:

> Every ethnic group has the right to preserve and develop its own culture and values within the Canadian context. To say that we have two official languages is not to say that we have two official cultures, and no particular culture is more "official" than another. A policy of multiculturalism must be a policy for all Canadians.

It was official: Canada's existing brew of "bilingualism and biculturalism" received a dose of something new – the notion that Canadian citizens ought to revel in cultural heterogeneity and even cosmopolitanism.[37]

What did Anglo-American liberalism mean in this context? To examine this question, I now turn to what might be called the politics of official multiculturalism in the naive era, my focus being the discourses and practices of the patriation of Canada's constitution in 1982 and Australia's bicentennial in 1988. Many nations have gone officially multicultural since Trudeau first spoke about it, but few have been able to keep up with Canada and its Anglo-American sister Australia.[38]

In the first instance, the patriation and the bicentennial both show how peoplehood is constructed – and contested – through public spectacle and spectatorship. What is remarkable is the similarity with which the central governments and the mainstream media protagonized and performed the doctrines of multiculturalism. In each event, official scripts produced Australians and Canadians as "unique" nations – deeply diverse in cultural terms, yet tightly bound by shared values and institutions.[39] The audiences were mostly unimpressed. Key constituencies – the indigenous organizations, opposition parties, and, in Canada, the powerful government of the province of Quebec – rejected unity-in-diversity claims as fantasies and political traps. More important, the events showed that even the most symbolic recognition of cultural rights could not avoid a resolute engagement with the myths of race, ethnicity, and nationhood as well as with the problem of racialized hierarchy that liberals thought they had left far behind.

Let us begin with the "patriation" of the Canadian constitution, an event that officially began as a conversation between the parliaments in Ottawa and London in the fall of 1980. Prime Minister Trudeau sent the draft of the constitution to Queen Elizabeth II and Canada's First Nations lodged legal actions against Trudeau's government with British judges, while Quebec's Premier René Lévesque queried Prime Minister Margaret Thatcher on the best ways to preserve his province, a "distinct society, enveloped in an Anglophone culture dominant in the entire North American continent."[40] Then, between December 1981 and March 1982, Westminster parliamentarians duly took "Canada Act, 1982" through several rounds of debate. The majority of speakers praised the former colony, but not all. Thatcher's disgruntled backbenches, left-leaning Labour MPs, Ulster Unionists, and Scottish Nationalists rose to carp about Canada's aboriginal rights record and even requested a delay of the constitutional reform on behalf of Quebec. In those months, London replayed the role of Canada's capital, with the federal government's envoys attempting to outwit First Nations and Quebec lobbyists.[41]

The Canadian media, also heavily represented in London, covered these developments with a mix of puzzlement and ridicule. How could those Brits (especially those unelected peers who had never set foot in Canada), judge us?! Yet the same (English language) media expressed nothing but excitement about the arrival of Canada's "very own" queen at Ottawa's Parliament Hill on 17 April, where she signed off the "constitutional proclamation" before thirty thousand delighted Canadians. The royal family spectacle has long been central to the production of Anglo-American peoplehood. The global dimensions of the House of Windsor were decisively demonstrated in 2011, when (by some accounts) more than two billion – one-fourth of all humanity – watched (parts of) the broadcast of the wedding ceremony of Prince William and Kate Middleton.[42] Within Anglo-America, however, the royal spectacle is amplified by a long, continuous history that goes back to 1860, when the teenaged Prince of Wales – who would later (briefly) rule as King Edward VIII – crossed the Atlantic to tour North America. Civic and officially unofficial in the republican USA, but very official in the British half of the continent, this visit was one of the major events at the time, mediated as it was every step of the way for nearly five months by both the metropolitan and the local press.[43]

The patriation party was carefully choreographed as a chance to celebrate Canada's complex diversity: its federalism, its dual democratic and constitutional-monarchical political identity, its Anglo-French duality, and its recent immigration record. The government and the media both played up the latter two themes by publishing photos of young people carrying conspicuous pro-Canada texts in French alongside Asian and African families, all spontaneously unified in one happy crowd. The US state, too, was invited and it quite hovered over the party – literally so: the spectators could enjoy the sight of two US Marines standing on the balcony of the nearby American embassy, saluting the proceedings under large Canadian and American flags.

In a parallel reading, it appears that the organizers of Australia's 1988 bicentennial had tried to adopt parts of Canada's patriation ceremony (demonstration effects are likely given that Australia's two-hundred-year anniversary had been continuously planned since 1980). Here, too, the same "very own" queen came to the capital city of a former colony to celebrate unity-in-diversity themes. By Canadian standards, the party was a flop. On 9 May, the queen proclaimed Australia's new Parliament building open for business; but the crowds were missing. Attention paid to political institutions in the normally dull national capital probably subtracted from the rather official attempt to emphasize sunshine, leisure, and "fun" – the ingredients that made Australia into a tourism superpower in the first place. The Australian government was not terribly embarrassed. The queen's visit to Canberra was neither the biggest show of the bicentennial, nor its only royal event: Brisbane hosted the World Expo and Sydney hosted everything else, including Prince Charles in January.

The bicentennial catered to a global audience. Luckily for Australia, its two "great and powerful friends" had much to celebrate themselves. Britain celebrated the Glorious Revolution (and the victory against Spain) and the USA its glorious Constitution (and the victory against Britain). Both nations sent official birthday gifts Australia's way: Britain dispatched a sailing ship thoughtfully named "Young Endeavor," while America invested $5 million toward a maritime museum in Sydney. Like the patriation, the bicentennial produced – and was produced by – Anglo-America, simply because no other community in the West or the East could ever come close to matching the intensity, longevity, and breadth of these exchanges for most Australians. In Britain, the USA, and Canada, public television and radio stations aired special programs about the bicentennial, and arts and history institutions sent their performers and exhibitions to Australia.

This was one lavish party, but not everyone was cheerful. National unity, the basic script of the Australian bicentennial, faced a major counternarrative from the beginning. The rags-to-riches story according to which the nation arose from a nasty and brutish convict colony to a prosperous multicultural nation uniting people from 120 countries was criticized as naive, even in the mainstream press. What defined the bicentennial on this front was a gigantic protest – between sixty and eighty thousand strong – against the Australia Day: January 26, argued the indigenous groups and their supporters, should more properly be called the Invasion Day.[44] According to one official newsletter:

> We could see the entire, diverse Australian community – including Aboriginal people, many of whom did not celebrate the Bicentenary but

whose successful march on 26 January showed the world that their spirit had survived 200 years.[45]

Various attempts to explain away the protest did not stick with the intended audiences, much to the embarrassment of authorities, including the ruling Australian Labor Party (ALC). The right-of-center Liberals and Nationals, led in the official opposition by John Howard, voiced strong concerns about official multiculturalism. In this discourse, which then had an aura of novelty, multi-culturalist policies perpetuated stereotypes (and therefore prejudices) and caused social isolation (or "ghettoes," "balkanization") among citizens. To minimize the damage done to the country, Howard publicly called for the review and reform of the government's immigration policies. (In the polls, the Liberal–National coalition was ahead of Labor on the question of immigration.) Critics to the left of the ALC point to the presence of lasting inequalities and divisions and therefore to the ironies of the official mottos "living together," "celebration of a nation," and "one land, one people."[46]

Perhaps the greatest challenge to the legitimacy of the bicentennial came from the left-wing coalitions for "racial justice," which mostly meant recognition of indigenous land rights. Recently published histories of Australia – mainly Henry Reynolds's *The Law of the Land* (1987), but also Robert Hughes's *Fatal Shore* (1986) – brought home the notions of conquest, invasion, occupation, internal armed conflict, martial law, forced displacement, and even genocide. This discourse went well beyond the critiques of unity-in-diversity as the referent object of the bicen-tennial and questioned the very moral and legal foundation of the Australian state. Among the critics, Australian republicans were perhaps the most coherent, calling for the end of the monarchy and the beginning of a new, post-national Australia. In this context, racial justice variously referred to an official apology, a new consti-tution, recognition of the spiritual status of the land, or full-blown territorial autonomy. The Barunga statement, the main contemporary manifesto for Aboriginal sovereignty, went virtually unaddressed by the ALC government that year.[47]

Much like Australia's bicentennial, Canada's patriation was defined by resistance to central authority. This was not surprising considering that the patriation process was initiated in reaction to the Quebec independence referendum of 1980. The Parti Québécois (PQ) government failed in its bid to win "sovereignty-association" with Ottawa, but the affair made Canada look like an improbable failing state. The patriation worsened the problem of national unity, a key issue being Trudeau's principled refusal to recognize the PQ's demand for making Quebec distinct in the constitution.[48] Viewed from the French-speaking province, it appeared that Trudeau was itching to kill the "Two Founding Nations" model that was foundational to the original Canadian confederation. The federal–provincial conference that came up with a workable draft of the new constitution in 1981 was dubbed the "night of the long knives" – a reference to a decisive bar-gaining session that took place behind the back of the Péquiste (PQ) negotiators.[49]

The result was another rump party. Like the bicentennial, the patriation had its own promotional campaign, which, too, skirted over the fact that a key part of the nation refused to celebrate.[50] The queen noticed the problem. In her Parliament Hill speech, she first expressed regret that the "government of Quebec" was absent from the festivities, then tactfully added that the patriation was only ever about bringing the constitutional process home, not about defining Canada once and for all. The Canadian government adopted this line, but only half-heartedly. Its pictorial story of the event, published a year later under the title "Constitution 1982," acknowledged the "intense" and "stormy" nature of the constitutional debate, adding a small side note: "Further negotiations will be needed to obtain the agreement of Quebec."[51] As Louis W. Pauly and Chris Reus-Smit explain in Chapter 6, that agreement is still missing.

Central to the patriation was the adaptation of the Charter of Rights and Freedoms, a document Trudeau later described as an expression of "purest liberalism."[52] Canada's version of the US Bill of Rights came with a set of clauses regarding differentiated citizenship. The Charter thus codified Canada's "foundational" Anglo-French duality through official bilingualism and minority language rights (Articles 16–23), but it also gave nods to three aboriginal groups ("Indian, Inuit and Métis," in Articles 25, 35) as well as to the "multicultural heritage of Canadians" (Article 27). These moves were consistent with Canada's existing institutions as well as with Trudeau's own theories of Canadian federalism: "In terms of realpolitik, French and English are equal in Canada because each of these linguistic groups has the power to break the country. And this power cannot be claimed by the Iroquois, the Eskimos, or the Ukrainians."[53]

What Trudeau was articulating was a view that each application of diversity liberalism as policy must first bow to politics and history. The Charter offered an early recognition that Canada's multicultural politics operated in what Will Kymlicka later metaphorized as three "silos" of Canadian diversity, each building upon different, and occasionally competing, sets of institutional codes and practices.[54] The Anglo-French "foundational" equality thus led to federalism, bilingualism and minority language rights; official multiculturalism accommodated the Ukrainians and similar "immigrant groups"; and aboriginal rights went for the "Iroquois and the Eskimos."

Among the three silos in 1982, only the first one was meaningful and it appeared to be falling apart yet again. Canada's version of the Invasion Day was the Marche du Québec, between fifteen and twenty-five thousand strong, held in Montreal on the day of the Ottawa ceremony.[55] The atmosphere smacked of another Quebec independence campaign, but what the protesters officially took umbrage to was the constitutional silence on French Canadian right to self-government as well as the way in which minority language rights protected the Anglophone minority in the province at the expense of the language of the Québécois majority.[56] Premier Lévesque went on radio and television to explain the concept of "cultural insecurity" to Quebeckers, while Le Devoir and other French-language newspapers dedicated full pages to the end of Canada's deux nations model. The appearance of the term multiculturalism in the Charter was added to the history of Trudeau's trickery – as yet another political move designed to dilute Quebec's nationhood. This argument resonates to this day in the province, in large part because Ottawa has so far failed to establish the terms of interaction among the laws and policies designed for each of the three silos.

The "Iroquois and the Eskimos" also staged protests concerning the patriation, albeit in remote places and in numbers small enough to be safely ignored by the mainstream media. The indigenous peoples had none of the country-breaking power which Trudeau sought to tame in the province of his birth, but their claims, too, demonstrated the limits of compartmentalizing diversity. The notion that First Nations had special rights beyond federalism or multiculturalism had prima facie support in the Royal Proclamation of 1763 and had also been affirmed by a Supreme Court ruling (the *Calder* case in 1973). However, no national political party or mainstream media outlet at the time went to question the continuity of the Indian Act, a nineteenth-century statute that empowered Canada's federal government to legislate on behalf of the indigenous peoples and manage them through the reserve system. Even the best liberals in Trudeau's Liberal Party were unwilling to erase the colonial line between peoples who have the capacity to govern themselves and those who require assistance.

Against the shrillness of Ottawa–Quebec relations, which the media so often personified as the clash of Trudeau and Lévesque, official multiculturalism lived a politically vestigial life. At the federal level, multiculturalism enjoyed bipartisan support precisely because it was regarded as a "symbolic" policy. If it was Trudeau's multiculturalists who in 1971 decided that Canadians should have "no official culture," then it was their Progressive Conservative opponents who solidified this idea by describing the country as a "community of communities."[57] Outside Quebec, provincial and municipal governments followed with further praise of the Canadian "mosaic." But there is another reason why Canadian elites were attracted to this discourse and it directly relates to Self–Other relations in Anglo-America. Much like "peace, order, and good government" and peacekeeping, to name two familiar symbols of the Canadian identity at the time, multiculturalism was useful in distinguishing Canada from its towering neighbor to the south. Arguably, without an image of America's assimilationist melting pot, Canada's love affair with its accommodationist mosaic would be mostly meaningless. So while the idea of multiculturalism had its share of critics among journalists and academics, many of whom associated it with national fragmentation, class segregation, and other public ills, most Canadians in fact found succor in the way it differentiated them from Americans.[58] A similar politics of identity explains the failure of Canadian leftists to articulate an argument their Australian counterparts made in 1988 with considerable ease – that monarchy contradicts multiculturalism in principle because it rests on medieval ideas of blue blood and belonging to a special white European family. The "Republic of Canada" is impossible precisely because of its closeness to the American republic.

That multiculturalism can serve as an important point of identification was also obvious in the rhetorical dance between Quebec and Ottawa. On the day of the constitutional proclamation, the PQ made sure that the provincial *fleurdelisé* was flown half-mast, at once symbolizing Quebec's displeasure with Ottawa and the long-standing victimhood and vulnerability of the Québécois. Another interpretation was that the Péquistes preferred history over liberal progress. If one were to judge by Lévesque's letter to Thatcher, Anglo-French relations seemed as discrete and as irreconcilable in the 1980s as they had been in the times of ancient New France. Predictably, the federalist side-jumped at an opportunity to tar the PQ as a nasty, archaic party and its supporters as old-fashioned bigots. Cultural minorities, one argument went, would always be better off in multiculturalism-loving English Canada than in a province bent on preserving its racialized settler identity. Eventually, the Quebec governments, separatists and otherwise, have found a response. While Ottawa has retained its commitment to multiculturalism, the province developed an alternative known as interculturalism, which seeks to strike the diversity balance away from the mosaic model and toward the preservation of the Francophone majority culture.[59]

The interactions between the Canadian mosaic and the American melting pot, or between the intercultural Quebec and the multicultural "rest of Canada," are indicative of a larger political trend that has come to distinguish Anglo-America anew. In evaluating their own policies for achieving civic integration, the English-speaking peoples are constantly comparing themselves to Others, such as France's republicanism or Germany's *Leitkultur*. Diversity models made in Anglo-America are sometimes put forward as a standard for good governance to which other communities should strive, in ways not unlike those in which "civilization" used to be set as a standard for good governance in the nineteenth century. "It does not seem accidental that Canadians," suggests Michael Ignatieff (who led Canada's Liberals between 2008 and 2011), "have been so centrally involved in the struggle to contain inter-ethnic war."[60] Whether diversity models can or should be promoted as an exportable commodity on a par with liberal democracy or the rule of law is of course questionable,[61] but the point is that pride in multiculturalism easily slips into claims of moral superiority similar to those examined in the previous section of this chapter. If good government once arose from the centuries of struggle for liberty against tyranny, it now continues in the form of struggle for equal recognition amid cultural diversity; either way, Anglo-America can position itself as the planetary leader.

The limits to differentiating peoples

In historicizing liberal Anglo-America, this chapter has taken several snapshots. In the first set, we have seen how English-speaking liberals once argued that humanity was at once universal and unequal. What connected these two abstractions in an elegant rule of thumb was a racialized idea that Anglo-Saxons ruled the world, while everyone else followed. For these American and British liberals in the 1880s,

Anglo-Saxon supremacy was necessary for global leadership and therefore for the progress of humankind. In advancing this argument, they legitimized Anglo-American expansion against various imperial and colonized Others, and thus helped sustain the old political, social, and cultural hierarchies against new democratizing forces. As a result, the majority of the human populace living under disparate Greater British authorities ended up being governed by illiberal means well into the twentieth century.

In the second set of snapshots, we have seen how late twentieth-century multicultural scripts in two Anglo-American societies challenged not only past notions of cultural superiority and democracy, but also the regnant forms of postcolonial memory. Both the Canadian patriation in 1982 and the Australian bicentennial in 1988 saw no shortage of political struggles among competing versions of multiculturalism, most typically pitting the official unity-in-diversity models against a variety of national and sub-national alternatives. These changes were deeply interconnected with the dramatic shift in liberal doctrines. In the 1880s, liberals inscribed social inequality onto the human body with the help of science, but in the 1980s they worked to dismantle the hierarchies of unequal opportunity by recognizing the significance of culture with the help of liberal constitutions.

Contemporary Anglo-American societies are sometimes described as "color-blind," "post-racial," or "raceless"; but these should be read primarily as programmatic statements about the future, not as descriptions of the present. The continuation of systematic discrimination against racialized groups of people in Australia, Britain, Canada, and the USA is evident from any number of recent national and international policy reports and scholarly studies. Laws cannot cover all discriminatory practices, and racism has the ability to perpetuate itself through social problems such as poverty cycles. These problems are often invisible. Already in the 1980s, many Australian and Canadian liberals were ready to congratulate themselves on building equitable societies, even while virtually every representative of the indigenous groups pointed fingers at the writhings of racialized oppression, showing those who wanted to see just how closely the inequities of opportunity followed the lines drawn by old-fashioned racisms.

Further, the mainstreaming of anti-racism has had the paradoxical effect of reifying racialized structures of meaning. Instead of erasing race, new and old racialized categories expressed in decennial censuses, education policies, and civil rights laws have kept it politically alive. For example, "visible minorities," the term Canadian policymakers introduced in 1984 to replace race (and coexist with "ethnocultural groups") gave new wind to the old skin-color game without much helping with anti-racist efforts. The paradox is strengthened by the inability of any liberal societies to protect difference against unwarranted calls for universality without privileging essentialist – and therefore reifying – categories of identity.

The political contestations over whether modern societies ought to be organized along cultural lines such that various cultural minorities – whether visible, invisible, ethnic, or ethnocultural – can protect their distinct values, histories, and territorial spaces has continued unabated since the 1980s, the general difference being that the critics of official multiculturalism are beginning to hold the upper hand, at least in some parts of the liberal world.[62] Viewed from the political and cultural left, official multiculturalism has perpetuated both racialized identities and racialized hierarchies. Already in the early 1980s, British sociologist Chris Mullard predicted that in official multiculturalism, "saris, samosas, and steel bands" would dominate over the actual politics of cultural recognition (and redistribution) or, as he put it, "resistance, rebellion, and rejection."[63] In the subsequent decades, this criticism has become standard for many leftists. For one, it resonates in Stanley Fish's famous provocation that official multiculturalism is "boutique" in the sense that it "stop[s] short of approving other cultures at the point where some value at their center generates an act that offends against the canons of civilized decency as they have been either declared or assumed."[64]

Judging by the attempts to curb select Islamic practices in Europe circa 2010, Mullard and Fish were prescient; the notion that "equal recognition" of cultural Others can and does clash with the basic principles of liberal polities has long gone mainstream. But there was another message in their critique: by consigning diversity to entertainment and commerce, official multiculturalism works to depoliticize radical differences as well as to obscure the persistence of old hierarchies. Rather than going mainstream, this point has mostly stayed within the confines of academia. According to the histories and ethnographies of Australian and Canadian multiculturalisms penned by several astute observers, all policies devised to "manage" cultural diversity tend to draw racialized boundaries.[65]

This effect is most clearly evident with respect to immigration control. After dismantling their racist immigration laws and policies, Canada and Australia have been at the forefront of developing the so-called immigration point systems that aim to match immigrant skills from a single global pool to the needs of the labor market at home. (Indeed, economic liberalizations contributed to a shift in the immigration debate, from whether or not immigrants are welcome, to which immigrant skills we most need.) The new immigration regimes have created new categories of people. Migrant status has now become a hierarchical and nested category that has highly skilled professionals on the top and asylum-seekers and undocumented migrants at the bottom. That this type of management of peoples can have explicitly racialized dimensions was dramatically illustrated by Australia under Howard's government, which in 2000 instigated armed naval patrols and offshore detention centers – the infamous "Pacific Solution" – to prevent "unauthorised arrivals" from Asia.[66]

Immigration control is but one realm of policies and institutions that constantly intersect with official multiculturalism, but it is central to the problem of managing diversity. From the perspective of liberal doctrines on differentiated citizenship, the easy way in which official policies partition society into racialized groups can be troubling. Consider the seamless conflation of immigrants with "ethnics" – groups that are identified as neither indigenous nor "founding," but (visibly or invisibly) ethnocultural. Australians with British origins are not regarded as ethnic, at least not in the way ethnicity is applied to Australians of Colombian, Lebanese, or

Vietnamese descent. For "ethnics," this rhetoric undermines not only official multiculturalism, but also the principle of equal citizenship. Even more problematic are racialized differentiations at the level of practices, as opposed to the level of texts, policies, laws, institutions, and other elements that make and break Anglo-American peoplehood. From this perspective, while Anglo-Saxonhood long ago became de-ethnicized and flattened as "whiteness" or as the colorless "mainstream," it still constitutes the standard against which the value and extent of diversity is measured. This standard comes with the official language or languages, which every state must codify, as well as a myriad of practices that conform to, or deviate from, assumed cultural norms, whether in speech, eating, dress, shopping, or recreation. And if race operates mainly as productive power, a collective property that affects individual action in both conscious and unconscious ways, then racialized inequalities can endure even in contexts in which the entire society subscribes to anti-racism.[67]

In the late twentieth century, racial supremacism is no longer possible, but the need to manage peoples can and does lead to racialized inequalities and hierarchies. Indeed, analytical constructs such as "cultural racism," "raceless racism," and "racism without racists" have been recently developed precisely for the study of these unhappy connections.[68] For some, the problem lies with liberalism. Critical social theorists, feminists, postcolonial historians, and many other scholars have long argued that liberal ideologies are unable to deal with the problem of membership in a political community without double standards, double visions, and doublethink. One of the more far-reaching critiques comes from the philosopher Charles W. Mills. The notion of the social contract, Mills contends, should be read as coexistent with, and even posterior to, the political, moral, and epistemological "racial contract" that structures white human subjects as more universal and more sovereign than nonwhites.[69] To go back to one of the themes discussed in this volume, classical liberal ideology foregrounds Locke's idea of the state of nature characterized by morals and private property, but it forgets that Locke conceptualized property as a function of industry and rationality. On this view, the liberal idea of responsible land use emerged as a normative rationale not only for the expropriation and colonization of the New World by the Old, but also for slavery.[70] My comparison of two Anglo-Americas separated by a century indicates that modern liberal states, nations, and societies were able to rewrite the racial contract and expand their definitions of peoplehood. But it also shows that the "universal creed" tends to lend itself to abuse by political actors searching for further specifications of who gets to enjoy freedom and equality, when, how, and in what proportion. Put provocatively, as long as the historical line between terra nullius and certain "silos of diversity" appears at least somewhat continuous, the Anglo-Saxon Atlantic will not fully dry out.

Notes

1 For written comments and criticism, I thank Richard French, Andrew Gamble, Alexandra Gheciu, Ronald Krebs, Patricia Lenard, Justin Massie, Jennifer Mitzen, Cindy

O'Hagan, Giles Paquet, Janice Gross Stein, Sarah Tarrow, and Elke Winter, as well as the contributors to this volume, especially Peter Katzenstein. All errors remain mine.

2 Anglo-America has had many aliases, the "Anglosphere" being the most recent. See Bell 2007a; Browning and Tonra 2010; Gamble 2007; Vucetic 2010a.

3 Churchill 1956–58.

4 Mead 2007, 19. To appreciate the centrality of Churchill in the contemporary reflections on history, see Mbeki 2005.

5 Mead 2007, part IV.

6 Burk 2007, 659; also see xiii.

7 Bellamy 1992; Clarke 1978; Dean 2002; Hindess 2004; Kautz 1995; Mantena 2010; Mendilow 1986; Mehta 1999; Smith 1999; and Pitts 2005.

8 Smith 1997, 15.

9 Hindess 2004, 28. Also see Rogers Smith's (2003, 12–15) discussion of political peoples as well as Duncan Bell's (2010b) distinction between the people and the public.

10 Accordingly, racism, racialism, and racial supremacy refer, respectively, to prejudice, inequality, and oppression based on racialized identity. On the concept of power and the underlying issues in the philosophy of race, see Barnett and Duvall 2005; Murji and Solomos 2005; Alcoff 2006; and especially Mills 1998. On the intersection of race/ ethnicity with age, class, gender, religion, see Hancock 2007. On the ways in which race and ethnicity relate to various forms of nationalism, see Balibar 1991 and Brubaker 2009.

11 Frantzen and Niles 1997.

12 Greene and Morgan 2009; Gabaccia 2004.

13 Churchill 1956–58, Vol. I, xiv.

14 Horsman 1981, 17–24.

15 Dilke 1869, Vol. II, vii.

16 Bell 2007a.

17 Cited in Hastings 2006, 93–4.

18 Belich 2009, 457. Also see Bell 2007a, 113–19; and Mandler 2006, 106–42.

19 Galton 1883, 25.

20 Jacobson 1998; Bell 2007a; Mandler 2006.

21 Bryce 1888, Vol. I, 28.

22 Lake and Reynolds 2008, 49–74.

23 Seeley 1883, 184, 195–7, 206; see also Bell 2007a.

24 Floyd 2004; Gossett 1997 [1963]; Jordan 1974; Lorimer 1996; Mandler 2006, 86–105; Tulloch 1977.

25 Horsman 1981; see also Drinnon 1980 and Hofstadter 1992.

26 For overviews, see Anderson 1981; Jacobson 1998; Kidd 2006; Kramer 2007; Roediger 2008 and Stein 1989.

27 Fiske 1885, 135.

28 Benjamin 1884, 4; Smith 1887, 2.

29 Pitt 2000, 153. See also Pitts 2005, ch. 6.

30 Parker 1981, 825.

31 Horton 2005, 37; Mandler 2006, 34; see also Collini et al. 1983, 223–5.

32 On the concept of power, see Barnett and Duvall 2005.

33 Elsewhere I have argued that Anglo-Saxonism laid the foundations for that elusive twentieth-century phenomenon – the Anglo-American "special relationship." Once the diplomatic dust raised by the American Civil War settled in 1872, the two empires found fewer and fewer reasons to fight. The "war scares" over Venezuela in 1894–95 and again in 1902–3 served to further delegitimize the Anglo-American war, and key imperial victories of the period – America's against Spain, Britain's in South Africa – were greatly facilitated by the mutual, racially grounded "benevolent neutrality" (Vucetic 2011; more generally, see Dumbrell 2006). The racial forms of cooperation subsequently became less racial, but they also expanded, deepened, and endured such that a Greater Britain obtained in the majority of hot and cold wars of the twentieth and twenty-first centuries.

34 Mandler 2006, 60.
35 Hume, like many writers examined here, usually used the term "English race." For a spirited semantic discussion, see Fiske 1885, 103–5.
36 Young 1990. On "diversity liberalism," see Kymlicka 1995; Laden and Owen 2007; Seglow 1998; and Taylor 1985. Cf. Hall 2000. On Anglo-Americanism as an antidote to "radical multiculturalism at home," see Windschuttle 2005.
37 Trudeau's government proceeded to identify around eighty ethnocultural groups in Canada as worthy of financial support from Ottawa, which lasted for at least a decade. On the origins of Canada's official multiculturalism, see McRoberts 1997; Winter 2005; and Day 2000, 179–98.
38 For an innovative index of official multiculturalism policies in which Australia and Canada emerge as trendsetters, see Banting et al. 2006, 51–63. Also see Hawkins 1982 and Vickers 2002.
39 On politics as performance, see Parker and Sedgwick 1995. My analysis builds on media representations of these events as well as on scholarly publications from the period. In the Australian case, spanning January and July 1988, I consulted *The Age*, *The Australian*, *The Sydney Morning Herald*, the news magazines *Bulletin* and *Quadrant*, plus four videos made by the Australian Broadcasting Corporation and the Australian Bicentennial Authority (accessed at the National Film and Sound Archives, Canberra). For Canada, covering the period from November 1981 to April 1982, I drew on the *Globe & Mail*, *Le Devoir*, *The Montreal Gazette*, *The Ottawa Citizen*, *The Toronto Star*, *The Vancouver Sun*, and *The Winnipeg Free Press*, as well as the news magazines *Maclean's* and *L'actualité*. I also analyzed one radio and five television reports produced by the Canadian Broadcasting Corporation in this period (available online at CBC Digital Archives).
40 Morin 1988.
41 To more fully appreciate the transnational nature of the patriation, consider that First Nation representatives began lobbying British politicians in 1980, went to the United Nations, and even considered going to the international courts in Strasbourg and The Hague (Sanders 1983, 310–14).
42 Lyall 2011.
43 Radforth 2004.
44 The numbers are unclear because the protest took place at three different locations, while Sydney Harbour simultaneously hosted a parade of ships for some two million spectators, the biggest gathering in Australia's history (*SM Herald*, 27, 28 Jan.).
45 Quoted in Spillman 1996, 161.
46 On the reception of the promotional campaign, see Crawford 2008; Cochrane and Goodman 1988; Spearitt 1988; Spillman 1996; and Carter and Mercer 1992. Also see Morris 1988.
47 For discussions, see Marcus 1988; Dessaix 1998; and White 2004. The power of Canberra to legislate on Aboriginal matters was overturned in the Supreme Court rulings in the 1990s.
48 Trudeau was back in his second stint as prime minister (1980–84) and steered the patriation process with the help of Justice Minister Jean Chrétien, future prime minister (1993–2003).
49 Bergeron 1983; Morin 1988. The terms of the new constitution were worked out mostly behind closed doors for a year, but a parliamentary committee devoted less than two months to public hearings by civic and minority groups, with 1,200 presentations in total.
50 Rose 2000.
51 Department of the Secretary of State 1983, 57.
52 Trudeau 1990, 363.
53 White Paper on Indian policy, 1968, cited in Weaver 1981, 55. For an overview of the first-cut impressions of the Charter, see Banting and Simeon 1983.
54 Kymlicka 2007a.

55 Numbers vary across historical sources. There was also a small protest in Hull, across the river from Ottawa's Parliament Hill (*Le Droit*, 17 Apr.).
56 Before the term "Québécois" emerged in the 1960s, Canada's "French fact" typically referred to "la nation Canadienne-Française," a nationwide entity. See Taylor and Sigal 1982 and McRoberts 1997.
57 The term belongs to their leader and Canada's one-time prime minister (1979–80), Joe Clark. The same party, but under a new leader, turned multiculturalism into law in 1988.
58 For elite opinions, see Buchignani 1982; Kallen 1982; Moodley 1983; Roberts and Clifton 1982. On the melting pot and mosaic metaphors, see Day 2000, ch. 7.
59 Bouchard and Taylor 2008; Pietrantonio et al. 1996.
60 Ignatieff 2000, 11.
61 On the pitfalls of exporting models of multiculturalism, see Kymlicka 2007b.
62 Vertovec and Wessendorf 2009. Cf. Banting et al. 2007; Hewitt 2005; Ryan 2010.
63 Mullard 1982, 130. Also see Paul 1997.
64 Fish 1997, 378.
65 Day 2000; Hage 1998, 2003; M. Smith 2003; Mackey 1999; Vickers 2002.
66 Hage 2003, 31.
67 Arguments of this sort are largely unintelligible outside of academia. Consider the 2000 furor in the British media over a report on "The Future of Multi-Ethnic Britain," whose academic authors suggested that "Britishness" and "Englishness" have "systematic, largely unspoken, racial connotations" (Parekh et al. 2000, 38).
68 Scholars writing about new racisms are too numerous to cite. For two examples, see Balibar 1991 and Bonilla-Silva 2010.
69 Mills 1997, esp. 56–7.
70 Ibid., 67–8.

PART III

6

NEGOTIATING ANGLO-AMERICA

Australia, Canada, and the United States[1]

Louis W. Pauly and Christian Reus-Smit

Introduction

At the core of the Anglo-American West, what some still imagine to be the cutting edge of modernity, lie unfinished cultural conflicts and persistent practices of political accommodation. Contests over collective identities, over the extent of commitments to the autonomy of the individual, and over the standing of distinct cultures within single polities – all are hardwired into the most basic social and political processes of a still promising and still potentially global project. Larger systemic implications may be drawn from the essentially pluralist practices, including open-ended negotiation, through which unique cultures defined, defended, and integrated themselves within Anglo-America. One promising way to draw out those implications is to look comparatively at the evolution of such practices within key bilateral relationships constitutive of something that may rightly be remembered as Anglo-American civilization.

This chapter compares and contrasts US–Canada and US–Australia relations over a long period of time. Conservative politicians, scholars, and political commentators place these three states at the heart of the "Anglosphere," attributing to them a robust cultural unity – one that is said to explain numerous political outcomes, from unparalleled levels of intelligence sharing and common assessments of diverse geopolitical challenges to remarkable economic openness and the diffusion of similar policy reforms.[2] Yet these two bilateral relationships have also been used to highlight differences, particularly in connection with aspects of complex interdependence in world politics. In what follows we take this emphasis on difference and variation one step further. We examine the deeper cultural and political histories of Canada and Australia, and their respective relationships with the United States, to show how processes of economic, security, and ideological linkages correlate with far-reaching internal political reconfigurations, which we contend are best captured in the concept of "complex sovereignty." Today, changes within these two bilateral relationships combine with unique geographies and histories to place Canada and Australia at the eroding psychological boundaries around Anglo-America itself, and at the fulcrum of the emerging global civilization of modernity.

From complex interdependence to complex sovereignty

Australia and Canada are longstanding allies of the United States; prior to the formation of those alliances, both constituted essential parts of the British Empire.[3] Even before the United States took on the role of systemic leader and the Empire began to recede, each had sought ever deeper integration into the American economy and into world markets eventually anchored in that economy. Each, moreover, has long professed a strong affinity with the liberal values championed by Washington. Yet these relationships, in some ways located at the cultural and geographic limits of the Anglo-American world, are marked as much by diversity as by similarity. In *Power and Interdependence*, Keohane and Nye drew a distinction between relationships characterized by complex interdependence – in which military power has become less relevant, there is no clear hierarchy of issues, and multiple channels connect societies – and those that come closer to realist expectations, in which military security dominates and social linkages are few. While the realist concept of "hegemony as dominance" applied to neither the Canada–US nor the Australia–US relationship, the former was a microcosm of complex interdependence, while in the latter "the protective role of military force has remained crucial, and distance has limited the multiple channels of contact."[4]

Much has changed in the two bilateral relationships since the original publication of *Power and Interdependence* in 1977. The Australia–US relationship, in particular, subsequently developed many of the attributes that Keohane and Nye associated with the complex interdependence of Canada–US relations, suggesting a degree of convergence between the cases. While the Australia, New Zealand, and United States (ANZUS) alliance remains central to the relationship, webs of interdependence now enmesh both societies, and no clear hierarchy of issues exists. Not only do Australia and the United States now engage across a broad spectrum of issues, from combating transnational terrorism to managing economic globalization and limiting climate change, but Australia must today balance efforts to preserve the alliance relationship with its key commitment to economic engagement with China.

Clearly, the bare architecture of complex interdependence is still apparent in both the Australian and the Canadian cases – military force is no longer central, multiple channels connect societies, and a plethora of issues compete for attention. But Keohane and Nye emphasized the "reciprocal effects among countries and among actors in different countries."[5] The degree to which states were affected by interdependence, positively or negatively, was determined by their relative "sensitivity" and "vulnerability," the former referring to "how quickly changes in one country bring costly changes in another," the latter to a state's "liability to suffer costs imposed by external events even after policies have been altered."[6] The underlying model treated states as relatively stable entities responding as rational actors to the incentives and constraints of interdependence. Although useful in terms of analytical brush-clearing, such a model fails to capture much of the actual contemporary complexity of the two bilateral relationships. More than this, the continuing convergence it suggests is now misleading.

Seen over time through alternate lenses, these two relationships evince considerable diversity. To begin with, if the concept of hegemony is to play any useful analytical role, the idea of dominance that provided the backdrop to Keohane and Nye's critique and analysis needs to be replaced by a more nuanced conception, one that integrates ideas of leadership, followership, and shared social purposes. Hegemony-as-dominance did characterize the prior relationship between the early English settlers and the earliest occupants of the two landmasses, namely aboriginal peoples in both cases and French settlers in the Canadian case. The troubled legacies of that original contact can hardly be denied; they certainly underlie current debates on indigeneity and its implications in both Canada and Australia. With regard to bilateral relations with the United States since the late nineteenth century, however, even the concept of structural hierarchy sheds little light. In fact, both Canadian and Australian elites from then on have shown inconsistent and often ambivalent attitudes toward political influence from abroad in the processes of defining their own novel senses of nationhood. In reality, both Canada and Australia have constantly renegotiated their relationships, first with the United Kingdom and then with the United States. Within frameworks characterized by increasingly diffuse hierarchies of power, these relationships have evolved to accommodate ongoing and regionally distinct reconfigurations of political authority.

The processes through which Canadians and Australians have built their polyglot nations and, in turn, been constrained by diverse geographies and cultural expectations, are dynamic. The idea of "complex sovereignty" today evokes these processes, this persistent, complicated, and never-completed negotiation over legitimacy. The need for effective problem-solving and risk-mitigation measures, combined with commitments to maintaining the maximum feasible degree of collective political autonomy, has by now taken policymakers in Canada and Australia to many places – some below, some alongside, and some above the analytical category of the nation state. The key observable feature of institutional adaptation and innovation in this regard is an increasingly difficult search for robust solutions to problems of collective action. It now often includes quiet acquiescence in tradeoffs among governing principles that are competing or even contradictory.[7] In bilateral relations with the United States, such tradeoffs today suggest much more than "complex interdependence."

Facing problems often but not always shared with their American counterparts, Canadian and Australian societies find themselves drawn more deeply into non-hierarchical and non-majoritarian modes of conflict resolution. To adopt Slaughter's language, they are embedded in networks that facilitate bargaining.[8] In short, their polities have lost the monopoly position to which they once aspired when it came to defining the common good of their citizens and making collectively binding decisions; they are profoundly engaged in a spatial and functional reconfiguration of public authority; and they are actively experimenting with new measures to endow that process with procedural and substantive legitimacy.[9] Although the United States faces particular and deeply rooted problems in publicly acknowledging its own engagement in such processes, the histories of Canada and Australia have long been marked by sometimes explicit and often implicit negotiations over the meaning and content of legitimate and effective political authority in both its internal and external dimensions. Indeed, those histories reflect a persistent effort to reconstitute sovereignty-in-practice through continual, multidimensional, often opaque negotiations.

In analytical terms, complex sovereignty is every day becoming more evident within the United States, Canada, and Australia as well as within their bilateral relationships. Does an increasingly militarized series of fences around the continental United States really protect American citizens from terrorist attacks, or is the threat already deeply internalized? Do freer trade and capital flows among the United States, Canada, and Australia really depend upon formal treaty arrangements, or in practical terms has deep integration of many regulatory standards and supervisory structures already superseded conventional inter-state legal agreements? Are joint military and intelligence operations involving the three countries seriously dependent on agreements dating back to the 1940s, or are habits of communication, interoperability, and burden sharing now deeply routinized, indeed rendered quite "special" in the sense used by Bow and Santa-Cruz when they discuss Canada–US diplomatic cultures in Chapter 7 in this volume? The most plausible answers to such questions suggest the ebb and flow of much more than sensitivity or vulnerability interdependence. Underneath contemporary relations across the territorial borders of three still formally separate states, a more fundamental working out of a shared social and political legacy now profoundly influences the day-to-day work of political leaders, government officials, businesspeople, travelers, and even citizens staying close to home.

Globalization

Australia's and Canada's relationships with the United States have been profoundly conditioned by processes of social, economic, and security globalization. Global webs of trade, production, and finance have produced new integrative dynamics, both within the bilateral relationships and beyond. Similarly, patterns of human migration have reshaped all three polities, pushing and pulling in directions often at odds with economic pressures. Lastly, significant changes have occurred in the global security environment, with the state-centric security challenges of the Cold War replaced by a far more complex mixture of traditional and non-traditional threats. Together, these forces have driven the simultaneous reconfiguration of Australian and Canadian self-understandings and their relations with the United

States. Globalization, in sum, is reconfiguring Canada and Australia as sovereign polities in ways unanticipated in early studies of interdependence.

Canada

Canada and the United States have been moving beyond interdependence for some time. Neither right-wing nor left-wing nationalists desire North American confederation, but their fears concerning just such an end-point are well grounded in Canadian history. As Cox cogently summarizes it, at the outset a competition between two visions of the future decisively shaped Canada's politics, an east–west vision and a north–south vision.[10] Creighton's commercial empire of the St. Lawrence articulated the former; it helped to rationalize both a foundational pact between Anglophone Upper Canada and Francophone Lower Canada, and an expansionist thrust to the Pacific.[11] Simultaneously, however, along with English business elites, Anglo-liberal intellectuals nurtured deep if complicated economic and cultural ties with the United States. Some, like émigré Cornell professor Goldwin Smith, even anticipated a future continental federation based on liberal principles and the idea of a wider union of Anglo-Saxon peoples.[12]

Although party politics would be influenced from the beginning by such antitheses, with Conservatives until the 1980s supporting the east–west vision and Liberals variants of continentalism, in 1867 the fathers of Canadian Confederation consciously stopped a North American political union from emerging in the aftermath of the American Civil War – a war in which nearly 50,000 Canadians fought on the Union side. They and their successors, at least until World War II, mainly aspired to build a country mindful of a fundamental British heritage but nevertheless durably distinct from the United States.[13] The founding policy line countenanced moderate protectionism in the cause of building a coherent east–west economy, accommodation of the culture and rising political demands of French Canadians, and continuation of essentially imperial strategies with regard to aboriginal peoples. In a basic sense, from the Quebec Act of 1774, to the failed American invasion of 1775, to the Constitutional Act of 1791 that divided Upper and Lower Canada, to the Act of Union in 1840, to the establishment of Confederation in 1867, a continuous struggle played itself out to establish a viable compromise among these three basic objectives.[14] Indeed, after assimilationist dreams were finally abandoned, that struggle focused ever more intently on the internal work of finding a viable modus vivendi between two distinct European cultures and many pre-existing aboriginal cultures, and on the external work of redefining ever more nuanced differences of identity and interest with the United States.

After 1945, and after the British connection had become mainly sentimental in many sections of the country, Canadians across the internal cultural divides still aspired to a high degree of political autonomy, but also to a level of economic prosperity reasonably close to the average in the northern section of the United States. In both Quebec and the rest of Canada, leaders favored the construction and maintenance of a fairer and safer society than the one widely perceived to exist to the south. In order to achieve such objectives, the more practical-minded among them knew that the country needed a novel kind of border with the United States.

Ideally, if not always in practice, that border would restrict the inflow of many kinds of problems, mainly problems associated with poor people, with guns, and with cultural influences unwanted by the national elite. It would have to be designed, however, in such a way as not to impede the inward flow of the people, money, goods, and ideas deemed desirable by most Canadians. In addition, such a border would have to accommodate certain kinds of outflows, not just of prosperity-creating exports and investments, but also of people. Some of those people – like students, skilled workers, and "snowbirds" seeking warmer weather in the winter – might eventually return home, but others would need to find opportunities in the United States that they could not find in Canada. Certain pressures potentially disruptive of the social and political balance sought release; the right kind of border then would provide a helpful sort of safety valve. Very importantly, that ideal physical boundary would also have to be porous enough to allow Canadians to benefit from American military preparedness, and for good policy ideas and artistic creations occasionally to filter out of Canada into the right American circles. But it would have to be not so porous as to render vacuous the historical claim of Canadians to legal sovereignty over a given territory.

This unique kind of border had to have an irreducible psychological dimension, what Gwyn evoked with the phrase "nationalism without walls."[15] It might be more accurate to call it deeply contested nationalism behind a well-constructed kind of fence. We return to the culturalist debates below, but in this regard even the idea behind a "common security perimeter" currently being discussed may be taken to represent the latest attempt to reconceive and rebuild such a fence.

Despite the end of the Cold War, Canadians remained willingly within a US-led security community. In the continuing absence of their own external spy service, for example, they were reliant on extensive intelligence-sharing arrangements with the United States.[16] Through the 1988 Canada–United States Free Trade Agreement and the 1994 North American Free Trade Agreement, moreover, they deliberately integrated themselves more deeply into a continental economy. Perhaps by then, even though they retained all the trappings of independent citizenship, many Canadians did not really view themselves as entirely alien in the territory of the United States.[17] In any event, they were apparently unwilling to commit themselves to large-scale national projects that might seriously lessen their deepening economic and social links across the border.[18]

Canadians continued, nevertheless, to have no formal standing in US legislative and regulatory processes. As an organized interest group, moreover, Canada had no more clout inside the US Congress than any other foreign country. But General Motors, Chrysler, Ford, Dell, Apple, and other business firms operating on both sides of the political border did have such clout, and so did the governors of border states sharing crucial interests with neighboring provinces. By the opening of the twenty-first century, many cross-border understandings had taken the bilateral relationship to new levels of complexity. At one level, economic union *within* Canada was arguably strengthened by shared prosperity, while at another level, the possibility of ultimate political dis-integration from the United States continued to recede. Where the interests of residents of border towns in Ontario ended and the interests of residents of their analogues in New York and Michigan began was less clear than ever. The concept of straightforward interdependence lying behind comparative economic and social indicators seemed quaint in such a context.

Australia

Prior to the late 1960s, it was plausible to cast the US–Australian relationship in conventional alliance terms. The wartime collapse of British power in the Asia-Pacific and Australia's embrace of the United States as its principal security guarantor were recent developments. Geostrategic competition and the use of military force in the pursuit of national ends were still prominent features of the Southeast Asian political landscape. The "China threat" was as yet undiluted by economic incentives for engagement. In this world, Keohane and Nye correctly characterized Australia's relationship with the United States as one in which military security issues dominated, and conventional state-to-state relations were uncomplicated by webs of society-to-society interaction. Since the early 1970s, however, Keohane and Nye's characterization appears less and less applicable to the relationship. Australia's ties with the United States remain both close and strong, with the leaders of both countries frequently stressing the "special" nature of the relationship, the common interests that bind them together, and the importance of their shared identities as liberal democracies. Yet the relationship, "special" as it is purported to be, has been transformed by three dimensions of globalization: economic, cultural/demographic, and security.

Over the past three decades, the center of gravity of Australian trade has shifted from the traditional centers of Europe and the United States to Asia, with China recently emerging as Australia's largest trading partner, displacing Japan and the United States.[19] Much of this has been trade in strategic commodities, binding Australia's economic fortunes to key sectors of the Chinese economy. Trade in services has grown significantly as well, however. Selling education to overseas students has become a key national industry, contributing some 19.1 billion AUD to GDP annually, with 31 percent of outbound students returning to Asia.[20] These economic trends have been matched by continued high levels of immigration, and by significant growth in immigration from Asia and Africa. Immigration from China is now the second largest component of the annual intake, only slightly behind immigration from the United Kingdom.[21] Meanwhile, economic globalization and changing patterns of migration have been matched by shifts in the global security environment. Since Keohane and Nye wrote, Cold War security challenges have been replaced by issues of transnational terrorism, failed states, and new threats to the nuclear non-proliferation regime, all of which have distinctive manifestations and expressions in Australia's primary region of concern, the

Asia–Pacific. Added to this, the ambiguities associated with the conjunction of America's post-Cold War ascendance and China's rise have generated a complex geostrategic environment deeply interconnected with the dynamics and imperatives of economic globalization.

These interconnected global processes have had a profound impact on Australia's relationship with the United States. The formal architecture of the ANZUS alliance remains, as does the bipartisan rhetoric of closeness and specialness. Dense networks of military and intelligence cooperation bind the two countries, and successive Australian governments have maintained the longstanding practice of providing moral and material support for Washington's overseas interventions. Ever deeper integration with the US economy has been pursued with persistent vigor, despite equally vigorous domestic debate about the merits of particular bargains, especially concerning bilateral free trade. Yet it is not at all clear that the old characterization of Australia as "a dependent ally" adequately captures the complexity of the relationship. In 1980, Joseph Camilleri wrote that "Nearly thirty years after the establishment of the ANZUS alliance, the American connection, reflected in a wide range of formal and informal arrangements, remains the single most important factor in Australia's integration into the capitalist world economy."[22] It would be difficult indeed to write this today.

Thirty years ago, Australian governments clung to the alliance as a solution to existential security fears bred of the Cold War. Over time, however, the connection between attachment to the alliance and actual security challenges has become increasingly attenuated. The role that the alliance plays in addressing the plethora of new security challenges that have emerged since the end of the Cold War (and the events of 11 September 2001) is either unclear or deeply contested, and as prominent commentators have observed, the alliance may well be an obstacle to Australia responding effectively to the rise of China.[23] Not surprisingly, defense of the alliance has been couched less in terms of its concrete contribution to ameliorating threats, and more in terms of deeply rooted friendship, commonality of values, and the benefits of living in the orbit of a unipolar power. For Labor governments (Hawke and Keating 1983–96, and Rudd and Gillard 2007 to the present), the emphasis has been on the first two of these, with the alliance being nested within broader commitments to multilateralism and augmented forms of global governance. For the Howard Conservative government (1996–2007), an argument about America's enduring primacy and the viability of war-fighting responses to transnational terrorism was alloyed to a nostalgic romanticism about Australia–US relations.[24] Oddly, the most heated subject of security debate in Australia over the last decade has been in an area almost completely disconnected from the alliance – the securitized debate about asylum seekers arriving by boat.

If changes in the security environment forced a recasting and relegitimation of Australia's relationship with the United States, economic globalization had an equally transformative effect. Drawn by the economic dynamism of East and now South Asia, the region has become the focus of Australia's political and economic attention. At the center has been Australia's determined, if ambiguous, engagement with China. For the past decade and a half, China's rise has featured as a persistent security concern for Australian governments, standing alongside globalization as a primary structural condition framing national policy. Yet, this concern has coexisted with a bipartisan commitment to tying Australia's economic future to the rapid development of the Chinese economy, a relationship that helped shield Australia from the worst of the global financial crisis. Australia has been positioned as a principal supplier of China's natural resource demands, with the supply of "strategic" energy and mineral resources at the center of the relationship. In the non-resource sector, Chinese students now constitute 23 percent of Australia's international education market. In addition to simply representing growth areas in Australian trade, the imperative of vigorous economic engagement with Asia – and China in particular – has transformed the nature of the Australian economy itself, fueling the development of the resource and service sectors and undermining innovation in manufacturing. As a result, Australian governments have been forced to balance and hedge their relationships with Washington and Beijing, an artful dance that succeeds only so long as tensions between these two powers can be contained.

One consequence of the above processes has been a significant reconfiguration of Australian understandings and practices of sovereignty. Prior to the 1970s, Australian sovereignty was "compromised" along two relatively simple axes. First, while Australian governments vigorously asserted Australia's international legal sovereignty and equally vigorously defended Australia's territorial integrity, Australia retained constitutional ties with Britain that formally bound Australia to the British Parliament, monarch, and Privy Council (ties that ended in 1986 with the passing of the Australia Act). Second, less formally, Australian governments regularly compromised Australian decision making in military–security relations with the United States. The most notable example was in the nuclear strategic realm. While nuclear weapons have never been stationed on Australian soil, key command, control, and communication (CCC) facilities were maintained at North West Cape, Pine Gap, and Nurrungar. American warships and submarines were also frequent visitors to Australian ports. In both cases, Australian governments deferred to US decision making, accepting US control over the CCC facilities and Washington's policy of neither confirming nor denying the presence of nuclear weapons on its naval vessels (a position contrary to that adopted by New Zealand).

By the 1980s, a far more complex form of sovereign reconstitution was under-way. As noted above, Australia gained constitutional independence from Britain in 1986, but almost immediately ratified a series of international legal instruments that "unbundled" its sovereignty (the 1980 ratification of the First Optional Protocol to the International Covenant on Civil and Political Rights being the notable example). Similarly, as successive Australian governments sought to enmesh Australia ever deeper within globalized economic processes, national sovereignty was renegotiated to accommodate a variety of multilateral and bilateral free trade instruments that bound Australia not only to the United States economy but also to key Asian economies. Lastly, as Australia grappled with the political implications of a greatly diversified immigration pool, Australian governments played political football with the issue of refugees, formally excising parts of Australian territory from the immigration zone and establishing offshore detention centers in nearby small island states, effectively creating new centers of extra-territorial authority. The partial sovereignty of the early post-independence period, and the compromised sovereignty of high Cold War, have thus been replaced in recent decades by a distinctively Australian variety of complex sovereignty in which both territorial and jurisdictional authority have been crafted to the diverse imperatives of multi-faced globalization.

Identity and engagement

As a legal principle, sovereignty allocates power and authority in distinctive ways as it defines bounded and independent political units. Organizing political life in this way, however, requires justification. It requires discourses and practices that make its political implications appear legitimate, even natural. In the context of rapid economic and social change, the task becomes more difficult, as actual political autonomy becomes attenuated. Because the Australia–US and Canada–US relationships have always demanded the artful calibration of the junior allies' sovereignty, changes in legitimation discourses and practices adopted by Canadian and Australian elites have had a significant impact on those relationships. They have worked at two interconnected levels: at the level of internal, corporate identity, and at the level of modes of international engagement.

Australia

Since the mid-1970s, Australia has undergone a profound shift in corporate identity, in the many ways in which Australians imagine themselves as a people and a sovereign polity. Indeed, it would be difficult to find another state – certainly an advanced Western state – that has undergone a greater revolution in self-understandings and attendant institutional structures and processes. Despite the fact that Australia was a country forged through mass migration, until this period Australia was culturally defensive, a society dominated by white Anglo Protestants. It maintained an explicitly "White Australia" immigration policy and denied its indigenous peoples full political rights and membership of the polity; Catholics met systematic, if informal, discrimination in the workforce and in their access to political power. After 1970, however, in response to a variety of factors (including actual changes in the composition of the Australian population over time and political pressure for indigenous rights), a revolution in social policy occurred.[25] In the mid-1960s, key elements of the White Australia policy were dismantled, opening the door to a wide range of new immigrant groups; later in that decade, Australian Aborigines gained full citizenship rights.[26] From the mid-1970s an explicit and vigorous policy of multiculturalism was adopted, a policy promoted most notably by the Conservative Fraser government through town hall meetings across the country. Over time, as well, the old divide between Protestants and Catholics disappeared, becoming little more than a curious historical fact most Australians would no longer recognize or identify with.

While sweeping in the scope and the depth in which they transformed Australian society, these changes have not been without ongoing challenges or contestation. Multiculturalism is now the deep norm of Australian society, a norm few politicians openly challenge, with debate confined to its meanings rather than its merits.[27] That indigenous peoples are, and ought to be, full rights-bearing members of the polity is also taken for granted, as is Australia's "color" blind immigration policy. Nevertheless, a series of "culture wars" erupted, principally after 1996 under the Howard government. Howard himself was a cultural conservative with a romantic attachment to the Australia of the 1950s. Earlier in his career he was roundly condemned for questioning the pace of Asian immigration, and while he never explicitly sought to reverse multicultural policy, he personally preferred "multiracialism," the idea that Australians celebrate their diverse origins while focusing on what unites them as a people. His was thus an ambivalent multiculturalism with strong assimilationist overtones, a view that rubbed up against prevailing pluralist interpretations and the complex institutional practices that had evolved to support such pluralism. Similarly, the rights of indigenous peoples had gained greater recognition, taken further with the High Court's "Mabo" decision on land rights; but the degree to which Australians should atone for violent and discriminatory past practices became hotly contested. How the new National Museum of Australia told the story of that past became a focal point for this contest, as did the issue of a formal apology to the indigenous peoples for the practice of forcibly removing aboriginal children from their families.[28]

It is important to note here that these debates came to the fore in a permissive environment cultivated by the Howard government, and the extent to which they reflect deep or profound divisions within Australian society is questionable. Australia's preferential voting system amplified the voice of the minority uncomfortable with the transformation of Australian society, providing a resource for less than scrupulous politicians to exploit. Furthermore, while the treatment of asylum seekers arriving by boat has been a focal point of such politics, it is noteworthy that the anti-refugee case has not been made in racial or ethnic terms (even if these were the underlying motives). Those seeking to turn back such refugees have made their case in the language of fairness: "the boat people are jumping the queue." Moreover, when the Rudd government made its highly publicized apology to the indigenous stolen generations, it received almost universal endorsement across Australian society.

These transformations in, and contestations over, Australia's corporate identity have been paralleled by a shift in Australia's modes of international engagement. There have been two dimensions to this shift. First, the old focus on military–security ties with the United States has been replaced by an oscillating foreign policy stance, in which Australian policy has moved between phases of strong liberal internationalism (generally, though not exclusively, under Labor governments) and a more traditional, alliance-focused stance. The Fraser government (1975–83) adopted the second of these, casting the alliance with the United States as crucial to the maintenance of a central, systemic balance of power. Under the Hawke and Keating governments (1983–96), the alliance receded into the background, displaced by an emphasis on cultivating global order and justice through international institutional development. Howard reversed this trend, reasserting the centrality of the alliance (with a number of notable exceptions, such as its support for the International Criminal Court). The Rudd/Gillard government has since returned to a more internationalist stance. Second, since the 1970s successive Australian governments have sought deeper engagement with Asia. This engagement has had political, economic, and cultural dimensions, but again there have been shifts in temper, an integrationist mode vying with an instrumentalist mode. The integrationist mode, most notably seen under the Hawke and Keating governments, has cast Australia as part of Asia, a move evident in everything from projects of regional institution building (the Asia-Pacific Economic Cooperation [APEC] for example) through to Keating's insistence that Australia "is an Asian country." This contrasts with the instrumentalist mode seen most prominently under the Howard government. Howard had no sentimental attachment to Asia, but had a strong sense that Australia's interests lay in deep integration with the burgeoning Asian economies, particularly China. The foreign policy of the Rudd/Gillard governments is an admixture of these two tendencies, producing at times a clumsy mode of engagement with regional powers.

While these shifts in corporate identity and international engagement have occurred in parallel, they have also been deeply interconnected. One of the great weaknesses of the literature on Australian foreign policy has been its near complete failure to recognize and explore this relationship, with the domestic and international realms treated as hermetically sealed social and political universes.[29] In reality, how Australian governments have sought to navigate changing global conditions has been inextricably entwined with the reconstitution of the Australian polity and its broader social and economic structures. Indeed, these two processes ought to be seen as different faces of a four-decade-long struggle to reconstitute the cultural, institutional, and economic nature of the Australian polity. Moreover, different phases of domestic transformation correlate with different phases of international engagement. Less internationalist approaches to global governance, and more instrumental approaches to engagement with Asia, map on to more conservative approaches to multiculturalism and indigenous reconciliation. Similarly, more internationalist and integrationist approaches have coincided, by and large, with more progressive and ambitious social policies. Seen from this perspective, Keating's narration of Australia as an "Asian" nation articulates with the construction of a multicultural Australia, as does Howard's sentimental re-embrace of the West's political heartland with assimilationist "multiracialism" and rejection of critical reinterpretations of the history of white colonization.

Canada

The decline of the old notion of Canada as a key element of the British Empire, and even of the more recent idea that the country represented the joint project of "two founding peoples," left Canadians after World War II with the task of reimagining the nature of their political community and the rationale for its distinctiveness in an economic and social context increasingly shaped by continentalist impulses.[30] The vast majority of the population remained in Ontario and Quebec, formerly Upper and Lower Canada. But just as raw political power was shifting westward and new patterns of immigration began changing the country's demographic profile, especially in big cities, the claims for justice of indigenous peoples throughout the land became ever more assertive. The task of reimagining an identity capable of sustaining the legitimacy of a separate polity within North America was, and remains, daunting. Anti-Americanism could still be a vote-getting palliative, as in the federal election of 2011 when the victorious Conservatives made much of the Liberal leader's lengthy prior residence in the United States; but no Canadian leader would try to extend such emotional reactions to actual policies designed to stop their constituents from seeking access to US private healthcare, connecting to US telecommunications systems, vacationing in Florida, or sending their children to American universities.

Still, basic structures of collective identity and individual autonomy were in motion across the bilateral relationship, even if shared traditions of liberal democracy obscured fundamental political issues. In the new environment, questions of identity and autonomy pointed to sites of tension and contestation within which that relationship was, and is, being redefined. Even pro-American leaders had now to seek new characterizations of, and rationalizations for, deeper continental integration.

"Responsible government" came to Canada in a long process beginning with rebellions in Upper and Lower Canada in 1837, the British North America Act of 1867, and the Statute of Westminster in 1931. But the very idea would be meaningless in the absence of the concept of autonomy.[31] Only individuals and groups possessing some requisite degree of autonomy can make decisions for which they will themselves henceforth be held responsible in any practical sense. Embedded mainly in two distinct but conjoined communities, Canadian elites in the modern period imagined themselves to be in a position to shape the conditions of their existence to the fullest extent possible and without external interference. Over time, the original "federal" division of powers along linguistic and cultural lines was supplemented by a dispersal of power along territorial lines as population expanded in the west.[32] Although the original Canadian constitution came home from the UK in 1982 with the assent of the descendants of New France – indeed, Francophone federalist leaders were prime movers in the process – later events developed in a manner that left Quebec's leaders unable to affirm political support for a fully elaborated settlement.[33]

The technical issues here are important in understanding the specific Canadian version of "complex sovereignty." The British North America Act, renamed the

Constitution Act 1867, was patriated and became the foundational Canadian law. In addition to the final act of patriation, provincial and federal leaders sought to address the need for an explicit charter of rights and for a constitutional amending procedure. They proposed, therefore, a *new* act – the Constitution Act 1982. The first 34 clauses contained the Charter, section 35 specified the rights of indigenous peoples, section 36 covered regional disparities and equalization (transfer) payments across provinces, and sections 37–52 contained the amending procedure and other items. Nationalists in Quebec were not opposed to the Constitution Act 1867, but the separatist government then in power in Quebec was upset by the Constitution Act 1982. Even though key concessions had been made to their cause, their stated aim was "sovereignty," or what later evolved into the idea of a formal "sovereignty-association" with the rest of Canada. Despite the defeat of related referenda in Quebec in 1980 and 1995, and despite frustrated efforts to accommodate demands for explicit acknowledgment of Quebec as a "distinct society" within Canada, the issue of Quebec's political assent to the Constitution Act 1982 remains unsettled. So, too, are many issues related to the place of indigenous peoples within the confederation, the legacy of imperialism and failed assimilationist experiments, and subsequent differences of views on precise measures to transcend that legacy.[34]

Meanwhile, economic and social integrationist pressures continue to build along a north–south axis. This has created new options for local populations looking simultaneously for new markets for their resources and production, not least in Quebec. As cooperation with the United States across a range of associated issues has deepened, the east–west pressures once binding the Canadian provinces have weakened. Continentalism is today being driven by various and coincident innovations in critical technologies, in communication and transportation systems, and in artistic and literary realms of social reimagining. Even for a cohesive group of human beings, such forces could in principle change quite profoundly perceptions of the common good and, since human beings exist as individuals-in-community, encourage basic transformations in social identity. But Canadians have never really constituted a cohesive people. Their state has therefore always been in the business of trying to construct a common identity adequate to the task of holding itself together and preventing complete envelopment by the United States. That task has lately become more difficult.

A few phrases evoke a set of practices through which successive national governments have approached it. These practices include: preservation of the idea of "the Crown" at the core of a parliamentary democracy; respect for the rule of law and the civil rights of the individual; tolerance of social difference across a vast landmass that supporters call openness and cynics can easily depict as indifference; an instinctive urge to avoid open conflict and a willingness to make tacit compromises in the name of collective cohesion; fiscal transfers to offset regional inequalities; an often deliberate draining of emotion from public policy debates; open-ended and often opaque bargaining among organized interests; a widely shared belief that many important social problems have no near-term solutions; a commitment to economic growth; a sense of irony. Therein lies the obvious inheritance from the past, a pluralist inheritance that simultaneously reflects the traditions of British pragmatism, abiding cultural diversity, and leaders determined to maintain the maximum feasible degree of political autonomy on a continent populated mainly by citizens of the United States.

In 2011 the Conservative Party won a majority of the seats in the federal parliament. A political coalition originally organized as the Reform Party of Alberta, and expressing both western alienation from central Canada and an American-style neoconservatism, superseded the old Tories, who had been out of power since 1993. The Liberal governments that followed finally collapsed in 2006. With social-democratic and Francophone nationalist parties now taking most Quebec seats, the rising power of energy-rich Alberta combined with the rightward movement of voters in Ontario to create the conditions for a pragmatic Alberta–Ontario alliance. On offer was a looser confederation, continued continental integration, and a vague kind of multiculturalism (discussed further below). Given the relative economic decline of Ontario, the traditional champion of pan-Canadian nationalism and perennial source of fiscal transfers, the challenge of holding the country together became more complicated. No alternative strategy, however, was offered by any of the country's main political parties.

The shifting limits of Anglo-liberal bonds

If the US–Australia and US–Canada relationships no longer strictly fit Keohane and Nye's ideal-type, and if internal and external environments have encouraged the development of complex sovereignty and malleable identities in both Canada and Australia (albeit in different specific forms), then what holds these relationships together? One possibility, hinted at above, is that it is their common Anglo-liberal heritage. Indeed, this, as we have observed, has become an increasingly important theme of those seeking to relegitimate these relationships under conditions of profound international and domestic change.[35] In reality, however, the common Anglo-liberal heritage of these states is as internally contradictory as it is coherent, and its causal and behavioral implications less straightforward or well varnished. The distinctive and constantly evolving cultural identities of Australia, Canada, and the United States stand in dynamic tension with a set of dominant Anglo-liberal norms that are themselves sufficiently broad to allow very real disagreements over the nature and development of a liberal international order, and equally significant differences in the evolution of their respective liberal democratic institutions.

Canada

As politics and effective decision-making became much more complex, the Anglo identity at the core of the post-1945 US–Canada relationship became more attenuated. In truth, it was never so simple, since Canadian identity was bicultural at its start, and even that was complicated by the nature of early contact with indigenous peoples. Tenuous from the beginning was the idea that Canada was ever an entirely coherent element in the effort to establish what Bell, in his seminal assessment of nineteenth-century British imperialism, labeled a global society centered on a powerful Anglo-Saxon bond.[36] As MacDonald and O'Connor in Chapter 8 of this book note in a comparison of New Zealand and Canada within Anglo-America, the existence of very significant non-Anglo ethnic groups, and their steadfast refusal to assimilate, ensured a mixed cultural foundation for future nation-building.

The French fact has long deeply influenced Canada's externally oriented policy decisions, most recently, for example, Canada's decision to oppose the US invasion of Iraq in 2003. What is involved here is the rearticulation of an internally already complex Canadian identity. Especially in the wake of new immigration flows, the broad label now commonly used to suggest the social foundations of contemporary Canadian politics is multiculturalism. That ideology needs further unpacking in the larger continental context.

Traditional Anglo-American – not to say, imperial or hegemonic – understandings are still evident in the bilateral Canada–US relationship when it comes to security, intelligence, and many economic issues. They are, however, increasingly obscure in issue areas in which a broad commitment to maintaining distinctiveness from the United States remains. Some, for example, see the widely shared interest of Canadians in publicly funded healthcare as defining one such issue area, and upon it today rests one attempt to revive a pan-Canadian nationalist vision.

Political institutions codify and make routine the creation of a public sphere and arrangements for governing activities within it. Over time, Canadian political institutions developed ever more complex and functionally differentiated organizational structures. When most people today refer to "society," they typically think about the populations of bounded and autonomous states. And the ideological foundation of most bounded states is nationalism, whether manifested in civic or ethnic forms. The evolving Canadian polity, from its beginning to its present, rests uneasily on both forms.

Anglo-Canadians traditionally considered their collective sentiments liberal or civic, not ethnic, a preference rendered ever more plausible over time with the deliberate admixture to their society of immigrants from all over the world. In the Ontario heartland, the very word "nationalism" applied to itself seems as alien as the word "imperialist" sometimes applied to it by Quebecers or by indigenous peoples. In contrast, notwithstanding demographic pressures associated with low birth rates and significant immigration flows, old stock Quebecers remain in control of their province and continue to assert the legitimacy of that control, sometimes subtly and sometimes not so subtly, on a distinct ethnic claim.

Indeed, since the Battle of the Plains of Abraham in 1759, the central political struggle for Canadians as a collectivity has been to find a way to accommodate the deep cultural distinctiveness of the descendants of New France. The two-founding-nations thesis and confederalism eventually provided a kind of answer. Until the late 1960s, various iterations of the British-derived discourses and pragmatic practices noted above sought to keep ethnic nationalism within Quebec contained. With the unexpected rise of Pierre Trudeau to the federal prime ministership in 1968, however, a radical reversal occurred as Parliament united around a strategy of "confronting and undermining Quebec nationalism."[37] This son of a Scottish mother and French Canadian father committed himself to bringing Quebecers out of ethnic, hierarchical, and territorial mindsets. He wanted them to see all of Canada as their own.

In 1971, reinterpreting a key recommendation from the report of the Royal Commission on Bilingualism and Biculturalism, Trudeau finally articulated a policy toward which he had been moving all of his adult life – the embrace of bilingualism from sea-to-sea-to-sea combined with a decisive rejection of biculturalism, which in his view was narrowly collectivist, unjustifiably historicist, and unnecessarily restrictive. The policy came to be labeled "multiculturalism." As Trudeau originally put it in Parliament: "although there are two official languages, there is no official culture, nor does any ethnic group take precedence over any other."[38] Leaving aside the debate between those who wanted to imagine the fire of 1759 still burning or to reinforce the later image of "two founding peoples," Trudeau asserted that "the individual's freedom would be hampered if he were locked for life within a particular cultural compartment by the accident of birth or language."[39]

> [In sum,] a policy of multiculturalism within a bilingual framework commends itself to the government as the most suitable means of assuring the cultural freedom of Canadians. Such a policy should help to break down discriminatory attitudes and cultural jealousies. National unity, if it is to mean anything in the deeply personal sense, must be founded on confidence in one's own individual identity; out of this can grow respect for that of others and a willingness to share ideas, attitudes and assumptions. A vigorous policy of multiculturalism will help create this initial confidence. It can form the base of a society which is based on fair play for all.[40]

The argument over the success or failure of Trudeau's policy continues, not least in referenda on the question of Quebec separation in 1980 and 1995, in subsequent failed efforts to amend the federal Constitution through a formula acceptable to Quebec, and in the rising assertiveness of aboriginal groups. Recently expanding immigration from the Caribbean, Africa, the Middle East, and Asia, moreover, changed the context for policy debate, partly by highlighting race in a country that had long sought to insulate itself from deeply racialized social problems in the United States.[41] Cox captured well the optimistic multiculturalist vision of the country's future: "A coexistence of cultures, not by assimilation to one standard model, but for the mutual enjoyment of diversity, is the emerging form of the pan-Canadian idea; this is the domestic counterpart to the geopolitical evolution of a plural world."[42] Nationalist Quebecers, on the other hand, saw the matter differently. It undercut their identity as a people with prior and irrevocable claims on power within a given territory, and it threatened to reduce them to the assimilated status of other French-speaking populations in the Anglo sea of North America. Although their fears failed to culminate in outright secession from the rest of Canada, separatist leaders from Trudeau's time to the present could count on near-majority support. They could also count on a reluctance from the rest of Canada to push Trudeau's project aggressively. As Ignatieff put it, "Since the 1995 referendum...the fervent desire to find either common ground or the terms of divorce has been replaced by a tacit contract of mutual indifference."[43]

To leading Quebec intellectuals, that indifference represents contemporary acquiescence by the rest of Canada to what some call "interculturalism." Rejecting multiculturalism as an attempt to deny Quebec a heritage that preceded the arrival of English-speakers, but also seeking to move beyond a simplistic and outmoded biculturalist vision of Quebec and Canada, in 2008 two prominent scholars from either side of Quebec's language divide, Gerard Bouchard and Charles Taylor, proposed interculturalism as a viable alternative to Trudeau's vision. In a report commissioned by the Government of Quebec, they characterized their central idea as at least applying in Quebec in such a manner as to: (a) institute French as the common language of intercultural relations; (b) cultivate a pluralistic orientation that is concerned with the protection of rights; (c) preserve the necessary creative tension between diversity, on the one hand, and the continuity of the French-speaking core and the social link, on the other hand; (d) place special emphasis on integration and participation; and (e) advocate interaction. The main implication they drew for policy was the need for "reasonable accommodation" of the desires of non-dominant groups in Quebec, now including many new immigrants, as long as such accommodation did not undercut "the continuity of the French-speaking core" or broader social cohesion.[44]

The debate remains unfinished, and contemporary Canadian society in fact remains influenced by biculturalist, interculturalist, and multiculturalist ideas. Ethnic nationalism in Quebec has not been decisively overcome, and Canada as a whole is hardly bilingual. At the same time, the economic opportunities spawned by deeper continental integration have nurtured visions in Quebec of sovereignty-association in practice if not in law. In this light, Anglophone Canada and Francophone Canada remain caught up in a supreme irony, for Trudeau's foundational anti-nationalism provided a key building block for a new and more complex kind of nationalism. As Forbes explains:

> [S]een from the perspective of its founder, [multiculturalism is] an experiment in creating a nation designed to show the world how to overcome nationalism and war. The confusing difficulty Trudeau faced was the need to foster a certain nationalism in the very act of trying to overcome it. Given the prevailing national organization of political life, any appeal to Canadians to embark on the experiment he favoured had to be cast as an appeal to their national pride and ambition.[45]

An uneasy federal union continues to rest on contested and diverse nationalist ideologies, but also on persistent and pragmatic practices of cross-cultural negotiation.[46] Charles Taylor himself many years ago diagnosed this as fundamentally representing a tense but persistent conversation between two incompatible views of liberal society, one based on proceduralism and the fundamental rights of individuals, the other respecting such rights within an overarching framework that accommodates the enduring identity of a distinctive and dominant group within a given territory.[47]

Beyond the perennial issue of reaching a final understanding between English- and French-speaking Canadians on the nature of their union, another incomplete conversation involving contradictory premises and much hypocrisy today centers on indigenous peoples, or "first nations." Debate on the actual political and cultural status of indigeneity is gathering force, having long been suppressed, most recently under the rubric of multiculturalism. Indigenous peoples in Canada received the right to vote only in 1960, but many would later come to see a fuller set of rights as grounded in claims to dignity and self-government pre-dating the establishment of Canada – or Anglo-America. In 2010 the Canadian federal government ratified the 2007 UN Declaration on the Rights of Indigenous Peoples and seemed to accept that fundamental point. What this actually means for contemporary political practice, in policy arenas under federal and especially provincial jurisdiction, remains to be seen.

Pragmatic practices for governing a society fundamentally marked by such abiding cultural differences undoubtedly provide distinct groups, and sometimes Canada as a whole, with useful tools for extracting benefits from economic and social integration across the North American continent. Surely helping to render such an outcome politically acceptable to the United States is the observation that the actual process of managing Canada's cultural struggles correlates with policies favoring a high degree of economic openness. Providing Americans with ever-expanding access to vast natural resources certainly helps Canadians counter an ancient external threat to their political integrity. The internal challenge remains.

Australia

Unlike in the Canadian case, where claims to common Anglo roots are complicated by the culturally divided nature of Canadian society, both the United States and Australia grew out of dominant British settler societies, English has remained their predominant language, and their societies have been culturally diversified by waves of post-1945 immigration. Similarly, both states embrace their identities as liberal democracies, maintain (with several notable lapses) robust democratic institutions, and remain committed to the preservation and development of a liberal international order.

The picture with respect to Australia is considerably more complicated, however. Australian democracy was not the product of revolutionary struggle – Australians gained their independence, as well as their democratic institutions, incrementally and with more than a little ambivalence and anxiety. If John Stuart Mill was correct that a people must struggle for their liberties if they are to understand and appreciate them, the absence of struggle has left Australians with neither a strong sense of ownership of their democratic institutions nor deep identification with their democratic rights. Fortunately, aspects of the Australian Constitution, such as compulsory and preferential voting, foster robust democratic practices. But the Constitution provides no explicit guarantees of individual rights, it falling to the High Court to identify a number of "implied rights." (This is clearly apparent in the Victorian state government's recent ban on swearing in public.) The policy and practice of multiculturalism is constructed on liberal norms of toleration and pluralism, but this domain of social policy has, if anything, been a vehicle for the articulation and diffusion of such norms, rather than a product of them. Current government statements about what Australian multiculturalism means state that what binds Australians of diverse cultural backgrounds together is respect for Australia's democracy and laws, and the rights and liberties of all individuals.[48] The nature and existence of such rights and liberties is generally not a matter of public discourse or debate: Australian liberalism lives in the realm of habitual practices, not self-conscious values, resulting in a notable (and laudable) general absence of preaching about political values. On the downside, it is hard to stir Australians in defense of fundamental liberties, as evident in the near total lack of public concern about elements of recent anti-terrorist legislation and the torture of Australian citizens in the conduct of the war on terror.

In addition to the distinctive nature of its liberal democracy, Australia's engagement with the Anglo-world has, since World War II, worked in moving concentric circles. After 1945, despite the shift in Australia's military–strategic dependence toward the United States, its closest ties were with Britain, reinforced by the persistence of imperial structures for the next two decades. During this period, the United States was the ally of necessity, but in terms of Anglo attachments it was one step removed from Britain. The complexities of these Anglo attachments were clearly apparent in the politics of postwar decolonization, where Australia often equated Anglo bonds with imperial bonds and found itself in an ambiguous relationship with the United States as Washington's position on decolonization oscillated between rhetorical support for colonial peoples and practical opposition to the self-determination movement in the United Nations. Since the mid-1970s – with the multicultural transformations of Australian society and identity and greater engagement with Asia – the romantic attachment of Australian elites to the Anglo-world, so evident in the Menzies era, has declined. While Howard's personal expressions of Australia's relations with the USA echo such romanticism, justifications for close ties have appealed either to strategic imperatives or to a history of friendship and common endeavor. As suggested earlier, the increased appeal to the latter kind of legitimation has coincided with the end of the Cold War and the decline in established justifications for the alliance relationship. Ever more frequent references to common liberal democratic traditions and values have accompanied this shift.

The rhetoric of shared liberal democratic identity, and the implication that this can inform shared foreign policy positions, is belied by the fact that liberal democracy can have multiple meanings and multiple institutional expressions, as can a "liberal international order" constructed and sustained by liberal democratic states. The relationship among the individual, society, and the state is central to liberalism, but there is no consensus among liberal democrats about what this means in concrete institutional terms, and "real existing" liberal democracies exhibit considerable political cultural and institutional variation (as evident in the differences between Australia and the United States). Similarly, the rights of the individual, a commitment to multilateralism and international law, and peace through free trade are emblematic liberal internationalist values. Yet how this translates into concrete policies and practices is open to considerable disagreement among liberal states. If mutual respect for sovereignty and sovereign equality undergirds a multilateral order and the rule of international law, can this be compromised to protect individual rights, for example? These inherent contradictions within the ideational complex of liberal internationalism have produced substantial policy divergence between Australia and the United States since the early 1980s, with the two states moving in and out of step with one another, particularly on key issues of global institutional development. While a baseline commitment to supporting the United States is a persistent feature of Australian foreign policy, a clear pattern has developed of Australian Labor governments (Hawke and Keating, then Rudd and Gillard) pursuing ambitious programs of international institutional development well ahead of Washington's consistent institutional ambivalence.[49] There have also been a number of key differences under Conservative governments, the Howard government's strong support for the International Criminal Court being the most notable example.

What, therefore, binds the US–Australia relationship together? If the geostrategic necessities of Cold War have gone, if economic engagement with China is pulling Australia in new directions, if discourses of friendship, specialness, and liberal democratic brotherhood have come to the fore in the context of weakening traditional bonds, then what undergirds the relationship? Conventional arguments hold that new security challenges have replaced the old ones, giving new life to the alliance. They also emphasize the military–technological and intelligence benefits that Australia gains from close, trusted relations with Washington. And, finally, these narrowly instrumental factors are often linked to arguments about the importance of common Anglo-American bonds.[50] Yet these things seem insufficient, and need augmenting with at least two other factors. The first has to do with recognition. For Australian political leaders, as well as senior bureaucrats, the close relationship with the United States has provided social recognition of Australia's identity and standing internationally. Indeed, it may well be that the pursuit of social recognition accounts for much of the emotion that appears to characterize Australia's discursive engagement with the United States. Second, the US–Australia relationship is now deeply institutionalized, and has become embedded in habitual practices. Like all institutions, even when they prove less than optimal on purely functional grounds, the costs of change can outweigh the benefits; without a cata-lytic crisis forcing change (the way the fall of Singapore prompted the turn from Britain toward the United States), institutionalized relationships can persist, with incremental evolution taking the place of revolutionary change.

Conclusion

At first glance, the relationships between the United States and Canada, and the United States and Australia, may appear to reflect a common and uncomplicated inheritance from the Anglo-American "West." Yet as the case histories surveyed in this chapter suggest, the actual legacy of Anglo-America is complex and fluid. In their pioneering work, Keohane and Nye tried to capture some of this complexity. Their distinctions between relations characterized by traditional power and secu-rity dynamics and those marked by deep interdependence nevertheless cannot adequately capture the enduring impact of the practices through which that legacy has been transmitted over time.

Canada and Australia have, over the past half-century and in explicit or implicit dialogue with the United States, struggled to reconstitute their sovereign identities through quite distinctive discourses and policy practices. The Anglo heritage, always contested, remains – but in forms much attenuated. The term "complex sovereignty" suggests the variegated nature of those discourses and practices, which by now have themselves globalized. Although similarities continue to exist across the Canada–US and Australia–US relationships, both have faced different impera-tives and adjusted in unique ways. The contrasting imperatives posed by distance and proximity are clear: Canada is navigating the complexities of physical close-ness; Australia those of regional dislocation from the United States. Yet contrasts also exist in areas of seeming convergence, the politics surrounding multicultural-ism providing the most prominent example. If multiculturalism is understood as more than a synonym for cultural diversification – as a distinctive kind of policy practice – then Canada and Australia are among the very few states to have adopted such practices, systematically and persistently. Their multicultural policies and prac-tices are very different, however, for they arise out of different social conditions and address different challenges. Canadian multiculturalism was a response to the fact of biculturalism and bilingualism, a still-incomplete attempt to incorporate Quebecers within a culturally pluralistic polity. Australian multiculturalism took inspiration from the Canadian experiment, but in response to a very different set of impera-tives. With the demise of the White Australia policy, a new policy regime was required simultaneously to provide a new narrative about Australian society and to set in place an array of practices acknowledging the increasingly diverse immigrant base of Australian society while fostering the development of a peaceful pluralism. But because of Australia's weakly developed sense of substantive national identity, this has mainly become a multiculturalism of the market place, where government sets in place policies and practices enabling cultural diversity with no mandated sense of "commonness." (The Gillard government's talk of shared rights and values is, as noted, a recent innovation.) In short, these contrasting forms of multicultural-ism lie at the heart of Canada's and Australia's very different expressions of complex sovereignty.

In describing civilizations, the intellectual historian William Goetzmann writes:

> They are syncretistic, chaotic, and often confusing information mechanisms.... Civilization advances beyond the set prescriptions of culture into a broader eclecticism, and to identify both the individual and the social is harder to discern.... Beneath the surface of apparent chaos and contradiction lies great efficiency in absorbing, organizing, and distributing the world's information.... Cultures and systems of idea are then, figuratively speaking, temporary bulwarks, stopping places, organizational makeshifts in the path of on-rushing civilizations that are the inevitable products of history in the same sense that learning is the inevitable product of individual experience.[51]

Canada–US and Australia–US relations remain embedded within something like what Goetzmann describes as a civilization. Nevertheless, our analysis casts doubt on his notion of cultures as "temporary bulwarks" eventually to be swept away by larger forces. It also suggests remarkable fluidity within and around the traditional core of Anglo-America. Even as the pressures of globalization now most clearly associated with the United States increase, the distinctive cultural and political identities within Canada and Australia continue to adapt and not to disappear. Idealists and economists remain convinced that they will ultimately be hollowed out. Our comparative overview casts doubt on any such expectation, even as it highlights successful means of taking some of the political sting out of cultural diversity. Those distinctive identities underpin commitments to political autonomy, commitments that continue to influence the scope of bilateral relations with the United States.

Complex sovereignty remains an apt descriptor of the overall situation. In Australia, expanding economic, political, and cultural engagement with Asia, and the associated and continuing transformation of Australian society through waves of non-Western immigration, have produced a collective identity in constant flux and renegotiation. This is entwined with an unresolved search for a stable liberal social identity within the international system, and particularly within the Asia-Pacific region. These processes of self-constitution draw in part on the cultural heritage of Anglo-America but take place in the liminal space between this civili-zational complex and the wider global social and cultural processes in which Australia is embedded. Similarly, Canada relies on the practical legacies of Anglo-liberalism to manage its domestic contradictions and to influence the nature and meaning of its territorial border with the United States. Even as power shifts within its confederal political system, open-ended cultural negotiation and distinctive internal compromises continue to condition the process of economic and social integration with the United States and the broader engagement of Canadians internationally.

Over the long sweep of modern history, Canada and Australia have often proven themselves to be less sensitive and less vulnerable to developments within the United States than to their own internal cultural dynamics. The discourses and policy practices through which they have held their distinctive polities together remain visible to all with eyes to see them. As the world's leaders seek practicable ways to protect common goods and address common challenges in an era when systemic power seems to be dispersing, an awareness of such practices and their enduring rationales may be instructive. Cultural distinctiveness and commitments to political autonomy place limits on deep integration, even among the inheritors of Anglo-American legacies. But the idea of complex sovereignty they embodied, and the practices they developed to sustain it, can provide an excellent starting point for thinking through pragmatic policy responses to the challenges humanity now faces at the global level. Immobilism remains an imaginable outcome, but our brief case histories suggest that cultural diversity and joint problem-solving can go together. The politics of complex sovereignty remain as open and open-ended as the psychological boundaries around and within polities still shaped by the memory of Anglo-America.

Notes

1 Acknowledgments: Pauly has benefited from resources provided by the Canada Research Chair Program of the Social Sciences and Humanities Research Council of Canada and from the exceptional research assistance of Joelle Dumouchel. Reus-Smit thanks the European University Institute for the award of a Fernand Braudel Senior Fellowship in 2008–9, and for the research support associated with the Chair in International Relations since August 2010. We are both grateful for the comments of the editor and participants in this project, of audience members at the International Studies Association meeting held in New Orleans in February 2010, of Robert O. Keohane at the American Political Science Annual Meeting in Washington the following September, and of William Coleman, Patricia Goff, David Haglund, Richard Simeon, Don Forbes, and Rob Vipond before, during, and after a final project meeting at the Munk School of Global Affairs in Toronto in May 2011.
2 Wesley 2010.
3 Blaxland 2006.
4 Keohane and Nye 1977, 166.
5 Ibid., 8.
6 Ibid., 12–13.
7 Grande and Pauly 2005, 5. The underlying idea derives from convergent political and legal research literatures that evolved rapidly if mainly separately during the 1990s. The term "complex sovereignty" or its equivalents were used, for example, in works like Ruggie 1993; Biersteker and Weber 1996; and Jayasuriya 1999. On related institutional manifestations, see Katzenstein 2005 and Pauly and Coleman 2008.
8 Slaughter 2004.
9 Grande and Pauly 2005, 15.
10 Cox 2005, 667–84.
11 Creighton 1937.
12 Cox 2005, 668.
13 This section draws on Pauly 2003, 90–109.
14 Bothwell 1998.
15 Gwyn 1997.

16 Known as the "Quinquepartite Partnership," this longstanding arrangement for extensive intelligence sharing includes the United States, Great Britain, Canada, Australia, and New Zealand. It parallels similar arrangements setting out shared doctrine for interoperability across the air, space, and naval services of the same five countries, and the continuing Quinquepartite Combined Joint Warfare Conference.

17 Granatstein 1999. Note that dual nationality has long been accepted in Canada, not least because of the long and gradual process of political separation from Great Britain.

18 On the policy debate, see Canadian International Council 2010.

19 Government of Australia, Department of Foreign Affairs and Trade 2010.

20 Government of Australia, Australian Education International 2011.

21 Government of Australia, Department of Immigration and Citizenship 2010.

22 Camilleri 1980, 135; see Bell 1988 and Camilleri 1987.

23 White 2010.

24 Garran 2004.

25 The best account of this transformation is Tavan 2005. For a contrasting viewpoint, see Windschuttle 2004.

26 On the incremental nature of the dismantling of the White Australia policy, and on the broad public support for the policy, see Tavan 2004.

27 The importance of the latter policy has been recently reaffirmed by the Gillard government. Government of Australia, Department of Immigration and Citizenship 2011.

28 See MacIntyre and Clark 2003. A very similar story played out in Canada around the same time.

29 A significant exception to this tendency is Lowe 1999.

30 See Clarkson 2002 and 2008; Bow 2009; Lennox 2009; Griffiths 2009.

31 This section draws on Coleman, Pauly, and Brydon 2008, 1–20.

32 Russell 2004.

33 David Smith 2010.

34 For clarity on this subject, we are indebted to William Coleman.

35 A good example is found in a book published by the current leader of the Australian opposition, Tony Abbott. See Abbott 2009.

36 Bell 2007a.

37 McRoberts 1997, 55.

38 Parliament of Canada 1971.

39 Ibid.

40 Ibid.

41 See Klotz and Vucetic, Chapters 4 and 5, respectively, in this book.

42 Cox 2005, 680.

43 Ibid., 154.

44 Bouchard and Taylor 2008, 121.

45 Forbes 2007, 41.

46 See Simeon 2006; Gagnon and Iacovinco 2007; Kymlicka 1996; and Taylor 1992 and 2004.

47 Taylor 1993, 176–7.

48 See Government of Australia, Department of Immigration and Citizenship 2010, 6.

49 See Evans 1991.

50 For one integration of these kinds of arguments, see Tow and Albinski 2002.

51 Goetzmann 2009, xiii.

7

DIPLOMATIC CULTURES

Multiple Wests and identities in US–Canada and US–Mexico relations

Brian Bow and Arturo Santa-Cruz[1]

What difference does the "Anglo-American" connection make to relations between states, and how exactly does it make that difference? Others have looked for answers by starting with the US–UK relationship and moving on to compare with other pairs.[2] We think we can get new perspective on the way the United States relates to the world, and more specifically about how the USA fits into "the West," through a focused comparison of the US–Canada and US–Mexico relationships. On the face of it, the comparison is straightforward: Canada and Mexico are both next-door neighbors to the USA, both dependent on the USA for security and economic growth, and both deeply interspersed demographically with American society. But whereas Canada shares in the same "Anglo-American" heritage as the USA, and US–Canada relations have historically been close and cooperative, Mexico comes out of an entirely different tradition – "western," but not "Anglo" – and US–Mexico relations have historically been distant and mutually exasperating. This first-glance characterization does capture some of the essential differences, but it misses some of the most interesting aspects in each of these complex and subtle diplomatic relationships. Each is characterized by both attraction and repulsion, and in each case, these conflicting impulses are reflective of underlying tensions within each society's concept of itself and its place in the world.

In this chapter, we explore the very different "diplomatic cultures" governing US–Canada and US–Mexico relations, in historical and comparative perspective. From its adversarial beginnings in the nineteenth century, the US–Canada relationship has evolved into one of the world's closest and most cooperative partnerships, characterized by consultation, self-restraint, and extensive and often deeply integrative policy coordination and collaboration. This "special relationship" seems to have become less so since the high point of bilateral relations in the 1950s and 1960s, but it is still generally extraordinarily "easy" and rewarding for both countries. US–Mexico relations, on the other hand, have historically been characterized by a sense of distance and mistrust. Though the scale and complexity of bilateral connections have grown immensely over the last twenty years, overall the US–Mexico relationship is still far less close and cooperative. These different modes of diplomacy are partly attributable to the different levels of economic development in Canada and Mexico, but they also stem from very different ideas about national identity and international relationship within each pair, and those ideas have evolved over time.

Diplomatic culture and national identity

We see the comparison of the US–Canada and US–Mexico relationships as especially useful for exploring one of the core problems in International Relations theory: understanding the bases for stable peace and cooperation between strong and weak powers. The conventional approach is to think about this in terms of a strategic bargain: the United States, as the dominant power in the international system, secures the compliance of less powerful states like Canada and Mexico by accepting limits on its own power and/or by opening up pathways for the smaller partners to influence collective decision-making.[3] This arrangement is often described by academics in terms of a transaction, based on sterile, free-floating interests – that is, the calculating and re-calculating of a quid pro quo. But policymakers tend to think about relations between states in terms of *relationships*, grounded in ideas about friendship, trust, and obligation, or the absence or violation of these elements.

These ideas about the nature of the relationship are rooted in the structural realities of the pairing, the history of the states' previous interactions, and each society's underlying beliefs about identity, community, and political and social "compatibility." The working out of grand bargains between strong and weak thus always takes place within a larger social context, and these structures shape the process and outcomes of bilateral bargaining.[4] The United States, as the stronger state, seeks to cultivate a sense of partnership with Canada and Mexico, and the recognition of an obligation to compliance, based on supposed common values and purposes. Canada and Mexico also try to play up shared identity and purposes in their dealings with the USA, to encourage it to accept an obligation to self-restraint. Where those arguments resonate with the other state's ideas about its own purposes and place in the world – as they often do in the US–Canada relationship – we see the development of a richer framework of bargaining norms, both in the sense that there are more norms in play and that compliance with those norms is more reflexive. Where they do not resonate – as in US–Mexico relations – they provoke a skeptical response and may reinforce a sense of difference and distance. Yet even where there is no mutual identification or obligation, states can still work out tacit understandings about how to avoid unintended provocations and where to look for acceptable trade-offs.

We refer to these relationship-specific bundles of bargaining norms as "diplomatic cultures," and our main aim in this chapter is to describe and explain the differences between the diplomatic cultures in which the US–Canada and US–Mexico relationships are rooted, and their evolution over time.[5] Scholars like Hedley Bull, Adam Watson, and James Der Derian have employed the phrase, but usually to refer to what we might call "the culture of diplomacy (or of diplomats)": a framework of diplomatic norms and practices that connects (and defines) the members of "international society" as a community of "civilized" states or (in some formulations) as the global community of states.[6] We also think about diplomatic culture as a framework of norms and practices; but whereas English School theorists are interested in the diplomatic community, we are interested in *the* variety of *diplomatic* communities across different groupings of states and in the way those cultures are grounded on wider notions of identity. Previous studies have outlined important differences in the diplomatic cultures of West and East, and the resulting frictions between them;[7] here, we highlight some of the variegation *within the West*, as a refraction of multiple traditions within western societies.

As in the pioneering work by Bull and Watson, we see diplomatic cultures as defined by practices, and thus closely related to what Emanuel Adler and others have called "communities of practice"[8] – in this case a set of shared bargaining norms and rituals that have been identified as supportive to the proper "management" of the bilateral relationship. Diplomatic culture is more encompassing (and so analytically slipperier) than Adler's communities of practice, because it refers not only to the specific practices that define and reproduce the relevant network of negotiators, but also the underlying conceptions of national identity and the broader symbolic landscape that informs their arguments and counter-arguments about practice. Diplomatic cultures are shaped by inter-state interaction, but because they ultimately depend on policymakers' ideas about national identity and community, they are also influenced by domestic political debates about national identity and the country's place in the world.

Conventional rational choice treatments of international relations tend to set diplomacy aside, and to see inter-state interaction as taking place in a social vacuum. But, as Harold Nicolson describes in his study of diplomacy's evolution, even societies with virtually nothing in common can develop common diplomatic practices, like raising a white flag to call for a ceasefire in war;[9] these are the most basic sorts of diplomatic cultures. Where diplomatic cultures are very "thick," as in US–Canada relations, negotiators share not only a store of common experiences that rationalize and reinforce specific diplomatic norms and practices, but also an overarching sense of common purposes and values. Where diplomatic cultures are "thinner," as in the US–Mexico relationship – and indeed in most international relationships – there is no such feeling of commonality and trust. Yet, through experience, diplomats may learn enough about one another's priorities and sensitivities to anticipate their responses to certain bargaining "moves," and thereby develop a set of tacit understandings about how to manage the diplomatic relationship and avoid conflict. The US–Mexico relationship is not like all others, or even exactly like US relations with other Latin American states: though bilateral relations are characterized by distance and mistrust, the two countries' diplomats have learned to signal their commitment to certain forms of self-restraint through discourse and practice.

Though there have been few attempts to parse it out, the diplomatic culture that has governed US–Canada relations is an especially rich and complex one, which has had important effects on bilateral bargaining outcomes over the last sixty years. Among the core elements are an expectation of continuous, informal consultation; a strong attachment to "quiet diplomacy"; and a norm against making coercive "linkages" between issues.[10] These follow from a general tendency to think about bilateral differences as common problems, and a shared inclination to seek "technical" (that is, not "political") solutions, either through informal coordination or via more formal kinds of integration. US self-restraint in relations with Canada is based in part on enlightened self-interest, but it also seems to reflect a genuine sense of obligation. In US–Mexico relations, there are far fewer of these diplomatic "rules of the game," and very little sense of mutual obligation. The "thinner" diplomatic culture that prevailed through most of the twentieth century was predicated on a tacit quid pro quo: the USA held back from blatant meddling in Mexican affairs and put up with Mexican criticism of US decisions, with the expectation that Mexican leaders would maintain domestic political stability, not interfere with US investments and other interests in Mexico, and refrain from challenging the USA on important regional issues.[11] US diplomats recognize that their arrangement takes this particular form because of Mexico's deeply rooted anxiety about foreign intervention; but the real basis for US self-restraint seems to be calculations about how best to avoid problems that would follow from instability on the southern border.

As an "exceptionalist" power, the USA has historically been torn between liberalism and empire, and the resolution of this apparent tension has been one of the defining themes in American diplomacy.[12] Students of US foreign policy often mistakenly see this as one dilemma, or assume that the USA responds to it in the same way in all contexts. But a comparison of the US–Canada and US–Mexico relationships helps us to see that the United States reconciles these conflicting impulses in different ways within the context of different international relationships, and the way that these differences are at least partly anchored in domestic debates about the nature of America's national identity and purposes. It can also help us with the more specific problem of the United States' place in the West, and the "Anglo-American" community as a pivotal grouping within it. As Peter Katzenstein explains in the introductory chapter to this volume, the West is both plural and pluralist, and the United States "fits" into the West in a variety of different ways, revealing different sides of itself in the process. In the nineteenth and early twentieth centuries, Americans tended to think about the West in much the same way that Europeans did, as a community of countries with ("western") European traditions, and in terms of "white" race and

Christian religion. But the USA also imagined itself as part of a new West: the western hemisphere, often referred to then as "the New World." In his farewell address, Thomas Jefferson expressed the hope that the countries of the hemisphere would coalesce "in an American system of policy"; a few years later, he wrote that the governments to be formed in the nascent states "will be American governments, no longer to be involved in the never-ceasing broils of Europe...America has a hemisphere to itself. It must have a separate system of interest which must not be subordinated to those of Europe." The defining characteristic of this "separate system of interests" would be the form of government for its constituent units: republicanism.[13] Jefferson's statements were, according to Arthur P. Whitaker, "the first flowering" of the Western Hemisphere Idea (WHI).[14] Thus, when the Monroe Doctrine was formulated a decade later, it was received by Mexico's first president, Guadalupe Victoria, as a "memorable promise" on Washington's part.[15]

There was, however, a deep fault line running through the hemisphere, between the United States and the Latin American states. For the latter, the principle of non-intervention was of equal or greater importance to the lofty ideals and commonality of interests that Washington emphasized. The USA came to unconditionally accept the non-intervention principle only in the second half of the 1930s. It was this composite understanding – as reflected, for instance, in the 1948 charter of the Organization of American States (OAS), which emphasizes both representative democracy and the sovereign independence of the American states – that has constituted the WHI.

Canada, on the other hand, was seen as a part of the other West – of "western civilization" – as defined by race, religion, and "shared history." As a fellow "settler" society, Canada was viewed as different from the European members of the community. Many Americans, especially the advocates of "manifest destiny," saw that shared experience as an important link with the USA.[16] But because Canada did not break away from the British empire, it was still seen by most Americans as an outpost of Europe in the New World and therefore separate from the rest of the hemisphere. By the time Canada emerged as an independent international player in the middle of the twentieth century, US and UK elites were struggling to build "western" alliances for World War II and the Cold War, and Canada was eager to support its two most important partners. Canada's membership in NATO helped to reinforce the alliance's claim to be a genuinely "transatlantic" community, and Canada hoped to serve as a bridge between the USA and its European allies. Though this arrangement sometimes put Canadian foreign policymakers in an awkward position – as during the tensions between the USA and UK during the Suez Crisis – for the most part they prized Canada's emplacement within the "transatlantic" community because it created opportunities to influence US strategy and diplomacy, increased the country's international stature and opened doors to influence in the UN and G8, and – equally importantly – served as a basis for national pride that appealed to both anglophone and francophone Canadians.

The end of the Cold War shook up US policymakers' map of the world, and regional dynamics became much more salient. Canada (reluctantly) joined the OAS, and Mexico began to experiment with democracy and freer markets. Since the North American Free Trade Agreement (NAFTA) came into effect in 1994, both Canada and Mexico have been increasingly recognized by their common neighbor as partners within a distinct subregion of the western hemisphere: a newly imagined, tri-national "North America." The consolidation of a robust North American regional community would be a historical development comparable with the integration of Europe, in the sense that it would depend on building sturdy bridges between several different, partially discordant "western" traditions. So far, however, those divergent worldviews have mainly been a source of tensions among the three governments, and have tended to work against meaningful regional integration.[17]

Americans have historically had a tendency to overestimate their similarities with Canadians, and their differences with Mexicans – not just in terms of their economic and political development, but also in terms of the more fundamental "civilizational" traits in which these second-order differences are thought to be rooted. In the nineteenth and early twentieth centuries, these differences were usually talked about in the language of race and religion, and since then more often in the language of "values." When Americans think about Canadians (which is not very often), they tend to imagine them as white, Anglo-Saxon, Protestant, individualist, liberal-market, and democratic; when they think about Mexicans, they often imagine them as not-white ("Hispanic"), Catholic, collectivist/corporatist, authoritarian, and corrupt. Those perceptions are grounded in real differences between the two countries, of course, but they gloss over the great diversity and contradictions in Canadian and Mexican societies. There is more going on here than simple stereotyping. Over-drawing those similarities and differences helps to reinforce a particular way of thinking about what defines the United States and its place in the world. The idea of a special relationship with Canada supports the image of the USA as an instinctively benevolent leader, bilaterally and within a larger Anglo-American or transatlantic community. Imagining that special relationship as one predicated on "shared values," echoing past formulations of the "Anglo-Saxon" idea, can – depending on the context – reinforce libertarian arguments about America's self-defining commitment to free markets and small government, and/or nativist arguments about the USA as a country defined by European (racial) origins and cultural traditions. And the image of Mexico as alien, backward, and dangerous serves to reinforce a traditionalist conception of the United States as a unitary society, defined by white, Anglo-Saxon, Protestant (WASP) values, and more generally supports a "clash of civilizations" view of America's place in the wider world. As we will explain below, however, there has been some rethinking of these old images of Canada and Mexico, and contention over those images has become more explicitly entangled in the United States' domestic culture wars.

Like their US counterparts, Canadian and Mexican diplomats have to be careful to reconcile what they say about the nature of the bilateral relationships with their own national identity narratives, and with domestic demands for the assertion of national distinctiveness and autonomy. Of course, the stakes are much higher (at least with respect to these particular bilateral relationships) in Ottawa and Mexico City. Both countries are naturally deeply concerned with their autonomy in the face of overshadowing American power; but Canadians are also worried about defining and reinforcing what makes Canada separate and distinct, and Mexicans are perpetually preoccupied with recognition and respect.

Canadian elites have long seen a special connection between their country, Britain, and the United States, based on language, religion, and ethnicity. In the late nineteenth and early twentieth centuries, Canadian policymakers were mainly concerned with improving their position within the empire, and their relations with the USA went through London. Many were receptive to arguments coming out of the USA and Britain during this period, about a natural community of "Anglo-Saxon" nations destined to play a leading role in world politics. But because of its substantial francophone population and the mythology of "two founding nations," the new country's leaders had to be careful about openly embracing this way of thinking about the relationship. During and after World War II, Canadian elites embraced the idea of a special relationship with the United States, as part of their efforts to secure US foreign direct investment (FDI) and gain influence on US foreign policy. The Cold War reinforced the perception of shared ("western") values and purposes, but it also brought about diplomatic clashes which tested it, particularly the war in Vietnam. Yet even after the end of the Cold War, bilateral tensions have always given way to an impulse to "restore" the relationship, and a renewal of narratives about shared values and purposes.

Yet there is also a powerful and enduring impulse in Canada to maintain difference and distance from the United States. Since the American Revolution, "English Canadian" elites have often fanned the flames of anti-Americanism, casting the USA as a threatening external Other, in order to reinforce their own particular conception of national Self – be it imperialist or nationalist, liberal or Tory, isolationist or internationalist. (Francophone Canadian elites have of course always had in mind an entirely different national Self, and for them it was English Canada that was the relevant Other, not the United States.) Since the 1980s, demographic and political changes in Canada seem to have attenuated the impulse to strike independent poses; yet US personalities and policies – like George W. Bush's rush to war in Iraq – can still trigger outbursts of anti-Americanism.

Mexicans have deep but conflicting feelings about their relationship with the United States. Some have seen the USA as a model for what Mexico could be, and as the natural leader of a broader hemispheric community. But the predominant view of the USA is as a threatening and disdainful external Other, whose aggressiveness and excesses help to define Mexico's more conservative and communitarian national Self.

After Mexico's devastating defeat by the USA in the 1846–48 war and the failed experience of a French-supported emperor (1863–67), its leaders hoped to establish a distant but cordial relationship with the United States, based on mutual recognition. After the Mexican revolution (1910–20), the USA did exercise some self-restraint in its dealings with Mexico (in marked contrast with many other Latin American states) – but only as a strategy to reinforce domestic stability in Mexico and avoid the disruptions that might follow from any serious weakening of the post-revolutionary regime. In the Cold War context, with Washington's aggressive anticommunist crusade in the continent, the tension between the two constitutive principles of the hemispheric normative structure was evident – and the Latin American states became highly sensitive about US intervention. As a Mexican diplomat and scholar on foreign relations put it ten years after the OAS had come into existence, "[w]hile this fear exists…the cornerstone of the [I]nter-American system, its guiding principle, will not be democracy, but intransigent non-intervention."[18] However, Mexican diplomats also tried to play up the two countries' common membership in the western hemisphere community, as when president Alemán referred to the United States as a "strong and prosperous" country that struggled with the "immense responsibilities" it had to bear "under the moral sign of democracy."[19] Over the last twenty years, Mexican leaders have struggled to reinvent the relationship and to try to secure greater influence and autonomy. There are some signs that their efforts might eventually pay off, but for now there is still a sense of estrangement and mutual frustration, which has seriously undercut efforts to tackle transnational challenges like immigration and organized crime.

US–Canada relations: rethinking the special relationship

The best place to begin thinking about the evolution of US–Canada relations is with US–UK relations. As the original "special relationship," the US–UK is sometimes touted as a model for others, having evolved in less than a century from enmity and violence into stable peace and close partnership.[20] But Americans' thinking about their relationship to Britain is much more subtle and complex than that, a fact that we must grasp before we can understand the United States' relationship with Canada. Before the American Revolution, most residents of the thirteen colonies identified with a very broad "British" or Anglo-Saxon community, made up of "mother England" and her far-flung settler "daughters" (that is, the territories that would become the USA, Canada, Australia, and New Zealand), often referred to collectively as a single, world-spanning "nation." Many colonists felt little attachment to the empire per se, and most had grievances of one kind or another against the crown; but their sense of a separate "American" identity was still unformed and directionless.[21] Unlike most subsequent national revolutions, the American Revolution could not be predicated on ethnic differences, so it had to be driven entirely by philosophical and institutional or legal claims. Revolutionary leaders focused most of their anger on crown and court, but there was also a stirring of animosity against the British people, and the depth of this estrangement was visible in the subsequent popular opposition to the Jay Treaty. After the war of 1812, US anxiety about another British attack faded, giving way to strategic rapprochement and formal demilitarization of the US–Canada border.[22] Though latent rivalry and diplomatic tensions endured through the century, by the close of the Venezuela Crisis in 1895 the prospect of war had dissipated, and the two powers had begun to forge a lasting partnership. This reconciliation made possible, and was in turn fueled by, growing enthusiasm for "Anglo-Saxonism" in both countries, and by elite support for the idea of some sort of Anglo-American union or association.[23]

Even after Canada was constituted as a (virtually) independent entity in the 1860s, most Americans tended to think of it simply as an extension of the British empire, and some of their new affection for Britain in the late nineteenth century was transferred to Canada. Because Canada remained in orbit around Britain, it was not until World War I that the USA and Canada began to develop a meaningful diplomatic relationship. World War II compelled the two countries to work very closely together, particularly with respect to joint production and transport of war matériel. Officials from the two governments found it exceptionally easy to work with one another, based on common language, priorities, and perceptions of major global issues. And politicians in both countries were generally inclined to allow career officials to work closely with their cross-border counterparts with relatively little political interference, fostering the creation of informal inter-bureaucratic and military-to-military networks across a wide variety of agencies and offices. These connections were extended and deepened in the early Cold War years, as Britain's decline forced Canada to actively pursue the USA as a security guarantor and source of FDI. Between 1945 and 1970, the share of Canadian exports going to the USA went up from about 50 percent to just under 70 percent; by 1966 the US share of all FDI in Canada had reached a staggering 82 percent.[24]

Reliance on Britain had been one thing, but deep interdependence with the United States was something else entirely, and Canadian elites made it known in Washington that they and their constituents were uneasy about this new arrangement. They therefore pressed their American counterparts for frequent demonstrations of self-restraint, through verbal reaffirmations of and practical adherence to a set of informal "rules of the game": continuous consultation, quiet diplomacy, and foreswearing of coercive issue-linkages.[25] Americans were receptive to these calls for reassurance, because they resonated with and reinforced their own national self-image as a generous and fair-minded alliance leader and trade partner. At the same time, Canada was taking a place within the newly imagined "transatlantic" community, anchored in NATO, and the framework of bargaining norms that undergirded it, including strong expectations of consultation and compromise.[26]

Within this set of shared understandings, US and Canadian officials were able to put together extraordinarily extensive and intensive forms of policy coordination.

Most of the strictly bilateral cooperation between them was informal, taking the form of negotiated "gentlemen's agreements" and special exemptions, predicated on flexible compromises and diffuse reciprocity. Other issues were managed through joint panels of experts such as the International Joint Commission, which could pass non-binding judgments on the governments' adherence to past agreements. A few were resolved through highly integrative formal regimes, such as the Auto Pact and the Defense Production Sharing Agreement – the most extraordinary of them being the North American Aerospace Defense Command (NORAD), which features an integrated "bi-national" command structure, with US officers serving under Canadian commanders, and vice versa.

Most of the American officials that dealt most often with Canadian issues had a good understanding of the basic political and developmental challenges that drove Canadian policy choices, but few really understood Canadian political culture or the differences between the two societies. American elites have always tended to oversimplify Canada and take it for granted, seeing it as pretty much the same as the United States. They do not do this out of disrespect; as Charles Doran has explained, "when Americans assert that Canadians are just like Americans, Americans think they are conferring an honor, or at least sharing something that is distinctive and valuable."[27] But the effect is nevertheless to deny Canadians the thing they are most insecure about: a coherent and distinctive national identity. When it comes to the diplomatic management of the bilateral relationship, this presumption of similarity has been a double-edged sword. On one hand, it has encouraged US policymakers to assume that the two countries' interests are naturally convergent, and therefore to give Canada the benefit of the doubt on controversial new initiatives and grant it special exemptions from US foreign and domestic policies. On the other hand, that same presumption has sometimes made them indignant and vindictive in response to divergent Canadian policies, particularly with respect to investment policy and international diplomacy. When Canada tried to play an active role in brokering a diplomatic compromise prior to the 2003 war in Iraq, for example, many in the Bush administration were genuinely surprised (despite Canada's track record of support for the UN system), and tended to interpret Canada's choices in terms of disloyalty and domestic political opportunism. Successive US governments have been supportive of Ottawa in its ongoing struggle to hold the Canadian federation together, since that is obviously in the United States' interest; but they often fail to understand the forces behind the sovereignty movement in Quebec, as well as the importance of provincial politics in driving Canadian trade and investment policies.

Just as the US presumption that the two societies were essentially similar was awkward for Canada as a country desperately seeking a rationale for its own separate existence, so too were early American allusions to a world-spanning "Anglo-American" nation – or to the US–Canada relationship as one cemented by WASP values – for a country with a large and politically coherent francophone population that was neither Anglo-Saxon nor Protestant.[28] These arguments became even more inflammatory in Canada in the 1960s, with the integration of a new cohort of talented francophones into the federal civil service, and the eruption of a radicalized independence movement in Quebec. Over the next couple of decades, moreover, Canada changed its immigration policies to admit more non-European immigrants and adopted official multiculturalism, recently moving to emphasize the importance of its native population within the multicultural mosaic. As Pauly and Reus-Smit argue in Chapter 6 in this volume, multiculturalism was useful for Ottawa as a way to deflect and submerge Quebec's claims to special rights and privileges, and to encourage the integration of new immigrants, without undercutting the social and political predominance of established "Anglo-Saxon" values. Whatever the domestic political rationale behind these policy choices, the diplomatic effect was to further undercut overtly racial and religious rationales for bilateral partnership with the USA, and to sublimate them in a new discourse referring to shared values. Whereas "English Canadian" elites had been receptive to arguments about racial and religious compatibility in the nineteenth and early twentieth centuries, by the early Cold War years they had begun to downplay these arguments, preferring instead to talk about a bilateral relationship predicated on partnership and "good neighborliness." But even these new rationales were almost always underpinned by themes and images rooted in the old symbolic land-scape, in references to family and kinship or to common values that had previously been touted as distinctively "Anglo-Saxon" (for example, individualism, rule of law, and free markets).

Many of the diplomatic frictions between the USA and Canada in the twentieth century stemmed from the two countries' different ways of thinking about the role of the state in the economy and in society. Like the United States, Canada is a generally liberal society, but historically Canadians have collectively been much more receptive to state intervention to organize and stimulate economic develop-ment, remedy regional inequalities, and protect the interests of minorities and the less fortunate. There is controversy about whether this is traceable to Canada's geographical and demographic challenges, to its parliamentary institutions, or to Tory or "Red Tory" influences inherited from the original British colonists.[29] Whatever the reasons, this philosophical divide has generated policy divergences that create the potential for diplomatic tensions. In the early Cold War years these differences were brushed under the carpet, to be "managed" through informal compromises and exceptions; but they triggered severe tensions after the early 1970s, particularly over Canadian investment regulations. After the clashes of the early 1980s, Canadian elites' worldviews moved to the right, following the shifts already going on in the UK and the USA, and with an eye to the implications of economic globalization, subsequent Canadian governments undertook a variety of policy changes designed to minimize or prevent these frictions. The divide seems to have narrowed, but it has not yet been closed, and we still see these kinds of differences in economic and social policies. This is jarring for some American pro-ponents of the Anglosphere idea, who want to argue that the "English-speaking" societies are joined by their shared commitment to free markets and small govern-ment, and yet are often confronted with Canadian (and British and Australian and

New Zealander) policies that seem to contradict this reading of what is distinctive about "Anglo" societies. Nevertheless, conservatives in both the USA and Canada still find such "shared values" arguments to be useful as a rationale for closer bilateral connections and for their own favored domestic policies.

The tensions of the 1970s and early 1980s opened the door for the free trade agreement and to even higher levels of economic and social interdependence. But they also undermined the "special" quality of US–Canada diplomacy. America's relative decline made it less tolerant of free-riding by allies and partners, and more likely to begrudge Canada for the "sweetheart" deals signed in the early postwar years. The post-Watergate fragmentation of foreign policy decision-making in the USA disrupted transgovernmental networks and made it harder for central foreign policy officials to "manage" the relationship according to the old norms and practices. There were also growing doubts – on both sides of the border – about the old rationales for partnership. The Trudeau government's efforts to strengthen the federal government through greater intervention in the economy triggered hostile responses in Washington. And the war in Vietnam and Reagan's "peace through strength" strategy provoked strong negative reactions from Canadians more committed to multilateral diplomacy. These shocks prompted many in Canada to second-guess their close relationship with the USA, and to wonder whether they might have more in common with Europeans or even with potential partners in the developing world.[30]

The recession of 1981–83 and the resulting wave of Congressional protectionism crushed Trudeau's interventionist ambitions and drove Canadian elites to think about how they might renew their partnership with the United States. The Mulroney government, in pursuing friendlier relations with the Reagan administration, returned to the language of shared values and purposes, citing "a common heritage of individual liberty, shared democratic values of freedom and justice, vast commercial links, and…an open and undefended border."[31] Mulroney's efforts were well received in Washington but raised suspicion at home, with critics arguing that his pursuit of free trade with the USA was a Faustian bargain that would undermine Canada's political autonomy and cultural distinctiveness. Opponents condemned Mulroney's pro-market agenda as a "parroting" of American ideas, and supporters were compelled to try to make the case that theirs was a legitimately "home-grown" free market liberalism. Even mainstream opposition to free trade was tinged with classic anti-American themes and sentiments, including portrayals of the USA as inherently lawless, rapacious, and domineering. Mulroney ultimately won re-election in 1988, however, and the free trade agreement was quickly ratified. The economic expansion that followed seemed to wipe away popular anxieties stirred up by the prospect of free trade, and some observers thought that debate might be looked back on as the "last gasp" for anti-Americanism in Canada.[32] Yet new outbreaks during the Iraq war and missile defense debates proved that anti-Americanism in Canada might be somewhat diminished, but it was not dead.[33]

American attitudes toward Canada are also in flux, with potentially profound implications for bilateral relations. After Canada scaled back its contributions to

NATO in the 1970s, American policymakers were less inclined to think of it as an important member of the transatlantic community; the winding down of the Cold War and subsequent tensions between the USA and European allies only reinforced that tendency. After the signing of the free trade agreements, US officials increasingly thought of Canada as part of the western hemisphere, and more particularly as a "North American" country. In 1998, the State Department formally pulled its Canada desk out of the European Affairs Bureau, shifting it to the Western Hemisphere Bureau, specifically into the Canada, Mexico, and NAFTA issues desk. This did not necessarily imply any weakening of the diplomatic relationship or any diminution of mutual identification between the two countries. But it does seem to reflect Canada's relegation to America's regional "backyard," and could mean that Canada can expect to be treated less like a transatlantic friend and more like a hemispheric neighbor. Some foreign policy figures in Canada have therefore urged their government to try to break out of the "North America" box, by rejecting trilateralism and trying to revive the old bilateral "special relationship," and/or by rebuilding Canada's profile as an international player.[34] Proponents of these strategies – especially advocates of bilateralism – have justified their positions, and recommended that Ottawa seek closer relations with the USA, with familiar references to a "special relationship" based on shared values and purposes.

At the same time, US elites have begun to recognize significant cultural differences between the two societies, as reflected in Canadian domestic policies. American conservatives have expressed deep frustration with Canadian policies on gun control, same-sex marriage, medical marijuana, and universal health care. These policy divergences, in combination with Canada's supposed "disloyalty" on Iraq and missile defense, prompted many to question whether Canadians were really "just like" Americans, and a few even to condemn the northern neighbor as a degenerate anti-model for the USA.[35] Ironically, some of those spouting this kind of "anti-Canadianism" have also been among the most prominent backers of the "Anglosphere" concept, and of the myth of a unified "Anglo-American" worldview and historical mission. Thus the question of what Canada represents, and how it relates to the United States, seems to have become more deeply entangled in America's own national identity debates, and that will no doubt have important effects on the long-term evolution of the bilateral diplomatic relationship.

US–Mexico relations: the other continental divide

The United States saw Mexico's independence in 1821 mainly as an opportunity for territorial expansion – one that was realized in 1845, 1848, and 1854 – but also as the emergence of a troubled neighbor that would require US tutelage and direction. By the late nineteenth century, although Mexico had largely ceased to be thought of as an opportunity for further aggrandizement, it continued to be perceived as a backward country in need of US guidance. In 1914, President Wilson noted that his government intended "to show our neighbors to the south that their interests are identical with our interests," and told a British diplomat that he planned to "teach the South American republics to elect good men."[36] Mexico, on the other hand, has from its inception as an independent country had a national obsession with the United States, an overshadowing figure, both feared and admired. By the end of the 1910–20 revolution, however, it had become clear that the USA also represented an opportunity – as a market for Mexican products, as a source of investment, and as a destination for migrants looking for work. The post-revolutionary regime therefore developed a pragmatic approach to its economic policy, undertaking a highly protectionist economic model while at the same time pursuing close contacts and cooperation with US economic authorities and investors.

The ideological and civilizational links between the United States and Mexico have been evident since the latter's establishment. US elites saw their country as naturally suited to be the nucleus of an emergent hemispheric community, united by republicanism and close economic relations. As Henry Clay put it in 1820: "It is in our power to create a system of which we shall be the center....In relation to South America, the United States will occupy the same position as the people of New England to the rest of the United States."[37] The idea that the United States should be at the center of the New World was at the core of the above-mentioned "Western Hemisphere Idea" (WHI). Washington's condescending attitude, a republicanism that was both "emancipatory and imperial," was part and parcel of the emerging hemispheric diplomatic culture.[38] In Mexico, on the other hand, as in other countries of the hemisphere, there was a tenuous sense of identity based on separation from Europe and the sharing of a distinct political space: (the) America(s). Moreover, the USA soon became a role model for some Mexican elites. Many influential independence leaders not only found its political system alluring, but also perceived the United States as a natural ally in their emancipatory struggle. Although Mexico indeed adopted the US constitution "as [its] model, and copied it with considerable accuracy" the problem was that, as de Tocqueville noted in 1839, Mexican leaders were "unable to create or to introduce the spirit and the sense which give it life."[39]

The cultural divide between Mexico and the United States was not all that surprising; it was a "transplanted frontier," a replay of the political–religious conflict that had plagued Europe two centuries before.[40] The fact that Catholicism remained the only valid religion in Mexico for decades after independence had a profound effect on the bilateral relationship, mainly because Catholicism was largely abhorred in the United States during the nineteenth century.

The racial element was also present in the New World context, with a range of white supremacist discourses becoming hegemonic both internally and in US relations with its hemispheric neighbors.[41] Though both conservative and liberal Mexican elites' perceptions of the indigenous population ranged from the condescending to the blatantly racist, miscegenation was widespread in mid-nineteenth-century Mexico. At the time of the 1846–48 war, the *Richmond Whig* described the hostilities between the two countries in terms of "the Caucasian and Anglo-Saxon, pure white blood, against a mixed and mongrel race, composed of Indians, Negroes, and Spaniards, all three degenerated by the admixture of blood and colors."[42] As John Calhoun noted in Congress in 1848, "Ours, sir, is the Government of the white race."[43]

Since the mid-nineteenth century, Mexico and Mexicans had become intertwined with domestic cleavages in the United States. As the New York *Gazette* warned in 1847, "[w]hen the foreign war ends, *the domestic war will begin*."[44] The annexation of Mexican territory thus deepened the political struggles that would lead to the Civil War, particularly through its impact on the slavery issue. In addition to the Mexicans already in the USA, the prospects of increased Mexican immigration were perceived as a threat to the US body politic.[45]

The war, however, had other effects on the US character and practices that were bound to impact the emerging diplomatic culture. As President Polk noted, "the results of the war with Mexico have given the United States a national character which our country never before enjoyed";[46] this newly gained self-confidence, in turn, contributed to the adoption of a more overt use of Anglo-Saxonist discourse in US relations with its southern neighbor.[47] As Theodore Roosevelt stated in 1896: "It is to the interest of civilization that the English speaking race should be dominant in South Africa, exactly as it is...that the United States...should be dominant in the Western Hemisphere."[48]

The divide between the USA and Mexico was also echoed in domestic politics within Mexico. The profound upheavals in Mexican society were driven by deep political and ideological cleavages – to some extent a reflection of the "great American dichotomy" between Anglo-America and (what would later came to be known as) Latin America.[49] While Mexican conservatives looked "back" to Spain for inspiration, liberals advocated constitutional republicanism and looked to the USA as a role model and ally. Even Mexico's devastating defeats in the mid-nineteenth century did not dissuade liberals from their admiration for the USA. The liberal government of Juarez (1858–64), for example, sought US support in its war against the conservatives, and was prepared to grant Washington unprecedented concessions at the Tehuantepec Isthmus.[50] During the *Porfiriato*. (1876–1910), the ascendancy of "conservative liberalism" largely put an end to the fierce conservative–liberal battles of the past five decades. Díaz's approach to the United States was both distant and pragmatic: while diplomatic relations were not warm, US economic activities in Mexico increased exponentially during his three decades in power.

It was during the *Porfiriato* that the discourse on the *mestizo* as the synthesis of what it meant to be a Mexican was developed; but it was not elevated to official ideology until after the revolution. Although Indians were a pervasive presence in the political tumult of the revolution, the movement contained no Indian "ideology" or "Indian" political project. Rather, the revolution brought forth an *indigenist* discourse whose goal was to incorporate the Indian into the body politic. Notwithstanding their deep misgivings about miscegenation in Mexico, American elites came to accept the Indian component – particularly the *mestizo* character – of its neighbor's much-cherished (new) identity.[51] As journalist and politician Ernest

Gruening put it in the early 1930s, the USA was still assimilating the "discovery" that Mexico was "an Indian land" next to which "[w]e are to live side by side."[52]

The revolutionary leaders – like Díaz before them – adeptly avoided alienating the American people or their government by refraining from blatant anti-American discourse. However, some provisions of the 1917 revolutionary constitution, particularly those limiting the rights of foreigners to own land in Mexican territory and those establishing the subsoil as national patrimony, not only caused concern in the United States but also contributed to Washington's withholding of recognition of the post-revolutionary regime. For the new Mexican government, obtaining US recognition was paramount, for two reasons: the need to establish solid diplomatic and economic relations with the wider international community, which generally awaited a signal from Washington to bestow its recognition on the new Mexican government; and the need for a guarantee that the USA would not sell arms or give refuge to rebel revolutionary factions.

Diplomatic relations were reestablished in late 1923. By then, Mexico City had clearly shown its willingness to accommodate US interests, while Washington demonstrated that it understood its southern neighbor's need for dignified treatment. The United States recognized as well the great strides the post-revolutionary regime had made in achieving social stability, and had come to realize that this stability was its primary interest in relations with its southern neighbor. From then on, the bilateral relationship would be defined by Mexico's recognition of some fundamental US interests and its regional ascendancy, and the United States' hands-off policy on Mexican political affairs. Thus, while many observers expected the USA to take forceful action when President Cárdenas nationalized the oil industry in 1938, Washington instead adopted a prudent, measured attitude, which kept the ensuing diplomatic conflict contained. Secretary of State Hull publicly affirmed US self-restraint in formal terms: "This government has not undertaken and does not undertake to question the right of the Government of Mexico in the exercise of its sovereign power to expropriate properties within its jurisdiction."[53] Franklin Roosevelt's government even referred to Mexico as a model for other poor countries, especially with respect to its agricultural sector.[54]

The fact that the post-revolutionary regime possessed all the trappings of democracy, including regular elections, was important – in terms of the WHI – to the peaceful coexistence the two countries had achieved by the early 1940s. But for Washington what was undoubtedly more important was Mexico's emergence as a pivotal arena for US regional security designs. US strategic planners were concerned about Nazi influence during World War II and then Soviet influence during the Cold War, and about securing Mexico's support (or at least avoiding its overt opposition) in deflecting extra-regional interference in the hemisphere.[55] In the longer run, though, the crucial consideration for the USA was the post-revolutionary regime's capacity to guarantee domestic political stability, and thereby guard against the extraordinary dislocations that might follow from a breakdown of order on the United States' southern flank. This combination of elements – formal democracy, tacit diplomatic support, and political stability – led

US policymakers to see Mexico's post-revolutionary regime as an asset, if not necessarily an ally or a real partner. Mexican negotiators played up the need to maintain the post-revolutionary regime's steady grip on power, and were thus able to persuade their US counterparts to refrain from (openly) intervening in Mexican affairs. Many in Washington continued to harbor condescending attitudes toward their southern neighbor, but gave up the practice of bluntly telling Mexico what was best for it.

Bilateral cooperation increased substantially during the war years and then lost steam, but the diplomatic relationship became more stable and predictable. The implicit understandings outlined above coalesced into a clear quid pro quo, which both sides came to accept as a set of (conditional) bargaining norms: the USA would refrain from (conspicuous) interference in Mexican domestic affairs as long as Mexico maintained political stability, and Mexico would accept US leadership on the continent as long as it was exercised within certain limits – for example, without violation of the norm of non-intervention. Indeed, Mexico became one of the hemisphere's staunchest supporters of the non-intervention principle. In the early 1930s, it promulgated the Estrada Doctrine, by which Mexico pledged to make no pronouncement regarding the granting or withholding of recognition to other governments, because that practice "hurts the sovereignty of the nations" whose regimes are being granted (or denied) recognition. Decades later, the non-intervention principle was formally enshrined in the constitution.

A bilateral diplomatic culture was taking form, but a very "thin" one, without a real sense of partnership or extensive compatibility of interests; yet it was clearly acceptable for both countries. And it was one that not only "fit" with the particular demands of the bilateral relationship, but also reflected the key premises of the WHI and helped to conceal some of the contradictions between those premises. There were, however, limits to public acknowledgment of these understandings, and of the bilateral cooperation that they enabled. For instance, although Mexico and the United States were in basic agreement on the threats that communism posed for the hemisphere, and collaborated fairly extensively in regional and international diplomatic forums, this cooperation was not openly talked about. Mexico thus maintained a nationalist rhetoric, a formally democratic regime, and a relatively independent foreign policy, while guaranteeing the USA a stable, non-communist neighbor.[56] Washington, for its part, replied in kind. In 1964, in the midst of a Mexican election, US Secretary of State Thomas Mann reminded his ambassador of "the magic words": "we do not intervene in Mexico's internal affairs."[57] Stability thus trumped democracy.

Mexico, however, remained suspicious and sensitive to the policies of its northern neighbor. The United States' 1969 "Operation Intercept" – which was ostensibly designed to stop drug trafficking at the border, but mostly created havoc in the movement of legal goods – and the 1971 "Nixon Shocks" undoubtedly contributed to mounting tensions within the bilateral relationship. When in the late 1970s the USA turned to Mexico for its recently discovered oil deposits, President López Portillo rebuked President Carter, noting that his country had "suddenly found itself in the center of American attention – attention that is a surprising mixture of interest, disdain and fear, much like the recurring vague fears you yourselves inspire in certain areas of our national subconscious."[58]

The already tense bilateral relationship was tested even further in the early and mid-1980s, when the Mexican economic model suddenly imploded. When it became known that the country was in dire straits, the Mexican finance minister was summoned to Washington. There, Treasury Secretary Regan warned him that Mexico faced a "serious problem," to which the Mexican official replied: "No, *we* [Mexico and the USA] face a serious problem." With Washington's help, Mexico was able to cope with the financial crisis, but it had become evident that its protectionist economic model had come to an end. A new group of government "technocrats" in Mexico began to push for a new paradigm, which emphasized exports, scaled back state intervention, and greater engagement with international economic institutions. US officials commended this change in the economic realm, and once more touted Mexico as a role model for other less developed countries. However, the United States' overall perception of its southern neighbor, and its foreign policy, were not substantially altered.

Another breakthrough came in the early 1990s. In a veritable about-face, President Salinas proposed to President Bush that their countries begin negotiations leading to a free trade area. This historic reversal was not driven by any new sense of closeness with the USA, but rather by fear that the opening of central and eastern Europe would draw western investment, and foreign capital would evaporate from Mexico. Surprisingly, though, Salinas's adventurous proposal was not poorly received domestically; for most Mexicans, signing a trade agreement with the northern neighbor meant first and foremost more investment and more jobs. The Bush administration was receptive to the Mexican initiative, considering it a "geopolitical priority" and hoping it might bring Mexican foreign policy more closely into line with that of the USA.[59] Given the historical legacy of mutual suspicion, the expediency and pragmatism with which both governments dealt with the new joint project was remarkable. As a European diplomat commented during the initial stages of the negotiation: "Call it the advantage of a special relationship, call it a double standard, but the United States clearly does treat Mexico differently [from other Latin American countries]."[60]

The USA and Mexico, however, were to remain "distant neighbors."[61] As the Mexican ambassador at the time would later admit, "The fact is that we will always be neighbors, we are partners now, but we will never be friends. For them, we do not have the stature to be treated as equals. That is the difference when they look north: they find the Canadians, who speak their language and reason like them; they are therefore offered the respectful treatment amity demands."[62] Indeed, during the debates surrounding the negotiation and ratification of NAFTA, opponents on the right and the left drew on a populist discourse which often portrayed Mexico as profoundly incompatible with the USA, in cultural or racial terms.

This historic restructuring of the bilateral relationship also raised difficult questions about Mexico's sense of national identity. The post-revolutionary regime's efforts to adapt to the transformation of the global economy by overhauling the relationship between state and market clearly conflicted with some of the Mexican Revolution's core ideals, undercut the corporatist institutions that kept the party in power, and threatened to intensify the deep tensions within the country between north and south, urban and rural, rich and poor. Even the question of race, long pushed out of view in Mexico, came again to the forefront on the very day that NAFTA came into effect, as the Zapatista rebellion in Chiapas state raised new demands from the indigenous peoples in the southern part of the country and challenged the "*mestizaje*" myth that the post-revolutionary regime had built decades before.

Economic relations became more institutionalized with NAFTA. The 1995 Mexico bailout was justified in the United States partly in terms of the new partnership, but also raised questions in the USA about Mexico's capacity to be a real regional partner. The advent in 2000 of the first government not to come from the post-revolutionary regime created great expectations for a broadening and deepening of economic, social, and political integration, but these did not materialize, creating frustration on both sides of the border. Mexico's standoffish position on its security relationship with Washington continued even after 9/11. And both the general public and the Mexican government refused to support Washington's push for military action in Iraq – even when the country was in the delicate situation of holding a temporary seat at the UN Security Council. In 2002, Mexico and the United States signed a "smart border" agreement, and in 2005 the two countries plus Canada entered into the rather modest if controversial Security and Prosperity Partnership (SPP). The 2007 Mérida Initiative does constitute a significant step in bilateral collaboration – including the transfer of financial resources from Washington to Mexico City – but it is nevertheless mostly confined to issues pertaining to drug trafficking and does not really address the broader security relationship.

Conclusion

This brief review of two very complex diplomatic relationships draws out at least four main insights. First, comparison of the US–Canada and US–Mexico relationships helps us to appreciate the multiplicity of "the West" as a civilizational clustering, both in the sense that there is more than one "western" community in play, and that there is great debate over the constitutive premises of each of these communities. As a settler society, the United States has (for the most part) always been torn between where it came from – Europe, and more specifically Britain – and where it found itself – the Americas. When Americans look north to Canada, they see a New World neighbor and junior partner, a "transatlantic" ally, and a fellow member of a more intimate club of like-minded "Anglo" societies. When they look south to Mexico, they see a potential partner struggling to catch up politically and economically, a bubbling cauldron of security challenges like crime and drugs, and a demographic and cultural threat to traditional ideas about American identity.

These images of Canada as compatible with the USA in civilizational terms, and Mexico as incompatible – or only partially compatible – help to reinforce the way in which many Americans think about the United States' defining features as a political community and as an international actor: constitutionalism, limited government, free markets, and international exceptionalism.

Second, state decision-makers' ideas about identity, community, and place matter, because they are the foundations for diplomatic cultures, and diplomatic cultures shape bargaining practices. We find that the US–Canada relationship, which is characterized by perceived cultural similarity and trust, is governed by a very rich and robust diplomatic culture, and the US–Mexico relationship, which is characterized by perceived difference and mistrust, is governed by a much "thinner" set of understandings. The result is not simply that US–Canada relations are "good" and US–Mexico relations are "bad." The identity-driven presumption of shared values and purposes in the US–Canada relationship has made possible the formation of a much more expansive latticework of bargaining norms, more confidence in one another's compliance with those norms, and therefore greater opportunity for more extensive and intensive forms of policy coordination. US–Mexico relations have also been powerfully imprinted by historical memories, their diplomatic engagements are charged with symbolism, and there is a clear recognition of interdependence on some issues. But within the US–Mexico relationship there is a lack of mutual identification, understanding, and trust, which make it more difficult to initiate or sustain bilateral cooperation.

Third, diplomatic cultures are not just "given" by structure or culture, but shaped over time by discourse. Diplomats reproduce the existing diplomatic culture by reaffirming established norms and practices in what they say and do. And the political elites who are the "carriers" for diplomatic cultures do not operate in a social vacuum. Their norms and practices are rooted in popular discourse about national identity, international community, and the obligations that go with them, which may also evolve over time. Canadian and American elites have frequently referred to the sheer scale of bilateral trade and investment and (prior to 9/11) to the "world's longest undefended border" as emblematic of the relationship. These dinner party and press conference clichés actually serve an important purpose, as affirmations of the established diplomatic culture. There are similar clichés in the US–Mexico relationship – for example, the frequent affirmation that the USA does not interfere in Mexico's domestic politics – and they serve similar purposes. When new circumstances raise questions about the relevance of the old diplomatic culture, policymakers and negotiators can try to defend the old norms and practices, adapt them to fit the new challenges, or pursue a more radical overhaul. As with international norms in general, change comes about when old ideas are challenged, and new ideas proposed that still resonate with underlying core premises.[63]

And finally, because the social context is responsive to changing circumstances and rhetorical pressures, diplomatic cultures can evolve over time. World War II and the Cold War pushed the USA and Canada together, and the diplomatic culture we recognize today took shape very rapidly in the late 1940s and 1950s.

Canadian officials improvised and learned by trial and error in developing a set of bargaining norms that worked for them, and in socializing their US counterparts to habits of self-restraint. After the fragmentation of US foreign policy-making in the 1970s, this network was disrupted and displaced, no longer able to manage the relationship the way it once had. But the core premises of the post-war diplomatic culture remained in place, and continue to shape the bilateral agenda even today.

The underlying rationale for partnership between the USA and Canada has changed over the last thirty years or so. In the early Cold War years, close relations were predicated on the perception of shared values and purposes stemming from their common origins as "Anglo-Saxon" societies. Thus both societies were seen to be genetically programmed for liberal democracy, free markets, and "open" diplomacy. Today the partnership is still predicated on these shared values, but those values are no longer explicitly attached to race and religion. In recent years, American conservatives have become increasingly frustrated with Canadian policies on issues like same-sex marriage, gun control, and health care. These policy divergences, in combination with recent diplomatic frictions over Iraq and missile defense, have shaken the longstanding American presumption that the two countries' values and interests are naturally convergent, thereby seriously undercutting the very idea of a coherent "Anglo-American" civilizational community.[64]

US–Mexico relations have been stubbornly resistant to change over the last hundred years. When Ralph Waldo Emerson warned that Mexico would "poison" the USA, his concern was that war with Mexico and the annexation of Texas would undermine American democracy and upset the domestic political balance on the issue of slavery. After the war, there was growing concern that the people living in the territories taken from Mexico and the subsequent influx of Mexican immigrants might "poison" the USA with different racial groups and religious practices. As suggested above, the inclusion of Mexicans in the US body polity did have an effect on domestic cleavages, some of which would in time contribute to the outbreak of the Civil War. Since that time, many Americans have continued to think of Mexico as culturally and politically incompatible with, and inherently disruptive to, American traditions and institutions, and to see Mexico as irretrievably backward and corrupt. The debates surrounding the NAFTA negotiation brought these old anxieties to the surface, but also raised hope for a transformation of bilateral diplomacy.

Some have argued that the sheer number of Mexican immigrants, and the anticipated "hispanicization" of the USA, might pave the way for a transformation of bilateral diplomacy. It is worth noting, however, that the sustained growth of the Hispanic population in the USA has been going on for a few decades now, and it is hard to argue that this has so far had an effect on the way bilateral diplomacy has been conducted. In any case, what seems more likely is a transformation of attitudes and practices at the elite level, with Mexican decision-makers adapting to a new set of negotiating practices that accommodate the American approach. As in Europe and Asia, regional dialogue in North America has been driven not only by a pragmatic effort to resolve policy frictions, but also by a search for common norms and practices. There has been a significant expansion of bilateral and trilateral diplomatic engagement since the signing of NAFTA, particularly after the negotiation of the post-9/11 border security accords and the 2007 Mérida Initiative. There is still a sense of distance and mistrust, and progress on key issues like immigration and crime has been held back by popular prejudices, bureaucratic rivalries, and Mexico's lack of state capacity. But regular summit meetings, more extensive and independent consultations among bureaucrats and military officers, and growing recognition of the real interdependence seem to have undercut the old presumption of political and cultural incommensurability, and to hold out the prospect of closer, more cooperative relations.

Committed regionalists have argued that North America is in the process of becoming a distinct and coherent regional community, held together by transborder flows of people, ideas, and commerce.[65] They do not deny the deep and enduring differences between these societies, but rather argue that these are – or must eventually be – superseded by common interests. But deepening interdependence is not enough by itself to make the US–Mexico relationship more like the traditional US–Canada relationship. Shared policy challenges may create "demand" for new diplomatic norms and practices; but the emergence and consolidation of a more robust, cooperative diplomatic culture depends upon underlying perceptions of mutual identification and obligation. Regional integration does not necessarily depend on the three countries becoming much more alike, but it does depend on their creating and sharing in new narratives of (regional and national) identity, which reject old markers of difference and mistrust. Just as Germans and French came to think of themselves as Europeans, so the USA and its neighbors may eventually come to think of themselves as "North Americans," perhaps based on some reworking of the core themes of the Western Hemisphere Idea. But for now, the "great American dichotomy" remains firmly in place.

Notes

1 For comments and advice on previous versions of this chapter, the authors would like to thank the contributors to this volume, especially Peter Katzenstein, plus David Haglund, Robert Keohane, and Richard Simeon. For financial and other support during the research and writing of this chapter, Bow would like to thank Fulbright Canada, the Canada Institute at the Woodrow Wilson International Center for Scholars, and the Center for North American Studies at American University.
2 See, for example, Dumbrell and Schäfer 2009b.
3 Ikenberry 2001; Kupchan 2002; Walt 2002.
4 Schoppa 1999.
5 The concept is introduced, and one key facet of the diplomatic culture joining the USA and Canada during the Cold War is developed, in Bow 2009.
6 The use of the term by these authors and others is reviewed in Neumann 2003, 349–51 and 364; see also Kappeler 2004.
7 For example, Acharya 2001.
8 Adler 2008.
9 Nicolson 1954, 9–11.
10 Holsti 1971; Keohane and Nye 1977; Bow 2009.
11 Ojeda 2001, 120.

12 Hartz 1955; Ikenberry 2004. We say "apparent" here, because many have argued that it is America's liberal ideals which have been the main drivers for its imperial impulses. E.g., Layne 2006, 118–33.
13 Jefferson 2009, 352.
14 Whitaker 1954, 29; Santa-Cruz 2005.
15 Victoria 1986, 299.
16 Horsman 1981, 264, 283.
17 Basañez et al. 2007.
18 Sikkink 1997, 727.
19 Respuesta de Alemán al discurso de bienvenida de Truman a Washington el 29 de abril de 1947, Archivo Histórico Diplomático, México, Secretaría de Relaciones Exteriores.
20 Kupchan 2010, 73.
21 The most pressing external challengers at this time were of course the native population and the French colonies to the north and west; many colonial elites looked to "their" imperial patrons in London for support in pushing these obstacles out of the way. After Montcalm's defeat at Quebec in 1759, the French presence faded as an oppositional foil for the colonies' sense of collective identity. Kagan 2007, 19–28.
22 Shore 1998.
23 Horsman 1981; Kohn 2004. See also Bell, Chapter 2, in this volume.
24 Hoberg 2000, 39–42.
25 Gotlieb 1982; Bow 2009.
26 Risse-Kappen 1995.
27 Doran 1984, 41.
28 Breton 1988.
29 Horowitz 1966; Lipset 1990; Finbow 1993; Preece 1980; Stairs 1982.
30 Clarkson 1968. These sentiments resurfaced in Canada during the 2002–3 diplomatic crisis over war in Iraq. See Resnick 2005, esp. the preface.
31 Mulroney 1984.
32 Granatstein 1997, 285.
33 Bow 2008.
34 Gotlieb 2007; Carleton University Canada–US Project 2009, 5.
35 Gecelovsky 2007.
36 Wilson 1918, 391; Smith 1986, 107.
37 Reinhold 1938, 351.
38 Rojas 2009.
39 Tocqueville 2002, 129.
40 Sullivan 2005, 5.
41 King and Smith 2005.
42 DeConde 1992, 33.
43 Merk 1970, 162.
44 Pletcher 1973, 581 (emphasis in original).
45 Note that at that time, Americans worried most about immigration from the north, from Catholic Quebec. See Haglund 2007, 84.
46 DeConde 1978, 189.
47 Horsman 1981, 208.
48 In DeConde 1992, 44.
49 O'Gorman 1977, 4.
50 The concessions did not go into effect, as the US Senate failed to ratify the treaty.
51 Merrill 2009, 97.
52 Gruening 1935, 2, 8.
53 Macmahon and Dittmar 1942, 39.
54 In Cullather 2009, 11.
55 The authors thank David Haglund for pressing us to emphasize this point. See Meyer 1981, 444.
56 Herrera and Santa Cruz 2011.

57 US Department of State 2004, 739.
58 Carter 1979, 275.
59 In *El Financiero*, 27 March 1991, 1; *Proceso* 758, 1991, 7.
60 In the *New York Times*, 10 June 1990, E4.
61 Riding 2000.
62 Montaño 2004, 71.
63 Schimmelfennig 2001.
64 There are similar tensions in US relations with Australia and New Zealand. See MacDonald and O'Connor, Chapter 8, in this volume.
65 Pastor 2011.

8

SPECIAL RELATIONSHIPS

Australia and New Zealand in the Anglo-American World[1]

David MacDonald and Brendon O'Connor

In this chapter, we argue that the extensive range of Australia's and New Zealand's (NZ) foreign policy activities – including their involvement in numerous foreign wars since the Boer War – can be best explained by the special relations both nations have maintained with the broader Anglo-American world. Strong bonds of shared interests, history, culture, and other commonalities have proven durable and demonstrably influential in determining the priorities and actions of both Antipodean countries. The "imagined community" of the Anglo-American world, strengthened by regular economic, military, and diplomatic interactions, possesses significant ideational power. Such bonds have also been affected by emotional beliefs, as Mercer puts it, "a generalization about an actor that involves certainty beyond evidence."[2] These beliefs are expressed either as positive sentiments towards fellow members of the Anglo-American world, or as distrust of "others" like Japan, Indonesia, or China.

The origin and nature of these emotional and ideational ties are key foci of our chapter. Arguably, European settlement of both countries has had a long-term impact, orienting both nations towards Britain, the USA, and other white settler societies (and to a lesser extent non-white British colonies and ex-British colonies) for most of their histories. The resulting strategic culture helps to explain the extremely close security and cultural alliances with the USA and Britain, which we will dissect in detail. Both of our case studies are clearly part of the "West," even if that West, to echo Peter Katzenstein, is a plural and pluralist entity, often difficult to define as it is evolving and changing.[3]

Throughout this chapter, we find the distinctions between functionalist and sentimentalist special relationships helpful for our analysis. This distinction allows us to highlight different aspects of the relations both countries maintain, at elite and popular levels. As we demonstrate, Australia's and NZ's relationship with the United Kingdom (UK) began as both functionalist and sentimentalist. The relationship is now primarily sentimentalist for both nations, although NZ maintains more sentimental ties than does Australia. The US relationship for both countries has been primarily functionalist, although in Australia it was imbued with significant sentimentalism during the Howard–Bush period. Both functionalist and sentimentalist elements inform the relationship between the Antipodean nations themselves. However, we also critique artificial divisions between these two distinctions, since identities and interests are often tightly bound together and in practice nearly impossible to separate. The best that can be said, then, is that functionalism and sentimentalism exist as two ideal types, with actors within the state expressing tendencies toward one more than the other.

We also take into consideration the complex interdependent relationships between NZ and Australia and other members of the Anglo-American world. As Keohane and Nye observed some time ago,[4] multiple channels connect societies; elite contacts are not all that count. In both cases, special relations occur between different segments of the population at different times. We draw distinctions between the national security apparatus – the political and business elites, and the general population. Migdal provides a useful means of drawing distinctions between the permanent or national security state and the general population or society. Going further than Max Weber, he argues that "The state is a field of power marked by the use and threat of violence and shaped by (1) the image of a coherent, controlling organization in a territory, which is a representation of the people bounded by that territory, and (2) the actual practices of its multiple parts."[5] Bearing this in mind, when dealing with special relationships we ask: "special for whom?" However, it falls beyond the ambit of this chapter to actively track public versus elite desires, attitudes, and policy preferences and their periods of convergence and divergence.

Our chapter proceeds as follows: in the first section, we present a theoretical overview of special relationships and alliance building, establishing a framework which we then apply to our case studies. In this section, we also engage briefly with the emerging literature on emotions in international relations. In the second, we highlight the importance of security in both Australia's and NZ's special relationships, with subsections on the UK and the USA. We follow this with a subsection on NZ's break with the ANZUS alliance, another evaluating the significance of NZ's foreign policy turn, and a third on the role of Australian public opinion in foreign policy. We conclude this section by examining the prospects for security convergence between both countries and the USA. In the third section, we offer a brief focus on economic relations (UK, USA, but also Asia). The final section concludes our analysis with a look at Australia's and NZ's bilateral relationships.

Special relationships and alliance building

Martin Wight provides a useful definition of what is assumed to make a special relationship: "associations between powers that seem to be deeper than formal alliances, to be based on affinity and tradition as much as interest."[6] Bow and

Santa-Cruz further define special relationships in their work on Mexican and Canadian relationships with the USA, listing features such as "mutual understanding, extensive and often informal policy coordination, and reflexive self-restraint under stress." Here, shared interests, as well as "a deeply-rooted sense of mutual identification and common purposes," play crucial roles.[7] In these definitions, there are different levels of analysis. Wight writes about governments, but also about affinities between populations. Bow and Santa-Cruz are more concerned with high-level contact between bureaucrats, military leaders, and politicians. In our case studies, we explore a range of relationships.

Measuring the "specialness" of a relationship between countries is not easy. It is even more difficult in the case of America, with whom so many nations are said to have a special relationship. As David Schoenbaum has written, the term has been applied to US relations with "Canada, Mexico, and Panama, Britain, France, and Germany, the Soviet Union and the Russia that reemerged from its ruins, at least one Korea, one Vietnam, and two Chinas, Cuba, Guatemala, Nicaragua, and El Salvador."[8] As we outline later, the standard-bearer remains the Anglo-American special relationship.

Specialness does not tell us much about the relative capabilities of those in the relationship. It may infer equality among similar peoples (a "band of brothers"), but it can also imply hierarchical relationships between imperial powers and colonial administrations. The term thus evokes comparisons to relationships between parent–child, husband–wife, siblings, or cousins, provoking a range of emotions such as "loyalty and betrayal, agony and ecstasy, and yearning and spurning."[9] Measuring why a "relationship" is special comes down to identifying which of the many factors in a special relationship are potentially the most important, be they cultural, military, economic, racial, religious, or linguistic. The question "special for whom?" alerts us to the fact that while a free trade deal may be special for business elites, or NATO special for military elites, neither may resonate with the general population.

Further, "special" does not imply "identical." Even in the UK–US relationship, similar values are offset by differences in geography, capabilities, and communications. The classic image of the Anglo-American relationship is of a series of concentric circles, with Britain located within the Commonwealth, Europe, and an imagined North Atlantic community. The UK operates as a "swing power" in John Dumbrell's phraseology, wielding power "as a fulcrum within a wheel."[10] Bridge imagery also played an important role in this relationship during Tony Blair's administration, as he signaled the UK's unique ability to act as intermediary between Europe and the USA. UK foreign policy was oriented towards striking the right balance, allowing one side to cross to the other bank, and back. The UK thus figured as a sort of glue that bound the two halves of the West together, albeit at an elite level.[11]

In Table 8.1, we have measured the state-centered special relations in the Anglo-American world by comparing eight key elements. This process helps illustrate the overall strength or weakness of each relationship, rather than focusing

TABLE 8.1 *State* special relations in the Anglo-American world

Country	Former colony	Trade	Military training	Intelligence sharing	Legal system	Wartime alliance	Political system	Proximity to either UK or USA
Canada	Y	Y	Y	Y	Y*	Y	Y	Y
NZ	Y	Y	Y	Y	Y	Y	Y	N
Australia	Y	Y	Y	Y	Y	Y	Y	N
USA	Y	Y	Y	Y	Y	Y	N	Y
UK	Y	Y	Y	Y	Y	Y	Y	Y
Mexico	N**	Y	N	N	N	N	N	Y
China	N	Y	N	N	N	N	N	N

Notes

* Quebec continues its civil law tradition while the rest of Canada is common law.

** Much of Mexican territory was incorporated into the USA in the nineteenth century.

on one strong aspect. For example, an emphasis on trade would make China appear to have a very strong special relationship with Australia and NZ. Yet China shares few significant commonalities in other areas, such as geographic proximity, system of government, legal system, and sharing of military equipment or intelligence. Conversely, while much further away from Australia and NZ, the USA, UK, and Canada have far more in common with them.

In Table 8.2 we focus on societal commonalities such as culture, ethnicity, language, religion, and other variables. These help isolate further similarities and differences. In both tables we include "wartime alliances," which refers to alliance building during the twentieth century and after. We argue that wars connect elites and society and have played a formative role in special relationship building. We have also included a colonial/imperial dimension since, for our cases, these shared histories and ties continue to be very important.

Functionalist and sentimentalist approaches to special relationships

What role do special relationships serve in a country's foreign policy and identity? The answer depends on whether you take a "functionalist" or a "sentimentalist" viewpoint, although in practice, as we have noted, this is largely a chicken and egg debate. In Danchev's "functionalist" interpretation, realism of either the classical or structural variety plays a key role: shared interests lead to negotiated compromise. Friction often surfaces in the relationship because it is not based on emotions or

TABLE 8.2 *Social* special relations in the Anglo-American world

Country	Culture	Ethnicity	Language	Religion	Wartime alliance	Shared empire UK
Canada	Y	Y*	Y*	Y	Y	Y
NZ	Y	Y*	Y*	Y	Y	Y
Australia	Y	Y	Y	Y	Y	Y
USA	Y	Y*	Y	Y	Y	Y**
UK	Y	Y	Y	Y	Y	Y
Mexico	N	N*	N	Y	N	N
China	N	N	N	N	N	N

Notes
* We have asterisked some of the countries in Ethnicity and Language because of large
French-speaking populations in Canada, indigenous Māori in NZ, and European settlers in Mexico.
** Until the eighteenth century.

shared culture, or even on a shared worldview. Rather, the relationship is practical
and seeks to avoid reliance on mythology about shared culture, language, or, perhaps at a subtextual level, race.[12] Table 8.1 illustrates how these special relations at
the elite level converge and diverge, together with economic, military, judicial,
and other institutional arrangements. Why does such mythology exist? This is
where Table 8.2 enters the analysis. Danchev submits that imagery of shared values
is often ritualistic and liturgical without always having much substantive content.
Like many cliché-ridden rituals, the language can be superficial, as it attempts to
paper over complex and contradictory histories. As Danchev puts it, the Anglo-
American special relationship "has formidable assets, some of them well hidden.
One of the greatest is the stories it tells to sustain itself. The real strength of shared
values is in the soul of historiography. The truth lies somewhere between monu-
mentalized past and mythical fiction."[13]

Generally, politicians rather than scholars have talked up the Anglo-American
special relationship, as evidenced by its origin in Winston Churchill's famous 1946
speech. David Watt notes the common trend for British prime ministers to routinely invoke "'our joint aims,' 'our common heritage,' and other emblems of 'the
unity of the English-speaking peoples'" to give such clichés "the patina of great
antiquity."[14] Official rhetoric has explained the rationale behind the closeness in
terms of common language, heritage, and history, as demonstrated in Table 8.2.
Many scholars, on the other hand, argue that common interests rather than shared
values sustained UK–US relations throughout the twentieth century, and thus
would see the specialness of the relationship primarily through the characteristics
listed in Table 8.1. Thus, the alliance between the two nations appeared in moments

of necessity, such as the shared threat of the Nazis and the Soviets.[15] It follows that contemporary scholars such as David Reynolds view the "special relationship" as largely a British diplomatic strategy to cope with and benefit from American power.[16]

However, we are still left with the question of why clichés and shared values provide public traction when rallying populations to support certain policies and countries. In contrast to Danchev, Dumbrell has proposed that sentiments *do* matter, and that the Anglo-American special relationship has largely been based on beliefs about shared kinship, culture, symbols, and values that people actually believe are important.[17] The argument is then that the general population finds these ties compelling and, to a certain extent, so do elites. Recent proponents of this argument include Niall Ferguson, Andrew Roberts, and Walter Russell Mead, all of whom see the Anglo-American world as a sentimentalist and functionalist project, with shared culture, language, values, legal, political, and philosophical principles as the core drivers of Anglo-American unity.[18]

We are presented with two overarching claims. The functionalist perspective posits that politicians pay rhetorical lip service to well-worn phrases about "the English speaking peoples," without believing in such rhetoric themselves – although there is the assumption that the populace feels these attachments are meaningful. Shared values and moral causes are plot devices used by politicians to sell wars and interventions abroad to populations who find emotional resonance with such claims. McDermott describes this process as the "calculated use of emotional entrepreneurship by leaders to create and craft particular kinds of political identity."[19] Sentimentalists, on the other hand, emphasize the importance of commonalities derived from shared racial, ethnic, linguistic, cultural, or historical attributes. For them, these shared attributes and the norms that arise from them makes cooperation naturally easier between Anglo-American states.[20] Thus both elites and the general population are included in these ties. We see a clear example of this merging of sentimentalism and functionalism in the Obama–Cameron summit in May 2011. Here the president and prime minister released a joint statement, which proclaimed of the US–UK special relationship that,

> Yes, it is founded on a deep emotional connection, by sentiment and ties of people and culture. But the reason it thrives, the reason why this is such a natural partnership, is because it advances our common interests and shared values. It is a perfect alignment of what we both need and what we both believe. And the reason it remains strong is because it delivers time and again. Ours is not just a special relationship, it is an essential relationship – for us and for the world.[21]

This merging of the two forms of special relationship, we suggest, also echoes the idea of "International Society" introduced by the English School. Hedley Bull and Adam Watson's classic definition describes well the broad outlines of the Anglo-American world:

> a group of states (or, more generally, a group of independent political communities) which not merely form a system, in the sense that the behavior of each is a necessary factor in the calculations of the others, but also have established by dialogue and consent common rules and institutions for the conduct of their relations, and recognize their common interest in maintaining these arrangements.[22]

The focus on "solidarism" by some English School theorists like Nick Wheeler works well towards explaining why black-letter legal sovereignty amongst members of the Anglo-American world seems less important than cooperation across a range of issue areas.[23]

Our chapter moves away from a strict dichotomy between functionalism and sentimentalism. Such a dichotomy is artificial, we argue, since it is virtually impossible to draw a dividing line between these forms of "specialness." Foreign policy decisions can be explained by both theories, to varying degrees, and at varying times. In the cases of NZ and Australia, sentimentalist rhetoric has often been used to achieve functionalist aims, while at the same time, polling data and anecdotal information make it clear that sentimental ties are very important for voters and decision-makers.[24] In both Australia and NZ, as well as in Canada, political leaders chose to reject full sovereignty. All three cases were marked by slowly evolving gray periods in which a series of acts (the Treaty of Waitangi in 1840, the British North America Act of 1867, and the Australian Constitution in 1901) seemed to give sovereignty in a sense; but it took a very long time to achieve. In Canada, for example, it only came with the Constitution Act in 1982.[25] The specialness of these relationships defies the normal black-box model of sovereign states. Since the nature of sovereignty differs considerably among these cases, so does the specialness of their relations with the UK, the USA, and each other.

Specialness for us also connotes the role of emotions in alliance politics. Sentimentalism in special relations implies a certain level of emotional attachment to certain countries and peoples, as well as repulsion from others. Mercer, Ross, and Crawford, amongst others, have argued that emotional beliefs can help cement alliances and promote cooperation, or can lead to inexplicably high levels of mistrust. Mercer, for example, has argued that emotions influence decision-making behavior both positively and negatively: "A preexisting feeling that a relationship is warm, or one that is characterized by empathetic understanding with the other, may help actors frame ambiguous behavior as neutral, positive, or motivated by circumstances rather than hostile intentions." "Conversely," he argues, "fear and antipathy may promote negative evaluations and make a neutral or positive reception of ambiguous behaviors and events less likely."[26] Ross adds to this that "empathy develops, exchanges are more effective, parties are more open to a range of options that speak to each party's interests, and viable agreements become more attractive to all." Summing up, Crawford notes that emotions act to "influence actors' understanding of the past and sense of what is possible in the future in four ways; emotions influence recall, the use of analogy, the evaluation of past choices, and the consideration of counterfactuals."[27]

Australia and NZ demonstrate in their respective histories how both affinity and distaste played important roles in alliance building. Affinity with fellow members of the Anglo-American club helped cement strong relations over and above any purely rational considerations, while fear of Asian countries, such as China and Japan, played a key role in the formation of Australia and NZ and helped create domestic identity, while shaping foreign policy attitudes. Yet while we can trace the military, economic, political, and diplomatic effects of emotional attachments, emotional beliefs are not always obvious, and can sometimes be impervious to study based on traditional social scientific methods. Reflecting Bleiker and Hutchison, we argue that in examining special relations we may need to "accept that research can be insightful and valid even if it engages unobservable phenomena, and even if the results of such inquiries can neither be measured nor validated empirically."[28]

Security relationships in Australia and New Zealand

In this section, we begin by highlighting some of the salient similarities and differences between Australia and NZ in their relationships to the UK and the USA from the nineteenth century through to the 1970s. This includes pro-British sentiments, Asia-skepticism, mutual attraction between the two countries, and ties to the rest of the Anglo-American world. The 1970s saw the UK enter the European Economic Community (EEC) and "push" NZ and Australia away, prompting the two Antipodean nations to engage more strongly with Asia. With regard to the USA, there are similarities but also divergence during the 1980s when NZ, for domestic political reasons (as well as party politics), instigated a partial break from the USA, pursuing (at least on the surface) its own foreign policy course. Overall, a recurring theme plays out in Australia–NZ relations: NZ feels it has a less vulnerable geographical position, which has allowed it the "luxury" of looser relations with the USA and a smaller defense budget. Consequently, in 2007, NZ's per capita defense spending was 1.1 percent of GDP, mirroring Canada's. In contrast, Australia sat at 1.9 percent and the USA at 4.0 percent.[29]

The British era

The nineteenth-century security environment was marked not only by external challenges (with Asia as a common "Other" that helped glue the colonies together), but internal ones as well. The empire was crucial in securing the rights and privileges of settlers in its Antipodean colonies. Special relationships, expressed in ethnic terms, were secured by military force. The colonists saw themselves as British and expected British protection, but reciprocally expressed great willingness to defend the empire in which they had common cause, not just in the Asia–Pacific but around the world, as Audie Klotz has noted in Chapter 4 in this volume. Ties were not just functional but strongly driven by sentiments as well. Different interpretations of the British relationship may be in part influenced by NZ's large Anglo-Saxon population (primarily English and Scottish), which still predominate today. By contrast, Australia had a larger proportion of Irish immigrants – 30 percent versus 20 percent in NZ. Roughly 80 percent of New Zealanders have some British ancestry, and an estimated 17 percent have the right to a British passport.[30]

While Australia was initially a penal colony in the eighteenth century and only later became a destination for settlers, NZ began in the nineteenth century as a planned settler colony. Edward Gibbon Wakefield, an architect of NZ's colonization, aimed, as he put it, to replicate "an entire British community" that would include such elements as "the manners, the institutions, the religion, the private and the public character" of the country they left behind.[31] The process of settlement continued well into the mid-twentieth century. Both Australia and NZ instigated passage schemes to encourage British immigration during the 1940s and 1950s in an effort to "maintain the Britishness."[32] Ethnicity and the British special relationship went hand in hand because, until at least the 1970s, most white New Zealanders saw themselves as British and saw Britain as their homeland. The same held true for Australia, although for a smaller percentage of the population.

NZ and Australian politicians avoided strident quests for independence during the nineteenth century and even late into the twentieth century on some fronts. Neither government saw this independence as the cue to take up autonomy in foreign affairs, with both nations largely following England's lead until the fall of Singapore in 1942. Evidence of these deep emotional ties in the general population comes in many forms, from the large number of New Zealanders and Australians volunteering to serve in World War I, through to the fact that the Australian parliament did not formally ratify and pass into effect the 1931 Statute of Westminster (which removed the British parliament's power to legislate for the dominions) until 1942. NZ left it until 1947. Further, until World War II, Australia and NZ operated their embassies from within the British embassy. Arguably, the ultimate link is the British monarch: Queen Elizabeth II is still the formal head of state for both countries.

How British or English were NZ and Australian societies? The vaunted Britishness of NZ has always been precarious, which has arguably influenced some of the boosterism of the past. It was only in the mid-nineteenth century that British settlers outnumbered indigenous Māori. Thus overt displays of "brotherhood" by settlers betrayed a fear that such an identity could easily be diluted by a large indigenous culture, with strong symbols, a unified language, and a fairly unified political movement in the North Island. Despite obvious efforts to strip Māori of their lands and legal rights, they fared comparatively better than other indigenous groups. This was due in large part to their numerical preponderance in much of the country, their strong military traditions, and their cohesiveness and discipline; it had little if anything to do with how "nice" the colonizers were.[33]

The story of Britishness is complicated in Australia by the large number of Irish immigrants who have been a feature of Australian immigration since the late eighteenth century. Both countries maintained restrictive policies against Asian immigration, and forms of Asia-skepticism continued well into the 1970s. Australia's White Australia policy, as it was known, operated from 1901 to 1973. NZ did not formally mirror this policy; nonetheless, in practice NZ accepted very few Asian migrants until the 1990s (and, unlike Australia, accepted few Southern Europeans in the immediate post-World War II period).[34] Through the mid-1980s, most of NZ's non-white migrants came from the Pacific Islands. The changing immigration patterns in the 1960s and 1970s intersected with shifting perceptions of Asia. As Asian immigration and investment increased rapidly, so did the focus on Asia as the locus of new relationships. This generally occurred first in Australia.

Until the 1940s, white Australians and New Zealanders did *not* see a special relationship between sovereign countries as much as they saw themselves as British and their countries as being part of a larger imperial system, even perhaps a "Greater Britain," a topic on which Duncan Bell lucidly elaborates in Chapter 2 in this volume. This was a qualitatively different sort of special relationship than one later sees, in the case of the USA for example, between sovereign, rational governments seeking to maximize their national self-interest. Thus we are not dealing with either sentimentalism or functionalism but something quite different – the lack of clear sovereign borders between states. As independent nations, NZ and Australia now have a sentimentalist special relationship with Britain. The idea of both countries as continued members of an Anglo-American "club" remains salient. One difference, perhaps, is that pro-monarchical sentiment is lower in Australia than in NZ, as witnessed in the (unsuccessful but fairly popular) push for Australia to become a Republic in the late 1990s.

With the arrival of immigrants from a broader range of nations in the 1970s, Britishness has lost some of its currency as a crucial part of Australian identity.[35] Australia has, however, struggled to mold a clear new identity. Part of this is due to a reluctance to break away from Britain as well as a natural skepticism about grand national symbols and expansive political pronouncements about the state of Australia.

The standard narrative about Australian alliance relations is that the Australian government shifted from Britain to America during World War II. The war undoubtedly strengthened Australia's ties with the USA, but it is incorrect to claim that relations with Britain soured. As we indicate in Table 8.2, for most Australians, such relations continued unabated. While there was clear tension between Churchill and Australian prime minister John Curtin over the return of Australian troops from North Africa to defend Australia, both Curtin and his successor Chifley reaffirmed their commitment to Britain time and again.[36] Through both the world wars, Australians had seen themselves as "Australian Britons"; it is a similar story in NZ. This support is borne out by the number of military casualties from these conflicts. In World War I military casualties for the UK were around 2.2 percent of the entire population; meanwhile for Australia about 1.4 percent of its entire population perished; and NZ was even higher at around 1.6 percent. Given the distance and lack of direct threat to the two nations, these figures are astonishing. World War II provides similar comparison – the UK lost close to 1 percent of its population as war casualties; in Australia military deaths accounted for approximately 0.6 percent of the population; and in NZ it was 0.7 percent. Eventually global events rather than a quest for independence pushed Australia and NZ away from this self-identity and interdependence. The key factors were the demise of the British empire, the concomitant rise of the USA, and the movement of the UK towards Europe, culminating with British entry to the EEC in 1973.

The American era

The British special relationship is often described in terms of a mother–child relationship, with Australia and NZ showing dependence, respect, and loyalty in return for economic, cultural, and military benefits. The US relationship with Australia and NZ is seen more as an alliance, or perhaps as a relationship between cousins.[37] In this section, we consider the evolution of the ANZUS security relationship but also contextualize it within a much larger intelligence framework.

In 1942, the British surrender in Singapore drew NZ and Australia into a close alliance with the USA. Consequently, 100,000 American troops were stationed in NZ and, by some estimates, up to a million in Australia. Japan had conquered much of East Asia. It was moving into Papua New Guinea and had bombed Darwin in 1942 and 1943, making this alliance grudgingly welcome for functionalist reasons. During the Cold War, the deepening alliance flowered, not because of any sentimentalism in either rhetoric or fact, but because of Australia's and NZ's security concerns and fear of geographical isolation. Where possible, both countries pushed to balance their new and evolving US ties with their traditional anchor: the UK. Australia and NZ signed up to the ANZUS Pact in 1951, as well as the Southeast Asia Treaty Organization (SEATO) in 1954, and participated in the Five Power Staff Talks in 1955.[38] This deepening relationship with the USA did not sit well with many New Zealanders. It is instructive that soon after signing ANZUS, the NZ parliament passed a bill recognizing the British monarch as Queen of NZ. A royal tour was also planned in 1953 to buttress these links to empire.[39]

In Australia, the push to embrace America was heavily promoted by what Wesley and Warren call the "traditionalists" within foreign policy-making circles,[40] associated with the sentimentalism of the Liberal Party and Prime Minister Robert Menzies. During the 1950s and 1960s, Australia and NZ hoped to establish a four-member alliance with the USA and the UK. Cabinet discussions and other documents from the time reveal this was a high priority for Menzies and other leading Liberal politicians, as it was for Keith Holyoake's government in NZ. Although a formal alliance that included the UK and the USA was not achieved under Menzies or Holt, Australia did became part of a special "Anglosphere" club (which included the USA, the UK, Canada, and NZ), particularly in intelligence sharing. We feel the word "club" is appropriate, as this group shared similar values and cultures which led to the larger players (particularly the USA) trusting the smaller players such as Australia and NZ with sensitive intelligence sharing. These smaller players reciprocated by hosting spy bases on their territory, which were critical to America's intelligence network during the Cold War.[41] Again there are emotive or sentimental elements to this relationship that cannot be explained by functionalism alone.

In March 1946, the BRUSA or UKUSA agreement was signed between the USA and UK or "the two partners." Further negotiations brought Australia, NZ, and Canada into the alliance as "second parties" in 1956. The National Security Agency put this in somewhat sentimentalist terms: "These relations evolved and continued across the decades. The bonds, forged in the heat of a world war and tempered by decades of trust and teamwork, remain essential to future intelligence successes."[42] This high level of trust arguably demonstrates how sentimentalism and functionalism are often inseparable. The history of such close intelligence sharing indicates an extremely high level of trust, as a document released in 2010 outlines: "Such exchange will be unrestricted on all work undertaken … Except when specifically excluded from the agreement at the request of either party and with the agreement of the other." This, as the principal records specialist at the UK National Archives concludes, "represented a crucial moment in the development of the special relationship between the two wartime allies (the UK and the USA) and captured the spirit and practice of the signals intelligence co-operation which had evolved on an ad-hoc basis during the Second World War."[43] Certainly, the so-called "Five Eyes" arrangement became an important staple of Cold War alliance building and continues due to a combination of sentimentalist and functionalist considerations.

NZ's suspension from ANZUS

Until 1985, NZ decision-makers remained committed to ANZUS and subscribed to the "domino theory," sending troops to fight in Vietnam as in Korea.[44] Overall, NZ expressed common cause with the Americans, maintaining extremely close intelligence and military links. Nevertheless, NZ Foreign Minister Frank Corner observed during the 1970s that New Zealanders were "still old-style British in their instincts." This implied "a certain style of British superciliousness towards Americans and American culture and foreign policies."[45] The Australian perception of the alliance was in some respects quite similar. Their interest in closer relations with the USA was functionalist; nonetheless, over time, relations grew much closer.

Australia's security relationship with the USA held firm during the 1980s, in contradistinction to NZ, which broke from ANZUS in 1985. The reasons for this break, we suggest, were largely political. However, the foreign policy divergence was not as great as some have alleged. Indeed, NZ's vaunted independence over the nuclear issue obscures the reality that their foreign policies over other matters did not diverge significantly from the USA. Further, the government's economic policies became far more "American" during the Lange years, and defense cooperation and coordination with Australia actually became closer.

In NZ, perceptions of the USA were broadly positive until the Vietnam War, when large-scale anti-war demonstrations rocked the country.[46] Australia, too, developed a very strong anti-Vietnam War movement. However, it was not anti-war sentiment that caused the decline in the relationship between NZ and the USA, but rather the issue of a US nuclear warship in a NZ harbor. America tested nuclear weapons in the Marshall Islands until 1962, and in the outback of South Australia and the Gilbert Islands in the 1950s.[47] The anti-nuclear movement in NZ and Australia also grew in response to French testing in the Pacific. Indeed, the Campaign for Nuclear Disarmament engaged in organized opposition after France began testing on its island colonies of Mururoa and Fangataufa.[48] There were secondary effects in terms of NZ–US special relations, and permanent repercussions on the ANZUS alliance.

In the "special relations" of Anglo-American societies, the circulation of ideas across the member nations is an important aspect highlighted by the anti-nuclear movement. In fact, it was US criticism of nuclear weapons that helped fuel the NZ anti-nuclear campaign. Only after a NZ tour by the Harvard University-based Australian physician Helen Caldicott, who screened a documentary made by the National Film Board of Canada, did Labour's anti-nuclear initiative became enshrined as party policy.[49] Responding to a high level of public support, in 1984 the Labour Party under David Lange proclaimed a strict anti-nuclear policy, forbidding the docking of ships with nuclear technology or weaponry. This conflicted with the American policy of neither confirming nor denying that its vessels had nuclear technology on board. This anti-nuclear stance helped Labour secure election from a moribund National Party government in 1984.

In February 1985, the "Port Access Dispute" presented a test case for the new policy. The US government made a public request for a navy destroyer, the *USS Buchanan*, to dock at a NZ harbor. Lange was on a tour of the Pacific. His foreign minister was in favor of the ship docking, but his acting prime minister, Geoffrey Palmer, was not, on the grounds that it might have nuclear weapons or power. Lange supported Palmer, and a standoff ensued.[50] Support for anti-nuclear policies was further galvanized in July 1985 when the French secret service blew up the Greenpeace ship *Rainbow Warrior* in Auckland Harbour, killing a crew member. NZ saw this as an act of war by France, but found little support for this proposition from either the UK or the USA. This incident galvanized support for the anti-nuclear position and led to a further breakdown in public relations with the USA.

The Lange government pressed on with its anti-nuclear legislation, eventually passing the "Nuclear Free Zone, Disarmament, and Arms Control Act," which is still official policy. It was during this period that negotiations broke down, and the USA suspended its treaty obligations under ANZUS.[51] By August 1986, the USA forged stronger bilateral ties with Australia, and NZ–US relations entered into an "indefinite coma," a clear example of what one might call "small power idealism."[52] In theory, the USA withdrew its obligations to defend NZ in the event of attack. Lange, however, and all other subsequent prime ministers, felt that the USA would indeed come to NZ's aid if attacked, if only to defend its own security interests.[53]

Why did NZ take this path? The break had long roots in domestic politics, especially in the aforementioned opposition to French nuclear testing. The period from 1960 to 1984 saw 148 visits by US warships, 13 by nuclear propelled ships. As part of the broader anti-nuclear movement, which primarily targeted France, the USA became seen as part of the problem. A core activist faction within the Labour Party, which included Jim Anderton and Helen Clark, had vocally protested against the Vietnam War and were keen to prohibit nuclear weapons and nuclear power. The decision to ban nuclear ships occurred at a time when the Labour government was riding a wave of popularity and the globally unpopular Reagan administration had created the almost perfect "David and Goliath" set-up. Yet, those who would argue that NZ made a decisive break from the Anglo-American world need to acknowledge a number of ironies, which we elaborate below.

The first irony of the anti-nuclear position is that it was driven not by anger at the Americans, but by objections to French testing of nuclear technology. This fueled the movement that led to the ban on American ships. A second irony concerns Lange's populist poll-oriented politics. Lange has admitted to little personal interest in the nuclear policy, reiterating in his memoir that he never saw nuclear propulsion as equivalent to nuclear weapons. As he put it, "weapons are made to destroy people and we have to learn to live without them. The rest [nuclear power] may be useful if properly managed."[54] Nevertheless, public sentiment against nuclear power was strong, and Lange did not believe NZ would be ejected from ANZUS. Indeed, no NZ prime minister before Lange seriously considered that ANZUS membership would be imperiled by an anti-nuclear stance.

A third irony was Lange's swing to the right in economic terms. While playing up the nuclear issue as a form of Goliath-bashing, Lange launched his country on a sharp neoliberal course of privatization and a decrease in controls on foreign investment. His government initiated one of the most revolutionary neoliberal reform packages of any western country – spurred on by Finance Minister Roger Douglas.[55] "Rogernomics" promoted one of the world's freest and most deregulated regimes, "unmatched internationally, except in former communist bloc countries after 1989."[56] This apparent dichotomy was not by accident. Lange was playing to both wings of the party, thus NZ simultaneously developed a nuclear-free policy and one of the most open economies in the OECD.[57]

A fourth irony is that while the NZ public was clearly anti-nuclear, it did not see its anti-nuclear stance as consonant with an anti-ANZUS stance. Polls conducted in 1986 demonstrated a paradox: while 71 percent of the public backed ANZUS, 73 percent also backed NZ as a nuclear-free zone, and 80 percent of the population wanted to have it both ways: to be nuclear free within ANZUS.[58] Caution is thus warranted in drawing too much from the policy divergences of the Australian and NZ governments during this period. Both wanted very much to remain part of the ANZUS alliance, and both sought close ties with each other.

A fifth irony is that, seemingly unbeknownst to Lange, NZ's intelligence cooperation with the USA actually increased following the break. Certainly, Lange was punished. US military intelligence was curtailed, but other intelligence continued to flow in. Journalist Nicky Hager puts it that "The United States government wanted other countries to see New Zealand punished for its nuclear-free policies, but the UKUSA alliance was too valuable to be interrupted by politics." The intelligence break was partially a stage show. For example, for a brief period, the "routing indicators," showing the destination and origin of intelligence within UKUSA, were removed from incoming reports. Once the bilateral situation calmed down, they were quietly put back on overseas documents.[59] A second slap on the wrist was the denial of weekly intelligence summaries formerly provided to NZ under ANZUS; but while the summaries ceased, access to all the intelligence on which they were based continued to flow freely.[60]

The supposed break between NZ and the USA brought an increase in intelligence coordination during this period, largely through the auspices of the Government Communications Security Bureau (GCSB).[61] Key advisors in the GCSB, more interested in NZ's long-term security interests as part of the western alliance, managed to keep their operations largely in the dark from Lange as well as later prime ministers Geoffrey Palmer and Jim Bolger.[62] Hager's analysis, supported by Lange – who penned the foreword to his book – suggests that many of the functional aspects of the special relationship continued, despite legislative ignorance and even potential opposition.

NZ's foreign policy turn

Despite the obvious continuation of NZ's ties within the Five Eyes alliance, the anti-nuclear decision changed the orientation of NZ foreign policy over time. The US decision to cut NZ from ANZUS training missions, military cooperation, and intelligence sharing forced NZ to develop a more independent and multilateral approach to its foreign policy. By the 1990s the anti-nuclear position, as well as ambivalence toward ANZUS, were viewpoints accepted by all major parties. NZ became an active player in UN-mandated interventions from Cambodia to Angola and Somalia. In 1992, NZ also became a temporary member of the UN Security Council. Support for the anti-nuclear policy remained relatively constant at 52 percent in 1989 and 54 percent by 1991. Support for a defensive alliance with the USA, by contrast, dropped from 47 percent in 1986 to 39 percent by 1989.[63] There is little chance that even a coalition center-right government, as NZ now has, will see fit to reverse Lange's policy. Prime Minister John Key has argued that the stance has become "hard-wired into the New Zealand DNA," a crucial symbol of national identity.[64]

Overall, NZ policymakers have adopted a more publicly responsive foreign policy than has Australia. On matters close to home, like Pacific security, nuclear testing, and relations with Pacific Island neighbors, the government at times defers to public opinion when it is politically expedient to do so. In part, this reflects the small size of NZ and the changing ethnic composition of the country. Foreign Minister Murray McCully describes his country as a "bridge between Asia and Europe," with national identity as a melding of three identities: "European, Polynesian and Asian."[65] In line with this evolving identity is a "tri-polar approach to the world": a focus on Asia and the Pacific for "reasons of geography," and a European focus for cultural reasons.[66] Current demographic trends indicate that the ethnic underpinning of this bridge identity will be accentuated. Based on 2008 projections, NZ's non-European populations will sustain the highest annual growth rates over the next 20 years to the extent that by 2026, almost half of NZ's population will be non-European.[67] When considering the social relationships expressed in Table 8.2, we feel the public will continue to push for NZ engagement with the Pacific.

How much successive governments respond to these demographic changes will be influenced by politics. There is little reason to suggest that NZ decision-makers will pursue a major reorientation of foreign policy, although the pro-Asia rhetoric has become more pronounced in recent years in elite circles. Certainly NZ's anti-nuclear position and its non-involvement in the Iraq War have created tensions with the USA. However, these should be seen merely as *brotherly* arguments within the Anglo-American family, not as signals of a permanent break in relations. Beneath these occasional spats, the deep (and enduring) trust and connection is best illustrated by the continued closeness of intelligence relations.

Australian public opinion and foreign policy

Australian perceptions of ANZUS have been different: the alliance was embraced in Australia at precisely the same time that NZ policy on nuclear ship visits put that nation's US alliance at risk. For Australia, the sense of living in a dangerous security environment has made the US alliance seem far more necessary.[68] History and geographic insecurity have created a security culture, supported by both sides of the political spectrum, in which special relations with Britain and now America are very highly valued. At the same time, due to its larger economy, territorial base, mineral wealth, and larger population, Australia feels less economically vulnerable than NZ. Opinion polls in Australia show high levels of public support for the US–Australia alliance (reinforcing the security culture/special relations argument).[69] These views have created a situation in which each new prime minister (and most new leaders of the opposition) feel compelled to make a speech affirming support for the US alliance.

For Australia, the strengthening of its US alliance has been its key foreign policy goal, since at least the drafting of ANZUS. Australia's "American alliance" was never seen as a temporary solution to such passing threats as international communism or Japanese revanchism. Rather, it has been viewed as a central pillar of Australian security policy. The desire to secure US loyalty largely explains Australia's involvement in Korea, Vietnam, and Iraq, and its strong ongoing commitment to the US-led war in Afghanistan. During the Howard era, Australia moved rhetorically to the heart of the Anglo-American world, while NZ sided with France, Germany, Canada, and other Bush critics. Howard was a traditionalist, an "Anglosphere" booster, and a strong believer in the view held by Menzies that Australia needs "great and powerful friends." Unlike NZ, which under the Labour government of Helen Clark refused to support the war, Australia was an enthusiastic member of the Coalition of the Willing. The official reasons Australia went to war were similar to the arguments presented in the USA and UK – principally to rid Iraq of Weapons of Mass Destruction. However, in Australia, most commentators also saw the decision as being significantly about alliance politics. Further, it could be argued that it was entirely in keeping with what could be called Australia's ongoing Anglospheric "strategic culture."[70]

Security convergence with the USA?

Arguably, assertions about the divergent paths of Australia and NZ can easily be overdone: both countries abide by longstanding multilateralist traditions, which have been pursued very actively at times by leaders within both the Australian Labor Party and the NZ Labour Party. In Australia this involvement in multilateral forums has been balanced (and at times compromised) by a desire to seek close alliances with strong and powerful nations. NZ has also largely adopted this balancing act for much of its history since World War II. The decision to pursue an antinuclear policy created a schism in this tradition but, as we have pointed out, no one expected NZ to break with ANZUS – including Lange – and aspects of the NZ–US special relationship continued throughout this period, at times indirectly through the mediating influence of Australia, the UK, and intelligence institutions. A recent US embassy memo prepared for Hillary Clinton's trip to NZ in 2010 makes clear that "New Zealand remained a member of the Five Eyes intelligence community" after 1985, and that "Our intelligence relationship was fully restored in August 29, 2009."[71]

Recent events may reduce these differences still further. Under Prime Minister Key and President Obama, the NZ–US relationship has become increasingly cordial. While Bush was roundly unpopular, New Zealanders were very supportive of Obama, who received a 65 percent favorable rating amongst respondents, compared with 11 percent for McCain.[72] This more open atmosphere may lead to a renewed special relationship. In mid-2010, Assistant Secretary of State for East Asian and Pacific Affairs Kurt Campbell emphasized a "very deliberate effort" by the new administration to develop closer relations with NZ. This includes areas of joint concern like climate change, security in the Pacific, and economic and other opportunities and challenges in Asia. This may also translate into joint military training exercises and a closer security relationship, although it is unlikely that NZ will join a formal military alliance with the USA.[73]

Economic relationships

In gauging the evolution of special relationships, economic relationships also merit consideration. As we have already argued, both countries were forced to reorient their trading patterns towards Asia in the 1970s. In this section, we argue that despite closer functional relations with Asian countries, the specialness of the UK and US relationships have changed little over the past three decades.

In both Australia and NZ, we can observe a three-stage process in developing relations with Asia. This evolution is classically presented as first, a narrow xenophobic view of Asia as "alien" and dangerous; second, acceptance and engagement; and finally, third, interdependence. From 1940 to 1960, as was typical for other Anglo-American states, Asia was seen as a homogenous "Other," with Australia and NZ western-oriented and "unequivocally not part of Asia." This perception shifted by the 1970s, due to two oil shocks and Britain's membership in the EEC. Asia now became a regional economic opportunity. From 1968 to 1980, NZ doubled its exports to Asia, with the region becoming almost as big a market for New Zealand as Europe.[74]

Growth in the Asian markets was even more pronounced for Australia, and this continues to be the case. During the third phase of relations from the 1990s, Australia and NZ increasingly saw themselves as interdependent parts of Asia, both economically and, to a degree, strategically. This has since developed into the view that both nations need to be "Asia-literate."[75] ASEAN, APEC, and a number of organizations became useful in grouping NZ and Australia with Asian economies to promote a greater degree of interdependence.[76] It would be easy to believe that Australia has had a more fraught relationship in this period than has NZ, given the history of the White Australia policy and rhetorical exchanges between Australian and Asian leaders. However, both NZ and Australian decision-makers realized that their future prosperity rested significantly on increasing not just exports, but a whole range of economic exchanges such as fee-paying students, business migration, and foreign investment from Asia.

In Australia, there has been a perception that the Labor Party has embraced a pro-Asia stance more than the Conservative parties, which have focused on the Anglo-American alliance. This is true at the rhetorical level; the Keating Labor government backed up its talk by being a key player in the establishment of APEC and signing a security treaty with Indonesia in 1995. Although the Howard government rhetorically pulled back from this engagement and talked up its desire to "reinvigorate" the Australia–US alliance, the reality is that both major parties in Australia wanted to, and largely have, increased integration into Asian markets while maintaining a strong security alliance with the USA.

NZ would arguably have taken a similar approach if it had still been an active member of ANZUS. However, rhetorically cast out of a close alliance by the USA, it became more adventurous in its foreign policy. This has made it more creative in its policy approach to China and led to its unprecedented free trade agreement with the PRC. However, the NZ tendency to oversell the significance and uniqueness of its achievements, and to highlight differences with Australia, means that any analysis should proceed with caution. For example, the NZ–China FTA could be less about NZ ingenuity than it is about China's desire to send a message to Australia and other pro-China FTA trading partners.

Bilateralism: Australia and New Zealand

In this section, we focus on the relationship between Australia and NZ. Anglosphere theorist James Bennett observes that the Anglo-American world contains many double acts: "Britain and Ireland, the U.S. and Canada, and Australia and New Zealand." He notes an obvious fact remarked upon by Seymour Lipset and others: "In each, the smaller partner has found close trade relations and some aspects of union with the larger partner to be desirable but also has harbored resentments and concerns about being swallowed and assimilated by its larger partner."[77] This mixture of cooperation, resentment, and concern characterizes NZ perceptions of Australia. In psycho-sociological terms, New Zealanders often resent being ignored by the Australian press and Australians in general, especially given that New Zealanders tend to be much more knowledgeable and familiar with Australia. In Freudian terms, this is a classic case of the narcissism of minor differences playing out in bilateral relations. This makes sense when one considers the history of these two countries. In the nineteenth century it was assumed that NZ would eventually merge with the Australian colonies, which were as different from one another as NZ was from them. Indeed, the 1900 Australian constitution provides for NZ to join the Australian commonwealth at any time upon application.[78]

In this context we need to understand claims that the two countries are polar opposites. Devetak and True, for example, see them sitting on opposing ends of a spectrum, with NZ's identity as: "an independent and principled player on the world stage, whereas Australia's is asserted most strongly through its self-image as a regional great power and close ally of the United States, and its decidedly realist, sometimes unprincipled, foreign policy."[79] Australian defense expert Hugh White contends: "But Australians need to realise that our trans-Tasman cousins do see the world differently from us. Australians are from Mars, Kiwis are from Venus."[80] Devetak and True overstate matters, but their first point does highlight a common self-perception held by New Zealanders, while the second is the view of many critics of Australian foreign policy.

More sensibly, if one looks at the relative size of NZ and Australia and their geographical locations, it is hardly surprising that their foreign policy priorities have differed in recent years. In truth, these differences have come from the same catalysts for both nations: a growing independence in thinking and less attachment to Britain from the 1970s onward, and a greater move towards Asia in matters of trade and regional cooperation. It would be incorrect to argue that the "Port Access Dispute" entirely defines NZ's relationship with the USA. As we have discussed, intelligence networking and coordination actually increased during the 1980s and 1990s (including NZ's entry into the ECHELON surveillance project), and NZ's break with ANZUS was mired in a number of ironies which suggest that events did not have to transpire as they did, and were not as narrowly "path dependent" as subsequent political commentators have suggested.

Indeed, many similarities characterize the self-identity and world outlook of both countries. The enduring (and increased) importance of the ANZAC tradition in Australia and NZ highlights the ongoing power of militarism and mythology. Australian commentators have frequently claimed that the increased importance accorded to the ANZAC national memorial day in the last decade was in part the result of efforts by the Howard government to boost militarism in Australian life. Such claims, however, fail to account for the rise of similar sentiments in NZ, amongst both Labour and National supporters. Reflecting something deeper than the political manipulations of symbols in the cultures of both societies, the memory of the World War I battle at Gallipoli evokes powerful emotions that straddle the Tasman and point to the strong influence of military history. Australia and NZ offered incredible loyalty to Britain during both world wars, but the nations' experiences of war are often described as the founding points in developing their own independent national character.

In terms of bilateral arrangements, the 1944 Australian–New Zealand Agreement or Canberra Pact was signed to create a separate sphere of influence over the southwest and South Pacific. It also paved the way for regular meetings between Canberra and Wellington, for common planning in defense, external relations, industry, and commercial policy, even social programs.[81] Australia and NZ later set up a Consultative Committee on Defence Co-operation in 1977. NZ followed this a year later in its *Defence Review* by seeing the two countries as a "single strategic entity."[82] And, as we have already discussed, relations continued to strengthen as NZ and Australia became members of the Five Eyes and participated in ECHELON.

Ironically, while Australian leaders took exception to Lange's posturing during the 1980s, relations with Australia became closer. This was due in part to Bob Hawke's fear that if a strong bilateral relationship was not maintained, NZ might fall out of the western orbit.[83] Certainly NZ seemed to follow suit on many Australian decisions thereafter. For example, NZ followed Australia in creating a Defence Electronic Warfare Data Base (DEWDAB), even adopting the same name. Both countries also coordinated an increase in the deployment of specialized SAS personnel for intelligence missions, shared research in towed arrays for anti-submarine surveillance, and converged on many aspects of "signals intelligence interception and analysis."[84] There was also the adoption of the Close Economic Relations (CER) agreement in 1983, which created something akin to the EEC in Australasia.

Until the Clark Labour government in 1999, Australia and NZ still maintained that they were a "single strategic entity," meaning that an attack against one would pose a security risk against the other, thus necessitating collective action. By 2000, the term was dropped. While the phrase did not indicate any sort of joint foreign policies, the Clark government felt it impeded the assertion of an independent foreign policy.[85] Nevertheless, the two countries cooperate on defense matters. During the conflict in East Timor, NZ and Australia formed the bulk of the UN-mandated UNIFET force sent there in 1999.[86] Both countries worked together to achieve a peace settlement in Bougainville and responded in a coordinated manner after George Speight overthrew Fiji's first Indian prime minister in a 2000 coup, jointly imposing "smart sanctions" on the coup leaders. Both countries have also been instrumental in making RAMSI peace-building initiatives effective in the Solomon Islands.[87]

The most recent indication of NZ's intentions come from the National government's 2010 White Paper, which puts the Anglo-American alliance into perspective. It highlights historical ties, but also alludes to potential divergence in the future. Regarding the past, the other four members of the Anglo-American world are described as being part of "longstanding and close security partnerships," which are in turn "grounded in common traditions, experiences, and values" and "maintained and strengthened by dialogue, personnel exchanges, training, exercises, technology transfer, intelligence sharing, and the application of military doctrine." These relationships are presented as being at the core of the NZ defense strategy.[88] The differences in perception as well as size will continue to have an effect on the relationship. The White Paper is clear that "Australia will remain New Zealand's most important security partner," but while there is a search for common interest, divergence will become more obvious in the future because NZ's defense budget is small, while "Australia continues to invest more heavily in high-end military capabilities."[89]

In outlining the NZ–Australia special relationship, the idea of a bridge identity between Asia and Europe is common. Both see themselves as having a common heritage, common democratic norms, common security interests in the Pacific, and common economic interests in trading with each other, with Europe, and, most importantly, with Asia. For all of the rivalry between the two nations (much of it relating to sports), there is significant affection and cooperation. They afford each other's citizens special treatment from immigration through to welfare, education, and generous health benefits.

A key difference, again tied to domestic politics and state attributes, concerns the importance of domestic identity politics to each case. In NZ, small size, historical vulnerability in economic terms, and a sense of a benign security environment have all contributed to its porosity in terms of trade, migration, and new ideas. Australia provides a puzzling mix of a far more multi-ethnic society. More open immigration policies to South Europeans in the post-World War II period, and the entry of a diverse range of migrants since the early 1970s, have led to many migrant success stories and a good deal of integration. Still, many Australians have struggled to shed traditional Anglo-Celtic understandings of who they are as a people. Politicians have zeroed in on this concern in their federal politics rhetoric. The populist debate over the supposed "flood" (in actuality a tiny proportion of the total immigrants to the country) of illegal refugees arriving by boat is a case in point. Their subsequent treatment in detention centers reflects the policy outcomes of this tension. Nonetheless, Australia's substantial annual intake of migrants from around the world asks Australians to integrate with new peoples every year. They largely do, but the impact in the medium- to longer term of shifting demographics on Australian foreign policy is difficult to judge.

At present, a more obvious conclusion is that politicians are still most comfortable taking a traditional approach to alliance relations (in other words, embedding security relations with the Anglo-American world). Immigration has undoubtedly had a noticeable impact on NZ in the last two decades and has led to the development of a tripolar identity forged amongst the mix of Europeans, Polynesians, and Asians. At this stage, the Asian dimension is more rhetorical than deeply felt, but it builds on a foundation of biculturalism that has long rejected open ideas of multicultural citizenship. Both countries face a chasm between the elite's discourse on integrating migrants and popular "shock jock" announcements, which are frequently xenophobic. NZ's recent touting of its tripolar identity and how this might allow "special relations" with China is not that different from rhetoric used in the 1990s by the Keating government towards Asian economic integration. Another example is provided by the claim that the Chinese-language ability of former Australian prime minister Kevin Rudd would create closer relations between China and Australia. Ultimately these predictions of closer ties are functional. Relations with Asia are not cemented nearly as strongly as the sentimental ties NZ and Australia enjoy with each other and with the wider Anglo-American world.

Australia and New Zealand: torn and tripolar Identities?

Samuel Huntington sharpened Australia's evolving post-Anglo identity to the furthest extreme when he called Australia a "torn country" pulled between its traditional position as part of "European civilization" and its desire to become part of "Asian civilization."[90] For a number of reasons his claim rings untrue. All Australian elites wanted greater entry into Asian markets and Asian regional institutions. But they were divided on whether this meant distancing Australia from its British heritage. And no significant political leader talked about making Australia part of Asian civilization. As for public opinion, it was firmly against the notion. Lastly, Asian leaders were not particularly supportive of Australia joining regional forums and certainly did not see Australia as Asian. Describing Australia in the 1990s as anywhere close to a "torn" country – caught between the East and the West – was thus a serious misreading of the politics and policies that simultaneously sought more independence from Britain and more opportunities in Asia.

Blame for the confusion and misunderstanding can be laid at the feet of the at times hyperbolic debates over Australia's future as a Republic and over immigration levels from Asia. The key figures in these debates were prime ministers Keating and Howard, and an independent Member of Parliament from Queensland, Pauline Hanson. The Labor Prime Minister Paul Keating set off both the push for greater Australian economic and political integration into Asia and the call for Australia to become a Republic. His rhetoric on a range of issues was often colorful and blunt: he regularly chided Conservatives for being too closely wedded to Britain and the USA, lacking sufficient pride in Australian achievements or the courage to pursue a more independent and forward-looking foreign policy that was open to new opportunities.[91] Even though he pursued a policy cultivating a close alliance with the USA once he came into office in 1996, Prime Minister Howard disagreed strongly with Huntington's claims about Australia. But he blamed Keating for having left himself open to misunderstandings, and saw the entire episode as the unfortunate by-product of a foolish and needlessly introspective debate about Australian identity and foreign policy.[92]

A lightning rod for this stormy debate was Pauline Hanson, who was elected to Parliament in 1996 and subsequently made her One Nation Party a force in Australian politics. Hanson opposed Asian immigration and what she saw as the breakdown of Anglo-Australia. Although she received limited support, through the use of exaggeration and the stoking of moral panic she gained enough publicity for her name and arguments to become well known, not only across Australia but also with Asian neighbors. John Howard sought to distance himself from both Keating's Asian engagement and Hanson's anti-Asian rhetoric, but he conveyed clearly that he understood the concerns of Hanson supporters and has often been accused of courting One Nation voters with his very tough policies on refugees.[93] Australia's struggle for a foreign policy vision and identity has been ongoing ever since British entry into the European Common Market in 1972. Former Malaysian leader Dr. Mahathir once jibed that, "When the British were rich, Australia wanted to be British. When the Americans were rich, Australia wanted to be American. Now that Asia is rich, Australia wants to be Asian."[94] Since the 1980s Australia's foreign policy shows the continuing pull of Anglo-American sentimentalism. Seen positively, since the late 1980s Australia has fashioned a pragmatic multicultural policy at home that breaks with its racist past and facilitates the growing importance of Asian markets and influence in Australia. Seen negatively, Australia has thought too little about developing a new approach to foreign affairs. Instead, it has instrumentally traded with Asia while neglecting to learn much about Asian societies and cultures. Although neither interpretation comes close to a definition of Australia as a "torn country," what exactly Australia's foreign policy identity is remains significantly unknown, even to itself.

New Zealand illustrates with even greater clarity such a domestic reorientation. Demographic trends illustrate important shifts in New Zealand's ethnic composition and identity politics. Chinese had been considered "friendly aliens" who could be naturalized as British subjects, but policy changed in 1908 and Chinese immigration virtually ground to a halt. Well into the 1950s there existed a highly restrictive quota system targeting Asian immigrants.[95] The changing immigration patterns in the 1960s and 1970s intersected with more open perceptions of Asia, as policy-makers moved from outright hostility to the pursuit of interdependence.[96] Over time, New Zealanders saw themselves less as British and more as something distinct. This is not to deny that the relationship between New Zealand remained close. But with the non-European population growing rapidly, a new kind of mix between the declining Anglo and the growing Māori, Pacific Islanders, and Asian populations will give non-Europeans a majority in a few decades' time.[97] Even more than Australia, New Zealand is forging ahead into a tricultural future.

That future has roots reaching back into New Zealand's past. The 1840 Treaty of Waitangi is the country's founding document. It provides the basis of an enduring myth of equality between Māori and white New Zealanders. In return for loyalty to the British Crown, Māori were to receive sovereignty over their lands and resources, and legal protection.[98] Currently, Māori have their own political parties (the Māori Party), widespread influence in other parties through the mixed member proportional representation (MMP) system, a national television station, and funding for Māori culture and tradition. The Māori language is an official language. Although ethnic relations are far from ideal, New Zealand's track record compares quite favorably with that of other western settler societies.

In the future, Asian influence will surely grow and further transform New Zealand's society. In fact, China sees itself as having a special relationship with New Zealand and promotes the idea of the "four firsts" in New Zealand's diplomacy: recognition of the PRC in December 1972, the first western country to sign a bilateral agreement with China after it joined the WTO in August 1997, the first western country to recognize China as a market economy in April 2004, and the first developed country to pursue free trade negotiations with China, a process announced in November 2004.[99] New Zealand's relations with China and Asia epitomize an evolution in its identity expressed in terms of emotional beliefs, from a fairly narrow and at times xenophobic outlook, to acceptance and engagement, followed by a hopeful interdependence. Sharp increases in Asian immigration are continuing to make the Asian population a larger part of New Zealand society. New Zealand's foreign policy will continue to be shaped by its emerging tricultural identity.

Conclusion

Understanding the importance Australian and NZ leaders and the general public attach to special relationships helps clarify some enduring elements of the foreign policy of both countries, in particular towards the USA and UK. We conclude with several points. First, the special relationship *primus inter pares* has been with Britain. This relationship with NZ and Australia was not at first a relationship between states, between equally sovereign entities. To a certain extent, Watson and Bull's work on "world society" helps us to understand some of the shared values and beliefs that allowed an imperial center and a collection of colonies, and later dominions, to exist in a closely interconnected web of cultural, economic, and military relationships. The solidarist view, which sees sovereignty as less important than shared norms and forms of cooperation, also slots well into our work on special relationships. Similarly, constructivist observations about norms help us to understand how former colonies in NZ and Australia retained their special relationships to the UK as they evolved into dominions and then, eventually, sovereign states.[100] At the level of popular opinion, ties to the UK remain very salient.

Second, for both cases, the US special relationship began as primarily functionalist, but developed sentimentalist overtones with time. These stemmed from the very real benefits the US alliance brought to western countries in the Asia-Pacific after 1942. These benefits continued during the Cold War. Both NZ and Australia had a tendency to play off one special relationship against another, choosing the UK over the USA or vice versa, depending on the time period and political event. NZ has been more prone to this than Australia, especially in cultural terms, where most things British are still perceived as being superior. The level of functionalism in the US–Australian special relationship has changed little with time, while levels of sentimentalism tend to vary. In both cases, the specialness of the US relationship exists primarily at an elite level.

Third, the evolving relationships with Asian countries, particularly China, offer some fascinating contrasts. For both countries, China offers the possibility of a special economic relationship rooted in very close trading ties and a level of economic interdependence that will rival the US–Canada, NZ–Australia, or UK–Australia–NZ trade relationships before the 1970s. These ties will continue to be functionalist for the foreseeable future, although a rhetoric of sentimentalism is evolving, at least in NZ. Again, as with the USA, such ties are primarily between political and economic elites, rather than the general population.

Fourth, the relationship between Australia and NZ is extremely close: probably the closest of all in the Anglo-American grouping. While there are obvious differences, it is easy to downplay the enduring history of cooperation between these two longstanding allies and friends. Critics tend to underemphasize the continued circulation of immigrants, tourists, businesspeople, conference attendees, and students from one Anglo-American society to the other. New Zealand's single most popular destination for resettlement is Australia.

Finally, both countries, at both elite and society levels, remain closely tied to the larger Anglo-American world. Tourism to Canada and the UK remains high amongst New Zealanders and Australians. For all of their changing trading relations and new immigrants, Australia and NZ remain, at least into the medium term, firmly part of the Anglo-American "civilization" as it changes and evolves in the new century. This will continue to be the case because most politicians and senior foreign policy bureaucrats, and much of the public, see both countries as part of an Anglo-American club. At the everyday level, this ideational power is supported by the fact that most television shows, films, popular music, magazines, newspaper and media stories in NZ and Australia are from the Anglo-American world.

In alliance and security relations, this clubbishness has led to the two nations seeking close relations with the UK for much of their histories, later turning to the USA. This new relationship has been less sentimental and more based on elite connections, but clubbish nonetheless, particularly in the area of intelligence sharing, an activity whose daily cable rewards make senior politicians and their staffers in Australia (and even NZ) complicit in, and often addicted to, American power. Anti-nuclear policy was undoubtedly a challenge for the NZ relationship. It caused tensions and led to more a multilateral instinct in NZ than Australia but, as we opined earlier, these are best seen as disputes within a family, a view which pertains both at state and society levels. There seems little to indicate that the alliance is in danger of receding. Indeed, the opposite is arguably the case, and as trade and security relationships become more interconnected and interdependent, we expect the ties between Anglo-American states to retain an enduring appeal, in both functionalist and sentimentalist terms.

Notes

1 Our thanks to Peter Katzenstein for creating this fascinating project and including us as part of it. We appreciate his patience, kindness, and mentorship throughout. We have also benefited from the comments of numerous contributors to this volume, especially Herman Schwartz, Audie Klotz, Brian Bow, Arturo Santa-Cruz, and Srdjan Vucetic. Thank you also to Todd Hall and Rose McDermott.
2 Mercer 2010, 2.
3 Katzenstein 2010b.
4 Keohane and Nye 1977.
5 Migdal 2001, 16.
6 Wight 1986, 123.
7 Bow and Santa-Cruz, 2010.
8 Schoenbaum 1998, 273.
9 Dumbrell and Schäfer 2009a, 4.
10 Dumbrell 2006, 11–12.
11 Gamble and Kearns 2007, 116.
12 Dumbrell 2006, 14–15.
13 Danchev 2005, 435–6.
14 Watt 1986, 1.
15 Smith 1990.
16 Reynolds 1989, 95–6.
17 Dumbrell 2006, 14–15.
18 For an overview, see MacDonald and O'Connor 2010.
19 McDermott 2010, 114.
20 Finnemore 1996, 22.
21 Obama and Cameron 2011.
22 Bull and Watson 1984, 330; Buzan 1993, 327–52.
23 See, for example, Wheeler 2001.
24 MacDonald and O'Connor 2010.
25 Champion 2010, 30–3.
26 Crawford 2000, 134–5.
27 Ibid., 135; 140.
28 Bleiker and Hutchison 2007, 4–5.
29 New Zealand Cabinet Office 2010, 3.
30 Foreign and Commonwealth Office UK 2009.

31 Zemka 2002, 446–7.
32 Webster 2006, 656–7.
33 Walker 1987, 96.
34 Pearson 2009, 37–8.
35 Curran and Ward 2010.
36 Curran 2011.
37 Janiewski 2009, 94.
38 McIntyre 1993, 45.
39 Miller 1987, 383.
40 Wesley and Warren 2000.
41 Stewart et al. 1999.
42 National Security Agency 2010.
43 Gardham 2010.
44 Walker and Henderson 1980, 195–6.
45 McGibbon 1999, 115.
46 Thomson 2000, 328.
47 Smith 2005, 181.
48 Bennett 1988, 92.
49 McGibbon 1999, 122.
50 Lange 2005, 204–5.
51 Hoadley 1989, 9.
52 Mulhall 1987, 66.
53 Van Ness 1986.
54 Lange 2005, 33; Hawke 2011.
55 Smith 2005, 211.
56 Edwards 2001, 186.
57 Hawke 2011.
58 Smith 2005, 223.
59 Hager 2007, 23–4.
60 Ibid., 211.
61 Ibid., 19–20.
62 Ibid., 220.
63 Hoadley 2000, 48.
64 Key 2007.
65 McCully 2009a.
66 McCully 2009b.
67 Statistics New Zealand 2008.
68 Renouf 1979; Burke 2008.
69 Jackman 2008; Jackman and Vavreck 2011.
70 O'Connor and Vucetic 2010.
71 Hager 2010.
72 New Zealand Press Association 2008.
73 New Zealand Press Association 2010.
74 Harland 1992, 17.
75 Hartdegen 1999, 5, 19–20.
76 McLean 2003, 196–7.
77 Bennett 2007b, 57.
78 Palmer and Hill 2002, 315.
79 Devetak and True 2006, 243.
80 White 2005.
81 McIntyre 1993, 41–2; McLean 2003, 132–3, 140.
82 Hoadley 2000.
83 Harland 1992, 61.
84 Hager 2007, 180.
85 McMillan 2008, 194.

 86 McLean 2003, 260–6.
 87 MacDonald 2005, 171–92.
 88 New Zealand Ministry of Defence 2010, 18.
 89 Ibid., 28.
 90 Huntington 1996, 151.
 91 Curran 2004.
 92 Switzer 2009.
 93 Carney 2003.
 94 Wesley 2007.
 95 Pearson 2009, 37–8.
 96 Hartdegen 1999, 5; 19–20.
 97 Statistics New Zealand 2008.
 98 Orange 1987, 2; Williams 1989, 65.
 99 Ministry of Foreign Affairs and Trade (NZ) 2010.
100 Beeson 2009, 78–9.

PART IV

PART IV

9

MANY WESTS AND POLYMORPHIC GLOBALISM[1]

Peter J. Katzenstein

Anglo–America, this book argues, is one important part of the West. There exist other parts, most importantly in Europe (in its French and Germanic variants) and in the Americas (in its Hispanic, Caribbean, and other variants). The relationship among these parts of the West is neither parallel, in the form of amicable coexistence, nor hierarchical, in the form of clear subordination. Rather, it is layered. The historical trajectory of this manifold West has no fixed point of destination, as I shall argue at the end of this chapter.

As for its origin, Greece and Rome were not the foundation of European and Western civilization. Rather, Western civilization mixed important Graeco-Roman with other civilizational influences. Athena was neither black nor white, but brown.[2] To regard Greece, Europe, and the West as set apart from their Islamic, Semitic, African, and Orthodox-Christian roots strains the historical record. For almost a millennium, Islam's contributions to science, technology, and the arts were much more important than that of Western Europe. Much of Aristotle's work, for example, would have been lost without the Islamic scholars who translated, preserved, and developed it. Arabic science, Jim al-Khalili argues, made the European Renaissance possible.[3] John Jackson argues similarly that by transporting them into the realm of Ancient Greece, European scholarship has either ignored African civilizations or Europeanized African achievements, especially Egypt's.[4] Judaism is arguably European, and so is the strain and stain of Western anti-Semitism. And Constantinople rivaled Rome as the second center of Western civilization. Between 1458 and 1821, Greece was incorporated into the Ottoman empire. This left a profound mark on the fiscal incapacities of the Greek state. Freed from the grip of a military junta in 1974, Greece rode a wave of European civilizational sentiment to full membership in the European Economic Community (EEC). Europe's *enfant terrible* has since exploited a system of financial largesse, helping to trigger Europe's sovereign debt crisis in 2010. From beginning to end, Greek history offers a perfect illustration of the existence of many Wests.

After briefly giving a conceptual overview of civilizational analysis, I discuss the West with specific reference to America and Europe and Americanization and Europeanization. I then turn to multiple modernities reflected in Islam and Anglo-America as two bridging civilizations, and end with a discussion of a polymorphic globalism that encompasses both of them.

Civilizational analysis: a conceptual overview

Civilizations provide us with the broadest social context and worldviews in both space and time; they equal "culture writ large."[5] Civilizations do not act; political entities act within civilizations. More specifically, as Lydia Liu writes, "civilizations do not clash; empires do."[6] In a similar vein Ian Morris insists that culture "is less a voice in our heads telling us what to do than a town hall meeting where we argue about our options."[7] It thus helps to shape everyday practice and policy through the exercise of power in institutions. As Gary Hamilton argues, "world images have decisive effects on how such spheres of activity are actually interpreted and organized as going concerns."[8] Actors in all civilizations engage in the illusion that they are singular and thus blind themselves to the existence of other ways of imagining and living life. It is, however, undeniable that we live in a world of plural and pluralist civilizations. The illusion of singularity is often fostered by intellectual and political entrepreneurs who seek to serve particular interests through discursive moves and political strategies. Under the cold light of evidence, past claims to singularity do not hold up.[9] Civilizations are distinctive and differentiated, not unique or unified. As for the future, it is conceivable that we will witness a clash between Civilization, capitalized and in the singular, and Nature. To survive that clash a new kind of singularity may evolve – lodged in what Jeremy Rifkin calls an empathic civilization – that would transcend East and West. A successor to the contested traditions and modernities of plural and pluralist civilizations, such empathic civilization may be humankind's best hope for avoiding global nightfall.[10] For now, however, it exists only in embryonic form.

Civilizations are indelibly bound up with political power – in both its visible–behavioral as well as its invisible–symbolic dimensions.[11] Materialist accounts of civilizations are inclined to stress the former, ideational ones the latter. In reality, both play their parts. Civilizational politics is partly driven by the interests of elites. Seeking to expand their power and prestige across geographic and symbolic spaces, these elites rely on civilizational imageries in an instrumental fashion. More characteristic and less straightforward is a second civilizational dynamic in which elite interests are defined by civilizational discourses and practices that impose their own logic over material structures, incentives, and the interests derived from them. Power in civilizations is primarily social, revealed in identities and interests and in the processes, policies, and practices that flow from them. In short, the broad social context that civilizations provide shapes how political actors, not civilizations, mobilize power.

Language and religion

The two most important and distinctive characteristics of a civilization are its religious and literary traditions. Separately and together, they provide ample raw material from which to fashion the multiple traditions that constitute civilizational life. Language is a central element of civilization. In Japan, Korea, and Vietnam for millennia Chinese was used for writing, even though these countries retained their indigenous languages and in some cases their own scripts.[12] In the eighteenth century, French language and court manners were epitomes of civilization emulated in polite society throughout Europe. Frederick the Great spoke German – but only to his dogs.

In India, language is also a central marker of civilization.[13] The very choice between "Hindu" or "Indian" civilizations poses a central question. "Hindu civilization" suggests religion as the one overarching cultural component that overrides all others. "Indian civilization" makes space for numerous cultural components and for healthy contestation among them. Susanne Hoeber Rudolph chooses the composite over the coherence view. The Indian subcontinent encompasses states that are divided in terms of religion but share linguistic, literary, and other cultural characteristics, thus giving credence to the concept of Indian civilization. Furthermore, Rudolph argues, India invalidates the distinction between civilized and uncivilized based on the existence of a written language. With Brahmins trained in an oral tradition of reciting the Vedas, Sanskrit survived for hundreds of years under the social convention of oral transmission; writing would have violated the sacred. Yet, the emphasis on language and elite culture, Rudolph also points out, overlooks the importance of language as a vehicle of xenophobic nationalism and, in the case of India, of imperialism and colonialism.

Bruce Lawrence argues similarly that Islamic civilization arose in the context of nomadism with strong oral traditions.[14] The absence of a written language at the origin, as in Islam, or over prolonged periods, as in India, shows that in the evolution of civilizations, language plays important though varying roles. Indian scholars continue to debate the question of what is the language of Indian civilization. As a practical matter, Indian elites rely widely on English. However, while this permits India's service sector to leap-frog over other developing economies, nobody thinks of it as India's language. Here, as in other linguistically fluid situations such as the Philippines, English is accepted as a lingua franca but not as a mother tongue.[15] What, then, is the precise status of English as the latest in a long history of world languages? Nicholas Ostler argues that the world is moving not to a monolingual but to a multilingual future, without a successor to English as a lingua franca.[16] For now, at least, that primacy is beyond doubt as English presents the lion's share of all published translations.[17] Still, Ostler's detailed analysis of the use of mother tongue and of English as a lingua franca suggests a world of linguistic diversity.[18]

Indeed, as a lingua franca English is experiencing a limited process of differentiation into distinguishable varieties.[19] English will not displace the diversity of mother tongues in a multicivilizational world marked by linguistic regionalism.[20] And it may itself be undermined or displaced by the evolution of language technologies that is now beginning to revolutionize processes of translation.

Religion is a second marker of civilization. Samuel Huntington, for example, refers to "Western religion" rather than "Western Christendom" as the successor to "Latin Christendom," the term of choice before the Enlightenment.[21] Western Christendom was in fact a deeply divided religious tradition. In the sixteenth and seventeenth centuries, that division was revealed in Protestant and Catholic mass slaughters during the Thirty Years War. As late as the turn of the twentieth century, Protestants viewed Catholics with much suspicion as a subversive transnational religion, just as many Catholics and Protestants today regard Muslims. James Kurth builds and elaborates on Huntington's argument about the importance of Reform Protestantism for the origin and evolution of Western and American civilization.[22] Especially provocative is Kurth's argument that the Protestant core of the American Creed has come to include the civil religion of a secularized Protestantism – what he calls the heretical, neo-pagan religion of America's secular elite. Religious diversity rather than universal religion marks the resurgence of religious vitality in many contemporary civilizations. Multiple traditions of secularisms, in the plural, point to the intensification or persistence of religious consciousness and politics with which these secularisms must engage. While Christianity and Islam have expanded in the twentieth century, so have various forms of nonreligious and atheistic belief systems. Varieties of religious and secular belief systems thus continue to exist side by side. African civilizations illustrate clearly this pluralist theme.

Africa[23]

The West has frequently been likened to an *Über-civilization* with global reach. It is not, however, as classical theories of Eurocentrism suggest, the fountain of civilization. Africa, not the West, is the world's *Ur-civilization*. It merits attention because of the deep connections between Western liberalism and the issue of race.[24] Although modern humans spread from Africa, people are pretty much the same wherever we find them.[25] This is not necessarily to argue that African civilizations emerged as self-contained entities with crystallized values which subsequently spread. Rather, they developed at various crossroads of a complex mosaic of different peoples and a bewildering array of language communities. African civilizations are defined by and evolved at the intersections of other civilizations.[26] Africa's name has variously been traced to Berber, Graeco-Roman, Phoenician, or Arab origins.[27] And geographically, like other civilizations, Africa is not easily delimited. North Africa, for example, can be regarded as a Western extension of the Arabian peninsula, a northern extension of Sub-Saharan Africa, or a southern extension of Europe.

Salah Hassan has argued that our understanding of Africa has been marked by three different African trajectories.[28] The first was shaped by colonial and orientalist thought and by the racialized hierarchies and arbitrary divisions within African histories, societies, and civilizations that it helped produce. The second trajectory took a continental view of Africa in two characteristic forms. It included the internalization of Western perception, for example of North Africa's presumed separation from the rest of Africa, the Arabian peninsula, and the rest of the Islamic world; and it expressed a region-wide consciousness of Africa that emerged in the context of the encounter between Africa and Western colonialism. Finally, a third diasporic trajectory has encompassed different strands of pan-Africanism and Afrocentrism, covering both internationalist and nationalist visions. What unites all three trajectories is the fact that in its various dimensions, Africa has always been closely connected to the West, Islam, and the world beyond.

V.Y. Mudimbe traces the idea of Africa as a story of European philosophical, literary, and cultural invention.[29] Even in the most explicitly Afrocentric analyses, interpretations of Africa have largely relied on a Western epistemological order. European explorers brought back from Africa a wealth of descriptive evidence that supported reified categories of thought distinguishing between civilized Europeans and savage natives. European soldiers fought often brutal military campaigns that presumed the existence of that divide. And the language of missionaries expressed a clear normative discourse grounded in the same distinction. Only after World War I and with the beginning of the negritude movement did the possibility of African discourses of "otherness" become relevant. Yet even that movement reflected multiple Western traditions as much as authentic African intellectual currents. Furthermore, in the interest of continued British colonial rule, a group of civil servants, missionaries, and social scientists contributed to the creation of an ideology of "Africanity."[30] In the nineteenth and twentieth centuries, the British system of indirect rule in both East Africa and Nigeria relied on the creation of an African continental narrative designed to facilitate the colonial project and legitimate British rule. In nineteenth-century Yorubaland, in East Nigeria, British colonial administrators reinfused with new political meaning an old social cleavage along ancestral city lines. They also reestablished traditional kings, in the interest of creating an aura of legitimacy for the social order they were shaping. And in the interest of efficiency, they hoped to rule indirectly.[31] During the interwar period, British colonial administrators invented in Tanganyika a largely fictitious narrative of Africa's past, culture, and social structure. They sought to co-opt some social sectors of the colonized population in the hope of bolstering Britain's position, weakened by an ideological crisis of Britain's "civilizing mission" after World War I and confronting widespread resistance.

In contrast, told from an African perspective, the history of African civilization unfolded in five phases. In its earliest phase, North Africa was constructed as part of the European world, leaving southern Africa as a barbaric and "dark" continent.[32] While "black" was a descriptive category in "Sudan," meaning "the Black ones," in European and Arab usage that term was judgmental and pejorative. In the second phase, Africa was shaped to the North through its interaction with Semitic-speaking peoples (Phoenicians and Hebrews) and classical Greece and Rome, and to the East, at the Horn of Africa, through its interaction with Black Semites such as the Amhara and the peoples of Eritrea and Ethiopia. The third period was marked by the spread of Islam in Africa. Facing persecution in Mecca, the earliest Muslims fled across the Red Sea to seek refuge in Ethiopia. East Africa subsequently developed a dynamic Swahili mercantile civilization linking Africa to Asia.[33] West Africa, well before European colonization, also evolved at the intersection of two civilizations: indigenous Africanity and Islam. The city of Timbuktu became the most celebrated intellectual center in the Black world. In the fourth phase, Africa emerged as a product of the dialogue among three civilizations – Africanity, Islam, and the West. And in the fifth and final phase, Africa is now seen as the historical origin of the human species. With a singular lack of good intentions, Europeans did a great deal to Africanize Africa. Their cartography created a space for territorial imagination. And their racism created a feeling of fellowship among many Africans.[34] Specifically, the slave trade tied Africa indelibly to the Americas. Today, one of every five people of African ancestry lives in North America and the Caribbean. By looking at Africa in a global context and at the history of the world from an African perspective, Afrocentricity has replaced the idea of a triple civilizational heritage. The human species had its origin in Africa, and humankind can now be conceived of as one global African diaspora.[35] If the concept of America incites the imagination because of what it promises for the future, Africa incites because of what it recalls from the past.

Pluralist civilizations in one civilization of multiple modernities or unitary civilizations in the international state system?

Civilizational analysis should avoid being trapped by the illusion of singularity.[36] There are two basic views on civilization. This book takes a pluralist view that sees civilizations as embedded in a more encompassing context. It thus extends further the perspective of pre-modern civilizations as a Eurasian or Afro-Eurasian ecumene.[37] Civilizations are grounded in and encompass the material infrastructure of world affairs – cities, commerce, travel, trade, alliances, and warfare. Scouring the scattered testaments of long-forgotten collectors of Indian and Egyptian artifacts in the eighteenth and nineteenth centuries, Maya Jasanoff is able to track "how much the process of cultural encounter involved crossing and mixing."[38] Ian Morris has argued similarly that over the long course of human history, all large groupings of peoples have been endowed with similar inherent capacities; understood in geographic terms, West and East have enjoyed variable ecological advantages leading to shifting advantages of one over the other; the recent lead of Western over Eastern civilizations will either reverse during the coming century or, more likely, be rendered irrelevant by transformative changes that will eliminate the significance of territory in the universal explosion of knowledge.[39] Today's civilization of modernity stands for the known world and the manifold connections between different civilizational complexes. Although it retains for now territorial roots, it is defined also by non-territorial processes that express a forever changing historical consciousness. And it constitutes a universal system of knowledgeable practices that are characteristic of contested, multiple modernities. The history of civilizations is one of mutual borrowing that does not endanger a civilization's character.[40] The movement of peoples between hills and valleys and across continents and oceans, as well as the tensions within and between religious and literary traditions, account for the plurality and pluralism of civilizations.

An alternative view of civilizations holds that they are unitary cultural programs, organized hierarchically around uncontested core values that yield unambiguous criteria for judging good conduct.[41] This view was a European invention of the eighteenth century. In the nineteenth century, it was enshrined in the concept of one standard of civilization. That standard was grounded in race, ethnic affiliation, religion, and a firm belief in the superiority of European civilization over all others. The distinction between civilized and uncivilized peoples, however, is not specific to the European past. It enjoys broad support today among many conservative supporters of Huntington's thesis of the clash of civilizations – a book that was translated into 39 languages.[42] Paradoxically, it is also held by many liberals who are committed to improving the rule of law and global standards of good governance. Furthermore, the unitary argument is widely used by non-Europeans in their analysis of civilizational politics. Everywhere and at all times, so-called barbarians have knocked on the doors of civilizations.[43]

Where civilizations appear to cohere around uncontested core values, we are witnessing political and intellectual innovations created for particular purposes rather than inherent cultural traits of unchanging collective identities and practices. Samuel Huntington's *Clash of Civilizations* restates the old, unitary thesis for our times. For Huntington, civilizations are coherent, consensual, invariant, and equipped with a state-like capacity to act. Huntington succeeded brilliantly in his objective of providing a new paradigm for looking at world politics after the end of the Cold War. His correct anticipation of 9/11 gave the book a claim to validity that helps account for its continued relevance. Less noticed in public than in academic discourse is the fact that Huntington greatly overstates his case. Numerous analyses have established beyond any reasonable doubt that clashes occur primarily within rather than between civilizations.[44] Furthermore, the book's appeal has not been undermined by the failure of the second of its two main claims. Since the end of the Cold War, the relations between Sinic and American civilizations are summarized best by terms such as encounter or engagement rather than clash.

A very similar, anti-Western counter-discourse, also steeped in Western reasoning, has long existed in Asia. Lee Kuan Yew and his advisor Tommy Koh are outspoken supporters of the Asian values view.[45] Another well-known public intellectual in Singapore, Kishore Mahbubani, is a champion of Asia. His recent book details a seismic shift in power from "West" to "East."[46] And then there is the dialogue between Mohammad Mahathir and Shintarō Ishihara, which develops the same point more stridently.[47] The voices proclaiming the dawn of Asia's civilizational primacy may shift from yesterday's Japan, to today's China and tomorrow's India. But these voices are growing louder. Like "Orientalism," "Occidentalism" characterizes East and West in the singular.[48]

Primordialism as political construction

The widespread use of East and West in the singular creates a discursive category that is endowed with actor-like dispositions. It is then deployed under specific political conditions and for specific political purposes.[49] It is not the category, but the act of reification or construction that is politically consequential and that requires political analysis. In convincing ourselves and others of a specific mental map, and aligning our identities and interests with that map, we rely on rhetorical constructions to impute meaning that otherwise eludes us.

Primordialism is a simplifying crystallization of social consciousness. It can focus on civilization as it does on gender, kinship, territory, language, or race. The specific collective identity invoked is defined either in terms of "civility" (drawing boundaries between "us" and "them" with a specific focus on rules of conduct and social routines) or in terms of sacredness (drawing boundaries between "us" and "them" with specific reference to the transcendental, defined as God or Reason).[50] We need to understand both: how civilizations become, and what they are. Indeed, in primordial constructions of Self and Other, action and speech are deeply entangled with one another rather than existing side by side. Our analysis thus needs to encompass both to capture the broad and deep consensus about the very term "civilization."[51]

Samuel Huntington's unitary conception of civilization illustrates this point. For Huntington, civilizations are competing in an international system rather than constituting one global civilization of multiple modernities. Hence, Huntington articulates as a policy maxim "the commonalities rule," pointing as an urgent need to something that exists already in abundance: the search for values, institutions, and practices that are shared across civilizations.[52] In his view, civilizations balance power rather than reflecting open-ended processes and a broad range of human practices. Neglecting all the evidence of a restless, pluralist, and at times seething West, Huntington's analysis sees the West as a civilizationally reactive status quo power that reluctantly engages the upsurge of revisionist non-Western civilizations. Rather than focusing on actors such as states, polities, or empires that are embedded in civilizational complexes, in Huntington's analysis civilizations themselves become actors. And, implausibly, he measures civilizational power solely by material capabilities such as population, GNP, and military expenditures. His clash of civilizations thus looks remarkably similar to a clash of large states or empires. In my view, instead, civilizations are the broadest cultural context for world politics.

Civilization of multiple modernities and a balance of practice

A civilization of multiple modernities as an encompassing context for all civilizations enhances the pluralism that inheres in a world of civilizations. That context is not the international system or global markets, frequently deployed concepts that suffer from excessive sparseness and abstraction. Recognition of the importance of this context is central to the trenchant self-critique that William McNeill wrote of in his brilliant *The Rise of the West*, more than a quarter of a century after he had completed it and six years before the publication of Huntington's book.[53] For McNeill, civilizations are internally variegated, loosely coupled, elite-centered social systems that are integrated in a commonly shared global context. He argues that his earlier path-breaking book was wrongheaded, based on the faulty assumption of the existence of civilizations conceived as separate groupings whose interaction was the main engine of world history. Instead, McNeill now insists that an adequate account must give proper consideration to the broader context in which all civilizations are embedded. Since civilizations are internally differentiated, they transplant selectively. And since they are loosely integrated, they generate debates and contestations that tend to make them salient to others. What historically was true for South Asia and the Islamic world, under the impact of modern communications technologies is even more true for all contemporary civilizations. All of today's civilizations are embedded in one all-encompassing civilization of modernity.

Civilizational politics is therefore syncretic in blending global and international processes with religious, secular, and national ones.[54] For Fernand Braudel, at first sight "every civilization looks rather like a railway goods yard, constantly receiving and dispatching miscellaneous deliveries."[55] Deeply meaningful to many members of the cultural elite, as self-conscious and lived identities, civilizations do not rank at the top for most people and typically do not manifest themselves in an everyday sense of strong belonging. Making civilizations primordial is arguably a political project aimed at creating a taken-for-granted sense of reality that helps in distinguishing between Self and Other, and between right and wrong. It requires elimination of the awareness that civilizations exist in plural forms and are constituted by multiple traditions creating diverse processes, policies, and practices.

In sum, the conceptualization I offer here is attuned to both the emergence of new political forces that reflect the richness of the political repertoires made available by various civilizations, and the political backlash that novelty and change will frequently create. Closely tied to political power, shifting balances of policies and practices are thus producing and reproducing behavioral and symbolic boundaries within and between civilizations.

Civilizational identities: America and Europe

Unitary and single-tradition theories do not help us to accurately understand either the West or Anglo-America. At the same time, however, the concept of the West continues to receive support from its use by "outsiders" who invoke the concept in complex ways to construct their own identity and thus prolong the existence of the West as a unitary category.[56] K.M. Heller argues that the unitary West is a political construct that "gathers an imaginary geography, geopolitical being, an historical destiny, and a commitment to a unique set of values....Naming something Western thus tends to take the form, however truncated, of a theory of the world-historical."[57]

America

In his analysis of democracy in America, Tocqueville offers an analysis of one national experience in light of the broader civilization to which it belongs.[58] Within that civilization Michael Lind sees different strands of nationalisms: left-wing multiculturalism, right-wing democratic universalism, and centrist liberal (stressing language or culture) or populist nativist (stressing race or religion) nationalism.[59] Both multiculturalism and democratic universalism contain elements of political–constitutional universalisms and cultural–racial localisms, thus creating an affinity with the global civilization of multiple modernities that embeds the West and other civilizations. But they also contain strands of American exceptionalism, celebrating America's "Obama-nation" as the most successful racial and ethnic melting pot of the contemporary world, as well as the incarnation of democratic institutions that are morally superior to all others. These two visions, Lind argues, "have almost monopolized recent discussions…[and] agree that the United States has never been a conventional nation-state."[60] Lind disagrees with this assessment as he builds his case for a liberal nationalism that blends heterogeneous subcultures and political and religious dogma into a concrete historical community defined by a common language, folkways, and a vibrant vernacular culture. For Lind it is noteworthy that American nationalism was dominated by ideas expressing important civilizational notions such as the American way of life – not to the exclusion of national sentiments, but as quintessential components of America's collective identity.[61] The historical mutations of America's collective identity from Anglo-Saxon (1789–1861), to Euro-American (1875–1957) and Multicultural (1972 to the present) put the basic building blocs of race, culture, and citizenship in different configurations, with a successive broadening and blending of racial, religious, and ethno-cultural boundaries of exclusion. Considering the intensity of conflicts over its history,[62] and on the evidence of the contested multiculturalism that marks Anglo-America as discussed in this book, it is unlikely that Lind's preferred cosmopolitan liberal "Trans-America" will ever come to pass.[63] If it did, however, it would overcome, finally, the divisions between multicultural liberalism and plutocratic conservatism, offering its own distinctive blending of civilizational–national identities that are color-blind, gender-neutral, and expressive of a strong commitment to individual rights and socioeconomic equality.

On the strength of Lind's analysis of America's numerous contested identities, it is implausible to view America as being endowed with one central set of values and one overarching tradition. In the area of foreign policy as well, America has numerous traditions.[64] The most recent reassertion of Jacksonianism under the presidency of G.W. Bush must be seen against the background of alternative Jeffersonian, Hamiltonian, and Wilsonian traditions. Until the middle of the twentieth century these traditions were tinged with a racism that was readily apparent in the different approaches the United States took to the construction of NATO and SEATO in the late 1940s.[65]

Woodrow Wilson exemplifies America's multiple traditions in domestic and international politics.[66] A man of the South, he was a consistent advocate of racial difference. As Stephen Skowronek argues, as politician and statesman, Wilson was consistent. His racial ideas made him rework received ideals and promulgate principles now associated with liberal democracy.[67] Wilson was a strong opponent of Congressional despotism over the South which, he believed, made a travesty of the doctrine of states' rights. His conviction that the South should have a right to self-determination in effect sanctioned the rule of the Ku Klux Klan. But since the system of institutional checks and balances had been overturned, Wilson became an advocate for strong presidential leadership based on direct popular appeal. At the same time, Wilson and Wilsonianism took a page from Edmund Burke's insistence on the centrality of organic evolution over contrived constitutional principles. Lacking a proper system of checks and balances and operating under the rule of a strong president, in the United States political self-restraint was the most important virtue. Abstract plans were less important than established norms and habits and the functioning of a contentious pluralism. Hence, Wilson resisted the leveling tendencies of concentrated power and opposed women's suffrage.

Internationally, too, Wilson favored an activist foreign policy and the spreading of American values. He is best known in Asia for supporting the veto of the racial equality clause at the Versailles peace conference at the end of World War I. Wilson was less interested in the universal application of his doctrine than in getting great powers to agree on stabilizing compacts. Since Wilson saw the League of Nations as a conservative force, many Republicans in the Senate opposed his policy, fearing that in a refurbished Concert of the Great Powers the USA might strengthen the forces of repression rather than act as a force of liberation. Their fears were not totally unfounded. Wilson made Burke's criticism of Britain's leveling rule in India his own. And since he held firmly to an organic view of progress toward independence – in which the more civilized can help the less civilized to accelerate their journey toward eventual self-rule – Wilson supported America's tutelary empire in the Philippines and the South's tutelary rule over black Americans. For him collective security was not static, as was the balance of power, but organic and evolutionary. Thus Wilson supported both the mandate system and a system constraining war in Europe.

Anatol Lieven argues that America's journey from "Herrenvolk democracy" to "civilizational empire" required shedding the tradition of racism that characterized America's first Wilsonian phase at the outset of the twentieth century.[68] At the end of World War II between the late 1940s and the mid-1960s, under the experience of the Holocaust and the decolonization movement, American leaders made a significant break with America's deeply entrenched racist legacy. Eventually this shift has been embraced widely, transforming the political role of the South as the pivotal region for different Left-of-Center and Right-of-Center internationalist strategies. America's civilizational empire thus is not merely a military empire steeped in racist doctrine, as was true to varying degrees of the Mongolian continental and European maritime empires. Instead, it follows closer to the tradition of Islamic and Sinic civilizational empires – and perhaps also of the Roman empire after it granted full citizenship to all of its free subjects in 221 CE.[69]

The new politics of multiculturalism points to related developments in some of America's other traditions and the influence they have had on America's civilizational empire. One of those developments is the strong impulse of America's religious fundamentalism on faith-based, human rights diplomacy, complementing the secular human rights movement.[70] Similarly, since the beginning of the republic, economic liberalism has both battled intensely and lived symbiotically with economic protectionism, in an unending contest between competing political ideologies and traditions with a strong sectional base.[71] At home, America's multiple and dueling traditions find expression in the victories of different political coalitions and the institutions that emerge over time. Abroad, they have helped create processes of Americanization that have contributed to the shaping of contemporary world affairs.

In his genealogical account of the history of the West, James Kurth tracks successive Classical, Christian, and Western phases that merge into a contemporary global civilization.[72] The American roots in the Reform Protestantism of English Puritans and Scottish Presbyterians as well as the British Enlightenment created a distinct offshoot that differed from developments on the European continent and made it a genuine alternative to nineteenth-century European conceptions of Western civilization. American political development furthered rule by contract and constitution, thus defining institutions of liberal democracy and market capitalism. Crystallized, in Kurth's view, as the American Creed, it has had a strong influence on one emerging global civilization of multiple modernities without, however, fully imprinting it. Ruthless Americanization of successive waves of immigrants at home and – with the decline of the European great powers – active international leadership abroad were both integral parts of this process. The unity of the American nation state and the Western alliance that marked the global confrontation with Fascism and Communism during the second half of the twentieth century are now giving way to new political coalitions and developments: fragile and contested multicultural arrangements inside America in competition with a reconfigured American Creed, and the establishment of a global civilization supportive of individual human rights and unfettered global markets furthering and undermining individual well-being.

One implication of the centrality of America's multiple traditions and the political conflicts they have engendered is to let go of the cherished myth of American exceptionalism.[73] Instead, it makes more sense to underline American distinctiveness, especially when viewed comparatively and in a global context.[74] America is not cut from one cloth. It is constituted instead by various traditions – liberal and illiberal, secular and religious. In the past, the toleration of religious differences was a critically important precondition for America's ascendance in global politics.

Today, greater ethnic and racial tolerance has coincided with America's position of global preeminence after 1945.[75]

Europe

Although in a very different political context, a similar blending of civilizational and national identities is also characteristic of the European version of the West.[76] There is rarely any doubt that in Europe the primary locus of identification is national rather than European. And where they exist, European sentiments are more often instrumental than emotional. As an emerging multilevel polity, the European Union (EU) attracts some political allegiance – strongly from Europe's elites, and weakly from Europe's mass publics. But these expressions of political allegiance typically complement rather than replace existing national sentiments. Most Europeans feel themselves as members of both their national communities and of Europe. Dying for Europe is not an issue for the average European. Not killing Europeans is.

Viewed against the backdrop of persistent strong national identification, the increasing politicization of identities in the process of European enlargement has created two very different European identity projects – one outward-looking and cosmopolitan, the other inward-looking and national-populist. Cosmopolitan conceptions are driven by elite-level politics, reflect the winners of market liberalization and integration, and focus on political citizenship and rights. Populist conceptions respond to mass politics, reflect the losers of economic liberalization and integration, and are concerned with social citizenship and cultural authenticity. Furthermore, the politicization of religion and religious identities reinforces the politicization of collective identities during the process of European enlargement. Toward the East, Christianity or Catholicism is regarded by many Europeans as an intuitively plausible dividing line, crystallized politically in the issue of Turkish accession to the EU. Furthermore, European civil societies try to come to terms with a rapidly growing Muslim minority that is itself divided in its allegiance between Islam, Euro-Islam and a global *umma*. At the same time, many Europeans also subscribe to the notion of a non-confessional and secular European identity that clashes with a religious fundamentalism often seen as defining the extreme, American fringe of Western civilization. In Europe, as in America, civilizational and national identities are thus intermingled. To deny one or the other would simplify unduly the complex reality of a civilizational complex that links America and Europe.

In the case of Europe, it is "the idea of Europe" that provides the uniform veneer for its multiple traditions and the different political practices that idea entails.[77] That veneer conceals diversity. Karl Deutsch has argued that medieval Europe was extremely variegated.[78] It featured six separate civilizational strands: monastic Christianity around the Mediterranean; Latin Christendom in Western and Central Europe; and Byzantium in South-eastern Europe. These three major civilizations were connected by the Afro-Eurasian trade networks of Islam, which for more than half a millennium took hold on the Iberian peninsula, as well as elements of two smaller trading civilizations, the Jews and the Vikings. Europe's multiple traditions constitute important sources for its collective identities.[79] Insisting on Europe as a historically unified civilization is not easily squared with this historical record. When contemporary European civilization, in the singular, is invoked today, it is typically in contradistinction to Islam and the presumed binary between Occident and Orient.

Gerard Delanty, whom I am following here, writes in the opening sentence of his book, "every age reinvented the idea of Europe in the mirror of its own identity."[80] Europe is not a self-evident entity but a construction that changes over time and expresses different political processes, policies, and practices. The idea of Europe has often been deployed as a unifying cultural frame and a universalizing projection. In this view Europe is a fantasy homeland besieged by external enemies. Such primordial constructions, however, confront stubborn facts on the ground that suggest otherwise. Europe is, by its very nature, a deeply contested concept evoking profoundly ambivalent reactions and often contradictory political impulses. At its core lies the tension between exclusive and inclusive collective identities.[81] There is no immutable European idea and set of political practices linked indelibly, as many of Europe's leaders and media elites argue today, to humanist values and liberal democracy. Imperialism and genocide, both inside and outside of Europe, are as much part of the European idea and practice as are its Graeco-Roman legacies, Latin Christendom, the Renaissance, and the Enlightenment. Europe's traditions have encompassed ideas and practices that have been used for good and ill.

Europe incorporates more than one civilizational constellation. The Orthodox and Islamic parts of Europe make Gerard Delanty talk of contemporary Europe as a constellation of three civilizations.[82] In an era of cultural pluralization, Europe contains three religious communities and traditions, which exhibit in their variegated practices both political contradictions and convergences. In a longer historical perspective, Europe is larger than its Graeco-Roman legacy. Specifically, such historical understanding overlooks the intermingling of Greek with Semitic and African influences at the outset of the European odyssey. It also neglects the fact that other parts of Europe's civilizational constellations, located further to the East, came to cultural rationalization later and perhaps with less enthusiasm. In the form of Communism and Republicanism, Eastern European states imposed Western European forms of political rationalization on agrarian and religious populations – in Russia with and in Turkey without a social revolution.

Europe is becoming more open, especially on its Eastern border. It is moving, in the words of Delanty, from postnationality to a potentially transformative encounter with Russian–Orthodox and Ottoman–Islamic civilizations.[83] Enlargement is not just about Europe growing bigger. It is also about Europe's reconfiguration, rooted in a civilizational encounter with its suppressed or forgotten parts. Today, the consequences of that encounter are far from clear. They may consolidate a European identity defined more clearly against "the Other" in the East.

Or they may redefine Europe's "Self" as it is expressed in social purposes and laws that give room to a looser sense of cultural association. Arguably, religious diversity will increase with the incorporation of two additional religious communities.[84] Political friction is likely to increase also, as the European periphery resists and seeks to redefine Europe's core.[85] It remains nonetheless true that today's battle lines are less clearly drawn than they were more than three centuries ago at the gates of Vienna.

Europe is a political model that differs from the United States. Emanuel Adler, for one, dissents from both an America-centric view of the West, and from the view of the emergence of a new global civilization of multiple modernities stamped in America's image.[86] In the United States, militarism and multiculturalism are locked in an unresolved domestic conflict that is reflected also in the ambiguous American influence on an emerging global civilization of multiple modernities. Under the impact of a catastrophic thirty years war that started in 1914 and ended in 1945, since the middle of the twentieth century Europe has meanwhile shed its militarist legacy. European civilization is in the midst of profound change. It is the first civilization, Adler argues, that has reinvented itself as a postmodern security community. This European civilization is providing a context that supports the development of novel practices seeking to sidestep and overcome traditional power politics. In comparison to those living in American and Islamic civilizations, European actors tend to practice political self-restraint.

Dennis Bark points out some profound differences that separate Europe from America. These differences are "not of principle but of practice." He writes that the difference is historical: Europe was built from the top down, the United States from the bottom up.[87] While Bark makes his essentialist argument in the context of an overarching shared collective identity, Robert Kagan goes one step further.[88] In the run-up to the Iraq war, he and other neoconservatives favoring the invasion contrasted America's military might and masculinity with Europe's political pacifism and femininity. Within a few months, as Mars was battered and bloodied in Iraq, supporters of Europe lost little time in articulating more fully the notion of Europe's civilian and normative power.[89] Mark Leonard, for example, argues that Europe, far from being weak, wields a new kind of power, with more than a billion people now living in a European sphere of influence that transforms itself not by spectacular displays of military power but by laws, regulations, and the attraction of doing things the European way.[90]

This political duality is both new and old. The apostles of power politics in the United States are retracing the path of Rome by forcefully projecting a unitary conception of sovereignty backed by military might. The new Europe, by contrast, is returning to the Holy Roman Empire of segmented sovereignty and consensual decision making in and around networks. At its core, this Europe now constitutes a security community marked by predictable expectations of peaceful change and an often self-consciously stylized "Self" that is seen to differ from the American "Other."[91] Although American neoconservatives like Kagan and his European critics differed sharply in their politics, they tended to agree on the underlying assumption that Europe stood for one set of uncontested values – be it unmanly pacifism or good moral norms informing an ethical foreign policy. Yet it is plainly wrong to define Europe in terms of a single value or consistent set of norms. "'Europe' cannot really be defined in terms of a single culture at all … a definition that embraces the whole continent – such as respect for human rights, the rule of law, care for the poor and love of liberty."[92] Europe's normative power is rooted today in the fact that the new Europe subscribes to the same values as did the old USA, and that the new USA holds firm to the same values as did the old Europe. The simple fact is that Europe and America have switched places as the balance of power and contested values have changed over time. For both Europe and America contained advocates of the value of power and of weakness. "Deeply embedded within Western civilization," writes David Hendrickson, "through some mysterious process bearing providential overtones, Europe has ended up where America began."[93] This switch was made possible by the existence of multiple civilizational processes, policies, and practices.

Americanization and Europeanization

Civilizational processes are typically self-chosen and imposed. Even when they radiate outward from one center, processes of diffusion of best civilizational practices typically affect actors in the civilizational center.[94] At the same time, actors in the civilizational periphery recombine and absorb civilizational influences into effective ensembles of routinized practices. Profoundly interactive, two-way processes thus can have positive and negative consequences for both civilizational center and periphery.

Americanization

Best conceived of as a two-way street, Americanization covers a broad range of practices through spontaneous diffusion in social networks and markets as well as through planned corporate and state policies. Contrary to Amy Chua's argument, Americanization is not only a source of opposition to but also a glue for America's imperium.[95] On the North American continent, Americanization has had a powerful assimilationist impact that has shown multiple political faces – liberal, creedal, sociocultural, and genocidal. Coupled in the second half of the twentieth century with its military might, America's cultural and economic dynamism has helped to build a civilizational imperium beyond its borders.

Susan Strange once remarked that globalization is nothing but polite party talk for what in fact is a process of Americanization. Perhaps. But in tracing the approximation of these two processes, Akira Iriye notes important variations.[96] At the outset of the twentieth century, both the mechanical, physical, and material, and the spiritual, mental, and ethical aspects of Americanization fascinated observers.[97] Even though the influence of American ideals persisted, during the first half of the twentieth century the importance of the material outstripped the ideational. In the second half the temporary conflation of globalization and Americanization was problematic, as the Cold War split the world into different parts experiencing Americanization, Sovietization, and a surge of Third World nationalism. The geopolitics of the Cold War elevated greatly the military (and militarist) features of America and pushed into the background both the materialist culture and the idealist aspects of processes of Americanization. Indeed, Iriye argues that the international society of states became less tied to Americanization processes and more to the expanding tasks of international organizations which, over time, ceased to be mere mouthpieces of America's geostrategic interests. The difference between the two processes has at times created a chasm so broad that it can no longer be bridged – illustrated by the fact that, on a number of salient political issues, the United States is now being outvoted repeatedly in the United Nations by the overwhelming majority of states.

Americanization has a domestic and an international face. Its domestic face – the process of making foreign influences American – consists of three parts. The first is to make immigrants of different class and ethnic backgrounds American, a contentious process as illustrated by the political conflicts surrounding illegal immigration. A second part refers to the modularity of American practices. According to John Blair Jr., across a broad range of life (including education, industrial assembly, architecture, music, sports, law, and religion), practices in nineteenth-century America revealed modular structures.[98] Modularity is an integral part of the process of modernization. It makes it possible, Blair argues, to conceive of organic cultural repertoires as the sum total of parts that can be combined and recombined in novel ways. John Kouwenhoven makes a related argument, abstracting from a list that includes the architecture of skyscrapers, the gridiron town plan, jazz, the Constitution, Mark Twain's writings, and Walt Whitman's *Leaves of Grass*.[99] American civilization is about simple and infinitely repeatable units, process not product, and open-endedness in time and space. A third part is the Americanization of modernism, of anti-traditional movements that established themselves in European art in the late nineteenth century. It, too, is central to processes of Americanization.[100]

In its international face, Americanization refers to a broad range of empirical phenomena spanning economic, social, cultural, political, and military affairs.[101] Elsewhere I have tracked Americanization empirically in the domains of popular culture and technology.[102] Shopping malls and intellectual currents illustrate the range of American cultural exports and the importance of cross-fertilization. As it commingles imports and exports, Americanization exhibits a complex mixture of hierarchical and egalitarian elements. Immigrants brought foods that American ingenuity in mass production and marketing converted to commodities with global appeal. Other products – some harmless such as the cartoon *Peanuts*, others harmful such as Marlboro cigarettes – succeeded by meeting consumer tastes and needs through marketing the appeal of America the imagined. In popular entertainment, American idioms, often fed by foreign sources as in the case of rap music, have had energizing effects on other parts of the world. In the area of technology, the observable pattern is not cross-fertilization, as in popular culture, but co-evolution. With the exception of some areas of advanced technology, the era of America's unquestioned technological supremacy has passed. Instead, piecemeal borrowing and selective adaptation are the norm. Americanization, when successful, refers more to the learning capacities of local actors than to the diffusion of standardized American technologies which foreign producers and consumers copy wholesale. Even in the basic sciences, Asia and Europe are closing the gap that existed a generation ago. Seattle and Detroit are two cities that illustrate the full range of the economic and political consequences of technological co-evolution.

In sum, Americanization refers to processes and practices that are widely admired (democratic capitalism, affluent modernity, enlightened tolerance) and widely despised (culturally inferior, superficial, materialist, profit-hungry, religiously zealous) traits.[103] Whatever the American reality, the American dream has managed to entice the human imagination, ever since the discovery of the New World.[104] It offers an idiom to debate both American and non-American concerns. And this capacity to entice is enormously consequential for the political salience of American civilization.

Europeanization

According to Norbert Elias, Europe experienced a civilizing process, in the singular.[105] But it is also the origin of a multitude of Europeanization processes that differ from Europe's regional integration.[106] At a maximum, Europeanization leads to structural change that affects actors and institutions as well as ideas and interests. The actors involved in Europeanization can be individual, corporate, or collective. At a minimum, Europeanization involves responses to the policies of the EU. It has a dynamic quality that is inherently asymmetric and relational. It varies by degree, and it is not necessarily permanent or irreversible. Typically, Europeanization is incremental, uneven, and irregular across both time and space. Johan Olsen characterizes Europeanization as "a multitude of coevolving, parallel and not necessarily tightly coupled processes."[107]

Social historian Hartmut Kaelble has mapped a whole series of emerging common European practices, among others in family relations, employment systems, consumption, and urban life.[108] Some of these have grown weaker, others stronger. Together, they define an ensemble of distinct European practices that have not – at least not yet – had a strong effect on a still embryonic European identity. In the second half of the twentieth century, decreasing national differences and increasing European commonalities were accompanied by growing intra-European connections and exchanges in areas such as occupation, education, marriage, consumption, cultural exchanges, and rising foreign language competences. Johan Olsen's trenchant analysis of Europeanization shows similarly that, in contrast to the past, most of the components of contemporary processes of Europeanization are inward-looking.[109]

Europeanization also has an external dimension. Historically, the Europeanization of the world has meant the wholesale export of Europe's institutional patterns and practices.[110] Many scholars have developed long inventories of the forms of everyday life and habits, production and consumption, fads and fashions, religion and language, principles and organizational forms that Europe has exported. This aspect of Europeanization generated mutually profitable economic exchange and one-sided exploitation, welcome institutional modernization and unwanted military conquest and occupation. The Old World conquered the New; only in the case of America did the New prevail over the Old in permanently shifting not only the balance of practice but also the balance of power. In the most recent past, Europeanization has primarily come to refer to a set of interrelated processes that are directed at Europe's emerging polity. Going far beyond traditional intergovernmental bargaining, these processes also include developments in civil society and changes in elite identifications.[111]

Having lost its erstwhile hegemony over world affairs, European cooperation since 1945 prepared the ground for an unprecedented period of exploration and innovation after the fall of the Berlin Wall. As it seeks to wield its soft and at times hard power, Europe is challenging established hierarchies in world politics. Exporting its politics through the enlargement of the EU is the clearest manifestation of this shift. Changes in the territorial reach of Europe are enlarging the scope of its rules through a variety of mechanisms, including a normative discourse that has entrapped actors whose interests might otherwise be opposed to enlargement.[112]

The export of European models of organization results in the adaptation rather than cloning of parts of the European model that fit local conditions. Contemporary Europeanization processes are no longer violently coercive. Instead, they offer a set of institutions for governance, including the welfare state and a security community, that makes the application of violence among its members unthinkable. Concerns for social justice, human rights, and environmental sustainability have found institutional forms that European states and the EU are seeking to advance in Europe and in world affairs. Europe is gaining experience with consensual methods of decision making in the form of its open method of coordination, soft law, and various forms of informal consultations. It prefers diplomatic and political approaches to purely military ones. These practices and policies put meat on what is a transatlantic bone of contention – Europe's normative power.

Bringing the domestic and international dimensions of Europeanization together in one framework, Kevin Featherstone distinguishes among four broad types: historical process, cultural diffusion, institutional adaptation, and policy responses centered on or around the EU.[113] In the past, Europeanization referred to exporting Europe's authoritative norms and practices to colonies all over the world. Who constituted and stood for "Europe," however, was highly variable, as region, religion, class, and nationality all set Europeans apart from one another. A second conceptualization focuses on transnational cultural diffusion of practices, ideas, norms, identities, and discourses within Europe. Third, as institutional adaptation,

Europeanization describes the pressures that are emanating from Europe. It operates through positive (with the EU prescribing institutional models or policies) and negative integration (with the EU altering domestic legislation). Additionally, affecting preferences and strategies and operating outside of the EU, European policy can alter the beliefs and expectations of domestic actors. Finally, Europeanization can also take the form of political responses that are shaped by the public policy impact of the EU on the central governments, subnational authorities, and policy networks of its member states. With respect to the EU, Europeanization is thus the result of multiple processes that reflect national vulnerabilities, the institutional capacities to respond, the fit of EU policies with national policy legacies and preferences, and the policy discourses that influence national preferences.[114] In its various manifestations, Europeanization captures processes that flow downward from the EU in terms of policy, as well as those that flow upward from spontaneously acting groups or individuals. In its various forms Europeanization does not have to be in contradiction to, or tension with, self-assertion. Instead, it can operate as an appropriate form of self-interested national action.[115] In Featherstone's words, Europeanization "can provide a gateway to developments across the continent that are both current and complex."[116]

Conclusion

In the study of civilizations Oswald Spengler describes as Copernican the discovery that Classical or Western civilization holds no privileged position compared to other civilizations, which "in point of mass count for just as much in the general picture of history as the Classical, while frequently surpassing it in point of spiritual greatness and soaring power."[117] The West is distinctive, but not superior or unique. Furthermore, America and Europe, Americanization and Europeanization point to the plural and pluralist character of the West. But it would be a mistake to simply put Western civilization in its various forms side by side with other civilizations. Instead, all civilizations are embedded in a common context that is larger and more encompassing than its constituent parts. Shmuel Eisenstadt calls this a civilization of modernity, William McNeill a global ecumene, and Jeremy Rifkin an empathic civilization.[118] Sharing Eisenstadt's, McNeill's, and Rifkin's intuition, I call it a global civilization of multiple modernities.

Multiple modernities and bridging civilizations: Islam and Anglo-America

I argue here that one global civilization containing multiple modernities encompasses all civilizations. Specifically, it brings together two bridging civilizations, Islam and Anglo-America, which have defied all attempts at political unification. "The idea of pan-Islamic unity," writes Ali Allawi, "as the realistic final goal of Muslims' political action is as chimerical as a union of, say, the English-speaking world."[119] Grounded in different localities that can be found in both East and

West, Islam is distinctive in its geographic spread from Senegal to Indonesia, as it endows political actors everywhere with authority when they invoke their civilizational authenticity. Anglo-America is also globe-spanning, but in a different way. Democratic capitalism links the West to core aspects of a global civilization containing multiple modernities. Islam in America gives a lie to the notion that in America's domestic affairs Islamic culture is somehow intrinsically different from American culture, thus putting a fundamental challenge to the sharp distinction expressed in the overused phrase "Islam and the West."[120] Islam connects horizontally to the global civilization that encompasses it across various world regions; Anglo-America connects vertically across different civilizational levels.[121] In different ways, both Islam and Anglo-America are bridging East and West.

Multiple modernities

Shmuel Eisenstadt argues that the global civilization is a product of the recent past, starting with fundamental changes in demography, literacy, and the scientific and technological revolution that the European Enlightenment helped bring about, generating an unprecedented openness to novelty and uncertainty.[122] Fernand Braudel calls this the "common heritage of humanity" in which all civilizations share, however unequally.[123] Youssef Courbage and Emmanuel Todd see in it a fundamental driver of the "meeting of civilizations," a rapid convergence of different patterns of demographic change, including in the contemporary Muslim world which is heading ineluctably toward a meeting point more universal than is commonly acknowledged.[124] Female literacy, not per capita GDP, is driving down fertility. Religious belief systems cannot stop the demographic revolution; instead, religious crises often precede declines in fertility rates. Where there are strong impediments to the demographic transition, as was true of the Catholic world in the past and is true in parts of the Sunni world today, they are rooted in specific institutional arrangements.[125]

Eisenstadt's comprehensive, comparative analyses of a number of civilizations show how religious crises provide occasions for the continual reconstruction of various traditions. The religious centers of civilizations thus continue to have a strong impact on unending processes of reinventing civilizational traditions. Furthermore, all world civilizations have generated proto-fundamentalist movements. In the West, Jacobinism became an oppositional movement in Europe that exploded in the twentieth century under the banners of Communism and Fascism. In today's America and Europe Islamophobic currents lead, for example, to the burning of the Qur'an in Florida, battles over headscarves and mosque minarets in Europe, and strong anti-Muslim and anti-immigrant movements throughout the West. Similarly, modern fundamentalism in Islam and other non-Western civilizations combines the impact of Western Jacobinism with indigenous fundamentalist movements. Jacobin impulses in modernity thus are not passing phenomena in the history of civilizations. They are permanent features constitutive of modernity.[126]

Fundamentalism is an engine of change in all civilizations and a core aspect of the global civilization of multiple modernities.

Early forms of modernities (between the sixteenth and the eighteenth centuries) are a transitional phase that exemplifies and deepens the theme of multiple modernities.[127] Language offers a good explanation of this period of transition. The turn to vernacular languages occurred in both Europe and India. In Europe, but not in India, it was accompanied by the emergence of more clearly defined territorial boundaries. In India, but not in Europe, vernacular languages complemented rather than replaced the sacred languages of Sanskrit and Pali.[128] In China and Japan, classical languages and political orders survived those turbulent centuries. While Chinese history records major breaks in the history of its various religions, such was not the case for the civilizational state of Japan. Yet in both China and Japan a public sphere evolved in early modernity – although one that was not tied, as in Europe, to civil society. Instead, China's public sphere became the world of academics and literati, which was tied closely to the official sphere.[129] In Tokugawa Japan, people and territory were united (*kokka*). But even in that holistic conception politically relevant distinctions emerged, between official and non-official and between social and non-social. As in China, the realm of the private was denigrated and widely regarded as undercutting the pursuit of the common good. In Islamic law, Sufi orders constituted a dynamic public sphere that operated quite independently from the political or official sphere. In charting this multiplicity of early modernities, Eisenstadt's civilizational analysis avoids Eurocentrism.[130] Europe is, as Eisenstadt and Schluchter argue, an analytical ideal type, not a normative reference point.[131]

Based on the Enlightenment and defined politically by the American and French revolutions, Western civilization evolved in reaction to European Christianity. It contained a bundle of cognitive and moral imperatives demanding more individual autonomy, fewer traditional constraints, and more control over nature. The first modernity was constructed and reconstructed in the specific context of Judeo-Greek-Christian cultural universalism and in the political pluralism of its various center–periphery relations and political protest movements. Subsequently, West European modernity was reinvented in Central and Eastern Europe, North and South America, and some other non-European settler territories. For Eisenstadt, the global civilization is defined not by being taken for granted, but by becoming a focal point of contestation, an object of uninterrupted conflict engaging both pre- and post-modern protest movements.[132] The global civilization thus embodies a multiplicity of different cultural programs and institutions of modernity.

Modern societies thus do not converge on a common path involving capitalist industrialism, political democracy, modern welfare regimes, and pluralizing secularisms. Instead, diverse religious traditions are cultural sources for the enactment of different programs of modernity. West European modernity was transformed in the United States under the specific circumstances of a settler and immigrant society. This has given fundamentalist religious movements a large weight in the evolution of America's multiple traditions and various dimensions of social structure, political institutions, and collective identities of the American state. A second example is offered by Japan's reconstruction of modernity. Japan is based on specific patterns of emulation and selection that evolved a distinctive set of sociopolitical structures and collective identities. Since the Meiji revolution, Japan's deeply anchored syncretism of religious belief systems has been highly eclectic in the values it has adopted and flexible in the interpretation of the dramatic shifts in political context it has confronted.

The legacies of different world religions thus create multiple modernities as sources of cultural innovation. In the evolution of the socioeconomic, political–legal and technical–scientific dimensions of the civilization of modernity, forces of convergence are always balanced against forces of divergence. Modernity is inescapably multiple and undergoing a constant process of reinvention in which all traditional elements that rebel against it have themselves a modern, Jacobin character. Although the aspirations of actors in the world's important civilizational states, polities, and empires may be totalistic, they are pluralistic in their cumulative impact on the multiple traditions that constitute one global civilization.[133]

Islam[134]

Islam is an Afro-Eurasian complex that bridges East and West as well as North and South. Stretching from West Africa to Southeast Asia, the tenth parallel marks a faith-based fault line between forever changing Christianity and Islam. Eliza Griswold concludes after years of travel that individuals defy easy distinctions because they have complicated identities that are sufficiently capacious to accommodate the conflicting worldly labels foisted on them by outsiders. A long tradition of religious coexistence has moved Christians and Muslims in their everyday lives beyond the easy binaries of Saved and Damned, Us and Them. Life is marked by both real and grim religious strife and the long experience of everyday encounter, as believers of different faiths shoulder together many earthly burdens. "Their lives bear witness," Griswold concludes, "to the coexistence of the two religions – and of the complicated bids for power inside them – more than to the conflicts between them."[135]

Eighty-five percent of the world's Muslims live outside of the Middle East, with the largest concentrations in Indonesia and in India. Hyphenated Islam, as in Afro- or Euro-Islam, speaks to the vitality of this civilization and its ability to ground itself in both East and West.[136] It also leads to apparent incongruities, such as the architectural absurdity of the Royal Mecca Clock. A kitsch rendition of Big Ben, blown up to grotesque proportions and situated adjacent to the Grand Mosque in Mecca, it anchors a gargantuan shopping mall, hotels, prayer halls, and apartment complexes. Visually, it clashes more relentlessly with its environment than do super-churches in America's suburban sprawl.[137]

Two facts stand out about Islamic civilization. The Islamic world is global. It consists primarily of networks of social relations, rather than nations or states. The concept of Islam connotes, particularly in contemporary American political debates, a monolithic myth. Nothing could be further from the truth. Islam inhabits, as Ira Lapidus writes in the opening sentence of his magisterial history, "the middle regions of the planet."[138] Lapidus builds on Marshall Hodgson's pathbreaking work, a reformulation of world history in terms of the Afro-Asian complex in which Europe, the Middle East, India, and East Asia emerged as loosely linked, identifiable civilizational spaces.[139] Before the transmutation and rise of Europe after 1600, and all that followed in its wake, Islam was the shining exemplar of a pre-modern interregional civilizational complex. Persian and Turkish complemented Arabic in giving Islam a profoundly cosmopolitan stamp. Islam's stateless ubiquity had enormous subversive potential, as testified to by its global spread across the Afro-Eurasian landmass, encompassing China and the Far East, Southeast and South Asia, the Middle East, the Balkans, Southern Spain, and North Africa. All of that changed after the rise of states and empires based on the power of the gun – Ottoman, Safavid, Mughal, and Western.

While Islam rarely sums to the totality of Muslim lives' experience, it "permeates their self-conception, regulates their daily existence, provides the bonds of society, and fulfills the yearning for salvation. The relevance of Islam to Muslim communities varies across the globe: as a religion, a political ideology, and a set of social practices. Yet, for all its diversity, Islam forges one of the great spiritual families of mankind."[140] Islam transcends the modern state system that has spread throughout the world during the last 350 years. The separation between mosque (as a place of prayer and learning) and state, and between divine and human law has been of fundamental importance.[141] This is not to deny the existence of multiple competing perspectives and vigorous contemporary debate on the nature and necessity of a secular state, the character of sharia law, the impossibility of imposed religious adherence by the state, and the centrality of voluntary compliance with sharia in various communities. While Islam and the state are separated, Islam and politics are not.[142] Secularisms, in the plural, thus are not necessarily barriers to the ideal, eventually to be realized, of one godly community that will live under Islamic rule, governed by God's law. The *umma* is both fundamentally apolitical and united, at least in theory. It offers a neutral position or sentiment between East and West. Pluralistic and multiform, it gives space to Arabic only as a unifying language for prayer. In practice, the *umma* and Islam offer a common culture in which particular cultures coexist.[143] The *umma*'s division under pre-modern empires and in today's nation states has been and continues to be an enduring political fact of life. Territorial pluralization is a deep legacy of Islam. At the same time, Islam remains a bridging civilization. Between the tenth and the eighteenth centuries, Muslim societies spread to far-flung corners of the globe. Variegated as these societies were, they all interacted with Middle Eastern Islamic states, religious and communal institutions, and local cultures. This created a world system of Islamic societies with significant shared cultural idioms and traditions.[144]

This unified community of believers had deep religious and political significance. Under the prophet and the first four righteous caliphates, it was a community both tightly knit in religious beliefs and endowed with imperial ambitions and universal claims. Thereafter, vigorous intracivilizational debate was the rule. "The process of forming Islamic civilization was not a passive assimilation but an active struggle among the proponents of different views."[145] Proponents of Arabic, Persian, and Hellenic literatures sought to shape the identity of the caliphate. Muslim urban communities stressed individual piety in the pursuit of Islamic life. Courtly Islam developed instead a cosmopolitan identity and worldview. The two would compete and collaborate for more than a millennium. Subsequent splits between and within Sunni and Shi'a communities and among a series of Islamic empires in Arabia, on the Indian subcontinent, and in the Middle East provided additional grounds for sharp disagreements. Religious attitudes were, and continue to be, varied – scripturalist, fundamentalist, conservative, puritanical, accommodationist, realist, and millenarian, each one the result of intense political debate and conflict. In the last two centuries, Islamic revivalism and Islamic reformism were political responses to intellectual and political tensions arising from within Islam. This continues to be true now. "Today's debates about the place and role of Islam in the world," writes Peter Mandaville, "are part of a complex genealogy of internal debates" that mark all of Islam's history.[146]

Islam's encounters with other civilizations have intensified such debates. In modern times, Western states in particular have had profound and differentiating effects on Muslim polities. One of these effects was to make the caliphate, as the human representation of Islamic unity, the target of increasing rivalries before Turkey finally abolished it in 1924. The territorial pluralism of modern Islam replaced the original bifurcation between the Muslim (*Dar al-Islam*) and the non-Muslim (*Dar al-Harb*) world; in contemporary thought these two concepts continue to resonate as descriptions, respectively, of liberation movements and colonialism.[147] With the growth of state and nation, and often under the impact of Western imperialism, hyphenated versions of Islam have sprung up as in Turkish-, Afro-, and Euro-Islam. And a global Islam is having a profound effect on the identity of the Muslim diaspora. As Muslims seek to attach themselves to a universal *umma*, neo-fundamentalism is not so much a backlash against the West as a consequence of Westernization that brings in its wake new forms of non-radical and at times radical politics. The modern Muslim world has adjusted wearily and to varying degrees – and on occasion not at all – to the world of states. And it still remembers its very different point of historical origin and cherishes its hoped-for, very different point of destination.[148] Muslim diasporic communities are far-flung and today are growing rapidly in all parts of the world. Insistence on unity thus clashes with the incontrovertible fact of diversity and the multiplicity of voices and traditions that diversity entails.[149] Lifting Islam out of the specific and manifold contexts in which it evolved historically is an act of reimagination undertaken by contemporary, at times extreme, factions that promote an essentialist view of Islam as a unified civilizational context and political community.[150] This it clearly is not. Instead, Islam is marked by internal contestations that can, but must not necessarily, generate conflicts when encountering or engaging with other civilizations.[151]

The decentralized network character of Islam makes Islamicization a dynamic set of interrelated processes. Indonesia's Islamicization, for example, began around 1300 CE and has continued ever since.[152] It was helped by Indonesia's position as a way station for trade between Canton, the largest seaport of the Tang dynasty, and the Muslim world. Islamicization was peaceful, the work of Sufi missionaries from Gujarat and Bengal whose outlook was quite compatible with Hinduism. Although almost 90 percent of Indonesia's population today is Muslim, Indonesia is not an Islamic state, and Islam is not the national faith. Yet it is in many respects an Islamic country, as Islam acts as a unifying force on a fragmented archipelago.

From its inception, Islamic theology and religious practice spread rapidly. Religious traditions, such as the Islamic revivalism of the eighteenth century articulated by Shah Walliullah and Muhammad Ibn Abdul Wahhab, extended to religious instruction and practices which are exported today from, and generously supported by, Saudi Arabia. Islamic reformism in the middle of the nineteenth century, and Jamal al-Din al-Afghani's creation of a pan-Islamist movement as an instrument to overturn colonial rule, are forerunners of current debates about the relations among different branches of Islam and various modern secularisms.[153] Islamicization has included all forms of long-distance trade and migration – both temporary, as in the haj, and long term.[154] It also describes, as frequently noted since 9/11, the activities of small sects of radical activists who are reacting to Western interventions and domestic oppression as they seek revolutionary change or a restoration of the caliphate.[155] In its contemporary manifestation, Islamicization encompasses not only the full gamut of consumption culture (such as food, dress, and popular music) exhibited by any modern shopping mall, but also transnational communication channels – radio in the era of pan-Arabism in the 1950s and 1960s, Al-Jazeera satellite television, and websites such as Islam Online today. Islamicization is thus an integral and vital part of Islam marked by the movement of people, goods, and ideas over long distances and across political borders: the first instance in world history of a civilizational complex encompassing all of Afro-Eurasia.

Anglo-America

Anglo-America both resembles and diverges from Islam.[156] Kees van der Pijl's trenchant historical analysis offers us an insight of how this came to pass.[157] Van der Pijl does not regard 1648 as the watershed separating the pre-modern from the modern period of international relations.[158] Instead, since 1688 international politics has become first and foremost an English-speaking transnational sphere of overseas settlement, with Britain and eventually the United States at its center. Secured by maritime supremacy, this "Lockean heartland" of Anglo-America has become the open center of the modern world order – not an agglomeration of liberal states but a larger "hetero-cultural and translingual" structure that embeds them.[159] It is, in fact, the most consequential such structure that global history has seen in the last three centuries. This liberal transnational society was only incompletely unified, first by Britain and then by the United States. Its strength lies in a capacity for autonomous reproduction: in the emergence of constitutionally similar states, through the military defeat and conquest of rival states, and by the peaceful incorporation of states supporting and expressing other social purposes.

The Glorious Revolution symbolized the end of a long historical process by which actors in civil society succeeded in constraining and containing the power of the Crown, a sharp contrast to the victory of absolutism on the European continent. Preoccupied by its civil war, England did not look south, to Europe and the Westphalian system of 1648. Instead it looked west, across the Atlantic toward "New England" and later to its other settler societies in the Dominions. Along this Atlantic, and later Pacific, axis, a self-regulating transnational Anglo-American society evolved, forcing continental Europe and subsequently most other parts of the world to rely on state sovereignty as the indispensible instrument with which to negotiate the various modernization processes that were foisted upon them. English language, property rights, the subordination of executive to legislative power, scientific and technological discovery and innovation, the rule of law, white racism, and Protestant religion became some of the most distinctive institutions and practices enshrined by Anglo-America. In the Lockean heartland, a chosen people was committed to maintaining maximum freedom from the state. That people was endowed with ample doses of greed and generosity, as it aimed at both exploiting and liberating others. Relatively autonomous settler colonies eventually spread those institutions and practices around the globe, from Britain to Ireland, North America, South Africa, Australia, and New Zealand. This Anglo-American heartland subsequently has contended with a parade of rivals in world politics – France, Germany, Japan, and the Soviet Union among them – that have been integrated, more or less successfully, into an expanding West that continues to be internally vibrantly pluralist and externally connected to a global civilization through transnational networks, international regimes, and mechanisms of global governance.

This expanding West has relevance for many, if not most, contemporary policy issues. That relevance expresses the most advanced form of the West's cultural domination over all of the states, including China and India, that are hoping to chart an independent development trajectory.[160] The West creates complex sovereignty as well as developing mechanisms for coping with complex interdependence. In a prescient article, Samuel Huntington recognized the United States as the contemporary center of this transnational Anglo-American structure.[161] The United States has been powered by the spread of transnational organizations. Access to foreign societies and economies, and the freedom to operate in this transnational space, matter more to it than territorial control. By and large, in the internationalized arenas of their own domestic politics Anglo-American actors practice what they preach.

Beyond being receptive to and engaged in various transnational processes and practices, Anglo-America has been connected closely, directly and indirectly, to one global civilization of multiple modernities. It provides that civilization with its lingua franca. English has displaced French as the language of diplomacy and

German as the language of science. And it has spread far and wide as a global medium of communication. Today, first, second, and foreign language users of English total about 1.4 billion people, or about one-fifth of the world's population. The majority of English users now live in China and India. This is a substantial number, especially if one considers that native English speakers number only about 400 million.[162] The cultural, economic, and political advantages that the status of a world language conveys are numerous and undeniable. Yet, the spread of English may prove to be self-limiting. New varieties of spoken English are emerging around the globe, such as Singlish (in Singapore), Estglish (in Estonia) and Chinglish (in China). Because they express multiple identities and imaginations, these "New Englishes" diverge greatly from standard English. Language is a living practice. And as languages spread, they change.[163] At least to some degree, English may eventually go the way of classical Latin, which was superseded by vulgar Latin and subsequent linguistic fractionalization.

Extending the reach of Anglo-America, English may become increasingly severed from its roots, thus making it a characteristic only of the global civilization of multiple modernities rather than of one of its constituent parts. Language will of course always retain some of its social context of meaning and will not be reducible simply to universal signs of signification.[164] However, computer-assisted translation and voice recognition may make it quite possible that English will become something like "Globish." Sooner rather than later, writes Nicholas Ostler, "everyone will be able to express an opinion in his or her own language, whether in speech or writing, and the world will understand."[165] This would make English accessible on a global scale and eliminate the need for English as a lingua franca. Although innovations such as Twitter and text messaging make orthography and syntax less important, American university students illustrate in their written work that language is situationally specific; they are more respectful of spelling and syntax in applications for openings at Goldman Sachs than in the world of new social media. The new world of Globish will probably have its own form of stratification depending on the degree of expressiveness, fluency, and diction.[166] For now, the only thing that is certain is that the multiplicity of languages and the ascendance of English as a limited lingua franca connect Anglo-America closely to the global civilization of multiple modernities.

Besides providing a common language, Anglo-America is linked closely in other ways as well. Finding a shared conceptual language is an important achievement in the articulation of commonalities that are often experienced as differences. Charles Beitz's analysis of the human rights revolution offers a compelling view of rights, not as the substantive embodiment of Western, liberal values that others should emulate, now that the West itself has finally come to acknowledge the existence of a common humanity. Rather, Beitz looks at human rights as a "common idiom of social criticism in global politics."[167] As an emergent discursive and political practice, human rights operate as a form of practical reasoning that consolidates several justifications of specific conduct. Engaging in that practice reveals a set of norms that frame both agreements and disagreements among members of a discursive community inhabited by state and non-state actors. The practice is not constituted by agreement on the content of norms or the behavioral consequences to which an acceptance of such norms would point. Encompassing different kinds of rights in different historical periods and contingent on historical circumstances, the normative content of these practices is open-ended, and its application to political practice is often contested.[168]

Like language and human rights, science and technology are a social process no longer controlled either by Anglo-Americans or by any other set of actors. Over the course of the twentieth century, Anglo-America has been a leading force in the advancement of science and technology. And science and technology have had a powerful effect on all societies. The speed and direction of technological and scientific developments are increasingly governed by ever more competitive global markets. As the preferred instrument for reaching goals of equity and efficiency, science and technology thus are by their very nature now largely global and publicly accessible. With limited success, some ministries of defense and police agencies, as well as some corporate actors, continue to protect secrecy in the name of national security and intellectual property. Worldwide availability of best technological practice is, however, spreading far and wide. What has happened during the last two centuries may be no more than a mild foretaste of what is to come in the next two, well beyond the end of the era of American preeminence. At the end of his analysis of East and West since the beginning of archaeologically recorded time, Ian Morris peeks into the immediate future and sees a world in which, for better and for worse, biology transforms humanity and its environment.[169] It is improbable, though not impossible, that such a world would be based on such weak hierarchies of power, knowledge, and prestige so as to warrant the readaptation of China's traditional "all-under-heaven" *tianxia* world order model, as Tingyang Zhao has argued.[170] Indeed, even though it contains the notion of "barbarian," this Chinese concept lacks, as Chih-yu Shih has argued, the notion of "the Other." Chinese theorists focus on self-rectification to chart a morally good path in world affairs, thus approximating partially and incompletely rationalist notions of "self-restraint."[171] For now, permitting considerable national and regional variation, and without any one defining center, one global civilization of multiple modernities provides a weak common context for world politics.

The popular culture industry points to still another avenue through which Anglo-America is linked to that global civilization.[172] Throughout the twentieth century, Hollywood's dream machine has been iconic as it has fed the imagination of the world. Hollywood is so powerful because American producers have enjoyed a strong grip on worldwide outlets. Yet, it has not been able to stop India's Bollywood from passing it in terms of sheer size, if not yet in global appeal. Non-American influences are important in Hollywood. A majority of America's major studios are foreign-owned, and many of Hollywood's major directors are foreign-born. Furthermore, particular markets, such as children's television, have proven highly receptive to foreign imports. And Hollywood movies are now conceived and produced for a global DVD market and thus must transcend

American specificities. Hollywood is both in America and of the world. In sum, without pointing toward convergence, the direct and indirect connections between Anglo-America and the global civilization of multiple modernities to which it belongs are numerous and far-reaching.

East and West

Islam's horizontal bridging of space and Anglo-America's vertical bridging of levels of civilizations illustrate the existence of manifold connections between East and West. Invoking East and West in common language is a convenient shortcut that conceals the obvious: multiple internal "Selves" typically contain important elements of the external "Other."[173] This is true of the profound influence that Islamic art, science, medicine, architecture, and literature have had on Anglo-America and other parts of the West. And it is also true of the influence that some parts of the West and Anglo-America have had on the internal debates of Islam, powerfully illustrated by the 2011 Arab spring. As both Islam and Anglo-America illustrate, civilizations come into existence and evolve through exchanges and relationships; they do not come into being as self-contained, coherent systems of values and unified sets of practices. In their historical trajectories civilizations are open-ended. They do not follow predetermined routes. But it is also true that the coherence of the internal "Self" of a civilization can be imposed by an external "Other" that is eager to articulate more firmly its own identity and thus contributes indirectly to the persistent notion of a civilization's coherence. Civilizational outposts can have galvanizing effects, illustrated by Andalusia in the western Mediterranean in medieval times and by Palestine in the eastern Mediterranean today. When flux and openness become politically inopportune, confusing, or threatening, civilizations thus can easily be imagined as something they are not, as the crystallization of values.

Such acts of imagination are deeply political.[174] An interconnected world of change and the yearning for stability thus can create the conditions that invite intellectual and political entrepreneurs to generate a civilizational politics that responds to felt needs but does not necessarily match empirical reality. *The Federalist Papers* (No. 2) provide a telling example.

> Providence has been pleased to give this one connected country, to one united people, a people descended from the same ancestors, speaking the same language, professing the same religion, attached to the same principles of government, very similar in their manners and customs, and who, by their joint counsels, arms and efforts, fighting side by side throughout a long and bloody war, have nobly established their general liberty and independence.[175]

As a matter of historical fact, in the late eighteenth century this description was absurdly mistaken. But if we understand this invocation as a self-conscious political attempt to bring a united American people into being, then it makes a lot of sense. Thus the empirical reality that John Jay purports to describe was very much a deliberate political project for the future. The same politics can be deployed to shape our images of the past. For example, in a 2004 interview, shortly before being elected Pope, Cardinal Ratzinger stated that "Europe is a cultural continent, not a geographical one. It is its culture that gives it a common identity. The roots that have formed it, that have permitted the formation of this continent, are those of Christianity....In this sense, throughout history Turkey has always represented another continent, in permanent contrast with Europe."[176] Ratzinger's view of European history is historically questionable and highly political. It overlooks the prominent role Islam played on the Iberian peninsula for half a millennium; it slights Islam's influence in parts of Southeast Europe; and it affirms and reinforces a linear view of history that often ends up labeling non-Western societies as backward.[177]

Jay's and Ratzinger's views are highly political. More generally, transcivilizational coalitions that advance the search for commonalities among differences are opposed by backlash coalitions that feel threatened by such a prospect. Pluralist and cosmopolitan coalitions, conceptions, and practices of world politics thus coexist with unitary and nationalist ones. In dialectical fashion they both reinforce and undermine each other. Extended forward into the future or backward into the past, primordial politics is an integral part of all civilizational politics. It is, however, far from defining its totality. A plural and pluralist world of civilizations is embedded in an encompassing civilization of multiple modernities that differs from both universalist liberal and nationalist conservative global orders. Internal plurality and external encounters, engagements, and occasional clashes co-evolve. As is true of all civilizations, the global civilization of multiple modernities is not rooted in any one, specific origin, such as the Western Enlightenment or the global *umma*. Open to both empirical and normative inquiry, it arises instead in different life worlds and at the interstices of and crossroads between different civilizations.

Toward a polymorphic globalism[178]

We live in a global civilization of multiple modernities marked by both convergences around emerging practices and divergences derived from the enactment of cultural programs grounded in different civilizational complexes. History tells us of liberalism's many struggles in finding commensurabilities among differences. Jennifer Pitts, for example, has traced how a tolerant and pluralist liberal universalism in the first half of the nineteenth century gave way in the second half to an imperialist liberalism that insisted on interventionist policies in colonial societies.[179] Uday Mehta has shown an analogous tension between two kinds of cosmopolitanisms. A cosmopolitanism of reason points self-confidently to generalizable certainties that derive from its abstract logic and align an opaque world with its paternalistic and progressive expectations; a cosmopolitanism of sentiment displays a pragmatic humility and a hope for mutual understanding that does not falter in its quest for decoding the inscrutably unfamiliar in its concrete and singular manifestations.[180] This predicament of liberal cosmopolitanisms has lasted to this day. Michael Barnett's discussion of contemporary humanitarian governance captures the tensions and contradictions that inhere in arrangements and practices that fall short of an empire of humanity in sheep's clothing, but that bear nonetheless unmistakable imperial markings.[181]

Commensurabilities are not made impossible by either a monovocal liberal tradition or the existence of diverging civilizational traditions and practices. They emerge instead from the partial overlaps created by the multiple secular and religious traditions that mark all civilizational complexes. Adapting Yasusuke Murakami's and Michael Mann's terminology, that partial overlap creates space for what I call here polymorphic globalism.[182] This globalism exists at various intersections of secularisms and religions, generating never-ending processes of peaceful negotiations and conflictual bargaining.

Two such intersections command our attention in particular. The first pits a secular against a religious politics. With the desacralization of Christianity and the rise of science and technology since the eighteenth century, the content of the emerging global polity has become more secular than religious. The historical foundations of the global polity and the continued or renewed vibrancy of several of the world's major religions have in recent decades made religious movements once again integral parts of a secular world politics. Religion and secularism seek to deny or undermine each other's existence. And in the past, both have offered radically different foundations for world orders.

Andrew Phillips inquires into the constitution, operation, and eventual decay of two such world orders: Latin Christendom before the mid-seventeenth century, and the Sinocentric world order in the nineteenth.[183] Latin Christendom and its decaying canon law were undermined by the confessional splintering that accompanied the Protestant Reformation. Sectarian violence increased at the very time that technological innovations increased the cost, scale, and destructiveness of warfare. After Habsburg had failed to shore up a unified Christendom along imperial lines, Europe's princes began enforcing confessional conformity in their own realms. Religious heresy came to be equated with political treachery, and a century of warfare ensued. At its end, the Westphalian system of sovereign states began the attempt to separate an international, secular order from private, religious ones.

Nineteenth-century China watched a similar split between a religious and a secular politics. The Sinocentric world order, however, confronted not only endogenous but also exogenous shocks. Dynastic decline was accelerated by millenarian peasant rebellions and an incipient military revolution that destroyed the East Asian world order and plunged China and much of the region into a century of upheaval. Emboldened by a revolution in naval warfare, imperialist Western powers opened China by force to satisfy their commercial and cultural interests. The Taiping rebellion was a puritanical millennial movement that incorporated evangelical Christianity into Chinese folk religion, thus creating a ferocious insurgency. Although it was ultimately defeated, this rebellion hollowed out

China's centralized state, thus opening the path toward the system's ultimate demise, Japanese occupation, and, after a bloody civil war, the Communist seizure of power.

Is today's international order likely to go the way of Medieval Latin Christendom or the Sinocentric world in the nineteenth century? The intermingling of secular and religious elements in contemporary world politics is not just a matter of the different types of actors – state versus non-state, secular versus religious – vying for primacy. It is also a matter of the principles that constitute contemporary world politics. Do secular or religious elements provide the core organizing principles?[184] Although the Westphalian system is organized along secular lines, the weakening of scores of states in recent decades has given more political space to religious actors. And in seeking to substitute religious for secular principles in the organization of world politics, a small number of these actors pose a radical challenge to secular authorities. The current wave of jihadist politics is one such effort. It does not seek to advance its preferred outcomes within the existing Westphalian order. It wants to create a new one. The secular state system is organized around multiple sovereign centers of authority that respect territorial borders, subscribe to the sanctity of law and the legitimacy of international organizations, and deny that there exists one single truth governing world politics. A religious world order would recognize only one center of authority, might not respect territorial borders, would deny the sanctity of law and the legitimacy of international organizations, and would insist on the existence of only one source of divine Truth. Calling for such an order poses a systemic and total, not national and partial, threat. Today there is no state seeking to affect such a dramatic change, and only a few non-state actors, among them the Al Qaeda-led jihadist movement and possibly Hizb ut-Tahrir.[185]

Polymorphic globalism exists also at a second and less familiar intersection.[186] Rather than dividing secularism from religion, Yasusuke Murakami underlines the similarities in the transcendental tendencies of historical religions *and* modern science in the West. Both science and religion are based on transcendental thought. Religious politics holds to an unquestioned belief in the divine. Secular politics has an unshaken belief in the attainability of ultimate truth. In their contrasting revolutionary aspirations and impact, both are in tension with the conservative historiological and hermeneutic tendencies of East Asian civilizations. The former is possessed by the belief in various forms of religious redemption or secular progress. The latter remains firmly grounded in the world of the profane, which lends itself to limitless reinterpretations and existence in multiple realities.

In developing his argument, Murakami follows Weber in his sociological treatment of historical religions. Distinctive of Christianity, and the Western civilizations based on it, is a transcendental orientation. Divided into a high-level, intellectual and a lowbrow, popular form, Eastern religions and civilizations lack this transcendental orientation. For Murakami, a decline in international liberalism and a rise in polymorphic globalism would not end history. It would merely end a historical era dominated by Western states – specifically two great empires, British and American, that have shaped world politics during the last three hundred years.

History will continue, sustained by the dialectical relations between these two types of reflexive practices: transcendental, scientific–religious on the one hand and hermeneutic, historical–practical on the other.

For Murakami the religions that are part of the Judeo-Christian tradition have an absolute character, promise salvation in the afterlife, and are prone to violence. In their highbrow, intellectual and lowbrow, popular forms, Eastern religions are marked instead by syncretism, promise salvation in the earthly life, and tend toward peaceful coexistence. The prospect for cultural commensurability in a polymorphic globalism, according to Murakami, depends on a partial move away from universal justice-based standards and a transcendental style of thought in a world dominated by Western states, to accommodate contextual, rule-based standards and a hermeneutic style of thought in a world inhabited also by East Asian and, we might add, a number of other civilizational states.

An analysis of polymorphic globalism is enriched by the institutional analysis that John Meyer has provided.[187] Meyer argues that the culture of Latin Christendom has shaped the organizational form as much as the substance of a secular world polity. Christianity brought together local mobilization of individual effort and general, universalistic long-distance relationships. It offered an institutional model of collective life that accorded political prominence to states as ideologically validated units, thus avoiding global segmentation and disintegration. For many centuries, the Church owned much of the world's productive land and provided the ideology that both defined the content of the political practices of princes and justified the management of the Church's vast worldly affairs. Christianity offered a general frame for Western civilization that brought together elites and mass publics as well as central and peripheral organizations of the global polity. It thus helped create and sustain the political and economic vitality and imperialist thrust of the West.

Karl Deutsch has provided a complementary and more materialist account of why the civilization of Latin Christendom was able to unite, and why subsequently it was fated to split apart.[188] He argues that the spiritual, linguistic, and cultural unity of medieval Christendom – its common Latin language, the shared legal and spiritual authority of the Pope, the common political leadership provided by the Holy Roman Emperors, and the collective enterprise of the crusades – was a transitory historical stage that was eventually destroyed by the very forces that gave rise to it. In this view, scarcity was the economic foundation of the international civilization of Latin Christendom – scarcity in goods, services, and skilled personnel. Scarcity permitted the growth of a thin web of supranational trading communities sharing in a common language, customs, spirit, laws, traditions, and family connections. In this web, specialized nodes of productive skill-sets diffused over long distances – provided, for example, by Irish monks, German knights, Lombard traders, French master builders, and Flemish peasants knowledgeable in advanced agricultural techniques. While at the local level the linguistic fractionalization of an immobile peasantry persisted, the thin web of supranationalism created the conditions for a superficial internationalization of three major civilizations – Christianity, Byzantium, and Islam – knit together by commerce, intellectual life, and politics. Over time, as the rate of national mobilization began to outpace the rate of international assimilation, increasing contacts between village, manor, and town eventually gave rise to the conditions that led to the demise of Latin Christendom.

Deutsch ends his discussion with two scenarios, which I am adapting here to the conditions of contemporary world politics. In the first, Nazi victory in World War II would have created a world built upon the concepts of "master race" and "high culture," based on a rigid system of social and political stratification organized around pan-European or global rules of exclusion of the diverse and unassimilated vast majority of mankind. Allied victory in World War II set the stage for the second scenario. The world has embarked on a prolonged period of international-ization and globalization that is spreading the notions of human rights and human economic well-being around the globe, while also permitting the flowering of dif-ferent civilizations and national cultures. Eventually, these processes may return world politics to conditions somewhat comparable to the thin internationalism of medieval European unity or polymorphic globalism.

Rémi Brague's historical analysis of the West provides an instructive analogy for our understanding of polymorphic globalism.[189] For Brague, Rome, not Athens or Jerusalem, has defined the West. He views Rome as an empty container lacking substantive content. "Romanity" makes its main contribution by transmitting what it receives rather than by making its own contribution. The Hellenization of Roman culture shows that by transplanting Greek ideas, Rome's innovation rested on the very act of transmission rather than any act of cultural creation from the many native, Etruscan, Anatolian, Punic, Hellenistic, and Egyptian influences that it received. The transplantation from Greece to Rome and then from Rome to a far-flung imperium was an act of replication and renewal. The same was true for the Roman Catholic Church in its relations with Israel. The church was Roman, but the novelty of the Christ on which it rested was not. Unlike Greek philosophy and Hebrew prophecy, Roman culture was primarily processual. For Brague, a Roman West invented nothing but transmitted much, comparing its pale self critically against more full-blooded originals.

Japan's popular entertainment industry offers a contemporary example from the East that reinforces the same analogy. The industry's huge success has rested on its ability to rid itself of any specific Japanese cultural content or "color." Instead, the industry has developed a distinctive capacity to translate for Japanese and East Asian publics Western and American leisure products and a lifestyle of urban consumer-ism that is creating a new sense of commonality connecting Japan and other parts of East Asia and beyond. Crossover markets and hybrid products lead to genuine innovation in a sophisticated marketing strategy, managing production cycles that can spin off thousands of individual products. Japanese success was grounded in the self-conscious decision to act as a cultural intermediary that required an entrepre-neurialism and imagination all its own.

Adhering to alternative arguments not focused on polymorphic globalism, conservatives insist on a unitary conception of civilizations but accept multiple standards of proper conduct in a world of numerous civilizations.[190] Liberals follow an inverse logic. They are often more willing to acknowledge the existence of diverse cultural programs in a given civilization but have a difficult time letting go of the notion of a single standard of good international and intercivilizational conduct. This is illustrated by vigorous and extended debates over failing states, standards of good governance, property rights, and transparent markets. On all of these issues, and many others, liberal arguments often proceed from the unquestioned assumption of the existence of a single standard of good conduct. In liberal American and European public discourse, the West thus is widely referred to in the singular: a universal, substantive form of perfectability that is integrating all parts of the world based on the growth of Western reason.

This view is implausible. Polymorphic globalism expresses not a common standard but a loose sense of shared values entailing often contradictory notions of diversity in a common humanity. This loose sense centers on the material and psychological well-being of all humans. "Well-being" and the rights of all "humans" are no longer the prerogative or product of any specific civilization or political structure. Instead, science and technology, which serve these ends, are deterritorialized processes that have taken on a life of their own and provide the script for all civilizations and polities. Polymorphic globalism does not specify the political route toward implementation. It does offer a script, often not adhered to, that now provides the basis for political authority and legitimacy everywhere. All polities claim to serve the well-being of individuals, and all individuals are acknowledged to have inherent rights. The existence of these processes enhances the pluralism that inheres in civilizations. It also undercuts both the imperialism of imposing single standards and the relativism of accepting all political practices.

Sigmund Freud reflected in his celebrated essay *Civilization and Its Discontents* on the tensions created by the indissoluble bonds that link an internally variegated Self to the external world. As part of a manifold West, Anglo-America exemplifies that it is deeply intertwined with a forever changing global civilization. As is true of all civilizational encounters and engagements, the intermingling that this global civilization encourages can breed in the Self rigidity and willful ignorance. Alternatively it can also lead to experiencing the Other openly and reexamining the Self critically. This is as true of Anglo-America as it is of Islam. Both encourage the bridging of East and West through evolving practices that help bring about a polymorphic globalism while grappling with the vexing problems of their multiple traditions. Political actors can be fearful, risking to stumble again into a deep abyss of inhumanity; and they can be courageous, daring to step forward onto uncharted common ground. Crossing the bridges that span East and West invites us to take journeys with destinations we can only guess at and look further than the eye can now see.

Notes

1 Earlier drafts of this chapter were presented at the 2010 annual meetings of the International Studies and the American Political Science Association. I would like to

thank the discussants at these meetings: Duncan Bell and Andrew Gamble at the ISA meetings, Robert Keohane, Ron Krebs, Jennifer Mitzen, and Herman Schwartz at the APSA meetings. I thank Martin Bernal for his detailed criticisms and suggestions, Bruce Lawrence for his acute insight and bibliographical references, and Hassan Hanafi for a set of detailed reactions that are likely to be important also for my future work. The anonymous readers for the publisher gave valuable advice on both matters of substance and important editorial decisions. Most importantly I thank the contributors to this book, from whom I have learned enormously and who have been generous to a fault with their comments, suggestions, and friendly criticisms. For their invaluable research assistance, I am indebted to Emma Clarke, Elisa Charbonnel, and Jill Lyon. Sarah Tarrow has, as always, helped smooth my prose. Finally, I would like to acknowledge with enormous gratitude the generous financial support that I received in 2009–10 from Louise and John Steffens Founders' Circle Membership at the Institute of Advanced Studies in Princeton.

2 Bernal 1987; Gilroy 1993; Cartledge 2004; Stivachtis 1998.
3 Al-Khalili 2011.
4 Jackson 1970; Bernal 1987; Davidson 1987.
5 Lawrence 2010, 157; Huntington 1996, 41; Müller, 1999, 31–4.
6 Liu 2004, 1.
7 Morris 2010, 568.
8 Hamilton 2010, 37.
9 Morris 2010.
10 Kurzweil 2005; Rifkin 2009.
11 Barnett and Duvall 2006. Knöbl (2007) stresses the importance of political power in civilizational analysis.
12 Kang 2010.
13 Rudolph 2010; Sen 2006, 46–9.
14 Lawrence 2010.
15 Ostler 2010, 20.
16 Ibid.
17 Ibid., 10.
18 Ostler's analysis is at odds with the three circle view that distinguishes among native English, official English, and English as a first foreign language, as developed by Braj Kachru (1985).
19 Ostler 2010, 47–55.
20 Ibid., 225–41.
21 Huntington 1996.
22 Kurth 2010.
23 I would like to thank Salah Hassan for helpful comments and suggestions on an earlier draft of this section of the chapter.
24 This view is in sharp contrast to Huntington's (1996, 47) unitary conception of civilizations, which leaves him undecided whether Africa is, or is not, a civilization in its own right.
25 Morris 2010, 73.
26 I am indebted to Sinja Graf for sharpening my thinking on this point. See also Diop 1974; Bernal 1987; Patterson and Kelley 2000.
27 Mazrui 2005, 74, 69–70.
28 Salah Hassan, personal communication, 1 March 2011.
29 Mudimbe 1988, 13, 20, 46–7, 81–7.
30 Chachage 1988.
31 Laitin 1986, 150–69.
32 Mazrui 2005, 70–1.
33 Middleton 1992.
34 Mazrui 2005, 74–5, 77.
35 Patterson and Kelley 2000.

36 I restate here some of the main arguments and themes first published in Katzenstein 2010b and 2010c.
37 Hodgson 1974 and 1993; McNeill 1990. See also Lawrence 2010, 157.
38 Jasanoff 2005, 7.
39 Morris 2010.
40 Braudel 1993, 8.
41 Bowden 2009.
42 Huntington's publisher signed 57 foreign contracts. Information provided by Valerie Borchardt, 1 December 2009, personal communication. Huntington amplified and extended a similar thesis first advanced by Bernard Lewis (1990).
43 Callahan 2010; Pocock 2005; Brody 2001.
44 Ben-Yehuda 2003; Chiozza 2002; Ferguson 2011, 312–14; Fox 2001; Henderson and Tucker 2001; Neumayer and Plümper 2009; Russett, Oneal, and Cox 2000; Schimmelfennig 2003, 150.
45 Zakaria 1994; Koh, Yeo, and Latif 2000.
46 Mahbubani 2008.
47 Mahathir and Ishihara 1995.
48 Chen 1992; Buruma and Margalit 2004.
49 See also Katzenstein 2010c, 11–13.
50 Eisenstadt and Schluchter 1998, 14–15.
51 Ferguson 2007, 191, 195.
52 Huntington 1996, 320; Brooks 2011.
53 McNeill 1990, 1963.
54 Haas 2000.
55 Braudel 1993, 29.
56 Browning and Lehti 2010a, 5.
57 Heller 2010, 13–14.
58 Swedberg 2007, 9.
59 Lind 1995.
60 Ibid., 4.
61 Lind 2006, 4, 252.
62 Moreau 2003.
63 Lind 1995.
64 Mead 2002.
65 Hunt 1987; Katzenstein and Hemmer 2002.
66 The next three paragraphs are reproduced from Katzenstein 2010a.
67 Skowronek 2006.
68 Lieven 2004, 41–7.
69 Chua 2007.
70 Hertzke 2004.
71 Trubowitz 1998.
72 Kurth 2010.
73 Lipset 1996; Ignatieff 2005.
74 Bender 2002 and 2006; Pagden 1995.
75 Chua 2007, 233–66.
76 Checkel and Katzenstein 2009b.
77 Pagden 2002.
78 This paragraph is adapted from Katzenstein 2010a. Deutsch 1944.
79 Hobsbawm 1983.
80 Delanty 1995, 1; 2003.
81 Checkel and Katzenstein 2009a.
82 Delanty 2003, 14–19.
83 Delanty 2003; 1995.
84 Katzenstein and Byrnes 2006.
85 Checkel and Katzenstein 2009a.

86 Adler 2010. See also Adler 2005; Adler et al. 2006.
87 Bark 2007, 2, 4.
88 Kagan 2002 and 2003.
89 Duchêne 1972; Harpaz 2007; Lucarelli 2007; Manners 2002 and 2006; McCormick 2006; Orbie 2006; Pace 2007; Reid 2004; Rifkin 2004; Scheipers and Sicurelli 2007; Sheehan 2008; Sjursen 2006b; Whitman 1998.
90 Leonard 2005, 4–7, 35–48. See also Moravcsik 2009.
91 James 2006, 118–40.
92 *The Economist* 2006.
93 Hendrickson 2006, 26.
94 Zeitlin 2000, 16–17.
95 Chua 2007, 328, 331–2.
96 Iriye 2007.
97 Ibid., 30.
98 Blair 1988, 2–6.
99 Kouwenhoven 1956.
100 Elteren 2006, 104, 110.
101 Elteren 2006, 101–24; Rosenberg 1982; Melling and Roper 1996; Aysha 2003.
102 Katzenstein 2005, 199–207.
103 Kazin and McCartin 2006.
104 O'Gorman 1961.
105 Elias 2000.
106 Featherstone 2003.
107 Olsen 1996, 271.
108 Kaelble 1987 and 2004.
109 Olsen 2007, 68–91.
110 Gong 1984; Bowden 2009; Koskenniemi 2001. In the English School's approach, international society is the product of Western civilization defined in terms of "an international social consciousness, a world-wide community sentiment" (Wight 1968, 96–7). The core values of that community are Christian notions of natural law which have spread, to different extents, from Europe to all other parts of the world (Krasner 1999, 47–8). See also Bull and Watson 1984, and Watson 1992.
111 Checkel and Katzenstein 2009a.
112 Schimmelfennig 2001; Sedelmeier 2000; Sjursen 2006a.
113 Featherstone 2003, 5–12.
114 Schmidt 2002.
115 Kohler-Koch 2000; Knodt 2000.
116 Featherstone 2003, 19.
117 Cox 2000, 218, fn5; Spengler 1939, 18.
118 Eisenstadt 2002a; McNeill 1990; Rifkin 2009. See also Bell 2006.
119 Allawi 2009, 154. I leave here unexamined the possibility that other civilizations, or other variants (French or Hispanic) of Western civilizations, also provide possible bridges to the global civilization.
120 Ghaneabassiri 2010, 4.
121 Inglis 2010, 141; Perdue 2008.
122 Eisenstadt 2002a. My summary of Eisenstadt's encompassing thought and voluminous writings is based on Katzenstein 2010c, Spohn 2001 and 2010, and Knöbl 2007. Eisenstadt's scholarship on this topic is a partial revision of his own writings on modernization dating back to the 1950s and 1960s, and a forceful dissent from contemporary globalization theory and the philosophical discourse on modernity and post-modernity.
123 Braudel 1993, 7.
124 Courbage and Todd 2007, xi–xiii.
125 Ibid. This analysis can run the risk of overlooking the contingency of modernization processes that Wolfgang Knöbl (2007) stresses in his analysis. Emmanuel Todd (2011)

can plausibly claim to have been one of the few to have anticipated the Arab spring. But in an earlier book (Todd 1987, xi) he linked a very similar demographic argument to the then stunning rise of Japan (and Germany). Twenty-five years later this looks less plausible than it did in 1987.

126 Pijl 2010, 178–222.
127 Eisenstadt and Schluchter 1998.
128 Pollock 2006, 259–80.
129 Woodside 2006.
130 Pasha 2007, 65, 70.
131 Eisenstadt and Schluchter 1998, 6–7, 15.
132 Eisenstadt 2002a; Kocka 2001, 6.
133 Arjomand and Tiryakian 2004, 3; Sternberg 2001, 80–1.
134 I am grateful to Bruce Lawrence, David Patel, and Shawkat Toorawa for their suggestions for this section.
135 Griswold 2010, 282, 11–12, 278.
136 Bulliet 2004.
137 Ouroussoff 2010.
138 Lapidus 1988, xix. See also Lawrence 2011; Salvatore 2010; Allawi 2009; Emberley 2007; Bulliet 2004; Roy 2004.
139 Hodgson 1974, 1993. See also Salvatore 2010; Arnason 2003, 229–31; Halliday 1996; Turner 1974, 53–66.
140 Lapidus 1988, xix.
141 Crone 2005.
142 An-Na'im 2008; Kelsay 2007.
143 I would like to thank Hassan Hanafi for sharpening my thinking on this point.
144 Lapidus 1988, 551.
145 Ibid.,121.
146 Mandaville 2007, 147. See also Tibi 2009.
147 I am indebted to Hassan Hanafi for this point.
148 Mendelsohn 2009, 37–88.
149 Ayoob 2008, 23–41.
150 Ibid., 2.
151 Tibi 1998, 1999a, 1999b, 2001, 2008.
152 Choi 1996.
153 An-Na'im 2008; Roy 2007.
154 Crone 1987; Chaudhuri 1990.
155 Mendelsohn 2009; Mandaville 2007, 237–74.
156 Ahmed (2010) and Ghaneabassiri (2010) remind us that African-American Muslim slaves were among the earliest immigrants of America.
157 Pijl 2006, 2007, 2010.
158 See also Teschke 2003; Krasner 1999.
159 Pijl 2006; Liu 2004, 211.
160 Pijl 1984 and 1998.
161 Huntington 1973, 338, 342–5.
162 Ostler 2010; Crystal 2004, 9; 1997; Roberts 2007; House 2003; Swaan 2001.
163 Crystal 2004, 21–41.
164 Wierzbicka 2006.
165 Ostler 2010, 261.
166 Ibid., 250–66; McCrum 2010; *The Economist* 2010b.
167 Beitz 2009, xi.
168 Ibid., 8–9, 212; Reus-Smit 2011.
169 Morris 2010, 590–608.
170 Zhao 2011; *The Economist* 2011.
171 Shih 2010.
172 Katzenstein 2005, 162–7; Iwabuchi 2002.

173 I thank Janice Stein for helping me to conceptualize this point.
174 I am greatly indebted to Stefano Guzzini, who pushed me to clarify and press forward the implications of my argument.
175 Hamilton, Madison, and Jay 1961, 38. I would like to thank Allison McQueen for pointing out to me the relevance of this quote for my larger argument.
176 Magister 2009. I would like to thank Arturo Santa-Cruz for this reference.
177 Zarakol 2011, 53–6, 240–55.
178 This section draws on Katzenstein 1997.
179 Pitts 2005, 21.
180 Mehta 1999, 17–19, 210–17.
181 Barnett 2011, 221.
182 Murakami 1996; Yamamura 1997; Mann 1993, 44–91.
183 Phillips 2011.
184 Mendelsohn forthcoming.
185 Ibid., 19–36 (manuscript).
186 Murakami 1996.
187 Meyer 1989.
188 Deutsch 1944.
189 Brague 2002.
190 See Katzenstein 2010a, 13.

REFERENCES

Abbott, Lyman (1898) "The Basis of an Anglo-American Understanding," *North American Review* 166: 513–21.

Abbott, Philip (2005) "Still Louis Hartz after All These Years: A Defense of the Liberal Society Thesis," *Perspectives on Politics* 3(1): 93–120.

Abbott, Tony (2009) *Battlelines*, Carlton: Melbourne University Press.

Abu-Lughod, Janet L. (1989) *Before European Hegemony: The World System A.D. 1250–1350*, New York: Oxford University Press.

Acharya, Amitav (2001) *Constructing a Security Community in Southeast Asia: ASEAN and the Problem of Regional Order*, New York: Routledge.

Adler, Emanuel (2005) *Communitarian International Relations: The Epistemic Foundations of International Relations*, New York: Routledge.

—— (2008) "The Spread of Security Communities: Communities of Practice, Self-Restraint, and NATO's Post-Cold War Transformation," *European Journal of International Relations* 14(2): 195–230.

—— (2010) "Europe as a Civilizational Community of Practice," in Peter J. Katzenstein (ed.), *Civilizations in World Politics: Plural and Pluralist Perspectives*, New York: Routledge, pp. 67–90.

Adler, Emanuel and Barnett, Michael (1998a) "A Framework for the Study of Security Communities," in Adler and Barnett (eds), *Security Communities*, New York: Cambridge University Press, pp. 29–65.

—— (1998b) "Security Communities in Theoretical Perspective," in Adler and Barnett (eds), *Security Communities*, New York: Cambridge University Press, pp. 3–28.

—— (eds) (1998c) *Security Communities*, Cambridge: Cambridge University Press.

Adler, Emanuel, Bicchi, Federica, Crawford, Beverly, and Del Sarto, Raffaella A. (eds) (2006) *The Convergence of Civilizations: Constructing a Mediterranean Region*, Toronto: University of Toronto Press.

Ahmed, Akbar (2010) *Journey into America: The Challenge of Islam*, Washington, DC: Brookings Institution Press.

Alcoff, Linda Martín (2006) *Visible Identities: Race, Gender and the Self*, Oxford: Oxford University Press.

Al-Khalili, Jim (2011) *The House of Wisdom: How Arabic Science Saved Ancient Knowledge and Gave Us the Renaissance*, New York: Penguin.

Allawi, Ali A. (2009) *The Crisis of Islamic Civilization*, New Haven, CT: Yale University Press.

Allen, H.C. (1954) *Great Britain and the United States: A History of Anglo-American Relations*, New York: St. Martin's.

Anderson, Stuart (1981) *Race and Rapprochement: Anglo-Saxonism and Anglo-American Relations, 1895–1904*, Cranbury, NJ: Associated University Presses.

Angell, Norman (1918) *The Political Conditions of Allied Success: A Plea for the Protective Union of the Democracies*, New York: Putnam.

—— (1942) "The English-speaking World and the Next Peace," *World Affairs* 105: 7–12.

—— (1943) "The British Commonwealth in the World Order," *Annals of the American Academy of Political and Social Science* 228: 65–70.

—— (1958) "Angell Sums up at 85 – Urges Union of the West," *Freedom & Union* (Dec.): 7–11.

An-Na'im, Abdullahi Ahmed (2008) *Islam and the Secular State: Negotiating the Future of Shari'a*, Cambridge, MA: Harvard University Press.

Appadurai, Arjun (1996) "Sovereignty without Territoriality: Notes for a Postnational Geography," in Patricia Yaeger (ed.), *The Geography of Identity*, Ann Arbor: University of Michigan Press, pp. 40–59.

Arjomand, Saïd Amir and Tiryakian, Edward A. (2004) "Introduction," in Arjomand and Tiryakian (eds), *Rethinking Civilizational Analysis*, Thousand Oaks, CA: Sage, pp. 1–13.

Arnason, Johann P. (2003) "East and West: From Invidious Dichotomy to Incomplete Deconstruction," in Gerard Delanty and Engin F. Isin (eds), *Handbook of Historical Sociology*, Thousand Oaks, CA: Sage, pp. 220–34.

Aydin, Cemil (2007) *The Politics of Anti-Westernism in Asia: Visions of World Order in Pan-Islamic and Pan-Asian Thought*, New York: Columbia University Press.

Ayoob, Mohammed (2008) *The Many Faces of Political Islam: Religion and Politics in the Muslim World*, Ann Arbor: University of Michigan Press.

Aysha, Emad El-Din (2003) "The Limits and Contradictions of 'Americanization,'" in Leo Panitch and Colin Leys (eds), (2004) *Socialist Register* 40, London: Merlin Press, pp. 245–60.

Balibar, Etienne (1991) "Racism and Nationalism," in Etienne Balibar and Immanuel Wallerstein (eds), *Race, Nation, Class: Ambiguous Identities*, London: Verso, pp. 37–67.

Balogh, Brian (2009) *A Government Out of Sight: The Mystery of National Authority in Nineteenth-century America*, New York: Cambridge University Press.

Banting, Keith and Simeon, Richard (eds) (1983) *And No One Cheered: Federalism, Democracy and the Constitution Act*, Toronto: Methuen.

Banting, Keith, Courchene, Thomas, and Seidle, Leslie (eds) (2007) *The Art of the State III: Belonging? Diversity, Recognition and Shared Citizenship in Canada*, Montreal: Institute for Research on Public Policy.

Banting, Keith, Johnston, Richard, Kymlicka, Will, and Soroka, Stuart (2006) "Do Multiculturalism Policies Erode the Welfare State? An Empirical Analysis," in Banting and Kymlicka (eds), *Multiculturalism and the Welfare State: Recognition and Redistribution in Advanced Democracies*, Oxford: Oxford University Press, pp. 49–91.

Baratta, Joseph Preston (1999) "The International Federalist Movement: Toward Global Governance," *Peace & Change* 24: 340–72.

—— (2004) *The Politics of World Federation*, 2 vols, Westport, CT: Praeger.

Barber, Benjamin (1986) "Louis Hartz," *Political Theory* 14(3): 355–8.

Bark, Dennis L. (2007) *Americans and Europeans Dancing in the Dark: On Our Differences and Affinities of Our Interests, and Our Habits of Life*, Stanford, CA: Hoover Institution Press.

Barnett, Michael (2011) *Empire of Humanity: A History of Humanitarianism*, Ithaca, NY: Cornell University Press.

Barnett, Michael and Duvall, Raymond (2005) "Power in International Politics," *International Organization* 59(1): 39–75.

—— (eds) (2006) *Power in Global Governance*, Cambridge: Cambridge University Press.

Bartelson, Jens (2009) *Visions of World Community*, Cambridge: Cambridge University Press.

Basañez, Miguel, Inglehart, Ronald, and Nevitte, Neil (2007) "North American Convergence, Revisited," *Norteamérica* 2(2): 21–61.

Basson, Lauren L. (2008) *White Enough to Be American? Race Mixing, Indigenous People, and the Boundaries of State and Nation*, Chapel Hill: University of North Carolina Press.

Beeson, Mark (2009) "Australia, the United States and the Unassailable Alliance," in John Dumbrell and Axel Schäfer (eds), *America's "Special Relationships": Foreign and Domestic Aspects of the Politics of Alliances*, London: Routledge.

Beitz, Charles R. (2009) *The Idea of Human Rights*, Princeton, NJ: Princeton University Press.

Belich, James (2009) *Replenishing the Earth: The Settler Revolution and the Rise of the Anglo-World, 1783–1939*, New York: Oxford University Press.

Bell, Coral (1988) *Dependent Ally: A Study of Australian Foreign Policy*, Melbourne: Oxford University Press.

Bell, Duncan (2006) "Beware of False Prophets: Biology, Human Nature and the Future of International Relations Theory," *International Affairs* 82(3): 493–510.

—— (2007a) *The Idea of Greater Britain: Empire and the Future of World Order, 1860–1900*, Princeton, NJ: Princeton University Press.

—— (2007b) "The Victorian Idea of a Global State," in Bell (ed.), *Victorian Visions of Global Order: Empire and International Relations in Nineteenth-Century Political Thought*, Cambridge: Cambridge University Press, pp. 159–86.

—— (2010a) "Democracy and Empire: J.A. Hobson, Leonard Hobhouse, and the Crisis of Liberalism," in Ian Hall and Lisa Hill (eds), *British International Thinkers from Hobbes to Namier*, Basingstoke: Palgrave, pp. 181–287.

—— (2010b) "Imagined Spaces: Nation, State, and Territory in the British Colonial Empire, 1860–1914," in William Mulligan and Brendan Simms (eds), *The Primacy of Foreign Policy in British History, 1660–2000*, New York: Palgrave, pp. 197–213.

—— (2010c) "John Stuart Mill on Colonies," *Political Theory* 38: 34–64.

—— (2012) "Dreaming the Future: Anglo-America as Utopia, 1880–1914," in Ella Dzelzainis and Ruth Livesey (eds), *The American Experiment and the Idea of Democracy in British Culture, 1776–1914*, Aldershot: Ashgate (forthcoming).

Bellamy, Richard (1992) *Liberalism and Modern Society: An Historical Argument*, Cambridge: Polity.

Bender, Thomas (ed.) (2002) *Rethinking American History in a Global Age*, Berkeley: University of California Press.

—— (2006) *A Nation among Nations: America's Place in World History*, New York: Farrar, Straus and Giroux.

Benjamin, Charles F. (1884) "The Future Relations of the English-speaking Communities." Essay read before the Eleventh Convention of the North America St. George's Union, Chicago, 20 Aug.

Bennett, Bruce S. (1988) *New Zealand's Moral Foreign Policy 1935–39*, Wellington: New Zealand Institute of International Affairs.

Bennett, George (ed.) (1962) *The Concept of Empire*, 2nd edn, London: Black.

Bennett, James C. (2007a) *The Anglosphere Challenge: Why the English-Speaking Nations Will Lead the Way in the Twenty-First Century*, Lanham, MD: Rowman & Littlefield.

—— (2007b) *The Third Anglosphere Century: The English-Speaking World in an Era of Transition*, Washington, DC: Heritage Foundation.

Bensel, Richard (2000) *The Political Economy of American Industrialization, 1877–1900*, New York: Cambridge University Press.

Ben-Yehuda, Hemda (2003) "The 'Clash of Civilizations' Thesis: Findings from International Crises, 1918–94," *Comparative Civilizations Review* 49: 28–42.

Beresford, Charles (1900) "The Future of the Anglo-Saxon Race," *North American Review* 171: 802–10.

Bergeron, Gérard (1983) "Quebec in Isolation," in Keith Banting and Richard Simeon (eds), *No One Cheered. Federalism, Democracy and the Constitutional Act*, Toronto: Methuen, pp. 59–73.

Bernal, Martin (1987) *Black Athena: The Afroasiatic Roots of Classical Civilization*, New Brunswick, NJ: Rutgers University Press.

Besant, Walter (1896) "The Future of the Anglo-Saxon Race," *North American Review* 163: 129–43.

Bevan, Vaughn (1986) *The Development of British Immigration Law*, London: Croom Helm.

Bhabha, Homi (ed.) (1990) *Nation and Nationalism*, London: Routledge.

Bhana, Surendra (1997) *Gandhi's Legacy: The Indian National Congress 1894–1994*, Pietermaritzberg: University of Natal Press.

Bhana, Surendra and Pachai, Bridglal (eds) (1984) *A Documentary History of Indian South Africans*, Cape Town: David Philip.

Biersteker, Thomas and Weber, Cynthia (eds) (1996) *State Sovereignty as a Social Construct*, Cambridge: Cambridge University Press.

Blackmon, Douglas A. (2008) *Slavery by Another Name: The Re-Enslavement of Black Americans from the Civil War to World War II*, New York: Doubleday.

Blair, John G., Jr. (1988) *Modular America: Cross-Cultural Perspectives on the Emergence of an American Way*, Westport, CT: Greenwood Press.

Blaxland, John (2006) *Strategic Cousins: Canadian and Australian Expeditionary Forces and the British and American Empires*, Kingston and Montreal: McGill-Queen's University Press.

Bleiker, Roland and Hutchison, Emma (2007) "Understanding Emotions in World Politics: Reflections on Method." Working Paper 2007/5, Canberra: RSPAS/Australian National University.

Bodenhorn, Howard (2002) *State Banking in Early America: A New Economic History*, Oxford: Oxford University Press.

Bonilla-Silva, Eduardo (2010) *Racism without Racists: Color-Blind Racism and the Persistence of Racial Inequality in the United States*, New York: Rowman & Littlefield.

Borgese, G.A. (1953) *Foundations of the World Republic*, Chicago, IL: University of Chicago Press.

Bosco, Andrea (1988) "Lothian, Curtis, Kimber and the Federal Union Movement (1938–40)," *Journal of Contemporary History* 23: 465–502.

Bothwell, Robert (1998) *Canada and Quebec: One Country, Two Histories*, Vancouver: University of British Columbia Press.

Bouchard, Gérard and Taylor, Charles (2008) *Building the Future: A Time of Reconciliation*, Commission Report, Quebec: Government of Quebec. Online. Available at: http://www.accommodements.qc.ca/documentation/rapports/rapport-final-integral-en.pdf (accessed 12 April 2009).

Bow, Brian (2008) "Anti-Americanism in Canada: Before and After Iraq," *American Review of Canadian Studies* 38(3): 141–59.

—— (2009) *The Politics of Linkage*, Vancouver: University of British Columbia Press.

Bow, Brian and Santa-Cruz, Arturo (2010) "Power, Identity, and Special Relationships: the US–Canada and US–Mexico Relationships in Historical and Comparative Perspective." Paper prepared for the Annual Meeting of the International Studies Association, New Orleans, February.

Bowden, Brett (2009) *The Empire of Civilization: The Evolution of an Imperial Idea*, Chicago, IL: University of Chicago Press.

Brague, Rémi (2002) *Eccentric Culture: A Theory of Western Civilization*, South Bend, IN: St. Augustine's Press.

Braudel, Fernand (1993) *A History of Civilizations*, New York: Penguin.

Brawley, Sean (1995) *The White Peril: Foreign Relations and Asian Immigration to Australasia and North America 1919–78*, Sydney: University of New South Wales Press.

Brenner, Robert (2003) *Merchants and Revolution: Commercial Change, Political Conflict, and London's Overseas Traders, 1550–1653*, London: Verso.

Breton, Raymond (1988) "From Ethnic to Civic Nationalism: English Canada and Quebec," *Ethnic and Racial Studies* 11(1): 85–102.

Brody, Hugh (2001) *The Other Side of Eden: Hunters, Farmers, and the Shaping of the World*, New York: North Point Press.

Brooks, David (2011) "Huntington's Clash Revisited," *New York Times* (3 Mar.). Available at: http://www.nytimes.com/2011/03/04opinion/04brooks.html?_r=2&pagewanted=print (accessed 25 May 2011).

Browning, Christopher S. and Lehti, Marko (2010a) "Introduction: New Tensions in a Troubled Partnership," in Browning and Lehti (eds), *The Struggle for the West: A Divided and Contested Legacy*, New York: Routledge, pp. 1–11.

—— (2010b) "The West: Contested, Narrated, and Clustered," in Browning and Lehti (eds), *The Struggle for the West: A Divided and Contested Legacy*, New York: Routledge, pp. 15–32.

Browning, Christopher S. and Tonra, Ben (2010) "Beyond the West and towards the Anglosphere?" in Christopher S. Browning and Marko Lehti (eds), *The Struggle for the West: A Divided and Contested Legacy*, New York: Routledge, pp. 161–81.

Brubaker, Rogers (2009) "Ethnicity, Race, and Nationalism," *Annual Review of Sociology* 35: 21–42.

Bryce, James (1888) *The American Commonwealth*, 2 vols, London: Macmillan [Digitized 2009].

—— (1897) *Impressions of South Africa*, London: Macmillan.

Buchignani, Norman (1982) "Canadian Ethnic Research and Multiculturalism," *Journal of Canadian Studies* 17(1): 16–34.

Buell, Raymond (1929) *International Relations*, New York: Henry Holt.

Bull, Hedley and Watson, Adam (eds) (1984) *Expansion of International Society*, New York: Oxford University Press.

Bulliet, Richard W. (2004) *The Case for Islamo-Christian Civilization*, New York: Columbia University Press.

Burgess, Michael (1995) *The British Tradition of Federalism*, London: Leicester University Press.

Burk, Kathleen (2007) *Old World, New World: The Story of Britain and America*, London: Little Brown.

Burke, Anthony (2008) *Fear of Security*, Cambridge: Cambridge University Press.

Burns, John F. (2009) "In Turbulent Time for Britain's Premier, a Hope to Bolster U.S. Ties," *New York Times* (3 Mar.): A11.

Burton-Adams, George (1919) *The British Empire and a League of Peace; Suggesting the Purpose and Form of an Alliance of the English-speaking Peoples*, New York: Putnam.

Buruma, Ian and Margalit, Avishai (2004) *Occidentalism: The West in the Eyes of Its Enemies*, New York: Penguin.

Bush, George W. (2010) *Decision Points*, New York: Crown.

Buzan, Barry (1993) "From International System to International Society: Structural Realism and Regime Theory Meet the English School," *International Organization* 47(3): 327–52.

Cabrera, Luis (2010) "World Government: Renewed Debate, Persistent Challenges," *European Journal of International Relations* 16: 511–30.

Cain, P.J. (2002) *Hobson on Imperialism: Radicalism, New Liberalism, and Finance 1887–1938*, New York: Oxford University Press.

Cain, P.J. and Hopkins, A.G. (2002) *British Imperialism, 1688–2000*, London: Pearson.

Callahan, William A. (2010) *China: The Pessoptimist Nation*, New York: Oxford University Press.

Callendar, G.S. (1902) "The Early Transportation and Banking Enterprises of the States in Relation to the Growth of Corporations," *Quarterly Journal of Economics* 17(1): 111–62.

Cameron, Maxwell A. (1997) "North American Free Trade Negotiations: Liberalization Games Between Asymmetric Players," *European Journal of International Relations* 3(1): 105–39.

Camilleri, Joseph A. (1980) *Australian–American Relations: The Web of Dependence*, South Melbourne: Macmillan.

—— (1987) *ANZUS: Australia's Predicament in the Nuclear Age*, Melbourne: Macmillan.

Canadian International Council (2010) *Open Canada*, Toronto: CIC.

Carens, Joseph (2003) "Who Should Get In? The Ethics of Immigration Admissions," *Ethics and International Affairs* 17(1): 95–110.

Carleton University Canada-US Project (2009) "From Correct to Inspired: A Blueprint for Canada–US Relations," 19 Jan. Online. Available at: http://www.carletonphotogallery.com/newsroom/d/292–2/canada-us-project_eng.pdf (accessed 1 March 2010).

Carnegie, Andrew (1893) *The Reunion of Britain and America: A Look Ahead*, Edinburgh: Andrew Elliott.

—— (1896) "The Venezuelan Question," *North American Review* 162: 129–44.

—— (1899) "Americanism versus Imperialism," *North American Review* 168: 1–13.

Carney, Shaun (2003) "Howard's Hanson Shuffle," *The Age*, 30 Aug. Online. Available at: http://www.theage.com.au/articles/2003/08/29/1062050663341.html (accessed 2 April 2011).

Carter, David and Mercer, Colin (eds) (1992) *Celebrating the Nation: A Critical Study of Australia's Bicentenary*, Sydney: Allen & Unwin.

Carter, Jimmy (1979) *Public Papers of the Presidents of the United States: Jimmy Carter 1977*, Washington, DC: US Government Printing Office.

Cartledge, Paul (2004) "What Have the Spartans Done for Us? Sparta's Contribution to Western Civilization," *Greece & Rome*, Second Series, 51(2): 164–79.

Cell, John (1982) *The Highest Stage of White Supremacy: The Origins of Segregation in South Africa and the American South*, Cambridge: Cambridge University Press.

Chachage, C.S.L. (1988) "British Rule and African Civilization in Tanganyika," *Journal of Historical Sociology* 1(2): 199–223.

Chamberlain, Joseph (1902 [1968]) *The Life of Joseph Chamberlain*, ed. J.L. Garvin and J. Amery, London: Macmillan.

Champion, C.P. (2010) *The Strange Demise of British Canada: The Liberals and Canadian Nationalism*, Kingston: McGill-Queen's University Press.

Chanock, Martin (2001) *The Making of South African Legal Culture 1902–36*, Cambridge: Cambridge University Press.

Chaudhuri, Kirti N. (1990) *Asia before Europe: Economy and Civilisation of the Indian Ocean from the Rise of Islam to 1750*, New York: Cambridge University Press.

Chebel d'Appollonia, Ariane and Reich, Simon (eds) (2008) *Immigration, Integration, and Security: America and Europe in Comparative Perspective*, Pittsburgh, PA: University of Pittsburgh Press.

Checkel, Jeffrey T. and Katzenstein, Peter J. (2009a) *European Identity*, Cambridge: Cambridge University Press.

—— (2009b) "The Politicization of European Identities," in Checkel and Katzenstein (eds), *European Identity*, Cambridge: Cambridge University Press, pp. 1–28.

Chen, Xiaomei (1992) "Occidentalism as Counterdiscourse: 'He Shang' in Post-Maoist China," *Critical Inquiry* 18(4): 686–712.

Chiozza, Giacomo (2002) "Is There a Clash of Civilizations? Evidence from Patterns of International Conflict Involvement, 1946–97," *Journal of Peace Research* 39(6): 711–34.

Chipman, John (1989) *French Power in Africa*, Oxford: Blackwell.

Choi, Dong Sul (1996) "The Process of Islamization and Its Impact on Indonesia," *Comparative Civilizations Review* 34: 11–26.

Chua, Amy (2007) *Day of Empire: How Hyperpowers Rise to Global Dominance – And Why They Fail*, New York: Doubleday.

Churchill, Winston (1956–58) *A History of the English-speaking Peoples*, Vols 1–4, London: Cassell.

Claeys, Gregory (2010) *Imperial Agnostics: British Critics of Empire, 1850–1920*, Cambridge: Cambridge University Press.

Clarke, G.S. (1899) "Imperial Responsibilities a National Gain," *North American Review* 168: 129–41.

Clarke, Peter (1978) *Liberals and Social Democrats*, Cambridge: Cambridge University Press.

—— (2011) "The English-speaking Peoples before Churchill," *British Scholar* 4: 199–231.

Clarkson, Stephen (1968) "Conclusions: The Choice to Be Made," in Clarkson (ed.), *An Independent Foreign Policy for Canada?* Toronto: McClelland and Stewart.

—— (2002) *Uncle Sam and Us: Globalization, Neoconservatism and the Canadian State*, Toronto: University of Toronto Press.

—— (2008) *Does North America Exist?* Toronto: University of Toronto Press.

Cochrane, Peter and Goodman, David (1988) "The Great Australian Journey: Cultural Logic and Nationalism in the Postmodern Era," *Australian Historical Studies* 23(91): 21–44.

Coleman, William, Pauly, Louis, and Brydon, Diana (2008) "Globalization, Autonomy and Institutional Change," in Pauly and Coleman (eds), *Global Ordering*, Vancouver: University of British Columbia Press, pp. 1–20.

Collini, Stefan, Winch, Donald, and Burrow, John (1983) *That Noble Science of Politics: A Study in Nineteenth-Century Intellectual History*, Cambridge: Cambridge University Press.

Collins, Randall (2004) "Civilizations as Zones of Prestige and Social Contact," in Saïd Amir Arjomand and Edward A. Tiryakian (eds), *Rethinking Civilizational Analysis*, Thousand Oaks, CA: Sage, pp. 132–47.

Conquest, Robert (2000) *Reflections on a Ravaged Century*, London: Norton.

Cotton, James (2009) "Realism, Rationalism, Race: On the Early International Relations Discipline in Australia," *International Studies Quarterly* 53: 627–47.

Courbage, Youssef and Todd, Emmanuel (2007) *A Convergence of Civilizations*, New York: Columbia University Press.

Cox, Robert W. (2000) "Thinking about Civilizations," *Review of International Studies* 26: 217–34.

—— (2005) "A Canadian Dilemma: The United States or the World," *International Journal* 60(3): 667–84.

Craig, Campbell (2003) *Glimmer of a New Leviathan: Total War in the Realism of Niebuhr, Morgenthau, and Waltz*, New York: Columbia University Press.

Crawford, Neta (2000) "The Passion of World Politics: Propositions on Emotion and Emotional Relationships," *International Security* 24(4): 116–56.

Crawford, Robert (2008) "Celebration of Another Nation? Australia's Bicentenary in Britain," *History Compass* 6(4): 1066–90.

Creighton, Donald (1937) *The Commercial Empire of the St. Lawrence, 1760–1850*, Toronto: Macmillan.

Crone, Patricia (1987) *Meccan Trade and the Rise of Islam*, Princeton, NJ: Princeton University Press.

—— (2005) *Medieval Islamic Political Thought*, Edinburgh: Edinburgh University Press.

Crystal, David (1997) *English as a Global Language*, Cambridge: Cambridge University Press.

——(2004) *The Language Revolution*, Malden, MA: Polity.

Cull, Nicholas (1996) "Selling Peace: The Origins, Promotion and Fate of the Anglo-American New Order during the Second World War," *Diplomacy & Statecraft* 7: 1–28.

Cullather, Nick (2009) "Model Nations: US Allies and Partners in the Modernizing Imagination," in John Dumbrell and Axel R. Schäfer (eds), *America's "Special Relationships,"* New York: Routledge.

Curran, James (2004) *The Power of Speech*, Melbourne: Melbourne University Press.

—— (2011) *Curtin's Empire*, Melbourne: Cambridge University Press.

Curran, James and Ward, Stuart (2010) *Unknown Nation*, Melbourne: Melbourne University Press.

Curtis, Lionel (1916) *The Problem of Commonwealth*, London: Macmillan.

—— (1937) *Civitas Dei*, 3 vols, London: Macmillan.

—— (1939) "World Order," *International Affairs* 18: 301–20.

—— (1951) "The Fifties As Seen Fifty Years Hence," *International Affairs* 27: 273–84.

Daalder, Ivo and Lindsay, James (2007) "Democracies of the World, Unite," *American Interest* 2: 5–15.

Danchev, Alex (2005) "Shared Values in the Transatlantic Relationship," *British Journal of Politics and International Relations* 7: 429–36.

Davidson, Basil (1987) "The Ancient World and Africa: Whose Roots?" *Race & Class* 29(2): 1–15.

Dawson, Robert (1937) *The Development of Dominion Status 1900–36*, London: Oxford University Press.

Day, Richard J.F. (2000) *Multiculturalism and the History of Canadian Diversity*, Toronto: University of Toronto Press.

Dean, Mitchell (2002) "Liberal Government and Authoritarianism," *Economy and Society* 31(1): 37–61.

DeConde, Alexander (1978) *A History of American Foreign Policy*, New York: Charles Scribner's Sons.

—— (1992) *Ethnicity, Race, and American Foreign Policy: A History*, Boston, MA: Northeastern University Press.

Delanty, Gerard (1995) *Inventing Europe: Idea, Identity, Reality*, New York: St. Martin's.

—— (2003) "The Making of a Post-Western Europe: A Civilizational Analysis," *Thesis Eleven* 72 (Feb.): 8–25.

Department of the Secretary of State (1983) *Constitution 1982*, Ottawa: Government of Canada Publishing Office.

Dessaix, Robert (1998) *Speaking their Minds: Intellectuals and Public Culture in Australia*, Sydney: ABC Books.

Deudney, Daniel (2007) *Bounding Power: Republican Security Theory from the Polis to the Global Village*, Princeton, NJ: Princeton University Press.

Deutsch, Karl W. (1944) "Medieval Unity and the Economic Conditions for an International Civilization," *Canadian Journal of Economics and Political Science* 10(1): 18–35.

Deutsch, Karl W. et al. (1957) *Political Community and the North Atlantic Area*, Princeton, NJ: Princeton University Press.

Devetak, Richard and True, Jacqui (2006) "Diplomatic Divergence in the Antipodes: Globalisation, Foreign Policy and State Identity in Australia and New Zealand," *Australian Journal of Political Science* 41(2): 241–56.

Dewey, Davis Rich (1915) *Financial History of the United States*, New York: Longmans Green.

Dicey, A.V. (1897) "A Common Citizenship for the English Race," *Contemporary Review* LXXI (Apr.): 457–76.

—— (1915) *Introduction to the Study of the Law of the Constitution*, 8th edn, London: Macmillan.

Dilke, Charles (1868) *Greater Britain: A Record of Travel in English-speaking Countries during 1866 and 1867*, London: Macmillan.

—— (1869) *Greater Britain: A Record of Travel in English-speaking Countries during 1866 and 1867*, Volume II, London, Macmillan [digitized 2009].

Diop, Cheikh Anta (1974) *The African Origin of Civilization: Myth or Reality*, New York: Lawrence Hill.

Doane, William Croswell (1898) "Patriotism: Its Defects, Its Dangers and Its Duties," *North American Review* 166: 310–23.

Doran, Charles F. (1984) *Forgotten Partnership? US–Canadian Relations Today*, Baltimore, MD: Johns Hopkins University Press.

Dos Passos, John Randolph (1903) *The Anglo-Saxon Century and the Unification of the English-speaking People*, 2nd edn, New York: Putnam.

Doyle, Arthur Conan (1891) *The White Company*, London: Smith.

—— (1892) "The Adventure of the Noble Bachelor," in *The Adventures of Sherlock Holmes*, London: Newnes.

Doyle, Michael (1986) "Liberalism and World Politics," *American Political Science Review* 80(4): 1151–69.

Drinnon, Richard (1980) *Facing West: The Metaphysics of Indian-hating and Empire-building*, Stillwater: University of Oklahoma Press (Reprinted 1997).

DuBois, W.E.B. (1903) *The Souls of Black Folk*, New York: Dover.

Duchêne, François (1972) "Europe's Role in World Peace," in R. Mayne (ed.), *Europe Tomorrow: Sixteen Europeans Look Ahead*, London: Fontana/Collins, pp. 32–47.

Dulles, John Foster (1939) *War, Peace, and Change*, New York: Harper.

Dumbrell, John (2006) *A Special Relationship: Anglo-American Relations from the Cold War to Iraq*, Basingstoke, Hampshire; New York: Palgrave Macmillan.

Dumbrell, John and Schäfer, Axel R. (2009a) "Introduction: The Politics of Special Relations," in Dumbrell and Schäfer (eds), *America's "Special Relationships,"* London: Routledge.

—— (eds) (2009b) *America's "Special Relationships": Foreign and Domestic Aspects of the Politics of Alliance*, London: Routledge.

Dunlavy, Colleen (1991) "Mirror Images: Political Structure and Policy US/Prussia," *Studies in American Political Development* 5 (Spring): 1–35.

Economist, The (2004) "How Anglo is America?" (13 Nov.): 39.

—— (2006) "Culture Wars – Fashionable Talk of a 'European Culture' Is Pointless and May Even be Damaging" (4 Feb.): 50.

—— (2008a) "Anglo-Saxon Attitudes" (29 Mar.): 71–3.

—— (2008b) "The Ties that Bind" (26 July): 66.

—— (2010a) "Europe and the Trojan Poodle" (24 July): 58.

—— (2010b) "Top Dog" (29 May): 83.

—— (2011) "Nothing New under Heaven" (18 June): 50.

Edelstein, Michael (1982) *Overseas Investment in the Age of High Imperialism*, London: Methuen.

Edwards, Brian (2001) *Helen: Portrait of a Prime Minister*, Auckland: Exisle Publishing.

Egnal, Marc (1988) *A Mighty Empire: The Origins of the American Revolution*, Ithaca, NY: Cornell University Press.

Eisenstadt, Shmuel N. (2002a) "Multiple Modernities," *Dædalus* 129(1): 1–29.

—— (2002b) "The Civilization of the Americas: The Crystallization of Distinct Modernities," *Comparative Sociology* 1(1): 43–61.

Eisenstadt, Shmuel N. and Schluchter, Wolfgang (1998) "Introduction: Paths to Early Modernities – A Comparative View," *Dædalus* 127(3): 1–18.

Elias, Norbert (2000) *The Civilizing Process: Sociogenetic and Psychogenetic Investigations*, rev. edn, Oxford: Blackwell.

Elteren, Mel van (2006) *Americanism and Americanization: A Critical History of Domestic and Global Influence*, Jefferson, NC: McFarland.

Emberley, Peter (2007) "Politics and Civilization: Recent Works in Political Theory," *International Political Science Review* 28(5): 517–30.

Emmanuel, Arghiri (1972) "White Settler Colonialism and the Myth of Investment Imperialism," *New Left Review* 73 (May): 35–57.

Esposito, John L. (1995) *The Islamic Threat: Myth or Reality?* New York: Oxford University Press.

Evans, Gareth (1991) *Cooperating for Peace*, Sydney: Allen and Unwin.

Falk, Richard A. (1975) *A Study of Future Worlds*, New York: Free Press.

Fanis, Maria (2011) *Secular Morality and International Security: American and British Decisions about War*, Ann Arbor: University of Michigan Press.

Fausto, Boris (1999) *A Concise History of Brazil*, New York: Cambridge University Press.

Featherstone, Kevin (2003) "Introduction: In the Name of 'Europe,'" in Kevin Featherstone and Claudio M. Radaelli (eds), *The Politics of Europeanization*, New York: Oxford University Press, pp. 3–26.

Feng, Yongping (2006) "The Peaceful Transition of Power from the UK to the US," *Chinese Journal of International Politics* 1: 83–108.

Ferguson, Niall (2004) *Empire: How Britain Made the Modern World*, London: Penguin.

—— (2011) *Civilization: The West and the Rest*, London and New York: Allen Lane and Penguin.

Ferguson, Yale H. (2007) "Pathways to Civilization," in Martin Hall and Patrick Thaddeus Jackson (eds), *Civilizational Identity: The Production and Reproduction of "Civilizations" in International Relations*, New York: Palgrave, pp. 191–7.

Finbow, Robert (1993) "Ideologies and Institutions in North America," *Canadian Journal of Political Science* 26(4): 671–97.

Finnemore, Martha (1996) *National Interests in International Society*, Ithaca, NY: Cornell University Press.

Fischer, Louis ([1951] 1982) *The Life of Mahatma Gandhi*, London: Grafton.

Fish, Stanley (1997) "Boutique Multiculturalism, or Why Liberals Are Incapable of Thinking about Hate Speech," *Critical Inquiry* 23(2): 378–95.

Fiske, John (1885) *American Political Ideas Viewed from the Standpoint of Universal History (The Town-Meeting, The Federal Union, "Manifest Destiny")*, New York: Harper & Brothers.

Fleming, John (1891) "Are We Anglo-Saxons?" *North American Review* 153: 253–6.

Fletcher, Ian Christopher (2003) "Double Meanings: Nation and Empire in the Edwardian Era," in Antoinette Burton (ed.), *After the Imperial Turn: Thinking with and through the Nation*, Durham, NC: Duke University Press, pp. 246–59.

Floyd, Richard (2004) "449 and All That: Nineteenth- and Twentieth-Century Interpretations of the 'Anglo-Saxon Invasion' of Britain," in Helen Brocklehurst and Robert Phillips (eds), *History, Nationhood and the Question of Britain*, Basingstoke: Palgrave Macmillan, pp. 184–96.

Forbes, Hugh Donald (2007) "Trudeau as the First Theorist of Canadian Multiculturalism," in Stephen Tierney (ed.), *Multiculturalism and the Canadian Constitution*, Vancouver: University of British Columbia Press.

Foreign and Commonwealth Office UK (2009) "New Zealand," 21 Apr. Online. Available at: http://www.fco.gov.uk/en/about-the-fco/country-profiles/asia-oceania/new-zealand/?profile=intRelations&pg=4 (accessed 15 December 2010).

Foucault, Michel (1983) "Afterword: The Subject and Power," in Hubert Dreyfus and Paul Rabinow, *Michel Foucault: Beyond Structuralism and Hermeneutics*, 2nd edn, Chicago, IL: University of Chicago Press, pp. 208–26.

Fox, Jonathan (2001) "Clash of Civilizations or Clash of Religions: Which Is a More Important Determinant of Ethnic Conflict?" *Ethnicities* 1: 295–320.

—— (2004) *Religion, Civilization, and Civil War: 1945 through the Millennium*, Lanham, MD: Lexington Books.

Frantzen, Allen J. and Niles, John D. (eds) (1997) *Anglo-Saxonism and the Construction of Social Identity*, Gainesville: University Press of Florida.

Freud, Sigmund (1961) *Civilization and Its Discontents*, New York: W.W. Norton.

Fukuyama, Francis (2006) *America at the Crossroads: Democracy, Power and the Neoconservative Legacy*, London: Yale University Press.

Gabaccia, Donna (2004) "A Long Atlantic in a Wider World," *Atlantic Studies: Literary, Cultural and Historical Perspectives* 1 (Apr.): 1–27.

Gagnon, Alan and Iacovinco, Raffaele (2007) *Federalism, Citizenship, and Quebec*, Toronto: University of Toronto Press.

Galton, Francis (1883) *Inquiries into Human Faculty and its Development*, London: Macmillan [digitized 2009].

Gamble, Andrew (2007) "From Anglo-America to the Anglosphere: Empire, Hegemony, and the Special Relationship," BISA US Foreign Policy Working Group Annual Conference, University of Manchester, 20–21 Sept.

Gamble, Andrew and Kearns, Ian (2007) "Recasting the Special Relationship," in David Held and David Mepham (eds), *Progressive Foreign Policy: New Directions for the UK*, London: Polity.

Gardham, Duncan (2010) "Document that Formalised 'Special Relationship' with the US," Daily Telegraph, 24 June. Online. Available at: http://www.telegraph.co.uk/news/worldnews/northamerica/usa/7852136/Document-that-formalised-special-relationship-with-the-US.html (accessed 15 December 2010).

Garran, Robert (2004) *True Believer: John Howard, George Bush, and the American Alliance*, Crows Nest, NSW: Allen and Unwin.

Gates, Paul (1960) *The Farmer's Age: Agriculture 1815–60*, New York: Holt, Rinehart and Winston.

—— (1968) *The Illinois Central Railroad and its Colonization Work*, New York: Johnson Reprint Corp.

Gecelovsky, Paul M. (2007) "Northern Enigma: American Images of Canada," *American Review of Canadian Studies* 37(4): 517–36.

Geertz, Clifford (1973) *The Interpretation of Cultures*, New York: Basic Books.

Ghaneabassiri, Kambiz (2010) *A History of Islam in America: From the New World to the New World Order*, Cambridge: Cambridge University Press.

Gilmour, David (2003) *Curzon: Imperial Statesman*, New York: Farrar, Straus and Giroux.

Gilroy, Paul (1993) *The Black Atlantic: Modernity and Double Consciousness*, Cambridge, MA: Harvard University Press.

Goetzmann, William H. (2009) *Beyond the Revolution*, New York: Basic Books.

Gong, Gerritt W. (1984) *The Standard of "Civilization" in International Society*, Oxford: Clarendon Press.

Gorman, Daniel (2006) *Imperial Citizenship: Empire and the Question of Belonging*, Manchester: Manchester University Press.

Gossett, Thomas F. (1997 [1963]) *Race: The History of an Idea in America*, New York: Oxford University Press.

Gotlieb, Allan (1982) "Canada–US Relations: The Rules of the Game," *SAIS Review* 2 (Summer): 172–87.

—— (2007) "Bring Back the Special Relationship," *National Post*, 17 Aug.

Government of Australia, Australian Education International (2011) *Research Snapshot: Export Income to Australia from Education Services in 2009–10*. Online. Available at: http://aei.gov.au/AEI/PublicationsAndResearch/Snapshots/2011011401_pdf (accessed 8 March 2011).

Government of Australia, Department of Foreign Affairs and Trade (2010) *Trade at a Glance*. Online. Available at: http://www.dfat.gov.au/publications/trade/trade_at_a_glance_2010.pdf (accessed 8 March 2011).

Government of Australia, Department of Immigration and Citizenship (2010) *Report on Immigration Program 2009–10*. Online. Available at: http://www.immi.gov.au/media/statistics/pdf/report-on-migration-program-2009-10.pdf (accessed 8 March 2011).

—— (2011) *The People of Australia: Australia's Multicultural Policy*. Online. Available at: http://www.immi.au.gov (accessed 18 March 2011).

Granatstein, J.L. (1997) *Yankee Go Home? Canadians and Anti-Americanism*, Toronto: HarperCollins.

—— (1999) *Who Killed Canadian History?* Toronto: HarperCollins Canada.

Grande, Edgar and Pauly, Louis (eds) (2005) *Complex Sovereignty*, Toronto: University of Toronto Press.

Greene, Jack P. and Morgan, Philip D. (eds) (2009) *Atlantic History: A Critical Appraisal*, Oxford: Oxford University Press.

Gress, David (1998) *From Plato to NATO: The Idea of the West and its Opponents*, New York: Free Press.

Griffiths, Rudyard (2009) *Who We Are*, Toronto: Douglas and McIntyre.

Griswold, Eliza (2010) *The Tenth Parallel: Dispatches from the Faultline between Christianity and Islam*, New York: Farrar, Straus and Giroux.

Grovogui, Siba (2006) *Beyond Eurocentrism and Anarchy: Memories of International Order and Institutions*, New York: Palgrave Macmillan.

Gruening, Ernest (1935), "The Meaning of Mexico," in Hubert Herring and Herbert Weinstock (eds), *Renascent Mexico*, New York: Coici-Friede Publishers.

Gunderson, Gerald (1974) "The Origin of the American Civil War," *Journal of Economic History* 34: 915–50.

Gwyn, Richard (1997) *Nationalism without Walls*, Toronto: McClelland & Stewart.

Haas, Ernst B. (2000) *Nationalism, Liberalism, and Progress, Vol. 2. The Dismal Fate of New Nations*, Ithaca, NY: Cornell University Press.

Hackett Fischer, David (1989) *Albion's Seed: Four British Folkways in America*, New York: Oxford University Press.

Hage, Ghassan (1998) *White Nation: Fantasies of White Supremacy in a Multicultural Society*, Annandale, NSW: Pluto Press.

—— (2003) *Against Paranoid Nationalism: Searching for Hope in a Shrinking Society*, Annandale, NSW: Pluto Press.

Hager, Nicky (2007) *Secret Power*, Nelson, NZ: Craig Potton.

—— (2010) "Wikileaks: Leaked US Cables Spill the Beans on NZ Ties," *Sunday Star Times*, 12 Dec.

Haglund, David G. (2007) "A Security Community – 'If You Can Keep It': Demographic Change and the North American Zone of Peace," *Norteamérica* 2(1): 77–100.

Hall, Stuart (2000) "Conclusion: The Multicultural Question," in Barnor Hesse (ed.), *Un/settled Multiculturalisms*, London: Routledge, pp. 209–41.

Halliday, Fred (1996) *Islam and the Myth of Confrontation: Religion and Politics in the Middle East*, London: I.B. Tauris.

Hamilton, Alexander, Madison, James, and Jay, John (1961) *The Federalist Papers*, ed. Clinton Rossiter, New York: New American Library.

Hamilton, Gary G. (2010) "World Images, Authority, and Institutions: A Comparison of China and the West," *European Journal of Social Theory* 13(1): 31–48.

Hammond, Bray (1934) "Long and Short Term Credit in Early American Banking," *Quarterly Journal of Economics* 49(1): 79–103.

—— (1936) "Free Banks and Corporations: The New York Free Banking Act of 1838," *Journal of Political Economy* 44(2): 184–209.

—— (1948) "Banking in the Early West: Monopoly, Prohibition, and Laissez Faire," *Journal of Economic History* 8(1): 1–25.

Hancock, Ange-Marie (2007) "When Multiplication Doesn't Equal Quick Addition: Examining Intersectionality as a Research Paradigm," *Perspectives on Politics* 5 (Mar.), 63–79.

Hancock, W.K. (1937) *Survey of British Commonwealth Affairs, Vol. 1: Problems of Nationality*, Oxford: Oxford University Press.

Hancock, W.K. and van der Poel, Jean (1966) *Selections from the Smuts Papers, Volume III, June 1910–18*, Cambridge: Cambridge University Press.

Hansen, Randall (2000) *Citizenship and Immigration in Post-war Britain: The Institutional Origins of a Multicultural Nation*, Oxford: Oxford University Press.

Hari, Johann (2010) "The Two Churchills," *New York Times* (12 Aug.). Available at: http://www.nytimes.com/2010/08/15/books/review/Hari-t.html?src=me (accessed 15 June 2011).

Harland, Bryce (1992) *On Our Own: New Zealand in the Emerging Tripolar World*, Wellington: Victoria University Press.

Harpaz, Guy (2007) "Normative Power Europe and the Problem of a Legitimacy Deficit: An Israeli Perspective," *European Foreign Affairs Review* 12: 89–109.

Harrison, Benjamin (1901) "Musings upon Current Topics II," *North American Review* 172: 352–66.

Hartdegen, S. (1999) "Perceiving Asia 1945–98: Shifts and Changes as Seen in Official Speeches," in Y. Zhang (ed.), *New Zealand and Asia: Perceptions, Identity and Engagement*, Auckland: Asia2000 Foundation.

Hartley, Livingston (1965) *Atlantic Challenge*, New York: Dobbs Ferry.

Hartz, Louis (1955) *The Liberal Tradition in America*, New York: Harcourt, Brace.

—— (1964) *The Founding of New Societies*, New York: Harcourt, Brace.

—— (1984) *A Synthesis of World History*, Zurich: Humanity Press (typescript manuscript).

Hastings, Paula (2006) "'Our Glorious Anglo-Saxon Race Shall Ever Fill Earth's Highest Place': The Anglo-Saxon and the Construction of Identity in Late-Nineteenth Century Canada," in Phillip Buckner and R. Douglas Francis (eds), *Canada and the British World: Culture, Migration, and Identity*, Vancouver: University of British Columbia Press, pp. 92–110.

Hatter, Lawrence (2010) *Channeling the Spirit of Enterprise: Commercial Interests and State Formation in the Early American West, 1774–1825*, Charlottesville: Unpublished Ph.D. Dissertation, University of Virginia.

Hawke, Bob (2011) "Interview with Paul Kelly, Sydney". Online. Available at: http://ussc. edu.au/events/past/Bob-Hawke-Reflections-on-the-Australia-United-States-Alliance (accessed 22 July 2011).

Hawkins, Freda (1982) "Multiculturalism in Two Countries: The Canadian and Australian Experience," *Journal of Canadian Studies* 17(1): 64–80.

—— (1989) *Critical Years in Immigration: Canada and Australia Compared*, Montreal: McGill-Queen's University Press.

Hazeltine, Mayo (1896) "The United States and Great Britain: A Reply to Mr. David A. Wells," *North American Review* 162: 594–606.

Headlam, Cecil (1933) *The Milner Papers: South Africa 1899–1905*, London: Cassell.

Heater, Derek (1996) *World Citizenship and Government: Cosmopolitan Ideas in Western Political Thought*, Basingstoke: Macmillan.

Heller, K.M. (Peggy) (2010) "The West as a Concept of the World-Historical." Paper prepared for the Annual Meeting of the International Studies Association, New Orleans, 17–20 Feb.

Henderson, Errol A. and Tucker, Richard (2001) "Clear and Present Strangers: The Clash of Civilizations and International Conflict," *International Studies Quarterly* 45: 317–38.

Hendrickson, David H. (2006) "Of Power and Providence: The Old U.S. and the New EU," *Policy Review* 135 (Feb.–Mar.): 23–42.

Herrera, Octavio and Santa Cruz, Arturo (2011) Historia de las relaciones internacionales de México, 1821–2010, America del Norte, México City: Secretaria de Relaciones Exteriores.

Hertzke, Allen D. (2004) *Freeing God's Children: The Unlikely Alliance for Global Human Rights*, Lanham, MD: Rowman & Littlefield.

Hewitt, Roger (2005) *White Backlash and the Politics of Multiculturalism*, Cambridge: Cambridge University Press.

Hindess, Barry (2004) "Liberalism: What's in a Name?" in W. Larner and W. Walters (eds), *Global Governmentality: Governing International Spaces*, London: Routledge, pp. 23–39.

Hoadley, Stephen (1989) *The New Zealand Foreign Affairs Handbook*, Auckland: Oxford University Press.

—— (2000) *New Zealand–United States Relations: Friends No Longer Allies*, Wellington: New Zealand Institute of International Affairs.

Hoberg, George (2000) "Canada and North American Integration," *Canadian Public Policy* 26 (supplement) (Aug.): 35–50.

Hobhouse, L.T. (1994 [1911]) *Liberalism*, ed. James Meadowcroft, Cambridge: Cambridge University Press.

Hobsbawm, Eric (1983) "The Invention of Tradition," in Eric Hobsbawm and Terence Ranger (eds), *The Invention of Tradition*, Cambridge: Cambridge University Press, pp. 1–14.

Hobson, J.A. (1997 [1902]) *Imperialism: A Study*, ed. Philip Siegelman, Ann Arbor: University of Michigan Press.

Hobson, John M. (2007) "Deconstructing the Eurocentric Clash of Civilization: De-westernizing the West by Acknowledging the Dialogue of Civilizations," in Martin Hall and Patrick Thaddeus Jackson (eds), *Civilizational Identity*, New York: Palgrave, pp. 149–66.

Hochschild, Jennifer and Weaver, Vesia Mae (2010) "'There's No One as Irish as Barack O'Bama': The Policy and Politics of American Multiracialism," *Perspectives on Politics* 8(3): 737–59.

Hodgson, Marshall G.S. (1974) *The Venture of Islam: Conscience and History in a World Civilization*, 3 vols, Chicago, IL: University of Chicago Press.

—— (1993) *Rethinking World History: Essays on Europe, Islam and World History* (edited with introduction and conclusion by Edmund Burke IV), Cambridge: Cambridge University Press.

Hofstadter, Richard (1992 [1955]) *Social Darwinism in American Thought*, Philadelphia: University of Pennsylvania Press.

Holsti, K.J. (1971) "The United States and Canada," in Steven Spiegel and Kenneth N. Waltz (eds), *Conflict in World Politics*, Cambridge, MA: Winthrop.

Horowitz, Gad (1966) "Conservatism, Liberalism, and Socialism in Canada: An Interpretation," *Canadian Journal of Economics and Political Science* 32(2): 143–71.

Horsman, Reginald (1981) *Race and Manifest Destiny: The Origins of American Racial Anglo-Saxonism*, Cambridge, MA: Harvard University Press.

Horton, Carol A. (2005) *Race and the Making of American Liberalism*, Oxford: Oxford University Press.

House, Juliane (2003) "English as a Lingua Franca and Its Influence on Discourse Norms in Other Languages," in Gunilla Anderman and Margaret Rogers (eds), *Translation Today: Trends and Perspectives*, Clevedon and Buffalo, NY: Multilingual Matters, pp. 168–79.

Hughes, Robert (1986) *The Fatal Shore: The Epic of Australia's Founding*, New York: Random House.

Hulliung, Mark (2010) "Louis Hartz, His Life and Writings," in Mark Hulliung (ed.), *The American Liberal Tradition Revisited: The Contested Legacy of Louis Hartz*, Lawrence: University Press of Kansas, pp. 1–7.

Hunt, Michael H. (1987) *Ideology and U.S. Foreign Policy*, New Haven, CT: Yale University Press.

Huntington, Samuel P. (1973) "Transnational Organizations in World Politics," *World Politics* 25(3): 333–68.

—— (1981) *American Politics: The Promise of Disharmony*, Cambridge, MA: Harvard University Press, Belknap Press.

—— (1993a) "If Not Civilizations, What? Paradigms of the Post-Cold War World," *Foreign Affairs* 72(5): 186–94.

—— (1993b) "The Clash of Civilizations?" *Foreign Affairs* 72(3): 22–49.

—— (1996) *The Clash of Civilizations and the Remaking of World Order*, New York: Simon & Schuster.

—— (2004) *Who Are We? The Challenges to America's National Identity*, New York: Simon & Schuster.

Huntley, James (1998) *Pax Democratica: A Strategy for the 21st Century*, London: St. Martin's.

Hutchins, Robert, et al. (1948) *Preliminary Draft of a World Constitution*, Chicago, IL: University of Chicago Press.

Huttenback, Robert (1966) "Indians in South Africa, 1860–1914: The British Imperial Philosophy on Trial," *English Historical Review* 81(319): 273–91.

—— (1971) *Gandhi in South Africa: British Imperialism and the Indian Question, 1860–1914*, Ithaca, NY: Cornell University Press.

—— (1976) *Race and Empire: White Settlers and Colored Immigrants in the British Self-Governing Colonies, 1830–1910*, Ithaca, NY: Cornell University Press.

Hyam, Ronald and Henshaw, Peter (2003) *The Lion and the Springbok: Britain and South Africa since the Boer War*, Cambridge: Cambridge University Press.

Ignatieff, Michael (2000) *The Rights Revolution*, Toronto: Anansi Press.

—— (ed.) (2005) *American Exceptionalism and Human Rights*, Princeton, NJ: Princeton University Press.

Ignatiev, Noel (1995) *How the Irish Became White*, New York: Routledge.

Ikenberry, G. John (2001) *After Victory: Institutions, Strategic Restraint, and the Rebuilding of Order after Major Wars*, Princeton, NJ: Princeton University Press.

—— (2004) "Liberalism and Empire: Logics of Order in the American Unipolar Age," *Review of International Studies* 30(4): 609–30.

—— (2011a) *Liberal Leviathan: The Origins, Crisis, and Transformation of the American World Order*, Princeton, NJ: Princeton University Press.

—— (2011b) "The Future of the Liberal World Order: Internationalism after America," *Foreign Affairs* 90(3): 1–14.

Ikenberry, G. John and Slaughter, Anne-Marie (2006) *Forging a World of Liberty under Law: U.S. National Security in the 21st Century* (Princeton Project on National Security). Online. Available at: http://www.princeton.edu/~ppns/report/FinalReport.pdf (accessed 22 July 2011).

Inglis, David (2010) "Civilizations or Globalization(s)? Intellectual Rapprochements and Historical World-Visions," *European Journal of Social Theory* 13(1): 135–52.

Iriye, Akira (2007) "Globalization as Americanization?" in Bruce Mazlish, Nayan Chanda, and Kenneth Weisbrode (eds), *The Paradox of Global USA*, Stanford, CA: Stanford University Press, pp. 31–48.

Iwabuchi, Koichi (2002) *Recentering Globalization: Popular Culture and Japanese Transnationalism*, Durham, NC: Duke University Press.

Jackman, Simon (2008) "Australians, Americans and the 2008 Presidential Elections," *US Studies Centre Survey*, 2000. Online. Available at: http://ussc.edu.au/s/media/docs/publications/081030_ussc_national_survey_2008.pdf (accessed 22 July 2011).

Jackman, Simon and Vavreck, Lynn (2011) "Americans and Australians Compared: Ten Years After 9/11." Online. Available at: http://ussc.edu.au/s/media/docs/publications/1106_911Survey.pdf (accessed 22 July 2011).

Jackson, Alvin (2004) "Ireland, the Union, and the Empire," in Kevin Kenny (ed.), *Ireland and the British Empire*, Oxford: Oxford University Press, pp. 123–53.

Jackson, G.E. (1923) "Emigration of Canadians to the United States," *Annals of the American Academy of Political and Social Science* 107(2): 25–34.

Jackson, John G. (1970) *Introduction to African Civilization*, New York: Carol Publishing.

Jackson, Patrick Thaddeus (2006) *Civilizing the Enemy: German Reconstruction and the Invention of the West*, Ann Arbor: University of Michigan Press.

Jacobson, Matthew Frye (1998) *Whiteness of a Different Color: European Immigrants and the Alchemy of Race*, Cambridge, MA: Harvard University Press.

James, Harold (2006) *The Roman Predicament: How the Rules of International Order Create the Politics of Empire*, Princeton, NJ: Princeton University Press.

James, Robert Rhodes (ed.) (1974) *Winston S. Churchill: His Complete Speeches, 1897–1963*, New York: Chelsea House, VII.

Janiewski, Dolores (2009) "Yearning and Spurning: New Zealand's Special Relationships with Britain and the United States," in John Dumbrell and Axel Schäfer (eds), *America's "Special Relationships,"* London: Routledge.

Jasanoff, Maya (2005) *Edge of Empire: Lives, Culture, and Conquest in the East, 1750–1850*, New York: Knopf.

Jayasuriya, Kanishka (1999) "Globalization, Law, and the Transformation of Sovereignty," *Global Legal Studies Journal* 6.

Jebb, Richard (1905) *Studies in Colonial Nationalism*, London: Edward Arnold.

—— (1908) "The Imperial Problem of Asiatic Immigration," *Journal of the Royal Society of the Arts* 61(2892): 585–610.

—— (1911) *The Imperial Conference: A History and Study, Vol. II*, London: Longmans, Green and Co.

Jefferson, Thomas (2009) *The Works of Thomas Jefferson, Vol. XI*, New York: Cosimo Books.

Jones, Charles A. (2007) *American Civilization*, London: University of London, School of Advanced Study, Institute for the Study of the Americas.

Joppke, Christian (1999) *Immigration and the Nation-State: The United States, Germany, and Great Britain*, Oxford: Oxford University Press.

—— (2009) *Veil: Mirror of Identity*, Cambridge: Polity Press.

Jordan, Winthrop D. (1974) *The White Man's Burden: Historical Origins of Racism in the United States*, Oxford University Press.

Jupp, James (2005) "From 'White Australia' to 'Part of Asia': Recent Shifts in Australian Immigration Policy towards the Region," *International Migration Review* 29(1), 207–28.

Kachru, Braj (1985) "Standards, Codifications, and Sociolinguistic Realism, The English Language in the Outer Circle," in R. Quirk and H. Widdowson (eds), *English in the World*, Cambridge: Cambridge University Press, pp. 11–30.

Kaelble, Hartmut (1987) *Auf dem Weg zu einer europäischen Gesellschaft*, Munich: C.H. Beck.

—— (ed) (2004) *The European Way: European Societies in the 19th and 20th Centuries*, New York: Berghahn Books.

Kagan, Robert (2002) "Power and Weakness," *Policy Review* 113 (June–July): 3–27.

—— (2003) *Of Paradise and Power: America and Europe in the New World Order*, New York: Knopf.

—— (2007) *Dangerous Nation: America's Foreign Policy from Its Earliest Days to the Dawn of the Twentieth Century*, New York: Vintage Books.

Kallen, Evelyn (1982) "Multiculturalism: Ideology, Policy and Reality," *Journal of Canadian Studies* 17(1): 51–63.

Kang, David C. (2010) "Civilization and State Formation in the Shadow of China," in Peter J. Katzenstein (ed.), *Civilizations in World Politics*, London and New York: Routledge, pp. 91–113.

Kappeler, Dietrich (2004) "The Birth and Evolution of a Diplomatic Culture," in Hannah Slavik (ed.), *Intercultural Communication and Diplomacy*, Geneva: DiploFoundation.

Katzenstein, Peter J. (1997) "The Cultural Foundations of Murakami's Polymorphic Liberalism," in Kozo Yamamura (ed.), *A Vision of a New Liberalism? Critical Essays on Murakami's Anticlassical Analysis*, Stanford, CA: Stanford University Press, pp. 23–40.

—— (2005) *A World of Regions: Asia and Europe in the American Imperium*, Ithaca, NY: Cornell University Press.

—— (2010a) "'Walls' between 'Those People'? Contrasting Perspectives on World Politics," *Perspectives on Politics* 8(1): 11–25.

—— (2010b) "The West as Anglo-America: Plural and Pluralist." Paper prepared for the Annual Meeting of the American Political Science Association, Washington, DC, Sept.

—— (2010c) "A World of Plural and Pluralist Civilizations: Multiple Actors, Traditions, and Practices," in Katzenstein (ed.), *Civilizations in World Politics: Plural and Pluralist Perspectives,* New York: Routledge, pp. 1–40.

—— (2012) "Sinicization in Comparative Perspective," in Katzenstein (ed.), *Sinicization and the Rise of China: Civilizational Processes beyond East and West*, London and New York: Routledge, pp. 209–241.

Katzenstein, Peter J. and Byrnes, Timothy A. (eds) (2006) *Religion in an Expanding Europe*, Cambridge: Cambridge University Press.

Katzenstein, Peter J. and Hemmer, Christopher (2002) "Why Is There No NATO in Asia? Collective Identity, Regionalism and the Origins of Multilateralism," *International Organization* 56(3): 575–607.

Katzenstein, Peter J. and Keohane, Robert O. (eds) (2007) *Anti-Americanisms in World Politics*, Ithaca, NY: Cornell University Press.

Kautz, Steven (1995) *Liberalism and Community*, Ithaca and London: Cornell University Press.

Kazin, Michael and McCartin, Joseph A. (eds) (2006) *Americanism: New Perspectives on the History of an Ideal*, Chapel Hill: University of North Carolina Press.

Kelley, Ninette and Trebilcock, Michael (1998) *The Making of the Mosaic: A History of Canadian Immigration Policy*, Toronto: University of Toronto Press.

Kelsay, John (2007) *Arguing the Just War in Islam*, Cambridge, MA: Harvard University Press.

Kendle, John (1967) *The Colonial and Imperial Conferences, 1887–1911*, London: Longmans/ Royal Commonwealth Society.

—— (1975) *The Round Table Movement and Imperial Union*, Toronto: University of Toronto Press.

—— (1997) *Federal Britain: A History*, London: Routledge.

Keohane, Robert O. and Nye, Joseph S., Jr. (1977) *Power and Interdependence: World Politics in Transition*, Boston, MA: Little, Brown.

—— (1987) "*Power and Interdependence* Revisited," *International Organization* 41(4): 725–53.

—— (2001) *Power and Interdependence: World Politics in Transition*, 3rd edn, New York: Longman.

Key, John (2007) "Speech to the United States/New Zealand Partnership Forum," 11 Sept. Online. Available at: http://www.johnkey.co.nz/index.php?/archives/232-SPEECH-Speech-to-the-United-StatesNew-Zealand-Partnership-Forum.html (accessed 15 December 2010).

Kidd, Colin (2006) *The Forging of Races: Race and Scripture in the Protestant Atlantic World, 1600–2000*, Cambridge: Cambridge University Press,

Kilgore, DeWitt Clinton (2003) *Astrofuturism: Science, Race and Visions of Utopia in Space*, Philadelphia: University of Pennsylvania Press.

King, Desmond S. and Smith, Rogers (2005) "Racial Orders in American Political Development," *American Political Science Review* 99(1): 75–92.

Klotz, Audie (1995) *Norms in International Relations: The Struggle against Apartheid*, Ithaca, NY: Cornell University Press.

—— (forthcoming) *Migration and State Identity in South Africa, 1860–2010*, New York, Cambridge University Press.

Klotz, Audie and Smith, Braden (2007) "State Identity as a Variable." Paper prepared for the Annual Meeting of the American Political Science Association, Chicago IL, September.

Knöbl, Wolfgang (2006) "Of Contingencies and Breaks: The US American South as an Anomaly in the Debate on Multiple Modernities," *Archives européennes de sociologie* 47(1): 125–57.

Knöbl, Wolfgang (2007) *Die Kontingenz der Moderne: Wege in Europa, Asien und Amerika*, Frankfurt/New York: Campus.

Knodt, Michèle (2000) "Europäisierung: Eine Strategie der Selbstbehauptung?" in Michèle Knodt and Beate Kohler (eds), *Deutschland zwischen Europäisierung und Selbstbehauptung*, Frankfurt/New York: Campus, pp. 32–54.

Kocka, Jürgen (2001) "Multiple Modernities and Negotiated Universals." Paper prepared for the conference on Multiple Modernities, Social Science Research Center (WZB), Berlin, 5–7 May.

Koh, Tommy, Yeo, Lay Hwee and Latif, Asad (2000) *Asia and Europe: Essays and Speeches*, Singapore and River Edge, NJ: World Scientific Pub. and Asia-Europe Foundation.

Kohler-Koch, Beate (2000) "Europäisierung: Plädoyer für eine Horizonterweiterung," in Michèle Knodt and Beate Kohler (eds), *Deutschland zwischen Europäisierung und Selbstbehauptung*, Frankfurt/New York: Campus, pp. 11–31.

Kohn, Edward P. (2004) *This Kindred People: Canadian–American Relations and the Anglo-Saxon Idea, 1895–1903*, Montreal/Kingston: McGill-Queen's University Press.

Koskenniemi, Martti (2001) *The Gentle Civilizer of Nations: The Rise and Fall of International Law, 1870–1960*, Cambridge: Cambridge University Press.

Kouwenhoven, John Atlee (1956) "What's American about America?" *Harpers* (July): 25–33.

Kramer, Paul A. (2007) *The Blood of Government: Race, Empire, the United States and the Philippines*, Chapel Hill: University of North Carolina Press.

Krasner, Stephen D. (1978) *Defending the National Interest: Raw Materials Investments and U.S. Foreign Policy*, Princeton, NJ: Princeton University Press.

—— (1999) *Sovereignty: Organized Hypocrisy*, Princeton, NJ: Princeton University Press.

Krotz, Ulrich (2007) "Parapublic Underpinnings of International Relations: The Franco-German Construction of Europeanization of a Particular Kind," *European Journal of International Relations* 13(3): 385–417.

—— (2010) "Regularized Intergovernmentalism: France–Germany and Beyond (1963–2009)," *Foreign Policy Analysis* 6(2): 147–85.

—— (2011) *Flying Tiger: International Relations Theory and the Politics of Advanced Weapons*, New York: Oxford University Press.

Kupchan, Charles (2002) *The End of the American Era: US Foreign Policy and the Geopolitics of the Twenty-First Century*, New York: Vintage.

—— (2010) *How Enemies Become Friends: The Sources of Stable Peace*, Princeton, NJ: Princeton University Press.

Kurth, James (2010) "The United States as a Civilizational Leader," in Peter J. Katzenstein (ed.), *Civilizations in World Politics*, London and New York: Routledge, pp. 41–66.

Kurzweil, Ray (2005) *The Singularity Is Near: When Humans Transcend Biology*, New York: Vintage.

Kymlicka, Will (1996) *Multicultural Citizenship: A Liberal Theory of Minority Rights*, Oxford: Clarendon Press.

—— (2007a) "Ethnocultural Diversity in a Liberal State: Making Sense of the Canadian Model(s)," in Keith Banting, Thomas Courchene, and Leslie Seidle (eds), *Belonging? Diversity, Recognition and Shared Citizenship in Canada*, Montreal, QC: Institute for Research on Public Policy, pp. 39–86.

—— (2007b) *Multicultural Odysseys: Negotiating the New International Politics of Diversity*, Oxford: Oxford University Press.

Labillière, Francis de (1894) *Federal Britain, or, Unity and Federation of the Empire*, London: Low.

Lachmann, Richard (2002) *Capitalists in Spite of Themselves*, New York: Oxford University Press.

Laden, Anthony Simon and Owen, David (eds) (2007) *Multiculturalism and Political Theory*, Cambridge: Cambridge University Press.

Laitin, David D. (1986) *Hegemony and Culture: Politics and Religious Change among the Yoruba*, Chicago, IL: University of Chicago Press.

Lake, Marilyn (2005) "From Mississippi to Melbourne via Natal: The Invention of the Literacy Test as a Technology of Racial Exclusion," in Ann Curthoys and Marilyn Lake (eds), *Connected Worlds: History in Transnational Perspective*, Canberra: ANU E Press, pp. 209–29.

Lake, Marilyn and Reynolds, Henry (2008) *Drawing the Global Colour Line: White Men's Countries and the International Challenge of Racial Equality*, Cambridge: Cambridge University Press.

Lange, David (2005) *My Life*, Auckland: Penguin.

Lapidus, Ira M. (1988) *A History of Islamic Societies*, New York: Cambridge University Press.

Lavin, Deborah (1995) *From Empire to International Commonwealth: A Biography of Lionel Curtis*, Oxford: Clarendon.

Lawrence, Bruce B. (2010) "Islam in Afro-Eurasia: A Bridge Civilization," in Peter J. Katzenstein (ed.), *Civilizations in World Politics*, London and New York: Routledge, pp. 157–75.

—— (2011) "Polyvalent Islam in the Public Sphere," *Middle East Journal* 65(1): 133–42.

Layne, Christopher (2006) *The Peace of Illusions: American Grand Strategy from 1940 to the Present*, Ithaca, NY: Cornell University Press.

Lebow, Richard Ned (1976) *White Britain and Black Ireland: Social Stereotypes and Colonial Policy*, Philadelphia, PA: Institute for the Study of Human Issues.

Lennox, Patrick (2009) *At Home and Abroad*, Vancouver: University of British Columbia Press.

Leonard, Mark (2005) *Why Europe Will Run the 21st Century*, New York: Public Affairs.

Lewis, Bernard (1990) "The Roots of Muslim Rage," *Atlantic Monthly* (Sept.): 47–60.

Lieven, Anatol (2004) *America Right or Wrong: An Anatomy of American Nationalism*, New York: Oxford University Press.

Lind, Michael (1995) *The Next American Nation: The New Nationalism and the Fourth American Revolution*, New York: Free Press.

—— (2006) *The American Way of Strategy: U.S. Foreign Policy and the American Way of Life*, New York: Oxford University Press.

Lippmann, Walter (1943) *U.S. Foreign Policy: Shield of the Republic*, Boston, MA: Little, Brown.

Lipset, Seymour Martin (1990) *Continental Divide: The Values and Institutions of Canada and the United States*, New York: Routledge.

—— (1996) *American Exceptionalism: A Double-Edged Sword*, New York: W.W. Norton.

Liu, Lydia H. (2004) *The Clash of Empires: The Invention of China in Modern World Making*, Cambridge, MA: Harvard University Press.

Lloyd, Lorna (2001) "'Us and Them': The Changing Nature of Commonwealth Diplomacy, 1880–1973," *Commonwealth and Comparative Politics* 39(3): 9–30.

Lloyd Prichard, M.F. (1970) *An Economic History of New Zealand to 1939*, Auckland: Collins.

Lodge, Henry Cabot (1895) "England, Venezuela, and the Monroe Doctrine," *North American Review* 160: 651–58.

Lorimer, Douglas A. (1996) "Race, Science, and Culture: Historical Continuities and Discontinuities, 1850–1914," in Shearer West (ed.), *The Victorians and Race*, Aldershot: Ashgate, pp. 12–33.

Lorne, Marquis of (1885) *Imperial Federation*, London: Swan Sonnenschein.

Lowe, David (1999) *Menzies and "The Great World Struggle,"* Sydney: University of New South Wales Press.

Lucarelli, Sonia (2007) "The European Union in the Eyes of Others: Towards Filling a Gap in the Literature," *European Foreign Affairs Review* 12: 249–70.

Lucas, Charles (ed.) ([1912] 1970) *Lord Durham's Report on the Affairs of British North America*, New York: Augustus M. Kelley Publishers.

—— (1915) *The British Empire: Six Lectures*, London: Macmillan.

Lucassen, Leo (2005) *The Immigrant Threat: The Integration of Old and New Migrants in Western Europe since 1850*, Urbana: University of Illinois Press.

Lustick, Ian (1993) *Unsettled States, Disputed Lands: Britain and Ireland, France and Algeria, Israel and the West Bank-Gaza*, Ithaca, NY: Cornell University Press.

Lyall, Sarah (2011) "A Traditional Royal Wedding, but for the 3 Billion Witnesses," *New York Times*, 29 Apr.: A1.

McCain, John (2007) "An Enduring Peace Built on Freedom," *Foreign Affairs* 86 (Nov./Dec.): 19–34.

McCarthy, Thomas (2009) *Race, Empire, and the Idea of Human Development*, Cambridge: Cambridge University Press.

McCormick, John (2006) *The European Superpower*, New York: Palgrave Macmillan.

McCrum, Robert (2010) *Globish: How the English Language Became the World's Language*, New York: W.W. Norton.

McCully, Murray (2009a) "New Zealand: A Bridge between Asia and Europe." Speech to the Swedish Institute of International Affairs, 17 Dec. Online. Available at: http://www.national.org.nz/Article.aspx?ArticleId=31698 (accessed 15 December 2010).

—— (2009b) "Speech to the German Council on Foreign Relations," 2 Dec. Online. Available at: http://www.national.org.nz/Article.aspx?articleId=31545 (accessed 15 December 2010).

McDermott, Rose (2010) "Emotional Manipulation of Political Identity," in W. LeChaminant (ed.), *Manipulating Democracy*, London: Routledge.

MacDonald, David B. (2005) "Regionalism: New Zealand, Asia, the Pacific, and Australia," in Robert G. Patman and Chris Rudd (eds), *Sovereignty Under Siege? The Case of New Zealand*, London: Ashgate.

MacDonald, David B. and O'Connor, Brendon (2010) "Australia and New Zealand – America's Antipodean Anglosphere Allies?" Paper prepared for the Annual Meeting of the International Studies Association, New Orleans, Feb.

McGibbon, Ian (1999) "New Zealand Defence Policy," in Bruce Brown (ed.), *New Zealand in World Affairs 1972–90*, Wellington: VUP/NZIIA.

MacIntyre, Stuart and Clark, Anna (2003) *The History Wars*, Carlton: University of Melbourne Press.

McIntyre, W. (1993) "A Review of the Commonwealth Factor in Foreign Policy Making: 1943–93," in Ann Trotter (ed.), *Fifty Years of New Zealand Foreign Policy Making*, Dunedin: University of Otago Press.

Mackey, Eva (1999) *The House of Difference: Cultural Politics and National Identity in Canada*, London: Routledge.

McLean, Denis (2003) *The Prickly Pair: Making Nationalism in Australia and New Zealand*, Dunedin: University of Otago Press.

Macmahon, Arthur W. and Dittmar, W.R. (1942) "The Mexican Oil Industry since Expropriation," *Political Science Quarterly* 57(1): 28–50.

McMahon, Deirdre (2004) "Ireland, the Empire, and the Commonwealth," in Kevin Kenny (ed.), *Ireland and the British Empire*, Oxford: Oxford University Press, pp. 182–219.

McMichael, Philip (1984) *Settlers and the Agrarian Question: Foundations of Capitalism in Colonial Australia*, New York: Cambridge University Press.

MacMillan, Margaret (2001) "Isosceles Triangle: Britain, the United States, and the Dominions, 1900–1926," in Jonathan Hollowell (ed.), *Twentieth-Century Anglo-American Relations*, Basingstoke: Palgrave, pp. 1–25.

McMillan, Stuart (2008) "Defending the Realm," in P.M. Smith, P. Hempenstall, and S. Goldfinch (eds), *Remaking the Tasman World*, Christchurch: Canterbury University Press.

McNeill, William H. (1963) *The Rise of the West: A History of the Human Community*, Chicago, IL: University of Chicago Press.

—— (1990) "*The Rise of the West* after Twenty-Five Years," *Journal of World History* 1: 1–21.

McRoberts, Kenneth (1997) *Misconceiving Canada: The Struggle for National Unity*, Oxford: Oxford University Press.

Magister, Sandro (2009) "Erdogan and the Christians. Few Promises, Zero Action." Online. Available at: http://chiesa.espresso.repubblica.it/articolo/1339804?eng=y (accessed 11 March 2011).

Mahan, Alfred T. and Beresford, Charles (1894) "Possibilities of an Anglo-American Reunion," *North American Review* 159: 551–73.

Mahathir bin Mohamad and Ishihara, Shintarō (1995) *The Voice of Asia: Two Leaders Discuss the Coming Century*, New York: Kodansha International.

Mahbubani, Kishore (2008) *The New Asian Hemisphere: The Irresistible Shift of Global Power to the East*, New York: Public Affairs.

Manchester, William (1983) *The Last Lion: Winston Spencer Churchill, Visions of Glory 1874–1932*, New York: Dell.

Mandaville, Peter (2007) *Global Political Islam*, New York: Routledge.

Mandler, Peter (2006) *The English National Character: The History of an Idea from Edmund Burke to Tony Blair*, New Haven, CT: Yale University Press.

Mann, Michael (1986) *The Sources of Social Power*, New York: Cambridge University Press.

—— (1993) *The Sources of Social Power: The Rise of Classes and Nation-States, 1760–1914*, Cambridge: Cambridge University Press.

Manners, Ian (2002) "Normative Power Europe: A Contradiction in Terms?" *Journal of Common Market Studies* 40(2): 235–58.

—— (2006) "Normative Power Europe Reconsidered: Beyond the Crossroads," *Journal of European Public Policy* 13(2): 182–99.

Mantena, Karuna (2010) *Alibis of Empire: Henry Maine and the Ends of Liberal Imperialism*, Princeton, NJ: Princeton University Press.

Mar, Lisa (2010) *Brokering Belonging: Chinese in Canada's Exclusion Era, 1885–1945*, Oxford: Oxford University Press.

Marcus, Julie (1988) "Bicentennial Follies," *Anthropology Today* 4(3): 4–6.

Martin, Ged (1973) "Empire Federalism and Imperial Parliamentary Union, 1820–70," *Historical Journal* 16: 65–92.

Mathy, Jean-Philippe (1993) *Extrême Occident: French Intellectuals and America*, Chicago, IL: University of Chicago Press.

Mazower, Mark (2009) *No Enchanted Palace: The End of Empire and the Ideological Origins of the United Nations*, Princeton, NJ: Princeton University Press.

Mazrui, Ali A. (2005) "The Re-invention of Africa: Edward Said, V.Y. Mudimbe, and Beyond," *Research in African Literatures* 36(3): 68–82.

Mbeki, Thabo (2005) "Address to the Parliament of the Republic of Sudan, Khartoum," 1 Jan. Online. Available at: http://www.dfa.gov.za/docs/speeches/2005/mbek1108a. htm (accessed 3 July 2008).

Mead, Walter Russell (2002) *Special Providence: American Foreign Policy and How It Changed the World*, New York: Knopf.

—— (2007) *God and Gold. Britain, America, and the Making of the Modern World*, New York: Knopf.

Mehta, Uday Singh (1999) *Liberalism and Empire: A Study in Nineteenth Century British Social Thought*, Chicago, IL: University of Chicago Press.

Melleuish, G.C. (2004) "The Clash of Civilizations: A Model of Historical Development?" in Saïd Amir Arjomand and Edward A. Tiryakian (eds), *Rethinking Civilizational Analysis*, Thousand Oaks, CA: Sage, pp. 234–44.

—— (2009) "The West, the Anglo-sphere and the Ideal of Commonwealth," *Australian Journal of Politics and History* 55(2): 233–47.

Melling, Phil and Jon Roper (eds) (1996) *Americanisation and the Transformation of World Cultures: Melting Pot or Cultural Chernobyl?* Lewiston, NY: Edwin Mellen.

Mendelsohn, Barak (2009) *Combating Jihadism: American Hegemony and Interstate Cooperation in the War on Terrorism*, Chicago, IL: University of Chicago Press.

—— (forthcoming) "God vs. Westphalia: Radical Islamist Movements and the Battle for Organizing the World," *Review of International Studies*.

Mendilow, Jonathan (1986) *The Romantic Tradition in British Political Thought*, London: Croom Helm.

Mercer, Jonathan (2010) "Emotional Beliefs," *International Organization* 64 (Winter): 1–31.

Merk, Frederick (1970) *Manifest Destiny and Mission in American History: A Reinterpretation*, New York: Alfred A. Knopf.

Merrill, Dennis (2009) *Negotiating Paradise: U.S. Tourism and Empire in Twentieth-Century Latin America*, Chapel Hill: University of North Carolina Press.

Metcalf, Thomas (2007) *Imperial Connections: India in the Indian Ocean Arena, 1860–1920*, Berkeley: University of California Press.

Meunier, Sophie (2007) "The Distinctiveness of French Anti-Americanism," in Peter J. Katzenstein and Robert O. Keohane (eds), *Anti-Americanisms in World Politics*, Ithaca, NY: Cornell University Press, pp. 129–56.

Meyer, John W. (1989) "Conceptions of Christendom: Notes on the Distinctiveness of the West," in Melvin Kohn (ed.), *Cross-National Research in Sociology*, Newbury Park, CA: Sage, pp. 395–413.

Meyer, Lorenzo (1981) *México y los Estados Unidos en el conflicto petrolero*, Mexico City: El Colegio de México.

Middleton, John (1992) *The World of the Swahili: An African Mercantile Civilization*, New Haven, CT: Yale University Press.

Migdal, Joel (2001) *State in Society: Studying How States and Societies Transform and Constitute One Another*, Cambridge: Cambridge University Press.

Mill, John Stuart (1861) "Considerations on Representative Government," in John Robson (ed.), *The Collected Works of John Stuart Mill, XIX*, Toronto: University of Toronto Press.

Millar, T.B. (1967) *The Commonwealth and the United Nations*, London: Methuen.

Miller, J. (1987) "The Special Relationship in the Pacific," in William Roger Louis and Hedley Bull (eds), *The "Special Relationship": Anglo-American Relations since 1945*, Oxford: Oxford University Press.

Mills, Charles (1997) *The Racial Contract*, Ithaca, NY: Cornell University Press.

—— (1998) *Blackness Visible: Essays on Philosophy and Race*, Ithaca, NY: Cornell University Press.

Milner, Alfred (1925) "Credo," *The Times*, 25 July.

Ministry of Foreign Affairs and Trade (NZ) (2010) "New Zealand–China Relations: 'Four Firsts,'" 2 July. Online. Available at: http://www.chinafta.govt.nz/3-Progressing-the-FTA/1-Why-China/Four-firsts.php (accessed 22 July 2011).

Montaño, Jorge (2004) *Misión en Washington 1993–95: De la Aprobación del TLCAN al Préstamo de Rescate*, México: Planeta.

Monypenny, W.F. (1905) "The Imperial Ideal" in Charles Goldman (ed.), *The Empire and the Century*, London: Murray, pp. 5–29.

Moodley, Kogila (1983) "Canadian Multiculturalism as Ideology," *Ethnic and Racial Studies* 6(3): 320–31.

Moravcsik, Andrew (2009) "Europe: The Quiet Superpower," *French Politics* 7(3–4): 403–22.

Moreau, Joseph (2003) *Schoolbook Nation: Conflicts over American History Textbooks from the Civil War to the Present*, Ann Arbor: University of Michigan Press.

Morefield, Jeanne (2004) *Covenants without Swords: Idealist Liberalism and the Spirit of Empire*, Princeton, NJ: Princeton University Press.

Morin, Claude (1988) *Lendemains piégés. Du référendum à la nuit des longs couteaux*, Montréal: Boréal.

Morris, Brian (1988) *Australia Take a Bow: A Photographic Salute to Australia on the Occasion of its Bicentenary*, New York: St. Martin's.

Morris, Ian (2010) *Why the West Rules: The Patterns of History and What They Reveal about the Future*, New York: Farrar, Straus and Giroux.

Mudimbe, V.Y. (1988) *The Invention of Africa: Gnosis, Philosophy, and the Order of Knowledge*, Bloomington: Indiana University Press.

Mulhall, Daniel (1987) "New Zealand and the Demise of ANZUS: Alliance Politics and Small-Power Idealism," *Irish Studies in International Affairs* 2(3): 61–77.

Mullard, Chris (1982) "Multiracial Education in Britain: From Assimilation to Cultural Pluralism," in J. Tierney (ed.), *Race, Migration and Schooling*, London: Holt, Rinehart & Winston, pp. 120–33.

Müller, Harald (1999) *Das Zusammenleben der Kulturen: Ein Gegenentwurf zu Huntington*, Frankfurt am Main: Fischer.

Mulroney, Brian (1984) *Notes for a Speech by the Prime Minister to the Members of the Economic Club of New York*, 10 Dec.

Murakami, Yasusuke (1996) *An Anti-Classical Political–Economic Analysis*, Stanford, CA: Stanford University Press.

Murji, Karim, and Solomos, John (2005) "Introduction: Racialization in Theory and Practice," in Murji and Solomos (eds), *Racialization: Studies in Theory and Practice*, Oxford: Oxford University Press, pp. 1–27.

Muthu, Sankar (2003) *Enlightenment against Empire*, Princeton, NJ: Princeton University Press.

National Security Agency (2010) "UKUSA Agreement Release 1940–56." Online. Available at: http://www.nsa.gov/public_info/declass/ukusa.shtml (accessed 15 December 2010).

Naylor, R.T. (1975) *The History of Canadian Business 1867–1914, vol. I: The Banks and Finance Capital*, Toronto: Lorimer.

Neumann, Iver B. (1999) *Uses of the Other: "The East" in European Identity Formation.* Minneapolis: University of Minnesota Press.

—— (2003) "The English School on Diplomacy: Scholarly Promise Unfulfilled," *International Relations* 17(3): 341–69.

Neumayer, Eric and Plümper, Thomas (2009) "International Terrorism and the Clash of Civilization," *British Journal of Political Science* 39: 711–34.

New Zealand Cabinet Office (2010) "Defence Review 2009," Wellington: New Zealand Cabinet Office.

New Zealand Foreign Policy Research Archive (2007) "Recent Polls of Public Opinion in New Zealand," Auckland: New Zealand Foreign Policy Research Archive, 1 May. Online. Available at: http://www.arts.auckland.ac.nz/departments/index.cfm?P=11014 (accessed 15 December 2010).

New Zealand Ministry of Defence (2010) "New Zealand Defence White Paper," Wellington: NZ Ministry of Defence.

New Zealand Press Association (2008) "NZers Overwhelmingly Support Obama for President," *National Business Review*, 24 Sept. Available at: http://www.nbr.co.nz/article/nzers-overwhelmingly-support-obama-president-35650 (accessed 15 December 2010).

—— (2010) "NZ–US Bond Set to Step Up with Talks," *NZ Herald*, 4 Aug. Available at: http://www.nzherald.co.nz/politics/news/article.cfm?c_id=280&objectid=10663621 (accessed 15 December 2010).

Nicolson, Sir Harold (1954) *The Evolution of the Diplomatic Method*, London: Constable.

Novkov, Julie (2007) "Mobilizing Liberalism in Defense of Racism," *Good Society* 16(1): 30–9.

O'Connor, Brendon and Vucetic, Srdjan (2010) "Another Mars/Venus Divide? Why Australia Said 'Yes' and Canada Said 'No' to Involvement in the 2003 Iraq War," *Australian Journal of International Affairs* 64(5): 526–48.

O'Gorman, Edmundo (1961) *The Invention of America: An Inquiry into the Historical Nature of the New World and the Meaning of its History*, Bloomington: Indiana University Press.

—— (1977) "La Gran Dicotomía Americana: Angloamérica e Iberoamérica," *Vuelta* (Sept.).

O'Hearn, Denis (2001) *The Atlantic Economy*, London: Palgrave Macmillan.

Obama, Barack, and Cameron, David (2011) "Shoulder to Shoulder against Terror," *The Australian*, 25 May.

Ojeda, Mario (2001) *Alcances y Límites de la Política Exterior de México*, México: Colmex.

Oliver, F.S. (1906) *Alexander Hamilton: An Essay on American Union*, London: Constable.

Ollivier, Maurice (ed.) (1954) *The Colonial and Imperial Conferences from 1887 to 1937*, Ottawa: Queen's Printer and Controller of Stationery.

Olsen, Johan P. (1996) "Europeanisation and Nation-State Dynamics," in Sverker Gustavsson and Leif Lewin (eds), *The Future of the Nation-State*, London: Routledge, pp. 245–85.

—— (2007) *Europe in Search of Political Order*, Oxford: Oxford University Press.

Orange, Claudia (1987) *The Treaty of Waitangi*, Wellington: Allen & Unwin.

Orbie, Jan (2006) "Civilian Power Europe: Review of the Original and Current Debates," *Cooperation and Conflict* 41(1): 123–8.

Ostler, Nicholas (2010) *The Last Lingua Franca: English until the Return of Babel*, New York: Walker.

Ouroussoff, Nicolai (2010) "Reshaping Mecca Turns to Garagantuan Glitz," *New York Times* (30 Dec.): A1, A7.

Pace, Michelle (2007) "The Construction of EU Normative Power," *Journal of Common Market Studies* 25(5): 1041–64.

Pachai, Bridglal (1971) *International Aspects of the South African Indian Question, 1860–1971*, Cape Town: Struik.

Pagden, Anthony (1995) *Lords of All the World: Ideologies of Empire in Spain, Britain and France, 1500–1800*, New Haven, CT: Yale University Press.

—— (ed) (2002) *The Idea of Europe: From Antiquity to the European Union*, Cambridge and Washington, DC: Cambridge University Press and Woodrow Wilson Center Press.

Painter, Nell Irvin (2010) *The History of White People*, New York: W.W. Norton.

Pakenham, Thomas (1979) *The Boer War*, New York: Avon.

Palen, Marc-William (2010) "Protection, Federation and Union: The Global Impact of the McKinley Tariff upon the British Empire, 1890–94," *Journal of Imperial and Commonwealth History* 38: 395–418.

Palmer, Geoffrey, and Hill, Kim (2002), *Constitutional Conversations: Geoffrey Palmer Talks to Kim Hill on National Radio 1994–2001*, Wellington: Victoria University Press.

Parekh, Bhikhu et al. (2000) *The Future of Multi-Ethnic Britain*, London: Profile Books.

Parker, Andrew and Sedgwick, Eve Kosofsky (1995) "Introduction," in Parker and Sedgwick (eds), *Performativity and Performance*, New York and London: Routledge, pp. 1–18.

Parker, C.J.W. (1981) "The Failure of Liberal Racialism: The Racial Ideas of E.A. Freeman," *Historical Journal* 24(4): 825–46.

Parliament of Canada (1971) *House of Commons Proceedings*, 8 October, 8545.

Parmar, Inderjeet (2002) "Anglo-American Elites in the Inter-War Years: Idealism and Power in the Intellectual Roots of Chatham House and the Council on Foreign Relations," *International Relations* 16: 53–75.

Pasha, Mustapha Kamal (2007) "Civilizations, Postorientalism and Islam," in Martin Hall and Patrick Thaddeus Jackson (eds), *Civilizational Identity: The Production and Reproduction of "Civilizations" in International Relations*, New York: Palgrave, pp. 61–79.

Pastor, Robert A. (2011) *The North American Idea: A Vision for a Continental Future*, Oxford: Oxford University Press.

Patterson, Tiffany Ruby and Kelley, Robin D.G. (2000) "Unfinished Migrations: Reflections on the African Diaspora and the Making of the Modern World," *African Studies Review* 43(1): 11–45.

Paul, Kathleen (1997) *Whitewashing Britain: Race and Citizenship in the Post-War Era*, Ithaca, NY: Cornell University Press.

Pauly, Louis (2003) "Canada in a New North America," in Peter Andreas and Thomas Biersteker (eds), *The Re-Bordering of North America*, London: Routledge.

Pauly, Louis and Coleman, William (eds) (2008) *Global Ordering*, Vancouver: University of British Columbia Press, pp. 1–20.

Peabody, Sue and Stovall, Tyler (eds) (2003) *The Color of Liberty: Histories of Race in France*, Durham, NC: Duke University Press.

Pearson, David (2009) "The Majority Factor," in Manying Ip (ed.), *The Dragon and the Taniwha: Maori and Chinese in New Zealand*, Auckland: Auckland University Press, pp. 32–55.

Pemberton, Jo-Ann (2001) *Global Metaphors: Modernity and the Quest for One World*, London: Pluto.

Perdue, Peter C. (2008) "Eurasia in World History: Reflections on Time and Space," *History Cooperative* 5(2). Online. Available at: http://www.historycooperative.org/journals/whc/5.2/perdue.html (accessed 23 February 2010).

Phillips, Andrew (2011) *War, Religion, and Empire: The Transformation of International Orders*, Cambridge: Cambridge University Press.

Phillips, Kevin (1969) *The Emerging Republican Majority*, New Rochelle, NY: Arlington House.

Pienaar, Sara (1987) *South Africa and International Relations between the Two World Wars: The League of Nations Dimension*, Johannesburg: University of Witwatersrand Press.

Pietrantonio, Linda et al. (1996) "Multiculturalisme ou intégration: un faux débat," in K. Fall et al. (eds), *Les convergences culturelles dans les sociétés pluriethniques*, Quebec: Presses de l'Université Laval, pp. 147–58.

Pijl, Kees van der (1984) *The Making of an Atlantic Ruling Class*, London: Verso.

—— (1998) *Transnational Classes and International Relations*, London: Routledge.

—— (2006) "Lockean Europe?" *New Left Review* 37 (Jan./Feb.): 9–37.

—— (2007) *Nomads, Empires, States, Vol. 1: Modes of Foreign Relations and Political Economy*, London: Pluto Press.

—— (2010) *The Foreign Encounter in Myth and Religion, Vol. 2: Modes of Foreign Relations and Political Economy*, London: Pluto Press.

Pitt, Alan (2000) "A Changing Anglo-Saxon Myth: Its Development and Function in French Political Thought, 1860–1914," *French History* 14(2): 150–73.

Pitts, Jennifer (2005) *A Turn to Empire: The Rise of Imperial Liberalism in Britain and France*, Princeton, NJ: Princeton University Press.

Pletcher, David M. (1973) *The Diplomacy of Annexation: Texas, Oregon, and the Mexican War*, Columbia: University of Missouri Press.

Pocock, J.G.A. (1975) *The Machiavellian Moment: Florentine Political Thought and the Atlantic Republican Tradition*, Princeton, NJ: Princeton University Press.

—— (2005) *Barbarism and Religion*, New York: Cambridge University Press.

Pollock, Sheldon I. (2006) *The Language of the Gods in the World of Men: Sanskrit, Culture, and Power in Premodern India*, Berkeley: University of California Press.

Pooley, Colin G. (1977) "The Residential Segregation of Migrant Communities in mid-Victorian Liverpool," Transactions of the Institute of British Geographers, 2.

Porter, Bernard (2006) *Empire and Superempire: Britain, America and the World*, New Haven, CT: Yale University Press.

Pratte, André (2011) *Wilfrid Laurier*, Toronto: Penguin Canada.

Preece, Rod (1980) "The Anglo–Saxon Conservative Tradition," *Canadian Journal of Economics and Political Science* 3 (Fall): 3–32.

Press-Barnathan, Galia (2009) *The Political Economy of Transitions to Peace: A Comparative Perspective*, Pittsburgh, PA: University of Pittsburgh Press.

Puchala, Donald J. (1997) "International Encounters of Another Kind," *Global Society* 11(1): 5–29.

—— (2003) *Theory and History in International Relations*, New York: Routledge.

Radforth, Ian (2004) *Royal Spectacle: The 1860 Visit of the Prince of Wales to Canada and the United States*, Toronto, Buffalo, and London: University of Toronto Press.

Reid, T.R. (2004) *The United States of Europe: The New Superpower and the End of American Supremacy*, New York: Penguin Press.

Reinhold, Frances L. (1938) "New Research on the First Pan-American Congress, Held at Panama in 1826," *Hispanic American Historical Review* 18(3): 342–63.

Renouf, Alan (1979) *The Frightened Country*, Melbourne: Macmillan.

Resnick, Philip (2005) *The European Roots of Canadian Identity*, Toronto: University of Toronto Press.

Reus-Smit, Christian (2011) "Struggles for Individual Rights and the Expansion of the International System," *International Organization* 65(2): 207–42.

Reynolds, David (1981) *The Creation of the Anglo-American Alliance, 1937–41: A Study in Competitive Cooperation*, London: Europa.

—— (1986) "Roosevelt, Churchill, and the Wartime Anglo-American Alliance, 1939–45," in William Roger Louis and Hedley Bull (eds), *The Special Relationship: Anglo-American Relations since 1945*, Oxford: Clarendon.

—— (1989) "Rethinking Anglo-American Relations," *International Affairs* 65(1): 89–111.

Reynolds, Henry (1987) *The Law of the Land*, Ringwood, Vic.: Penguin Books Australia.

Rhodes, Cecil (1902) *The Last Will and Testament of Cecil J. Rhodes*, ed. W.T. Stead, London: Review of Reviews.

Rich, Paul (1986) *Race and Empire in British Politics*, Cambridge: Cambridge University Press.

Riding, Alan (2000) *Distant Neighbors: A Portrait of the Mexicans*, New York: Vintage Books.

Rifkin, Jeremy (2004) *The European Dream: How Europe's Vision of the Future is Quietly Eclipsing the American Dream*, New York: Tarcher.

—— (2009) *The Empathic Civilization: The Race to Global Consciousness in a World Crisis*, New York: Jeremy P. Tarcher/Penguin.

Riley, Patrick (1988) "Louis Hartz: The Final Years, the Unknown Work," *Political Theory* 16(3): 377–99.

Risse-Kappen, Thomas (1995) *Cooperation among Democracies: The European Influence on US Foreign Policy*, Princeton, NJ: Princeton University Press.

Roazen, Paul (1990) "Introduction," in Louis Hartz, *The Necessity of Choice: Nineteenth-Century Political Thought*, edited, compiled and prepared by Paul Roazen, with a preface by Benjamin Barber, New Brunswick, NJ: Transaction Publishers, pp. 1–24.

Roberts, Andrew (2007) *A History of the English Speaking Peoples since 1900*, New York: HarperCollins.

Roberts, Lance W. and Clifton, Rodney A. (1982) "Exploring the Ideology of Canadian Multiculturalism," *Canadian Public Policy* 8(1): 88–94.

Roberts, Priscilla (1997) "The Anglo-American Theme: American Visions of an Atlantic Alliance, 1914–33," *Diplomatic History* 21: 333–64.

—— (2009) "The Transatlantic American Foreign Policy Elite: Its Evolution in Generational Perspective," *Journal of Transatlantic Studies* 7: 163–83.

Rodgers, Daniel (2000) *Atlantic Crossings: Social Politics in a Progressive Age*, Cambridge, MA: Harvard University Press.

Roediger, David (2008) *How Race Survived U.S. History: From Settlement and Slavery to the Obama Phenomenon*, New York: Verso.

Rojas, Rafael (2009) *Las Repúblicas de Aire: Utopía y Desencanto en la Revolución de Hispanoamérica*, México, Taurus.

Rose, Jonathan W. (2000) *Making "Pictures in Our Heads": Government Advertising in Canada*, Westport, CT: Praeger.

Rosenberg, Emily S. (1982) *Spreading the American Dream: American Economic and Cultural Expansion, 1890–1945*, New York: Hill and Wang.

Roy, Oliver (2004) *Globalized Islam: The Search for a New Ummah*, New York: Columbia University Press.

—— (2007) *Secularism Confronts Islam*, New York: Columbia University Press.

Rudolph, Susanne Hoeber (2010) "Four Variants of Indian Civilization," in Peter J. Katzenstein (ed.), *Civilizations in World Politics*, New York: Routledge, pp. 137–56.

Ruggie, John Gerard (1993) "Territoriality and Beyond," *International Organization* 47(1): 139–74.

Russell, Peter (2004) *Constitutional Odyssey: Can Canadians Become a Sovereign People?* Toronto: University of Toronto Press.

Russett, Bruce (1963) *Community and Contention: Britain and America in the Twentieth Century*, Cambridge, MA: MIT Press.

Russett, Bruce M., Oneal, John R., and Cox, Michaelene (2000) "Clash of Civilizations, or Realism and Liberalism Déjà Vu? Some Evidence," *Journal of Peace Research* 37(5): 583–608.

Ryan, Henry Butterfield (1987) *The Vision of Anglo-America: The US–UK Alliance and the Emerging Cold War, 1943–46*, Cambridge: Cambridge University Press.

Ryan, Phil (2010) *Multicultiphobia*, Toronto: University of Toronto Press.

Salvatore, Armando (2010) "Repositioning 'Islamdom': The Culture–Power Syndrome within a Transcivilizational Ecumene," *European Journal of Social Theory* 13(1): 99–115.

Sanders, Douglas (1983) "The Indian Lobby," in K. Banting and R. Simeon (eds), *And No One Cheered: Federalism, Democracy and the Constitutional Act*, Toronto: Methuen, pp. 301–32.

Santa-Cruz, Arturo (2005) *International Election Monitoring, Sovereignty, and the Western Hemisphere Idea: The Emergence of an International Norm*, New York: Routledge.

Scheipers, Sibylle and Sicurelli, Daniela (2007) "Normative Power Europe: A Credible Utopia?" *Journal of Common Market Studies* 45(2): 435–57.

Schimmelfennig, Frank (2001) "The Community Trap: Liberal Norms, Rhetorical Action, and the Eastern Enlargement of the European Union," *International Organization* 55: 47–80.

—— (2003) *The EU, NATO and the Integration of Europe: Rules and Rhetoric*, New York: Cambridge University Press.

Schmidt, Vivien A. (2002) *The Futures of European Capitalism*, Oxford: Oxford University Press.

Schoenbaum, David (1998) "More Special than Others," *Diplomatic History* 22(2): 273–84.

Schoppa, Leonard (1999) "The Social Context in Coercive International Bargaining," *International Organization* 53(2): 307–42.

Schwartz, Herman (2009) *States vs. Markets: The Emergence of a Global Economy*, Basingstoke: Palgrave.

Sedelmeier, Ulrich (2000) "Eastern Enlargement: Risk, Rationality and Role-Compliance," in M.G. Cowles and M. Smith (eds), *The State of the European Union*, Vol. 5: *Risk, Reform, Resistance and Revival*, Oxford: Oxford University Press, pp. 164–85.

Seeley, John R. (1883) *The Expansion of England; Two Courses of Lectures*, London, MacMillan (reprinted 1914).

Seglow, Jonathan (1998) "Universals and Particulars: The Case of Liberal Cultural Nationalism," *Political Studies* 46(5): 963–77.

Sen, Amartya (2006) *Identity and Violence: The Illusion of Destiny*, New York: W.W. Norton.

Senghaas, Dieter (1998) *The Clash within Civilizations: Coming to Terms with Cultural Conflicts*, New York: Routledge.

Shaw, Timothy (2008) *Commonwealth: Inter- and Non-state Contributions to Global Governance*, London: Routledge.

Sheehan, James (2008) *Where Have All the Soldiers Gone? The Transformation of Modern Europe*, Boston, MA: Houghton Mifflin.

Shih, Chih-yu (2010) "The West That Is Not in the West: Identifying Self in Oriental Modernity," *Cambridge Journal of International Affairs* 23(4): 537–60.

Shore, Sean M. (1998) "No Fences Make Good Neighbors: The Development of the US–Canadian Security Community, 1871–1940," in Emanuel Adler and Michael N. Barnett (eds), *Security Communities*, Cambridge: Cambridge University Press.

Short, Nicola and Kambouri, Helen (2010) "Ambiguous Universalism: Theorising Race/Nation/Class in International Relations," *Journal of International Relations and Development* 13(3): 268–300.

Sikkink, Kathryn (1997) "Reconceptualizing Sovereignty in the Americas: Historical Precursors and Current Practices," *Houston Journal of International Law* 19(3): 705–29.

Simeon, Richard (2006) *Federal–Provincial Diplomacy*, Toronto: University of Toronto Press.

Sjursen, Helene (2006a) *Questioning EU Enlargement: Europe in Search of Identity*, London: Routledge.

—— (2006b) "The EU as a 'Normative' Power: How Can This Be?" *Journal of European Public Policy* 13(2): 182–99.

Skowronek, Stephen (2006) "The Re-association of Ideas and Purposes: Racism, Liberalism, and the American Political Tradition," *American Political Science Review* 100(3): 385–401.

Slaughter, Anne-Marie (2004) *A New World Order*, Princeton, NJ: Princeton University Press.

Slicher van Bath, B.H. (1963) *The Agrarian History of Western Europe, A.D. 500–1850*, London: E. Arnold.

Smith, David E. (2010) *Federalism and the Constitution of Canada*, Toronto: University of Toronto Press.

Smith, Goldwin (1887) *The Schism in the Anglo-Saxon Race*, New York: American News Co.

Smith, Jeremy C.A. (2010) "The Many Americas: Civilization and Modernity in the Atlantic World," *European Journal of Social Theory* 13(1): 117–33.

Smith, Malinda S. (2003) "Race Matters and Race Manners," in Janine Brodie and Linda Trimble (eds), *Reinventing Canada: Politics of the 21st Century*, Toronto: Prentice Hall, pp. 108–29.

Smith, Philippa Mein (2005) *A Concise History of New Zealand*, Melbourne: Cambridge University Press.

Smith, Robert F. (1986) "Latin America, the United States and the European Powers, 1830–1930," in Leslie Bethell (ed.), *The Cambridge History of Latin America, Vol. IV, c. 1870 to 1930*, Cambridge: Cambridge University Press.

Smith, Rogers M. (1988) "The 'American Creed' and American Identity: The Limits of Liberal Citizenship in the United States," *Western Political Quarterly* 41(2): 225–51.

—— (1993) "Beyond Tocqueville, Myrdal, and Hartz: The Multiple Traditions in America," *American Political Science Review* 87(3): 549–65.

—— (1997) *Civic Ideals: Conflicting Visions of Citizenship in U.S. History*, New Haven, CT: Yale University Press.

—— (1999) "Liberalism and Racism: The Problem of Analyzing Traditions," in David Ericson and Louisa Bertch Green (eds), *The Liberal Tradition in America*, New York: Routledge, pp. 9–27.

—— (2003) *Stories of Peoplehood: The Politics and Morals of Political Membership*, New York: Cambridge University Press.

—— (2007) "Studies in American Racial Development: An Interim Report," *Perspectives on Politics* 5(2): 325–33.

Smith, Rogers M., King, Desmond S., and Klinker, Philip A. (2011) "Challenging History: Barack Obama and American Radical Politics," *Dædalus* 140(2): 121–35.

Smith, Steve (1990) "The Special Relationship," *Political Studies* 38: 126–36.

Smith, William Roy (1921) "British Imperial Federation," *Political Science Quarterly* 36: 274–97.

Smuts, Jan Christian (1930) *Africa and Some World Problems*, Oxford: Clarendon Press.

Sohn, Louis and Clark, Grenville (1958) *World Peace through World Law*, Cambridge, MA: Harvard University Press.

Spearitt, Peter (1988) "Celebration of a Nation: The Triumph of Spectacle," in Susan Janson and Stuart Macintyre (eds), *Making the Bicentenary*, Melbourne: Australian Historical Studies, pp. 3–20.

Spengler, Oswald (1939) *The Decline of the West* (one volume edition), New York: Knopf.

Spillman, Lyn (1996) "'Neither the Same Nation Nor Different Nations': Constitutional Conventions in the United States and Australia," *Comparative Studies in Society and History* 38: 149–81.

Spohn, Willfried (2001) "Eisenstadt on Civilizations and Multiple Modernity," *European Journal of Social Theory* 4(4): 499–508.

—— (2010) "Political Sociology: Between Civilizations and Modernities – A Multiple Modernity Perspective," *European Journal of Social Theory* 13: 49–66.

Stairs, Denis (1982) "The Political Culture of Canadian Foreign Policy," *Canadian Journal of Political Science* 15(4): 667–90.

Stanley, Katri A. (2006) "A Look at Africa through French Identity," Government Department, Cornell University, Senior Honors Thesis.

Statistics New Zealand (2008) "National Ethnic Population Projections: 2006–26." Online. Available at: http://www.stats.govt.nz/browse_for_stats/population/estimates_and_projections/nationalethnicpopulationprojections_hotp06–26.aspx (accessed 15 December 2010).

Stead, W.T. (1901) *The Americanization of the World; Or the Trend of the Twentieth Century*, New York: Markley.

Stears, Marc (2007) "The Liberal Tradition and the Politics of Exclusion," *Annual Review of Political Science* 10: 85–101.

Stein, Judith (1989) "Defining the Race, 1890–1930," in Werner Sollors (ed.), *The Invention of Ethnicity*, New York: Oxford University Press, pp. 77–104.

Sternberg, Yitzak (2001) "Modernity, Civilization and Globalization," in Eliezer Ben-Rafael with Yitzak Sternberg (eds), *Identity, Culture and Globalization*, Leiden: Brill, pp. 75–92.

Stewart, Cameron et al. (1999) "US Aussie Spy Base Revelations," *The Australian*, 18 Feb. Available at: http://www.hartford-hwp.com/archives/24/167.html (accessed 15 December 2010).

Stivachtis, Yannis A. (1998) *The Enlargement of International Society: Culture vs. Anarchy and Greece's Entry into International Society*, New York: St. Martin's.

Stovall, Tyler and van den Abbeele, Georges (eds) (2003) *French Civilization and Its Discontent: Nationalism, Colonialism, Race*, Lanham, MD: Lexington Books.

Strauz-Hupe, Robert, Dougherty, James, and Kintner, William (1963) *Building the Atlantic World*, New York: Harper.

Streit, Clarence (1938) *Union Now: A Proposal for a Federal Union of the Democracies of the North Atlantic*, New York: Harper.

—— (1941) *Union Now with Britain*, New York: Harper.

—— (1953) "Atlantic Union – Freedom's Answer to Malenkov," *Annals of the American Academy of Political and Social Science* 288: 2–12.

—— (1956) "Lionel Curtis – Prophet of Federal Union," *Freedom & Union* (Jan.): 10.

—— (1961) *Freedom's Frontier: Atlantic Union Now*, New York: Harper.

Studdert-Kennedy, Gerald (1995) "Christianity, Statecraft and Chatham House: Lionel Curtis and World Order," *Diplomacy & Statecraft* 6: 470–89.

Sullivan, Henry W. (2005) "The Border that Refused to Go Away: The Rio Grande as Replication of the Rhine–Danube Frontier," in Raúl A. Galoppe and Richard Weiner (eds), *Explorations on Subjectivity, Borders, and Demarcation*, Lanham, MD: University Press of America.

Swaan, Abram de (2001) *Words of the World: The Global Language System*, Malden, MA: Blackwell.

Swedberg, Richard (2007) "Civilizations, Economies and Social Mechanisms: Some Central Themes." Paper delivered at the conference on "The Economic Performance of Civilizations: The Role of Culture, Religion and the Law," University of Southern California (23–24 Feb.).

Switzer, Tom (2009) "The Fall of a Civilisation, or Just a 'Torn Country'?" *The Spectator*, 4 Feb. Online. Available at: http://ussc.org.au/s/media/media/09/02/090204_spectator_switzer.pdf (accessed 22 July 2011).

Sylla, Richard (1972) "American Banking and Growth in the Nineteenth Century: A Partial View of the Terrain," *Explorations in Economic History* 9 (Winter): 197–227.

Tavan, Gwenda (2004) "The Dismantling of the White Australia Policy," *Australian Journal of Political Science* 39(1): 109–25.

—— (2005) *The Long, Slow Death of White Australia*, Melbourne: Scribe Publications.

Taylor, Alan (2001) *American Colonies: The Settling of North America*, London: Penguin.

—— (2010) *The Civil War of 1812: American Citizens, British Subjects, Irish Rebels*, New York: Knopf.

Taylor, Charles (1985) "Legitimacy, Identity and Alienation in Late Twentieth Century Canada," in Alan Cairns and Cynthia Williams (eds), *Constitutionalism, Citizenship and Society in Canada*, Toronto: University of Toronto Press, pp. 183–229.

—— (1992) *Multiculturalism and the Politics of Recognition*, Princeton, NJ: Princeton University Press.

—— (1993) *Reconciling the Solitudes*, Montreal: McGill-Queen's University Press.

—— (2004) *Modern Social Imaginaries*, Durham, NC: Duke University Press.

Taylor, Donald M. and Sigal, Ronald (1982) "Defining 'Québécois': The Role of Ethnic Heritage, Language, and Political Orientation," *Canadian Ethnic Studies* 14: 59–70.

Teschke, Benno (2003) *The Myth of 1648: Class, Geopolitics and the Making of Modern International Relations*, London: Verso.

Thompson, J. Lee (2007) *A Wider Patriotism: Alfred Milner and the British Empire*, London: Pickering & Chatto.

Thomson, John (2000) *Warrior Nation: New Zealanders at the Front 1900–2000*, Christchurch: Hazard Press.

Tibi, Bassam (1998) *The Challenge of Fundamentalism: Political Islam and the New World Disorder*, Berkeley: University of California Press.

—— (1999a) *Kreuzzug und Djihad: Der Islam und die christliche Welt*, Munich: Bertelsmann.

—— (1999b) "International Morality and Cross-Cultural Bridging," in Roman Herzog (ed.), *Preventing the Clash of Civilizations: A Peace Strategy for the Twenty-First Century*, New York: St. Martin's, pp. 107–26.

—— (2001) *Islam between Culture and Politics*, New York: Palgrave.

—— (2008) *Political Islam, World Politics and Europe: Democratic Peace and Euro-Islam versus Global Jihad*, New York: Routledge.

—— (2009) "Bridging the Heterogeneity of Civilisations: Reviving the Grammar of Islamic Humanism," *Theoria* (Sept.): 65–80.

Tinker, Hugh (1993) *A New System of Slavery: The Export of Indian Labour Overseas 1830–1920*, second edn, London: Hansib.

Tocqueville, Alexis de (1862 [1835–40]) *Democracy in America*, trans. Henry Reeve, 2 vols, London: Longman.

—— (1904) *Democracy in America*, trans. Henry Reeve, New York: D. Appleton & Co.

—— (2002) *Democracy in America*, Washington, DC: Regnery Publishing.

Todd, Emmanuel (1987) *The Causes of Progress: Culture, Authority and Change*, Oxford: Blackwell.

—— (2011) "Al-Qaida war schon tot," *Der Spiegel* 20: 138–42.

Tomes, Jason (1997) *Balfour and Foreign Policy: The International Thought of a Conservative Statesman*, Cambridge: Cambridge University Press.

Tourgée, Albion (1899) "The Twentieth Century Peacemakers," *Contemporary Review* 75: 886–908.

Tow, William, and Albinski, Henry (2002) "ANZUS – Alive and Well After Fifty Years," *Australian Journal of Politics and History* 48(2): 153–73.

Toye, Richard (2010) *Churchill's Empire: The World That Made Him and the World He Made*, London: Macmillan.

Trubowitz, Peter (1998) *Defining the National Interest: Conflict and Change in American Foreign Policy*, Chicago, IL: University of Chicago Press.

Trudeau, Pierre (1971) "Statement on Multiculturalism, House of Commons, 8 October." Online. Available at: www.culturescanada.ca (accessed 12 December 2009).

—— (1990) "The Values of a Just Society," in Thomas Axworthy and Pierre Trudeau (eds), *Towards a Just Society, the Trudeau Years*, Markham, ON: Viking, pp. 357–85.

Tulloch, Hugh (1977) "Changing British Attitudes towards the United States in the 1880s," *Historical Journal* 20(4): 825–40.

Turner, Bryan S. (1974) *Weber and Islam*, London: Routledge & Kegan Paul.

Turner, John (ed.) (1988) *The Larger Idea: Lord Lothian and the Problem of National Sovereignty*, London: Lothian Foundation.

United States Bureau of the Census (1921–23) Fourteenth Census of the United States Taken in the Year 1920, Washington, DC: Government Printers Office.

United States Census Office (1791) *Return of the Whole Number of Persons within the Several Districts of the United States*, Philadelphia, PA: Childs and Swaine.

United States Department of the Census (1860) *Recapitulation of the Tables of Population, Nativity and Occupation, Census of 1860*, Washington, DC: Government Printers Office.

US Department of State (2004) *Papers Relating to the Foreign Relations of the United States 1964–68: Volume XXXI*, Washington, DC: US Government Printing Office.

Van Ness, Peter (1986) "An Introduction to the Articles on New Zealand," *Bulletin of Concerned Asian Scholars* 18.

Verma, Dina Nath (1968) *India and the League of Nations*, Patna: Bharati Bhawan.

Vertovec, Steven and Wessendorf, Susanne (2009) *Backlash against Multiculturalism: Public Discourses, Policies and Practices*, London: Routledge.

Vickers, Jill (2002) "No Place for 'Race'? Why Pluralist Theory Fails to Explain the Politics of 'Race' in 'New Societies,'" in Stephen Brooks (ed.), *The Challenge of Cultural Pluralism*, Westport, CT: Praeger, pp. 215–38.

Victoria, Guadalupe (1986) *Correspondencia diplomática*, México City: Secretaría de Relaciones Exteriores.

Vitalis, Robert (2005) "Birth of a Discipline," in Brian Schmidt and David Long (eds), *Imperialism and Internationalism in the Discipline of International Relations*, Albany: State University of New York Press, pp. 159–82.

—— (2010) "The Noble American Science of Imperial Relations and Its Laws of Race Development," *Comparative Studies in Society and History* 52(4): 909–38.

Vucetic, Srdjan (2010a) "Anglobal Governance?" *Cambridge Review of International Affairs* 23(3): 455–74.

—— (2010b) "The Anglosphere, Liberalism and Race." Paper prepared for the Annual Meeting of the International Studies Association, New Orleans, 17–20 Feb.

—— (2011) *The Anglosphere: A Genealogy of a Racialized Identity in International Relations*, Stanford, CA: Stanford University Press.

Wagenberg, R.H. (1966) "Commonwealth Reactions to South Africa's Racial Policy 1948–61." Unpublished Ph.D. dissertation, London School of Economics.

Waldstein, Charles (1898) "The English-speaking Brotherhood," *North American Review* 167: 223–38.

Walker, Darryl and Henderson, John (1980) "China: A Study in Changed Perceptions," in John Henderson, William Keith Jackson, and Richard Kennaway (eds), *Beyond New Zealand: The Foreign Policy of a Small State*, Auckland: Methuen.

Walker, R.B.J. (1992) *Inside/Outside: International Relations as Political Theory*, Cambridge: Cambridge University Press.

Walker, Ranguinui (1987) *Nga Tau Tohetohe – Years of Anger*, Auckland: Penguin.

Wallerstein (eds), (1991) *Race, Nation, Class: Ambiguous Identities*, trans. Chris Turner, London and New York: Verso, pp. 37–67.

Walt, Stephen (2002) "Keeping the World 'Off-Balance': Self-Restraint and US Foreign Policy," in G. John Ikenberry (ed.), *America Unrivaled: The Future of the Balance of Power*, Ithaca, NY: Cornell University Press.

Watson, Adam (1992) *The Evolution of International Society*, London: Routledge.

Watt, David (1986) "Introduction: The Anglo-American Relationship," in William Roger Louis and Hedley Bull (eds), *The Special Relationship: Anglo-American Relations since 1945*, Oxford: Clarendon.

Weaver, John (2003) *The Great Land Rush and the Making of the Modern World, 1650–1900*, Montreal: McGill-Queen's University Press.

Weaver, Sally (1981) *Making Canadian Indian Policy: The Hidden Agenda 1968–70*, Toronto: University of Toronto Press.

Webster, Wendy (2006) "Transnational Journeys and Domestic Histories," *Journal of Social History* (Spring): 651–66.

Weisberg, Jacob (2007) "George Bush's Favorite Historian: The Strange Views of Andrew Roberts," *Slate* (28 Mar.), available at: http://www.slate.com/id/2162837/ (accessed 26 July 2011).

Weiss, Thomas (2009) "What Happened to the Idea of World Government?" *International Studies Quarterly* 53: 253–71.

Wells, Alan (1989) *Constructing Capitalism: An Economic History of Eastern Australia, 1788–1901*, Sydney: Allen & Unwin.

Wells, H.G. (1925) *The Outline of History: Being a Plain History of Life and Mankind*, London: Cassell.

—— (1935) *The New America: The New World*, London: Cresset.

—— (1999 [1902]) *Anticipations of the Reaction of Mechanical and Scientific Progress upon Human Life and Thought*, Mineola, NY: Dover.

Wendt, Alexander (2003) "Why a World State is Inevitable," *European Journal of International Relations* 9: 491–542.

Wesley, Michael (2007) "Location, Location, Location," *Griffith REVIEW* 18.

—— (2010) "Don't Dismiss Abbott's Anglosphere," *The Interpreter*. Online. Available at: http://www.lowyinterpreter.org/post/2010/08/12/Dont-dismiss-Abbotts-Anglosphere.aspx (accessed 8 March 2011).

Wesley, Michael and Warren, Tony (2000) "Wild Colonial Ploys," *Australian Journal of Political Science* 35(1): 9–26.

Wheeler, Nick (2001) *Saving Strangers*, Oxford: Oxford University Press.

Whitaker, Arthur P. (1954) *The Western Hemisphere Idea: Its Rise and Decline*, Ithaca, NY: Cornell University Press.

White, Arthur Silva (1894) "An Anglo-American Alliance," *North American Review* 158: 484–93.

White, Hugh (2005) "New Zealand's Niche Force Is Smart Defence," *The Age*, 10 May.

—— (2010) "Power Shift: Australia's Future between Washington and Beijing," *Quarterly Essay* 39.

White, Leanne (2004) "The Bicentenary of Australia: Celebration of a Nation," in Linda K. Fuller (ed.), *National Days/National Ways: Historical, Political, and Religious Celebrations around the World*, Westport, CT: Praeger, pp. 25–40.

Whitman, Richard G. (1998) *From Civilian to Superpower? The International Identity of the European Union*, New York: St. Martin's.

Wierzbicka, Anna (2006) *English: Meaning and Culture*, New York: Oxford University Press.

Wight, Martin (1968) "Western Values in International Relations," in Herbert Butterfield and Martin Wight (eds), *Diplomatic Investigations: Essays in the Theory of International Politics*, Cambridge, MA: Harvard University Press, pp. 89–131.

—— (1986) *Power Politics*, London: Penguin.

Williams, David (1989) "Te Tiriti o Waitangi – Unique Relationship between Crown and Tangata Whenua?" in I.H. Kawharu (ed.), *Waitangi: Maori and Pakeha Perspectives of the Treaty of Waitangi*, Auckland: Oxford University Press.

Williams, Paul (2003) "A Commonwealth of Knowledge: Empire, Intellectuals and the Chatham House Project, 1919–39," *International Relations* 17: 35–58.

Willkie, Wendell (1943) *One World*, New York: Cassell.

Wilson, Woodrow (1918) *President Wilson's Foreign Policy: Messages, Addresses, Papers*, New York: Oxford University Press.

Windschuttle, Keith (2004) *The White Australia Policy*, Sydney: Macleay Press.

—— (2005) "Sphere of Influence?" *National Review*, 14 Mar.

Winter, Elke (2005) "Debating Binationalism and Multiculturalism in Canada: Toward a Sociology of Ethnic Pluralism." Ph.D. dissertation, York University.

Wolfe, Allan (2005) "Native Son: Samuel Huntington Defends the Homeland," *Foreign Affairs* 83(3): 120–5.

Woodside, Alexander (2006) *Lost Modernities: China, Vietnam, Korea, and the Hazards of World History*, Cambridge, MA: Harvard University Press.

Wooley, Wesley (1988) *Alternatives to Anarchy: American Supranationalism since World War II*, Bloomington: Indiana University Press.

Wright, Gavin (2006) *Slavery and American Economic Development*, Baton Rouge: Louisiana State University Press.

Yamamura, Kozo (ed.) (1997) *A Vision of a New Liberalism? Critical Essays on Murakami's Anticlassical Analysis*, Stanford, CA: Stanford University Press.

Young, Iris Marion (1990) *Justice and the Politics of Difference*, Princeton, NJ: Princeton University Press.

Zakaria, Fareed (1994) "Culture is Destiny: A Conversation with Lee Kuan Yew," *Foreign Affairs* 73(2): 109–24.

Zarakol, Ayse (2011) *After Defeat: How the East Learned to Live with the West*, New York: Cambridge University Press.

Zeitlin, Jonathan (2000) "Introduction," in Jonathan Zeitlin and Gary Herrigel (eds), *Americanization and Its Limits: Reworking US Technology and Management in Postwar Europe and Japan*, Oxford: Oxford University Press, pp. 1–50.

Zemka, Sue (2002) "Erewhon and the End of Utopian Humanism," *ELH* 69: 439–72.

Zhao, Tingyang (2011) "All-under Heaven and Methodological Relationalism: An Old Story and New World Peace," Beijing, Chinese Academy of Social Sciences, unpublished paper.

Zolberg, Ari (2006) *A Nation by Design: Immigration Policy in the Fashioning of America*, Cambridge, MA: Harvard University Press.

INDEX